Daybreak of Freedom . . .

Daybreak of

The

University

of North

Carolina

Press

Chapel Hill

and London

Freedom ...

... The Montgomery Bus Boycott

Edited by Stewart Burns

Library of Congress Cataloging-in-Publication Data
Daybreak of freedom : the Montgomery bus boycott / edited by Stewart Burns.
p cm.   Includes bibliographical references (p.   ) and index.
ISBN 0-8078-2360-0 (alk. paper) — ISBN 0-8078-4661-9 (pbk.: alk. paper)
1. Montgomery (Ala.)—Race relations—Sources.   2. Segregation in transportation—Alabama—
Montgomery—History—20th century—Sources.   3. Afro-Americans—Civil rights—Alabama—
Montgomery—History—20th century—Sources.   I. Title.
F334.M79N39   1997   97-7909
305.8'00976147—dc21   CIP

01 00 99 98 97   5 4 3 2 1

For Claudette Colvin,
Jo Ann Robinson,
Virginia Foster Durr,
and all the other
courageous women
and men who made
democracy come alive
in the Cradle of the
Confederacy

We are here in a general sense because first and foremost we are American citizens, and we are determined to apply our citizenship to the fullness of its meaning. We are here also because of our love for democracy, because of our deep-seated belief that democracy transformed from thin paper to thick action is the greatest form of government on earth. . . .

And you know, my friends, there comes a time when people get tired of being trampled over by the iron feet of oppression. . . . But the great glory of American democracy is the right to protest for right.

We are not wrong in what we are doing. If we are wrong, the Supreme Court of this nation is wrong. If we are wrong, the Constitution of the United States is wrong. If we are wrong, God Almighty is wrong. If we are wrong, Jesus of Nazareth was merely a utopian dreamer that never came down to earth. If we are wrong, justice is a lie. Love has no meaning. And we are determined here in Montgomery to work and fight until justice runs down like water, and righteousness like a mighty stream. . . .

We, the disinherited of this land, we who have been oppressed so long, are tired of going through the long night of captivity. And now we are reaching out for the daybreak of freedom and justice and equality. . . .

Right here in Montgomery, when the history books are written in the future, somebody will have to say, "There lived a race of people, a *black* people, fleecy locks and black complexion, a people who had the moral courage to stand up for their rights. And thereby they injected a new meaning into the veins of history and of civilization."—Martin Luther King Jr., December 5, 1955, Montgomery

. . .

I believe that God is using Montgomery as his proving ground. It may be that here in the capital of the Confederacy, the birth of the ideal of freedom in America and in the Southland can be born.
—Martin Luther King Jr., March 22, 1956, Montgomery

Contents . . .

Maps and Illustrations

A section of illustrations follows page 136

Preface . . .
The Spirit of Montgomery

The Montgomery bus boycott looms as a formative turning point of the twentieth century: harbinger of the African American freedom movement, which in turn inspired movements for freedom around the globe; springboard for the leadership of Martin Luther King Jr. in civil rights, human rights, and peacemaking; launching pad for the worldwide era of upheaval known as the "sixties," which lasted nearly two decades and dominated the rest of the century; marker of the midcentury divide between modern and postmodern. The bus boycott stands for all times as one of humankind's supreme democratic moments, a monumental struggle to actualize the American dream of freedom, equality, and constitutionalism. The nonviolent uprising of 1955 and 1956 represented a new founding of American democracy that pushed the nation a quantum leap closer to keeping faith with its parchment principles.

The Declaration of Independence and the Constitution gave birth to the United States as a promise of freedom, something new in the eighteenth-century world. At that time American freedom meant independence from Great Britain and liberties for propertied Anglo-Saxon men. It remained an unfulfilled promise for nine out of ten inhabitants of the new world. African Americans, white women, wage workers fought to make their birthright real. They constructed a handle on freedom that they called "equal rights," a rallying cry that ascended from hush arbor and soap box, pulpit and tea table, penny press and fiery tract, to the Capitol and the White House.

Abraham Lincoln crystallized the nation's second founding halfway through the holocaust of Civil War when he emancipated slaves and spoke the incantation of Gettysburg. The Gettysburg Address gathered the "full measure" of the war's death and devastation—hauntingly reflected by the awful battlefield backdrop—to illuminate and consecrate the watchword of equality that had been raised up for a generation by abolitionists black and white, transcendentalists, women's rights activists, and other disturbers of the peace. Just as the Declaration of Independence had been concretized by the Constitution, so Lincoln's linking of liberty and equality was incorporated in the three Civil War amendments that abolished slavery, gave citizenship and legal rights to African Americans, and enfranchised black men. But the unfolding of freedom was far from finished.

For the freed people freedom and equal rights, even the very words, were twisted into new forms of enslavement and exploitation. The Jim Crow caste system of segregation, at first an expedient and then a whole culture and way of life, persisted for nearly a century, empowered by the systematic disempowerment of black men and women (and poor whites) by force, fraud, and reform. Black protests were sporadic, isolated, and short. Federal court decisions began undoing segregation slowly, in measured paces. Then in the mid-1950s a newly urban community of African Americans in the Alabama capital rose up to challenge Jim Crow. Organizing and mobilizing their people for over a year, black citizens dramatized in everyday life the popular sovereignty envisioned by the Declaration of Independence and the Constitution's preamble. They injected the energy and spirit of democracy—living grassroots democracy—into their bittersweet inheritance of freedom and equality.

The actions of Montgomery's black citizenry, along with the words leaders spoke from pulpits that ennobled and immortalized the mass protest, constituted the nation's third founding—the first in Philadelphia, the second at Gettysburg, the third in the "Cradle of the Confederacy." The Montgomery bus boycott made democracy tangible and heartfelt for those who took part in it and for wider circles swayed by its ripples—a shared communal awakening that commingled politics, emotion, and spirituality. Montgomery's democratic moment was its own, unique, unrepeatable, and far from flawless, but its vital elements took hold as standards for the epic black freedom movement that grew from it—and to some degree in later struggles for liberation, from South Africa to Prague to Tienanmen Square.

Montgomery showed that democracy cannot bloom without community. The richer the communal soil, the stronger its democratic shoots. The bus boycott exemplified an unparalleled unity across class lines that black movements have dreamt about since. The driving force of it all was thousands of African American women, middle class and working class, active in churches, clubs, and sororities. They transplanted democracy from their sheltered sanctuaries to public streets and squares. They turned faith and friendship from the healing balm of survival into the fire of defiance and transformation.

Blocked from voting by and large, lacking representation in the political arena, Montgomery's black citizens understood that, like their nineteenth-century forebears who fought slavery, democracy meant that they "must themselves strike the blow." They must act as their own agents of change. They came to believe, as their preeminent leader told them, that "the great glory of democracy is the right to protest for right." Just as they and their ancestors had tilled hard soil, planted seeds, harvested crops, hewn wood, repaired tools, cooked food, sewn clothes—for whites but also for themselves—so democracy, they found, was something palpable to hold and mold in their own hands, to carry forward step by step. Democracy too had its seasons and cycles. The journey mattered. Democracy was more than a right, more than a responsibility. It was a pantheon of hope and faith.

These citizens' reach for democracy was rooted in the churches, scriptures, and spirituals that tied them to their divinity and to generations past and not yet born. They made Montgomery a praying movement, a testament to their faith in God and, through God, faith in themselves. A testament to God's grace.

Their Bibles and preachers taught them that they were God's chosen people like the children of Israel. The bus boycott consummated this faith, made it surge alive in mass meetings, car pools, and weary soulful walking. Every day they were moving toward the Promised Land. The mass church-based protest exalted them as makers of history, bearers of God's will. The sense of divine mission catapulted their self-esteem, their dignity, their collective self-confidence. They believed that they were building, through toil, sacrifice, and sharing, a "new Jerusalem" in Montgomery and "a new heaven and a new earth" in the dispirited South. In this land of fulfilled promises, justice would "roll down like waters and righteousness like a mighty stream." Every person would be revealed as a child of God.

Black people of Montgomery believed that they were breaking a new day.

Acknowledgments . . .

Daybreak of Freedom is the first comprehensive history of the Montgomery bus boycott. It originated in my work as an editor of the Martin Luther King Jr. Papers at Stanford University. I spent five years producing the third volume of the King Papers, *Birth of a New Age* (University of California Press), which examines King's life and leadership during the bus boycott period, 1955–56. While acquiring documents for and editing the King volume, I found that "King-related" documents told only part of the epic story of the Montgomery movement, presenting a particular and incomplete perspective on events. Many of the richest, most revealing, and most significant documents from or about the bus boycott could not be published in the King volume according to our selection criteria. A more complex and multidimensional tale insisted on being told. As editor I tried to extend the definition of "King papers," but considerations of length and of precedents for subsequent volumes compelled me to scale down my broader vision of the King volume. When my efforts to include non-King documents were challenged by more pragmatic colleagues at the King Papers Project, senior editor Clayborne Carson encouraged me to produce a separate volume on the Montgomery bus boycott.

A number of people have assisted me during the two years that I have devoted to *Daybreak of Freedom*. Several remarkable Stanford undergraduates conducted research and transcribed documents: Julie Leadbetter, Anita McLane, Jane Wu, Wendy Lovejoy, Kris Baber, Karlyn Adams, and Michael Sessoms. Artist Jennifer Butler, also a Stanford student, created the map of Montgomery. My colleague James Tracy commented perceptively on numerous drafts, drawing on his expertise in civil rights and radical pacifism. I owe a special debt of gratitude to three pathbreaking historians of the bus boycott, J. Mills Thornton III, David J. Garrow, and Steven M. Millner, who generously provided advice, criticism, and research materials. I am grateful to Coretta Scott King and to the late Glenn Smiley for important interviews that I conducted with them. I am appreciative of telephone interviews that I conducted with other participants, including Mary Fair Burks, Virginia Foster Durr, Norman W. Walton, and Maude L. Ballou.

I want to thank the numerous individuals, archives, and repositories that provided me with photocopies of documents, without whose help this book could not have come to fruition: American Civil Liberties Union Collection, Princeton University; Archives of the Southern Regional Council, Woodruff Library, Atlanta University; Bayard Rustin Papers, Library of Congress; Clifford J. Durr Papers, Alabama Department of Archives and History, Montgomery; Montgomery County Circuit Court, Montgomery County Records, Montgomery; Dexter Avenue King Memorial Baptist Church Collection, Montgomery; Dwight D. Eisenhower Papers, Dwight D. Eisenhower Library, Abilene, Kansas; Fellowship of Reconciliation Papers, Swarthmore College Peace Collection, Swarthmore, Pennsylvania; David J. Garrow; Glenn E. Smiley Collection; Hazel Gregory Papers, King Library and Archives, King Center for Nonviolent Social Change, Atlanta; H. J. Palmer Papers, King Library and Archives; Highlander Research and Education Center Records, State Historical Society of Wisconsin, Madison; Martin Luther King Jr. Papers, King Library and Archives; Martin Luther King Jr. Papers, Mugar Library, Boston University; Montgomery County District Attorney's Files, Montgomery County Courthouse, Montgomery; National Association for the Advancement of Colored People Papers, Library of Congress; Norman Thomas Collection, New York Public Library; Pacifica Radio Archive, Los Angeles; Preston Valien Collection, Amistad Research Center, Tulane University, New Orleans; Robert Graetz; Roy Wilkins Papers, Library of Congress; Southeast Region, National Archives; and Virginia Foster Durr Papers, Schlesinger Library, Radcliffe College, Harvard University.

I am grateful to the King family and estate and to the King Library and Archives at the King Center for Nonviolent Social Change, for making available several King-related documents.

Jane Benson and James Tracy gave me encouragement and support throughout the preparation of this book. At Stanford University I wish to thank the staffs of Green Library, Meyer Media Center, and Residential Education, especially former director Alice Supton. At the Martin Luther King Jr. Papers Project, where my scholarship on the bus boycott began, I learned a great deal about documentary editing and computer-based research in collaborating with Clayborne Carson, Susan Carson, Peter Holloran, Dana Powell, and

Judy Wu. Special thanks to Clay Carson for suggesting that I undertake this work and for deepening my understanding of the black freedom struggle. Finally I would like to thank my fine editors at the University of North Carolina Press, Lewis Bateman and Mary Caviness, for their support and diligence in guiding the book to publication.

Stewart Burns
Stanford University

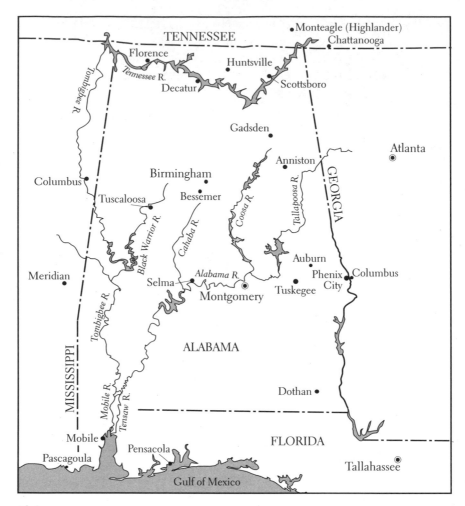

Alabama

Key to Montgomery, Alabama, Map

1. Empire Theater, Montgomery St.
2. Court Square
3. Montgomery County Courthouse
4. Dexter Avenue Baptist Church
5. Alabama State Capitol
6. First Baptist Church
7. Federal Courthouse

8. Greyhound Bus Station
9. King Parsonage, 309 S. Jackson St.
10. Mt. Zion AME Zion Church
11. Holt Street Baptist Church
12. Trinity Lutheran Church
13. Cleveland Apartments: Home of Rosa Parks
14. Alabama State College

ALABAMA RIVER

N

COLUMBUS

JEFFERSON

WATER

COMMERCE

COOSA

MOLTON

TALLAPOOSA

6

MADISON

MONROE

LEE

5

DEXTER

CATOMA

BIBB

MONTGOMERY

2

3

4

WASHINGTON

1

CHURCH

8

ADAMS

WILKINSON

7

ALABAMA

CLAYTON

SCOTT

9

HIGH

COURT

PERRY

LAWRENCE

McDONOUGH

HOLL

DECATUR

UNION

RIPLEY

JACKSON

STONE

12

10

HOLT

11

13

GROVE

JEFFERSON DAVIS

14

CLEVELAND

SOUTH

MONTGOMERY, ALA.
ESTABLISHED 1819

LB 97

Overview . . .
The Proving Ground

"Our leaders is just we ourself."
—Claudette Colvin, sixteen, Montgomery
federal court, May 11, 1956

On the morning of December 5, 1955, the black citizens of Montgomery, Alabama, inaugurated a year-long boycott of the racially segregated city buses. That afternoon, the boycott leaders elected Martin Luther King Jr., twenty-six-year-old pastor of Dexter Avenue Baptist Church, as president of the Montgomery Improvement Association (MIA), which they formed to direct the protest. Although King did not start the bus boycott, he grasped its significance at once. Chosen more because of existing leadership divisions than his own perceived strengths, he confidently took charge. When the mass protest persevered against unrelenting pressures from city hall, county courts, and white extremists, King emerged as a national and international symbol of the African American freedom struggle and was embraced by white and black media alike. While newspapers and magazines promoted an image of the young Baptist preacher as the bus boycott's prime mover, he acted within a broad structure of grassroots leadership that had been preparing the ground for black community mobilization long before he arrived in the Cradle of the Confederacy.

Founded in 1819 and designated the Alabama capital in 1847, the city in the heart of the fertile Black Belt in the southern half of the state sat on a bluff overlooking the winding Alabama River. Montgomery had served as a center for cotton marketing and slave auctions before the Civil War. In February 1861 ex–Mississippi senator Jefferson Davis chaired a meeting in Montgomery of white leaders from six southern states, including Alabama, that had decided to secede from the Union. These slaveholders drafted a constitution for the new Confederacy, elected Davis president, and made Montgomery the first Confederate capital. Although during the next century the city diversified its economy and developed manufacturing industries that included lumber, furniture, and fertilizer, its industrial base remained much smaller than that of Birmingham, 100 miles north and three times the population, where in the 1950s black families had almost twice the median income than they had in the capital.

From World War I onward, thousands of rural Alabama blacks relocated to Montgomery, searching for a better life. White supremacist interference combined with agricultural mechanization, foreign cotton competition, and the boll weevil plague made it increasingly difficult to survive as a farmer or sharecropper. In the 1940s and 1950s African Americans were drawn to Montgomery because of its emergence as a major industrial, commercial, and military hub, offering jobs, better schools, and a wider world. Unlike many southern cities, however, Montgomery's black influx did not keep pace with the arrival of rural whites and the departure of Montgomery blacks for northern cities. While the city's counted black population doubled from 20,000 in 1920 to 42,750 thirty years later (total population was 109,000 in 1950), its proportion declined during this period from 45 to 40 percent of the total (37 percent in 1955). During the 1940s alone, the white population grew by about 50 percent while the black community gained half that much.[1]

Most Montgomery blacks in the 1950s worked in service jobs or as laborers, many at the two neighboring air force bases. More than half of employed black women worked as domestic servants in white households. A majority of African American adults could be classified as "working poor"; black median income was $1,000 in 1949, less than half of that of the total city population.[2] Their needs for education, religion, medical and dental care, and other professional and business services—which due to racial barriers were not met by whites—fostered the growth of a small but relatively prosperous black middle class. This group benefited materially to some degree from the segregated social structure, while sharing its inequities and humiliations with the less well off whose needs they served. The core of this emerging professional class was city public school teachers and faculty at the black Alabama State College, which was established in Montgomery in 1887 primarily to train black teachers. The most civic-minded and politically active of these educators tended to be women.

Alabama's African American citizenry could take pride in a strong tradition of political activism that began during slavery and was first openly expressed during Reconstruction in local "union leagues" asserting civil and economic rights and in successful black legislative campaigns. In the 1880s and 1890s impoverished Alabama sharecroppers and tenant farmers formed chapters of the semicovert Colored Farmers Alliance and joined a short-lived electoral coalition with white Populists. In 1901 black petitions and other pressure failed to sway the state constitutional convention from disenfranchising black citizens.

The hardening of white supremacy at the turn of the century enhanced the popularity of Alabama educator and politician Booker T. Washington, whose accommodationist strategy held out hope for economic progress in the teeth of intensified oppression. Thousands of rural black families sought to escape racial subjugation by migrating to cities and to the North. Those who stayed tried to avoid white hostility, which was accentuated by the Ku Klux Klan resurgence of the 1920s. A small minority of Alabama blacks dared to resist the suppression of rights. Most notable was the early 1930s campaign to defend the "Scottsboro boys," nine youths who were improperly convicted of raping two white women. This campaign coincided with creation of the Alabama Sharecroppers Union in Tallapoosa and other southern Alabama counties near Montgomery; the union attracted several thousand members and organized an effective strike of cotton pickers in 1935 but did not survive violent attacks by sheriffs and vigilantes. In Montgomery and other Alabama cities black activism during the 1930s and 1940s centered on voter registration efforts, which were bolstered by the Supreme Court's decision in *Smith* v. *Allright* outlawing the South's white-only primary elections.[3]

The sudden Montgomery uprising of December 1955 did not take black Americans completely by surprise. In the decade since World War II black leaders had felt the pulse of their people's surging aspirations for freedom and fairness. These aspirations were vitalized and legitimized by the Supreme Court's public school desegregation decision in May 1954, which also heightened white resistance. But to the white mainstream, North and South— still sleepwalking through the nightmare of McCarthyism—the mass protest seemed as foreign as revolutionary upheavals in Africa and Asia. And that was the point: King was one of numerous contemporary blacks who came to view the Montgomery movement as part of a worldwide struggle of peoples of color against colonialism and white supremacy. Jamaican Marxist historian and activist C. L. R. James wrote in March 1957 that the bus crusade was as "revolutionary . . . profoundly so" as Ghana's successful independence campaign and the autumn 1956 Hungarian anticommunist revolt—despite all three movements' departure from proper Leninist principles. "Here is something that is new," he observed about Montgomery, in his opinion "one of the most astonishing events in the history of human struggle."[4] Toward the end of the protest King himself heralded "the birth of a new age."

The bus boycott was a thoroughly local movement, despite its external support. It served for a decade as the model community movement, influencing activists in southwest Georgia, Birmingham and Selma, Alabama, northern Florida, along the Mississippi Delta, and many other places. Unlike his outsider role everywhere else, King was the chosen representative of the Montgomery black community, which created, legitimated, and sustained his leadership. Never again would he participate in a local movement with such solid, nearly total, black community support. Never again would a movement of this era, black, white, or brown, be so effective in uniting a community across class, gender, and age.

The secret of success? A network of intrepid organizers, situated in overlapping black institutions, organized the entire community that was fractured both economically and geographically. Backing ranged from top to bottom, from the black elite—notably, Alabama State College president H. Councill Trenholm, who criticized tactics while proffering advice through his wife—to winos living on the streets who religiously guarded car pool fleets from nighttime sabotage. It might have been expected that the small cadre of activist ministers, professionals, and business owners would go all out for the cause. But this vanguard harnessed women's clubs, sororities, fraternal orders, ministers' associations, and other groups and corralled nearly all preachers, even the most apolitical or conservative, along with teachers, physicians, dentists, barbers, beauticians, undertakers, and shop owners. Led by this black middle class, and leading it by turns, marched the movement's foot soldiers from the class of working poor, the great majority of participants. Of these, female domestic workers (maids and cooks) predominated.[5]

Indeed, the bus boycott carried forward and consummated the communitarian lifeblood of the African American freedom struggle. For a century and a half black leaders had invoked direct action and protest when necessary, but communal support and resource sharing were the mainspring of both survival and change. Black resistance to white supremacy had always been most compelling when community building and protest activity infused and reinforced each other. More than any other instance of the twentieth century, the bus boycott mobilized black community institutions and resources as tools of reform and used protest as catalyst for community uplift and moral and spiritual regeneration. In every sense the bus protest was driven by, and fully expressed, the energy of collective self-help. Even the name Montgomery Improvement Association, which might have been inspired partly by Marcus Garvey's United Negro Improvement Association of the 1920s, conveyed the convergence of community and movement. Leaders understood that improving or elevating the black community would have been merely cosmetic without structural renewal, which entailed reshaping mores, customs, and power relations between black and white and among blacks themselves. If in the larger American culture liberalism and communitarianism spoke different languages, the black world, exemplified by the Montgomery experience, could not afford a dichotomy between fighting for individual rights and fortifying the community bonds that made it possible to actualize human rights in everyday life.

When it grew evident that the bus boycott would have to endure past a few days or weeks, King extended his leadership beyond city and state limits. The leaders learned that segregation could not be reformed, which was their initial goal, and certainly not in isolation. It would have to be abolished, throughout the South. This new abolitionism, they came to realize, would ultimately require a coordinated Southwide movement with major northern support. King spoke frequently at church and community rallies in the North not only to raise funds but also to solidify a growing community of black and white activists around the country and to marshal the backing of the black church, particularly his own National Baptist Convention, USA. He forged ties with an established black leadership network of preachers, politicians, educators, and journalists. He allied with white liberals and progressives in pacifist, labor, and religious circles. Partly by design but more by the dynamic of events, leaders built the bus boycott such that it set the stage organizationally, intellectually, and spiritually for the massive national movement that sprung out of Montgomery. King's oratorical leadership proved as vital in this regard as the new structures, networks, and alliances he helped create.

But King did not make the movement, as civil rights leader Ella Baker pointed out later, "the movement made Martin."[6] This was especially true in Montgomery. As veteran organizer E. D. Nixon put it, the question was not what "King did for the people of Montgomery, it's what the people of Montgomery did for Reverend King."[7] Citizens who had bravely organized for years before he came to town vaulted him to overall leadership while holding on to their own leadership identities. Setting the tone for the coming decade, grassroots activists revered King as the central figure but did not uncritically follow his lead or always acknowledge his practical as opposed to symbolic leadership. When plaintiff Claudette Colvin, a high school student, was asked in the federal court hearing that led to the nullification of bus segregation who was the protest leader, she testified, "Our leaders is just we ourself."[8]

She meant what she said. On March 2, 1955, the fifteen-year-old eleventh grader boarded a city bus outside King's Dexter Avenue Baptist Church and refused to give up her seat for a white passenger when ordered by the driver. Colvin replied that she was "just as good as any white person" and was not going to move. She told a policeman summoned by the driver: "I didn't know that it was a law that a colored person had to get up and give a white person a seat when there were not any more vacant seats and colored people were standing up."[9] Colvin was legally correct about the city ordinance, which required a Negro to relinquish a seat only if a vacant one was available; the state statute, however, had no such provision. As two officers roughly dragged her from the bus, she insisted: "It's my constitutional right to sit here. . . . You have no right to do this."[10] They handcuffed and jailed her.

Colvin's arrest, which fortuitously occurred amid a municipal election campaign, galvanized Montgomery's African American community. Two black civic organizations, the Women's Political Council (WPC) and the Citizens Coordinating Committee, met with city commissioners and bus officials. The delegation was led by WPC president and Alabama State College English professor Jo Ann Robinson and included E. D. Nixon, Rufus Lewis, Mary Fair Burks, Rosa Parks, and King. At the first meeting the officials appeared conciliatory, but at the second one they were intransigent. Bus company attorney Jack Crenshaw spurned any modification of the seating policy as illegal under the city's bus segregation ordinance. Former WPC president Burks recalled that the prospect of "a boycott was mentioned," apparently by Robinson.[11]

Authorities threw the book at Colvin, charging her with violating the state segregation law, disorderly conduct, and resisting arrest. "Instead of being exonerated as we anticipated," Robinson wrote in her memoir, she was convicted and placed on indefinite probation. "She had remained calm all during the days of her waiting period and during the trial, but when she was found guilty, Claudette's agonized sobs penetrated the atmosphere of the courthouse." After the verdict, "blacks were as near a breaking point as they had ever been. Resentment, rebellion, and unrest were evident in all Negro circles. For a few days, large numbers refused to use the buses" in a spontaneous protest.[12] King reported that "the long repressed feelings of resentment on the part of the Negroes had begun to stir. The fear and apathy which had for so long cast a shadow on the life of the Negro community were gradually fading before a new spirit of courage and self-respect."[13]

On October 21, 1955, eighteen-year-old Mary Louise Smith was arrested for refusing to give up her bus seat for a white woman. "I was sitting behind the sign that said for colored," she testified as a plaintiff in the *Browder* v. *Gayle* federal lawsuit. "A white lady got on the bus and she asked the bus driver to tell me to move out of my seat for her to sit there. He asked me to move three times, and I refused. So he got up and said he would call the cops. . . . I told him: 'I am not going to move out of my seat. I am not going to move anywhere. I got the privilege to sit here like anybody else.' So he say I was under arrest, and he took me to the station."[14] She was jailed briefly, then tried in city court and fined nine dollars—not for violating the segregation law, since she apparently had not, but for failing to obey an officer. Community leaders did not find out about her inconspicuous arrest and conviction until several weeks later. Both Colvin and Smith believed that they were not breaking the law.

By the early 1950s ill treatment on city buses had emerged as the most common and acute black community problem, since so many thousands, especially working women and schoolchildren, depended on the bus for daily transport. It inflicted, and symbolized, the injustice of Jim Crow apartheid; it proved the impossibility of "separate but equal" accommodations.[15] Resentment and anger intensified, fueled by expectations of better race relations in the post–World War and post-Korea era. Women's Political Council leaders were chiefly responsible for converting the personal pain of abusive treatment on buses into a visible public issue. Burks, chair of Alabama State's English Department, had founded the WPC in 1949 after experiencing allegedly racist conduct by Montgomery police. Dexter congregants like Burks and Robinson comprised the core of the group's membership of middle-class professional women, many of whom taught at Alabama State or in public schools. The WPC's initial purposes were to foster black women's involvement in civic affairs, to promote voter registration through citizenship education, and to aid rape victims.

During fall 1949 Robinson joined the newly formed women's group, having just begun teaching at the black college. Upon completing her first semester, she boarded a bus to the airport to spend Christmas holidays with family in Cleveland, Ohio. Unfamiliar with seating rules, the young professor sat down in the front white section of the almost empty bus. The driver yelled at her and nearly struck her. She fled in terror. Shaken by the incident, she vowed to remedy such racial abuse. When she succeeded Burks as WPC president in the early 1950s, the group focused more on bus treatment and other everyday concerns, such as police brutality and inferior parks and playgrounds. Robinson persuaded Mayor W. A. Gayle to allow WPC leaders to attend all city meetings that affected black residents. They learned how to lobby white officials face to face.

The WPC was the largest, best organized, and most assertive black civic organization in the Alabama capital. It cooperated with other community groups and individuals that had been organizing longer but had prioritized voter registration and electoral politics, particularly after the Supreme Court abolished southern primaries that excluded black voters.[16] E. D. Nixon, a Pullman train porter and longtime head of the Alabama region of A. Philip Randolph's Brotherhood of Sleeping Car Porters, founded the Montgomery

Voters League in 1943 to promote black registration and voting. In June 1941, the month of a threatened black march on Washington against racial discrimination in war industry, he led several hundred African Americans to the county courthouse in an attempt to register, which was blocked by county officials. Registration efforts gathered steam after World War II, when black combat veterans came home with raised confidence and self-esteem. They expected to be rewarded for fighting for freedom overseas with more freedom at home.

Nixon hammered away at a host of rights issues as president of the Montgomery NAACP branch (1946–50) and the state NAACP conference (1947–49).[17] Rufus Lewis, an undertaker who had coached a championship Alabama State football team in the 1930s, made voter registration a single-minded crusade. In the late 1940s he formed the Citizens Club to promote registering and voting among veterans and other young people. A handful of ministers too had battled racial injustice. In 1949 Rev. Solomon S. Seay sought redress without success for a young black woman raped by two white police officers. After the Supreme Court's 1954 decision in *Brown* v. *Board of Education* he led a campaign to desegregate public schools. For four years, through 1952, Vernon Johns railed against segregation from the pulpit of Dexter Avenue Baptist Church. To promote black economic development he helped set up and sponsored a produce marketing cooperative for local farmers. Owing partly to friction among African American leaders, such as that between the middle-class Lewis and working-class Nixon, and to resignation in the black community, but more because of monolithic resistance by the white elite, none of these ameliorative efforts made much headway by mid-decade. Black leaders faced a strategic dilemma that would bedevil the freedom movement for years to come. They lacked political power and knew that they could not really change their circumstances until they were fully enfranchised. But electoral initiatives toward this end, vital for long-term progress, did not offer immediate solutions to the community's pressing problems.

Early Thursday evening, December 1, 1955, after a long day of pre-Christmas tailoring at Montgomery Fair department store, Rosa Parks was arrested on a city bus when, ordered by the driver, she refused to give up her seat in the unreserved midsection to a white man. As with Colvin, no vacant seat was available, so she would have had to stand, carrying her packages. The forty-two-year-old seamstress was a civil rights activist of long standing who had served as secretary of both the Montgomery and Alabama state NAACP. For years she had advised the local NAACP Youth Council, which she had helped found in the 1940s; she persuaded Colvin to join the activist youth group after her March arrest. Although Parks had not planned her calm, determined protest, she later recalled that she had "a life history of being rebellious against being mistreated because of my color." The time had come "when I had been pushed as far as I could stand to be pushed. . . . I had decided that I would have to know once and for all what rights I had as a human being and a citizen."[18] Reflecting later on her motives, Parks said that she refused to obey the driver's command "because I was so involved with the attempt to bring about freedom from this kind of thing. . . . I felt just resigned to give what I could to protest against the way I was being treated, and felt that all of our meetings, trying to negotiate, bring about petitions before the authorities . . . really hadn't done any good at all."[19]

Nixon, whom Parks had worked with for a dozen years in the NAACP and as his secretary in his union's regional headquarters, bailed her out of city jail. Two liberal whites accompanied him: local attorney Clifford Durr, who had served as federal communications commissioner during the New Deal, and his wife, Virginia Foster Durr, a leader of the antisegregation Southern Conference Educational Fund (SCEF), a crusader against the discriminatory poll tax, and sister-in-law of Supreme Court Justice Hugo Black. The influential justice and ex-Alabama senator would play a crucial role in the boycott saga later in the year. The four returned to Parks's small apartment on Cleveland Avenue where Nixon persuaded her, over her husband's opposition, to use her arrest to challenge the constitutionality of city and state bus segregation laws.[20] Parks's unblemished character and high stature in the African American community made her the ideal representative of black grievances and hopes.

Later that evening Nixon conferred on the telephone with Jo Ann Robinson, who had learned of the arrest from Fred Gray, one of two black lawyers in town and a protégé of Clifford Durr. Robinson and Nixon agreed to bolster a slow-moving legal challenge with a one-day bus boycott on Monday, December 5, the date of Parks's trial, to dramatize the issue and demonstrate black unity and determination. But while Nixon wanted first to enlist backing of black ministers, Robinson and her WPC colleagues kicked off the long-discussed bus boycott on their own. They did not want it held back by more cautious leaders. Near midnight Robinson typed a flyer calling for direct action and drove to the Alabama State campus. She and a business professor spent the night mimeographing thousands of copies of the half-page flyer. The next day, between and after classes, two students helped her deliver bundles throughout black neighborhoods.

While flyers circulated around town, Nixon called the preachers. Hesitating at first, King offered his support and agreed to host a meeting of the city's black leadership at his church. Later that day ministers joined with the WPC, Citizens Coordinating Committee, Nixon's Progressive Democrats, and other black groups to prepare for the Monday protest and a mass meeting at night.

On Sunday morning preachers urged participation from dozens of pulpits. A front-page article about the protest in the Sunday paper, intended to alert the white community, further spread the word to blacks.

Scarcely any African Americans rode the buses on Monday, December 5. Most walked to work or school, carpooled with friends, or hitchhiked. Hundreds rode taxis; black cabdrivers voluntarily cut fares. In the morning Parks appeared in Recorder's Court with her supporters. Judge John B. Scott convicted her and fined her ten dollars plus court costs. Gray, her lawyer, appealed the verdict to a higher state court. Meeting that afternoon at Mount Zion AME Zion Church, eighteen leaders created a new organization, the Montgomery Improvement Association (MIA), to direct the protest. They quickly elected officers, set up committees, decided on demands, and drew up an agenda for the 7 P.M. mass meeting. Rufus Lewis nominated King, his pastor, for MIA president; participants elected him without opposition. They chose him because of his reputation as an orator—he was known locally as a compelling social gospel preacher—and because of his independence, as a relative newcomer, from long-running quarrels and rivalries among community leaders.

That evening, with little time to plan it, King delivered his first major political address at Holt Street Baptist Church in a black working-class section. He combined "the militant and the moderate," he later reflected, in encouraging the overflowing audience of several thousand to find "the moral courage to stand up for their rights," but to use the weapon of Christian love. "Let us be Christian in all of our actions," he said. "But I want to tell you this evening that it is not enough for us to talk about love. Love is one of the pivotal points of the Christian faith. There is another side called justice. And justice is really love in calculation. Justice is love correcting that which revolts against love. . . . Not only are we using the tools of persuasion but we've come to see that we've got to use the tools of coercion."[21] After Rev. Ralph D. Abernathy read the boycott resolutions from the podium, the vast audience rose as one and with great cheering expressed their resolve to continue the boycott "until some arrangement has been worked out" with the bus company.[22]

Leadership wore many faces during the Montgomery bus boycott. Much of it came from ordinary people acting in extraordinary ways, such as Claudette Colvin, Jo Ann Robinson, E. D. Nixon, Georgia Gilmore, Ann Pratt, and Mother Pollard. In particular, individuals exercised leadership when they purposely influenced others to challenge injustice on the buses. A pivotal act was Robinson's initiation of the mass protest by producing and distributing her flyer. Half a decade of nonconfrontational grassroots leadership, especially persistent organizing by the Women's Political Council, culminated in this breakthrough. Subsequently several dozen mainly middle-class organizers were assisted in leadership tasks by hundreds and then thousands of working-class bus riders. The latter encouraged, cajoled, and prodded family, friends, and neighbors to stay off buses, find other transportation, attend mass meetings, and donate hard-earned cash. Many with an automobile or spare time aided the car pool. Spontaneous leadership of various sorts transpired in packed autos and waiting lines at dispatch and pick-up stations. Those who lost jobs or sacrificed in other ways inspired their friends to give more and risk more. Personal example played a critical role in the spreading of leadership.

Three levels of leadership interacted and overlapped. King, Abernathy, and several other charismatic Baptist and African Methodist Episcopal (AME) preachers were mobilizers. Nixon, Robinson, and several dozen others, mostly women, comprised the organizers, including a score of ministers. As many as several thousand activists led at the microlevel of extended family, neighborhood, church, and workplace. The followers were the majority of the black population, at least 20,000 people, who, even if they seldom or never attended a mass meeting, participated by refusing to ride buses.

How did King fit in to the Montgomery movement's rich mosaic of leadership? Rooted in religious and biblical contrasts, his leadership embodied both the lion and the lamb, the patriarchal prophet and the suffering servant. On one hand, the leadership legacy that he inherited from his great-grandfather, a slave preacher, his grandfather, and his father lent him charismatic authority, poise, self-possession, and capability to marshal resources, especially money. On the other hand, a more informal leadership style that derived from less acknowledged sources—his mother and maternal grandmother, sensitive, even mystical, ministers like Howard Thurman, his encounter with humanistic psychology, his scrutiny of the Gospels, his growing identification with Jesus, his apparently genuine humility—instilled in him a genius for listening, learning, mediating, and finding sharable ground; for engaging and amplifying the needs, longings, and aspirations of the people who elevated him to his high station.

King's protest leadership spun out of his pastoral, priestly, and prophetic roles as Baptist preacher. He arrived in Montgomery one of the best educated of a rising generation of activist African American clergy, shaped by mentors like Thurman, Benjamin Mays, and William Holmes Borders, who wanted to apply the black church's power and resources to promoting racial justice. King's speaking abilities were the fruit of his immersion in Baptist church culture since early childhood, seasoned by several years of preaching in At-

lanta, Boston, and Montgomery. Although other dynamic orators like Abernathy fired up mass meetings, "no person could inspire the people like him,"
Rufus Lewis averred.[23] His verbal wizardry epitomized the preacher's tradi-
tional role as moral guide of the black community, galvanizing followers behind shared moral purposes of reform, uplift, and salvation. He insistently reminded his extended congregation that their movement was a unique chance
to make history; that by taking part in this great moral cause they served as
agents of freedom and justice. He inculcated a sense of personal responsibility
to fight evil and to further good.

From the time of slavery the test of a black preacher's leadership was his
capacity to lift the self-esteem and transform the self-perception of his audiences. King was so effective in mobilizing Montgomery blacks because his
visionary moral appeals empowered them to act to better their lives and see
themselves anew—as somebodies, as historical, even biblical actors, as a special, chosen people. Their heady sense of making history in the here and now
and of helping to fulfill God's plan for His kingdom, gave them feelings of self-
worth, efficacy, and sacred purpose. Jo Ann Robinson was struck by King's
ability to foster moral courage; she saw participants grow to the extent they
learned from him how to "maintain themselves under pressure." He taught,
she recalled, that if one loses one's equilibrium, one loses one's power and
sense of self.[24] King often rhapsodized about the "new Negro" emerging in the
South who had "replaced self-pity with self-respect and self-depreciation with
dignity. . . . In Montgomery we walk in a new way. We hold our heads in a new
way."[25] The young minister's gift for translating everyday wants, needs, and
longings into compelling universal principles and for dramatizing lofty moral
ideas in vivid, down-to-earth word pictures made his oratory irresistible not
only to all segments of the black community but also to open-minded white
audiences.

King's inspirational and instructional role as preacher carried over into his
moral leadership of the Montgomery black community. And his hands-on
managing of Dexter and his work in the broader Baptist network molded his
institutional leadership of the MIA. He ran the movement like a church writ
large. His administrative style was previewed by the recommendations for
Dexter's reorganization that he had pressed upon congregants a few days after
moving to town. Stressing the pastor's nearly absolute authority, he had explained that leadership "never ascends from the pew to the pulpit, but it
invariably descends from the pulpit to the pew."[26]

The Dexter recommendations highlighted his delegation of authority to a
select few, his reliance on an extensive committee structure, and the centrality
of fund-raising. Just as Martin Luther King Sr., in the depth of the Depression,

had lifted Atlanta's Ebenezer Baptist Church from the prospect of foreclosure to prosperity, his son was determined to keep the MIA solvent and ensure sufficient funds for its costly car pool system, paid staff, and relief to victims of economic reprisal. The legacy of his father that weighed heaviest on him was the imperative of sound fiscal management and financial security. King took major responsibility for the MIA's aggressive fund-raising, although Nixon and others shared this burden. King's frequent speaking trips garnered hefty sums, setting the tone for the rest of his career. In the early months, however, MIA funding relied on local people. Pitches by King and other mobilizers raised on average two to three thousand dollars at each weekly or twice-weekly mass meeting. More came from local churches and community groups. At the end of the bus boycott the MIA faced the future with a substantial surplus, which it tried to use as capital to launch a cooperative savings and loan bank. Although the amount of outside money was significant, the boycott earned enough from its own participants to cover regular expenses (but not legal costs).

At home in his dominant position, King delegated much authority to a handful of trusted ministers, particularly the heads of the Finance and Transportation Committees. When in late spring 1956 the car pool system ran into major problems of driver shortages and profiteering—some drivers defrauded the MIA for gasoline, tires, and repairs, and even charged passengers—King pressured a reluctant Rev. Benjamin J. Simms, an Alabama State professor, to take over the faltering Transportation Committee. "It had reached the point," Simms later remembered, "that our transportation system needed full-time supervision and complete reorganization. The MIA board called an emergency meeting. We were gravely concerned that blacks would be forced to ride those buses if we didn't get ourselves organized." Simms arrived late to the meeting, and King asked him to step outside the room. "People respect you," he recalled King buttonholing him, "people know that you're a pastor and that when you say something, that's that. And you can handle this thing. We need you, Brother B. J., don't fail us." Simms still was not convinced. King said: "Do it for me and for your people." "Mike, I'll do it if you'll let me run it," Simms replied. "If I have to have any interference from the front office up there . . . I can't handle it. If you let me run it, you can draw up certain guidelines, and I'll consult with the board, but I've got to have the last words within the limits." King said that he would back him "to the hilt."[27]

Simms's vigorous leadership turned the car pool into a model of efficiency. He set up three repair shops, designated official gas stations, instituted a uniform pay scale for drivers and a system for keeping track of them, oversaw dispatchers working around the clock, and demanded meticulous record keeping. The car pool tried to ensure every black person transportation when and where they needed it. "It was just beautiful," recalled Ann Smith Pratt, a hair stylist who served as Simms's chief dispatcher. "Beautiful blacks seeing one another perform efficiently on a big scale. There was something electrifying about our collective success. We developed a smooth working operation and as we got better and better, the city fathers downtown began to really panic. Most of us in transportation stayed charged up spiritually. It must have been God working. . . . That's where the strength must have come from."[28] Nevertheless, frustrated by the executive board meddling he had feared, Simms resigned several months later.

As the bus boycott carried on in the face of legal repression, white intimidation, and sporadic violence, King relied increasingly on his inner circle of pastors, all Baptists except for AME ministers Solomon S. Seay and W. J. Powell. Although sometimes resentful of King's rising stardom, these loyal lieutenants backed his efforts to tighten control over the MIA. For example, they authorized him to communicate to the media or negotiate with white officials without the executive board's prior approval. In fact the board decided that *only* King could speak to reporters and that leaders who represented the MIA outside Montgomery "will follow a given pattern prepared by a committee for such specific speeches or submit his speech in writing to the speakers' bureau."[29] Thus the MIA president largely controlled the movement's flow of information to the outside world.

Hierarchy and authoritarian control told only part of the story of King's leadership, however. They contrasted with, yet paradoxically provided structure and space for, his ability to listen, to pay attention, to learn. Top-down control interacted with democratic intimacy to engender a mode of leadership whose authority—claim to obedience and loyalty—was rooted in King's engaged relationship with subleaders and followers, a bond deeper than mere consent. His leadership offered a stable framework for volatile, freewheeling deliberation and dissent, encouraging conflict but keeping it in bounds. King's charisma and power, like that of Abraham Lincoln, another master of the authority and democracy dialectic, proved more compelling because these qualities were grounded in a sense of personal connection, felt as mystical by some. He strove to create with participants the "I-thou" relationship (as opposed to "I-it") that, following Jewish philosopher Martin Buber, he held up as a personalist ideal.

According to those who knew him, King's humility—the root meaning of the word is closeness to the earth—was not just an image that he learned how to dramatize on the public stage; it was sincere. It allowed him to suspend his elite mindset and enter others' worlds, meeting them on their levels and drawing them into his own. He established trust by self-revelation, admitting shortcomings and sins. His veiling of ego and eschewing of arrogance endeared him to the black masses and enabled him to transcend internecine quarrels that limited other leaders' effectiveness. His humility fertilized his folk humor—masterful joke telling and bantering—that disarmed opponents, bolstered morale, and restored group harmony. Ever the conciliator, his mediating skills were enhanced by his patience and attentiveness. In meetings he insisted on hearing out and considering everyone's view before making a decision. He typically achieved consensus by blending disparate views or finding an acceptable middle ground.

Jo Ann Robinson later recalled: "There was no other leader there with the humility, with the education, with the know-how of dealing with people who were angry and poor and hungry. . . . If King had not been prepared to talk with all of them, make all of them feel that they were making a contribution—and they were. Even that man who couldn't give a straight sentence was letting you know how he felt, and maybe representing the people from his area. And you had to have knowledge of all of it, in order to be able to work with all of it."[30] Knowledge is the telling word. King's responsiveness to ordinary people, his determination to learn from them and to absorb their varying perspectives, represented a distinguishing mark of his leadership from Montgomery until the end of his life. Projecting himself as a Christlike role model of courage, compassion, and humility, King motivated participants to embrace the cause with its risk and sacrifice, to stick with it and with each other. He struggled to reconcile his faith and moral certitudes with the doubting and questioning fostered by his honest soul searching, respectful learning from others, and the inexorable contingency of human life. Subleaders and foot soldiers not only strengthened his commitment but also emboldened him to take further risks and to rise above his comfort zone and socialization. "We really pushed him a whole lot," Nixon later recalled.[31]

In fact, initiative and direction came as much from less visible organizers as from King and his ministerial inner circle—especially from women. Because of sexism, protection of vulnerable jobs, and deference to a long tradition of leadership by black ministers, female leaders such as Robinson stayed in the background and rarely served as speakers at mass meetings or at assemblies out of town. In his Montgomery memoir, which generally minimized others' leadership, King singularly praised Robinson's contribution. "More than any other person," he wrote, she "was active on every level of the protest."[32] Besides her influential role as strategist on the executive board and major committees, she served as a key MIA negotiator since she had accrued the most experience lobbying white officials. She also edited the MIA newsletter and, despite a full teaching load, drove in the car pool mornings and afternoons.

She was one of very few women, perhaps the only one, whose voice carried weight in policy making.[33]

Yet women did most of the everyday organizing that kept the boycott going. "We really were the ones who carried out the actions," MIA financial secretary Erna Dungee remembered. "We organized the parking lot pick-ups" and much else. Women "passed the ideas to men to a great extent." Although Robinson and Mary Fair Burks "were very vocal and articulate, especially in committee meetings," Dungee recalled that in the mass meetings women "let the men have the ideas and carry the ball. They were kind of like the power behind the throne."[34]

Reciprocal leadership suffused the spirited mass meetings, where boycotters, many of whom were illiterate, learned, practiced, and even invented skills of participatory democracy that became integrated with familiar church rituals like call and response, praying, and singing hymns. Democratic practices included debating goals, strategies, and tactics; voting on important decisions; reaffirming or revising the leaders' mandates; training in nonviolent tactics; and fanning enthusiasm. Rev. Robert Graetz recalled that the "maids were the soldiers" who "rallied" and prodded the leaders. "Maids would stand up at mass meetings and tell about the arguments at employer's house. Maids would tell stories and people would cheer."[35]

Georgia Gilmore, a cook, nurse, and midwife, formed the "Club from Nowhere" (the name to preserve anonymity), which sold sandwiches, pies, and cakes and donated the proceeds at mass meetings. Gilmore and her friends had chosen to give their culinary skills to the cause. "We collected $14 from amongst ourselves," she said later, "and bought some chickens, bread and lettuce, started cooking and made up a bundle of sandwiches. . . . When we'd raise as much as $300 for a Monday night rally, then we knowed we was on our way for $500 on Thursday night. Then other ordinary folks like us started doing the same thing in their neighborhoods—competing with us, trying to raise more than us."[36] When Inez Ricks set up a rival club, the two women's friendly jousting enlivened the meetings. In creative tension with its authoritarian center, the movement's fluid structure spread opportunities for grassroots leadership that empowered many working-class participants.

At times the foot soldiers lifted leaders' faltering morale, sometimes the other way around. King and fellow mobilizers absorbed from participants the growing moral passion that they had helped galvanize, and they reflected it back verbally as eloquent, easily grasped justifications for their struggle and sacrifice that further fortified morale. The leaders and the foot soldiers kept each other from giving up.

At least once King edged to the brink of giving up. It took all of his spiritual resources and reassurance by activists to repair his courage and equilibrium. Late at night on January 27, 1956, hounded by phone calls threatening death, unable to sleep, he sat down at the kitchen table and confessed his despair to a personal God. "I am here taking a stand for what I believe is right," he remembered praying. "But now I am afraid. The people are looking to me for leadership, and if I stand before them without strength and courage, they too will falter. I am at the end of my powers. I have nothing left. I've come to the point where I can't face it alone."

"At that moment," he recalled, "I experienced the presence of the Divine as I had never experienced Him before. It seemed as though I could hear the quiet assurance of an inner voice saying: 'Stand up for righteousness, stand up for truth; and God will be at your side forever.' Almost at once my fears began to go. My uncertainty disappeared. I was ready to face anything."[37]

Three nights later, while presiding at a mass meeting, his house was bombed. Dynamite sticks damaged the front of the house but did not harm his wife, their two-month-old daughter, Yolanda, or a companion. They had rushed to the back bedroom when they heard the bomb hit the porch. King returned to find a furious throng of several hundred blacks outside his house, many armed, who "came to do battle," his wife later recalled. Calmly, appearing free of anger, he stood on his porch with Mayor Gayle and Police Commissioner Clyde Sellers and persuaded the aroused crowd to put away their guns and go home.

"It could have been a riot, a very bloody riot," Coretta Scott King remembered. "If that had happened I think the whole cause could have been lost, and it would have been very tragic for everyone." Moreover, her husband's leadership "would have been tarnished." She saw the incident as "a turning point in the movement, a very significant moment in terms of injecting the nonviolent philosophy into the struggle." The movement might not have survived had King "not made such a forceful statement that night on our porch."[38] This was the most dramatic and public but not the only time that he almost single-handedly steered the civil rights movement from turning violent. Acting spontaneously in the heat of the moment, he gracefully transformed the Montgomery protest's first direct encounter with violence into a public declaration of commitment to nonviolent principles, grounded in Christian faith. His action and words set a defining tone for the next decade.

Overcoming the bombing crisis buoyed King's confidence to cope with difficult trials in the months ahead. Martin and Coretta King helped each other to accept that he or she or both of them might be killed, an especially frightful prospect because of their infant child. They sustained themselves by strong faith, friends' and family support, and keeping busy. Besides caring for

Yolanda and cooking for endless guests, Coretta King monitored movement news in the media, took part in meetings, advised her husband, and preserved piles of movement documents. Her best stress reliever was resuming her singing career, which she had suspended while pregnant. She gave recitals of spirituals and classical music in Montgomery churches and elsewhere during 1956 that culminated in a New York benefit concert for the bus boycott in early December, where she shared star billing with Harry Belafonte and Duke Ellington.[39]

If the bus boycott was so rich in leadership, what difference did King make? Was he more than an eloquent "mouth piece" that the people "employed," as Aurelia Browder testified in the federal lawsuit that bore her name? He himself admitted, minutes before his house was bombed, that "if M. L. King had never been born this movement would have taken place. I just happened to be here. You know, there comes a time when time itself is ready for change. That time has come in Montgomery, and I had nothing to do with it."[40] His involvement was important but not essential for strategizing, policy making, managing, fund-raising, and community organizing. As much as the other mobilizers combined, his oratorical leadership nurtured people's morale, commitment, courage, endurance, solidarity, and faith. The one area where he made all the difference, however, was in shaping the movement's non-violent character.

This meant more than keeping his followers from resorting to violence out of frustration or rage, a remarkable achievement in itself. Many participants were prepared, as a last resort, to uncork the bloodshed Coretta King feared. Beyond adhering to the ethic of noninjury to opponents that Mahatma Gandhi called *ahimsa*, King pioneered the first explicitly nonviolent mass movement in U.S. history. Such nonviolent action did not appease, avoid, or stifle conflict but faced and fostered it. It did not constrain or inhibit force but deployed it creatively, with moral economy and strategic efficiency, for transformative ends. Nonviolent theorist Richard Gregg, who influenced King's thinking, called this force "moral jujitsu." Guided by Gandhi, Gregg, and other teachers, King crafted a coherent *philosophy* of nonviolent engagement that incorporated others' ideas about strategy, tactics, and technique into a larger ethical and spiritual framework. In Montgomery he tested the philosophy in the raw experience and uncharted terrain from which he formed it. He threw all of his freshly minted authority, stature, and prestige, all of his moral capital, into the daunting task of winning support for it from organizers, activists, and the black community as a whole. Rarely has a leader melded theory and practice so successfully as King did during the bus boycott; more so certainly than he did later in his career. For this new public philosophy, which until his death he elaborated, deepened, and rearranged to fit historical developments, he owed much to circumstance and locale, more to experienced organizers who mentored him, and more still to the black church culture that he refashioned to serve his nonviolent ideal.

The MIA leaders' initial aim was not to eliminate segregated bus seating but to make it more tolerable. In several negotiating sessions with city and bus company officials in December and January, they proposed a "first come, first served" seating arrangement that the parent bus company was using in Mobile and other southern cities. Blacks would sit from back to front, whites from front to back, preserving segregation but without prereserved sections. When it became evident that white officials would not accept so modest a reform, and when the city commissioners instead imposed what they called a "get tough" policy in January, black leaders abandoned hope of a quick settlement. They shifted course. After several discussions, the MIA Executive Board decided on January 30—in the afternoon before King's house was bombed—to file a federal lawsuit, aided by NAACP lawyers, to challenge the constitutionality of the city and state bus segregation statutes.

Next they debated whether to call off the bus boycott. Many ministers were tired and frustrated and sought a graceful exit. King was ambivalent but felt swayed by the foot soldiers' sentiment. "From my limited contact," he confided to the board, "if we went tonight and asked the people to get back on the bus" (he said this *before* the near riot that night) "we would be ostracized. They wouldn't get back. . . . I believe to the bottom of my heart that the majority of Negroes would ostracize us. They are willing to walk."[41] Feeling strong pressure from below, the leaders voted to continue the bus boycott. They may have hoped that the disruption and media attention would penetrate the minds and hearts of federal judges holding court a few blocks away. What did King mean by "ostracize?" No doubt he worried that the aroused mass following might repudiate the leaders. He might have feared too that participants would replace the current leadership with others more militant, more responsive to the people's will, perhaps advocates of violent tactics.

Several days after MIA attorney Fred Gray filed the federal lawsuit, whose plaintiffs were Claudette Colvin, Mary Louise Smith, and two other black women alleging discriminatory bus treatment, Judge Eugene Carter of Montgomery Circuit Court convened the county grand jury to examine evidence that bus boycott leaders were violating an obscure 1921 Alabama statute outlawing conspiracies to disrupt lawful business.[42] Some white opinion leaders, such as *Montgomery Advertiser* editor Grover Hall Jr. and even the district attorney at first, opposed prosecution as an extreme and counterproductive response. Nevertheless, on February 21 the grand jury indicted eighty-nine bus boycott leaders, including King and two dozen fellow ministers, on conspiracy charges.

The mass indictments coincided with the arrival of two seasoned radical pacifists who came to Montgomery to help out. On separate missions, Bayard Rustin and Glenn Smiley brought two closely linked traditions of nonviolent activism into the heat of battle. Rustin, a New Yorker, championed the application of Gandhian nonviolence to American race relations on the level of *mass* direct action. Rooted in labor movement militancy during the Depression, this nonviolent tradition was born in the March on Washington Movement conceived and led by A. Philip Randolph in the early 1940s that forced President Roosevelt to ban racial discrimination in war industry hiring and to create the Fair Employment Practices Committee (FEPC) to enforce the ban. Randolph, whom some called an "American Gandhi," had founded the Brotherhood of Sleeping Car Porters in 1925 and was widely considered the most influential black leader of his time. Both the 1941 campaign to bring tens of thousands of blacks to protest in Washington, which was called off when Roosevelt signed Executive Order 8802, and the wartime rallies and "Negro mass parliaments" in northern cities organized to fight racism, had tried to combine Gandhian satyagraha with mass direct-action tactics that CIO-affiliated unions had employed creatively during the 1930s. After the war Randolph used the threat of large-scale noncooperation with peacetime conscription to pressure President Harry Truman to issue a 1948 executive order that desegregated the armed services.

The other nonviolent tradition was developed by the pacifist Fellowship of Reconciliation (FOR) and its offshoot, the Congress of Racial Equality (CORE). Founded in England in 1914, FOR was an international Christian-based organization that sought nonviolent solutions to war and social conflict aiming at reconciliation. Under A. J. Muste's leadership, the American branch of FOR made racial justice a high priority in the 1940s. It midwifed CORE's creation in 1942 to experiment with interracial civil disobedience against segregation in the North and Upper South. The FOR tradition was white and middle class, explicitly shaped by Gandhian practice, rigorously pacifist; it focused on small group actions, prioritized interracialism, and was anchored in the Christian faith. By contrast, Randolph's "nonviolent good-will direct action" was shaped as much by the American labor movement as by the Gandhian independence struggle. It stressed mass action, aimed at mobilizing African Americans as an autonomous force, and was working-class, democratic socialist, and secular.

The two traditions nevertheless had shared values and goals and to some extent a common language, style, and ethos.

In the early weeks of the bus protest, King contacted J. Oscar Lee, head of the Department of Racial Justice of the National Council of Churches, to find out what resources might be available for training in nonviolent tactics. Lee referred him to FOR and to Bayard Rustin, executive secretary of War Resisters League (WRL), a secular and more radical pacifist group founded in 1923. Just after King's house was dynamited, a meeting took place in Randolph's New York office to decide whether Rustin should go to Montgomery. Participants included Muste, Socialist Party leader Norman Thomas, and James Farmer, a CORE founder.

Rustin's experience and skill in nonviolent direct action was unequaled in American pacifist circles. Not only had he worked closely with Randolph as youth organizer of the March on Washington Movement, but he had also served for twelve years as FOR's race relations director, helped create CORE, and among other protest actions was jailed in the "Journey of Reconciliation," CORE's 1947 effort to desegregate interstate bus travel in the Upper South. During these formative years he was mentored by Muste as well as Randolph. Muste guided him more in personal, ethical, and spiritual ways, and Randolph more in strategy and ideology. Rustin's stature among pacifists was marred, however, by his involvement in the Young Communist League in the 1930s (although by now anticommunist) and by a 1953 arrest for alleged homosexual activity in Los Angeles, which forced him to resign from FOR. Despite fears that Rustin's past, if disclosed, might harm the Montgomery movement, especially with McCarthyism rampant, Randolph and Muste swallowed their own doubts and persuaded colleagues that he was worth the risk.

When Rustin arrived in Montgomery on the day the indictments came down, he lost no time convincing leaders to submit freely to arrest in Gandhian fashion. Over the next week he tutored King in nonviolent theory and practice and advised MIA strategy sessions. Questions about the charismatic outsider's affiliations soon raised suspicion among a few local black leaders and white reporters, however. At a second New York meeting on February 28, Randolph and associates decided to ask him to leave town. From a distance, in and out of the shadows cast by both McCarthyism and homophobia, he served for half a decade as King's most influential adviser. During the bus boycott, even at arm's length, he seemed to have a hand in everything. Besides advising on strategy and tactics, he promoted education on nonviolent resistance among participants and the public and, to help spread the protest, he trained black leaders from other southern cities in nonviolent methods. In the

North he organized rallies, raised funds, and built support, especially from organized labor. Most important, he introduced King to Gandhian non-violence and its community of practitioners, and he initiated King's alliance with Randolph.

Independent of Rustin, the FOR sent Smiley, its national field secretary, into the Montgomery cauldron. A white Methodist minister raised in Texas, Smiley had worked with FOR since 1942 and like Rustin (whom he considered "my guru" in nonviolence) had been imprisoned as a draft resister during World War II. Already immersed in southern civil rights support, Smiley met with King, who asked him to "teach me all you know about nonviolence" and, according to the visitor's recollection, to teach nonviolent methods in Montgomery and across the South and to organize support groups of white ministers.[43] When Smiley asked what he knew about Gandhi, King reportedly replied: "I have read some statements by him," but "I know very little about the man," although "I've always admired him."[44]

Committed to racial justice but empathetic to concerns of southern whites, Smiley saw himself as a troubleshooter seeking nonviolent solutions to racial disputes and fostering local reconciliation. Rustin, in contrast, perceived his mission in larger, longer-range, and more strategic terms, as helping to launch a nonviolent revolution throughout the South. For him resolving the immediate bus dispute was not as crucial as using the bus boycott to catalyze further campaigns to advance the movement. Like Randolph, he sought to carry forward the goal of the March on Washington Movement, interrupted by the Cold War and McCarthyism, to build a national crusade of mass nonviolent action to abolish racial segregation.

Rustin reported to WRL that the bus boycott leaders were exploring non-violent principles and tactics and "are clear that they will have no part in starting violence. There is, however, considerable confusion on the question as to whether violence is justified in retaliation to violence directed against the Negro community. At present there is no careful, non-violent preparation for any such extreme situation." Nevertheless King was "developing a decidedly Gandhi-like view and recognizes there is a tremendous educational job to be done within the Negro community."[45]

Smiley wrote to FOR superiors on February 29 that King told him he "had Gandhi in mind when this thing started," that he was "aware of the dangers to him inwardly, wants to do it right, but is too young and some of his close help is violent. King accepts, as an example, a body guard, and asked for permit for them to carry guns. This was denied by the police, but nevertheless, the place is an arsenal. King sees the inconsistency, but not enough. He believes and yet he doesn't believe. The whole movement is armed in a sense, and this is what

I must convince him to see as the greatest evil. . . . If he can *really* be won to a faith in non-violence there is no end to what he can do."[46]

His developing ideas shaped by these related American Gandhian traditions, King forged during 1956 an amalgam of Gandhian nonviolence and black Christian faith, both in oratory and mass action. This was exactly fifty years after Gandhi invented satyagraha ("truth force" or "soul force") in South Africa. If, as King later wrote, "Christ furnished the spirit and motivation, while Gandhi furnished the method," black Protestant practice provided much of the methodology as well, particularly such mobilizing rituals as call and response preaching, praying, and singing spirituals.[47] Although refined by FOR's faith-based pacifism (which itself blended Gandhian with Christian ideas), King's resolutely Christian nonviolence did not derive so much from the white moral reform tradition of evangelical Protestantism, of which FOR was an offshoot, with its accent on moral perfectibility. Rather, he fashioned it more from values, themes, language, rituals, and other resources of the African American religious experience rooted in slavery. This included the black social gospel tradition he had picked up from his father, grandfather, and other activist preachers. His signal contribution to nonviolent protest was to incorporate Gandhian principles and techniques into the black church culture that had nurtured him, and to do so in ways, sometimes subtle and nuanced, that did not distort or disrupt this church culture but instead enabled it to manifest effectively its latent legacy of resistance.

In particular, King brought together Randolph's Gandhian mass action with black social gospel to create a synthesis of visionary but pragmatic nonviolent politics. Like blues or jazz, this was a fundamentally African American concoction that injected black intellectual and cultural elements into the larger American cultural and political mosaic and reshaped it. If Randolph's goodwill direct action was more instrumental, applied social gospel unleashed the prophetic fire.

Unlike its better-known white counterpart, the black social gospel tradition was driven more by the Old Testament than by the New. It sought to merge the two bibles in ways that much of white Christianity shied away from. One reason that King was so drawn to Reinhold Niebuhr's neoorthodox theology was that in his reclaiming of Hebrew Scriptures Niebuhr began in roughly the same place as did the black Christian belief system: with the problem of evil, its omnipresence in human life, and the prophetic resistance to it. If the basis of the white social gospel of Walter Rauschenbusch and others was that humans were naturally good, original sin notwithstanding, and were corrupted by sinful social structures—therein the potential for human perfectibility— then the basis of black social gospel was that evil had overtaken the world and its peoples. God was commanding humankind, especially black people, to pursue a messianic mission to fight the Devil and win the world back for God and goodness. Black spirituality took the Devil seriously. It was presently Satan's world as much as, or more than, God's. This cosmic injustice had to be rectified.

Human fighters for good and justice had to wield prodigious power, as proxies or conduits for God, to vanquish the evil Goliath. This power had to be equivalent to the power God wielded to part the Egyptian sea, which brought "the death of evil upon the seashore," the theme of a sermon King gave during the bus boycott; power at least metaphorically on a par with lightning and thunder, storms and floods. Mere moral witness, while useful and necessary (especially as a long-run corrective), was hardly sufficient as a weapon against evil. Nonviolent methods had to be more powerful than violent ones, applications of greater mass and energy. Mass nonviolent power fused physical with psychological, moral, and spiritual force: the Godlike power of moral absolutes, certitudes, and commandments, fueled by fervent faith. Such sacred force had to be tempered and bounded by compassion, understanding, and humility—qualities compressed in what King called goodwill. The grace of goodwill (theologically, "the love of God working in the lives of men") not only rendered righteousness a power that could be wielded safely by mortal beings. It also magnified this power by making it a force for personal conversion and transformation, for realizing one's higher self.

Traditional pacifism and Gandhian nonviolence stressed the power of love alone to effect social change. The nonviolent philosophy King synthesized aspired to be more dynamic, multidimensional, and dialectical. It combined two divinely originated forces, as King interpreted them, into one—the power of justice and righteousness and the power of agape, or creative goodwill. If the power of love could transform individual hearts and minds, righteousness grappled with collective evil. If love was tangible and interpersonal, justice was transpersonal. King sought to merge these two powers, incompatible on the surface, into a seamless union more potent than the sum of its parts; in theory and rhetoric, if not easily in action.

"Love must be at the forefront of our movement if it is to be a successful movement," he told Smiley in late February 1956. "When we speak of love, we speak of understanding goodwill toward *all* men. We speak of a redemptive, a creative sort of love." His words then shifted subtly: "So that as we look at the problem, we see that the real tension is not between the Negro citizens of Montgomery and the white citizens, but *it is a conflict between justice and injustice, between the forces of light and the forces of darkness*, and if there is a victory—and there will be a victory—the victory will not be merely for the

Negro citizens and a defeat for the white citizens, but it will be a victory for justice and a defeat of injustice. *It will be a victory for goodness in its long struggle with the forces of evil.* This is a spiritual movement."⁴⁸ Love necessitated justice and vice versa. The bus protest served as proving ground for the faith that good would ultimately triumph over evil.

The Montgomery movement was more spiritual than Gandhi's but it was not quite as principled. In his March 1956 conspiracy trial King and his lawyers put bus segregation on trial, somewhat in Gandhian fashion. Yet, whereas Gandhi insisted on truth telling in the courtroom and a willingness to go to prison, King's and fellow leaders' sworn testimony was riddled with evasions and prevarications to gain acquittal. Gandhi, a British-trained lawyer, put his faith in direct action to topple the British Empire. King and the participants in the civil rights movement, however, relied upon legal tools afforded by the Constitution and its Fourteenth Amendment, which Britain lacked, to supplement and reinforce mass protest and to defend themselves from what they perceived to be unconstitutional legal assaults.

Leaders of the MIA turned the crisis of the conspiracy indictments into a fortuitous opportunity to strengthen the movement. Judge Carter and prosecutors agreed to a defense request to try the many defendants separately, without juries. That King would be tried first and alone meant that media coverage of his trial would magnify his leadership mystique and emerging role as preeminent national symbol of black advance. After a four-day trial with several dozen witnesses, Carter convicted him of conspiring to disrupt the bus system "without just cause or legal excuse" and sentenced him to a $500 fine plus court costs. The judge converted the sentence to a year in jail at hard labor when King indicated he would not pay it. His lawyers appealed the verdict, sentence was postponed, and black people everywhere hailed King as a hero. Fund-raising for the MIA surged, with half of its year-long total garnered in the next two months. The spectacle of the trial as a David beaten by Goliath enabled King to tap existing black leadership networks, North and South, along with northern-based white and biracial civil rights groups. While his main purpose in cultivating this support network was to generate backing and money for the MIA, he drew upon these diverse allies during the boycott aftermath, when southern leaders utilized the Montgomery victory to launch a Southwide organization to combat segregation.

During the 1950s as in the prior half century, the locus of African American leadership lay in a professional subculture of black-run institutions: churches, colleges, newspapers, fraternal and women's orders, and civic groups like the NAACP. Because he had grown up in this middle-class milieu in Atlanta and his parents had close links to ministers, educators, and journalists throughout the land, King was well positioned to win support from the black elite, many of whom were acquaintances and some his mentors. The two most influential leaders with whom he formed enduring ties were Randolph and Roy Wilkins, the new NAACP chief—both men of his father's generation whom he had not known before. Although his maternal grandfather, A. D. Williams, had headed the Atlanta NAACP branch after World War I, his father was active in it during the 1930s and 1940s, and he himself served on the Montgomery NAACP Executive Committee, he had yet had little if any contact with the NAACP national leadership. The national office in New York initially refused to support the bus boycott because MIA demands did not include eliminating segregation. After MIA lawyers Fred Gray and Charles Langford filed the *Browder* v. *Gayle* lawsuit with NAACP legal help, Wilkins covered most legal costs for the lawsuit and the conspiracy trial. Still, tensions arose over King's concern that the NAACP might exploit the bus boycott in fund-raising and Wilkins's fear that the MIA would capture NAACP funding sources.

King's desire to stand as an equal with established civil rights leaders showed also in his first contacts with Randolph, who had been battling for black people's rights, especially on the labor front, well before King's birth. Although he valued Randolph's support, which opened the door to backing by several national labor unions (Randolph served as first black AFL-CIO vice president) and other progressive groups, King did not always reciprocate. He respected but rarely deferred to his elders. Despite Randolph's repeated appeals, King did not participate in the April 24 "State of the Race" Conference in Washington of seventy-five African American leaders, which Randolph called to respond to segregationist leaders' attacks and chart future strategy; nor did he speak at a major civil rights rally in New York's Madison Square Garden a month later that featured the Montgomery struggle.

In early March 1956, a week after Randolph asked Rustin to leave Montgomery, his protégé met with King in Birmingham to discuss "How Outsiders Can Strengthen the Montgomery Nonviolent Protest." Rustin left the meeting convinced that "an ad hoc committee is essential" to organize northern support for the bus boycott and stimulate similar protests.[49] He joined A. J. Muste, James Farmer, and other FOR and War Resisters League activists to create the Committee for Nonviolent Integration (CNI), a support group geared to furthering the Montgomery movement. The CNI's most useful contribution was holding workshops on nonviolent methods for southern black leaders. The short-lived committee complemented In Friendship, a group founded in February by Ella Baker and other New York–based activists to "provide economic assistance to those suffering economic reprisals in the efforts to secure civil rights."[50] Besides giving financial, technical, logistical, and intellectual aid, Rustin, Baker, and other figures in the boycott's expanding support network helped convey King's ideas to likely allies among liberals, labor, and the religious left.

Support for the bus boycott in the white world came mostly from its progressive fringe, but backing among blacks, centered in mainstream black institutions, was pervasive. King had grown up not only in Atlanta's Ebenezer Baptist Church but also in the nation's largest black organization, the National Baptist Convention, USA—with its thousands of preachers, several million lay members, and its myriad missions, services, ministers' and Sunday school teachers' training programs, seminaries, and affiliated colleges like King's alma mater, Morehouse. His leadership of the bus boycott propelled his rise in this religious empire in which his father and grandfather had been prominent. During 1956 two senior ministers promoted his candidacy, at twenty-seven, to challenge autocratic incumbent J. H. Jackson of Chicago, an old family friend, for the NBC presidency. More important, King used his growing clout in this body to further the bus boycott and the civil rights cause within the black religious world. Yet, while his emphasis early on was mobilizing the black church South and North, his religious outreach was also ecumenical and interracial. He planted the seeds of enduring alliances with white Protestants, Catholics, and Jews that bore fruit in the 1960s.

On June 5, 1956, after a mid-May hearing, a special three-judge federal court panel in Montgomery ruled two to one in favor of the *Browder* v. *Gayle* lawsuit. The court declared unconstitutional the Montgomery and Alabama bus segregation statutes as violations of the Fourteenth Amendment's equal protection clause. The decision hinged on how the three judges interpreted the Supreme Court's two-year-old school desegregation decision. Federal appeals judge Richard T. Rives's majority opinion, in which district judge Frank M. Johnson Jr. concurred, found that the *Brown* decision's rejection of the 1896 *Plessy* v. *Ferguson* "separate but equal" doctrine reached beyond public schools to other forms of legalized racial segregation. District judge Seybourn H. Lynne's dissent argued it did not. The federal court deferred enforcement of its decree until the Supreme Court could rule on the city of Montgomery's appeal. The boycott carried on through summer and fall.

On November 13, the same day that the city finally secured a state court injunction shutting down the MIA car pool, the Supreme Court unanimously affirmed the federal court's June *Browder* ruling, giving constitutional sanction to Rives's broad interpretation of *Brown*. In fact, unlike the *Brown* decision, the high court's eleven-word summary disposition now specifically overturned the sixty-year-old *Plessy* decision since, like *Plessy*, it applied to segregated public transport, buses in place of trains. Next evening several thousand participants at two simultaneous mass meetings voted to approve the MIA Executive Board's motion to halt the bus boycott as soon as the Supreme Court ruling was implemented. Due to a final city appeal and procedural delay, the court's enforcement order did not arrive in Montgomery until December 20. After spirited mass meetings that night, the black community returned to the buses in the morning, 381 days after the boycott began. Shortly after dawn King sat next to Glenn Smiley in the front of a city bus right behind Ralph Abernathy. The first two days of desegregation brought little open resistance, but late Saturday night, December 22, someone fired a shotgun through King's front door. Three days after Christmas three buses were fired on, injuring a black passenger. City commissioners suspended evening bus service.

King stressed that the outcome of the boycott ought to be seen not as a victory of blacks over whites but of justice over injustice; that it would benefit both races, in the long run anyway. "The end is reconciliation," he told the Institute on Nonviolence and Social Change, which the MIA organized in early December to further the movement and deepen its understanding of nonviolence. "The end is redemption; the end is the creation of the beloved community."[51]

During the immediate aftermath, in which participants' heady feelings of triumph and vindication mingled with fear and foreboding, King turned his attention to how his acclaimed leadership might catalyze a broad new civil rights structure to support local struggles across the South. It was needed as much for protection of fragile gains as for further progress. This goal had been central for Bayard Rustin from the outset and had begun to be realized with the Committee on Nonviolent Integration.[52] Smiley too had felt the need for a Southwide vehicle to promote communication, coordination, and teaching of nonviolent methods to local leaders. He had organized an FOR-sponsored conference of southern black leaders at Morehouse College on May 12 that evaluated the protests in Montgomery and Orangeburg, South Carolina, where black college students were striking in response to white economic retaliation.

King conferred often during the bus boycott with leaders of sister movements, sharing information and advice and arranging mutual aid, particularly with fellow Alabama preachers Fred Shuttlesworth of Birmingham and Joseph Lowery in Mobile. The state's June 1956 court injunction barring Alabama NAACP operations made such interchange all the more urgent since the state NAACP had provided what little coordination had previously linked Alabama activists. He also kept in touch with Baptist ministers C. K. Steele, leader of the concurrent Tallahassee, Florida, bus boycott, and T. J. Jemison in Baton Rouge, Louisiana, who had led a short, effective bus boycott in June 1953; the MIA emulated its car pool system. Lowery recalled that he, King, and Shuttlesworth "saw this need to get together and then we just talked about how we ought to broaden it to include Steele, Jemison, and the other guys."[53]

Having nudged King's thinking all year about the need for a regional organization, Rustin began active planning in the second half of November with two New York colleagues, Ella Baker, of the NAACP and In Friendship, and Stanley D. Levison, a white left-wing attorney and civil rights supporter. In correspondence to King on December 23 Rustin suggested: "Regional groups of leaders should be brought together and encouraged to develop forms of local organization leading to an alliance of groups capable of creating a Congress of organizations."[54] Several days later on a speaking trip to Baltimore, Martin and Coretta King shaped plans with Rustin and Levison, who were accompanied by attorney Harris Wofford and his wife, Clare, authors of *India Afire*, a first-hand look at the Gandhian independence movement and its aftermath.

On January 7, 1957, the MIA issued a press release announcing an "emergency conference call" sent out on New Year's Day by King, Steele, and Shuttlesworth to about 100 southern leaders in a dozen states asking them to gather in Atlanta on January 10–11. Despite recent legal victories in Montgomery and Tallahassee, the Southern Negro Leaders Conference on Transportation and Non-violent Integration convened in a crisis mood. In Tallahassee, the seven-month bus boycott, which had been precipitated in May 1956 by the arrest of two female Florida A&M students, Wilhelmina Jakes and Carrie Patterson, for sitting in the white section of a bus (in the only vacant seats), had just been suspended by its leaders after a federal judge, at the bus company's request, restrained the city from enforcing bus segregation. After a week of desegregated riding, on January 1 Florida governor LeRoy Collins declared a local state of emergency and halted bus service in the capital.[55] In Birmingham, Shuttlesworth had formed the Alabama Christian Movement for Human Rights (ACMHR) after the June outlawing of the Alabama NAACP, of which he had been a leader. On Christmas night his home was destroyed by dynamite, but he and his family escaped serious injury. The next morning, as planned, he led about 250 black citizens to challenge segregated seating on Birmingham buses, backed by King. He and twenty others were arrested. Bus desegregation campaigns were taking place also in Atlanta, Miami, Mobile, New Orleans, and other cities.

Martin Luther King Sr. hosted the two-day Southern Negro Leaders Conference at his Atlanta church. Martin and Coretta King stayed at his parents' home along with Abernathy.[56] At two A.M. the night before the meeting began, Juanita Abernathy telephoned her husband to tell him that their home and church had been bombed, along with the Graetz parsonage and three other black churches. King and Abernathy rushed back to Montgomery. In their absence Coretta King, Steele, and Shuttlesworth chaired the conference, with Rustin and Ella Baker orchestrating in the wings.

Sixty representatives from twenty-nine communities in ten southern states spent the first day discussing several "Working Papers" that Rustin had drafted. A large majority were black clergy, only a handful were black women, and only one, Rev. Will Campbell of Mississippi, was white. Besides Coretta King none of the bus boycott's women leaders, not even Robinson, attended the Atlanta conference. Rustin's brief mimeographed papers addressed issues such as responding to violence, the role of nonviolence and of law, and the relationship of voting-rights organizing to direct action. Rustin's first paper raised the key questions: "Do we need a coordinating group for advice and council among the present protest groups?" And "should such a council try to stimulate bus protests in other areas of the South?"[57] Conferees answered the first question affirmatively by constituting themselves a continuing group and choosing King chairman when he returned on the second afternoon. They did not resolve the second, thornier question. The consensus seemed more to press for federal intervention against violence and violation of court rulings than to launch new protests. For the time being they wanted to forestall terrorist reprisals brought on by more confrontational efforts.

Upon adjourning, the leaders issued a wide-ranging "Statement to the South and Nation," appealing to Christian principles of love and reconciliation. It seemed aimed chiefly at the white majority, particularly to "white Southerners of goodwill" and white churches and clergy. "We advocate nonviolence in words, thought and deed, we believe this spirit and this spirit alone can overcome the decades of mutual fear and suspicion that have infested and poisoned our Southern culture." They called for federal action: for President Eisenhower to speak in a southern city urging southerners to abide by Supreme Court decisions; for Vice President Richard Nixon to make a fact-finding tour of the South like the European trip he made for Hungarian refugees after the Soviet invasion; and for Attorney General Herbert Brownell Jr. to meet with their representatives about the Justice Department's responsibility to preserve law and order in the Deep South.[58] They got only perfunctory response.

In early February 1957 King sent telegrams to conferees asking them to reconvene on Valentine's Day in New Orleans at New Zion Baptist Church. Its pastor, A. L. Davis, had been a leader of the New Orleans bus desegregation campaign. Ninety-seven mobilizers and organizers from thirty-four cities created a formal organization, the Southern Leaders Conference, and elected King president.[59] More than a coordinating body, the association emerged as a regionwide equivalent to the MIA: a hierarchically structured organization of black leaders, mostly ministers, to link church-based movements sprouting across the South. The mass base of the black church, with its tiers of organizers, activists, and participants in each locality, was incorporated into the organization through its preacher leaders. A clergy-led association composed of affiliates like the MIA, Birmingham ACMHR, and Tallahassee Inter-Civic Council could not only foster leaders' collaboration but also enhance their ability to mobilize their own communities behind shared goals. The leaders decided not to make it a mass membership organization, mainly so as not to compete with the NAACP, but this decision would have major implications for organizing options and fund-raising down the road.

Glenn Smiley had tried to set up a different brand of organization: a biracial group of southern activists, including white and black clergy, educators, and college students, that would have been more explicitly grounded in non-violent principles.[60] Although King trusted Smiley and FOR and appreciated their help, his Baptist orientation combined with the success of the MIA model drew him toward forming a more indigenous, all-black structure in which preachers, himself at the center, would run the show. He and his colleagues christened it the Southern Christian Leadership Conference (SCLC) at a third gathering in Montgomery in August 1957. Thus, movement leaders chose for their strategic vehicle the nonviolent tradition of Randolph and Rustin, which called for a black-led organization and mass action, rather than FOR's pacifist tradition that sought interracial leadership and more spontaneous, smaller-scale activism.[61]

As it took shape in 1957, the new organization chose not to foster further bus boycotts or other direct action against segregation. This would come later. In the next few years, even in Montgomery, black citizens made little progress in desegregating schools, parks, or other public facilities. Conference leaders decided to concentrate on voting-rights education and organizing in southern cities, hoping to launch a Southwide mass movement to gain the franchise. This strategy was idealistic in that achieving universal suffrage would require not only changes in official practices but also in black attitudes, customs, and culture; and the amelioration promised by black voting power would take time. It was practical in that, being less of an immediate threat to white supremacy, it would not provoke as much violent opposition (outside of Mississippi) nor be impeded by the mythology of "separate but equal." Moreover, the right to vote was mandated unequivocally by the Constitution.

At the February 14 New Orleans meeting King and his colleagues made plans for a "Prayer Pilgrimage" to Washington on May 17, the third anniversary of the *Brown* decision. Cosponsorship with the NAACP was negotiated with Randolph's help. King's speech to the rally of 25,000 at the Lincoln Memorial, culminating in a call to "Give us the ballot!," prefigured his famous address six years later at the same spot and solidified his preeminence as symbolic leader of the rising black movement.

Despite this dramatic start, SCLC floundered in carrying out its voting-rights campaign. Although it faced daunting obstacles, its failure to build a mass movement in the late 1950s was rooted in a little-acknowledged organizational identity crisis. Was SCLC to center around and capitalize on King's fame and prestige, as some had intended? Or was it to be the congress of local organizations that would nurture and coordinate grassroots activism—modeled by Montgomery—throughout the South? Was its priority to build up King, or to build up the affiliates and their indigenous leadership, dynamic organizers like Jo Ann Robinson, E. D. Nixon, and Fred Shuttlesworth? It could not do both; centralism clashed with decentralism. The gulf between King and the local affiliates not only hindered the latter's efforts but undermined SCLC's own development.

An astute recruiter of leadership, King had the good sense to hire seasoned organizer Ella Baker to manage SCLC's operations; Baker's organizing prowess was in a league of its own. But King erred in not backing her efforts to craft the grassroots-based movement that he rhetorically advocated. In early 1958 SCLC launched the Crusade for Citizenship, aimed at doubling southern black voters by 1960, but it failed to adopt Baker's strategic and tactical proposals. By the end of the first year the crusade had run aground.

If SCLC had forged firmer ties with its affiliate "movement centers," in Nashville for example, it might have realized that, as Montgomery had presaged, protest against the immediate evil of segregation—rather than a push for suffrage—was the strategy needed at this historical moment to ignite and fuel a sustained large-scale movement for black freedom. The unanticipated explosion of southern student activism in 1960 compelled King's organization to downplay voting for the time being and to pursue the path of mass protest not taken at its founding meetings in 1957. Even so, SCLC stumbled before finding its footing; but the brilliant Birmingham campaign and the "Negro Revolution of 1963" led to achievement of civil rights reforms that abolished legal segregation and enforced voting rights. All across the South, as Montgomery had heralded, ordinary citizens proved themselves the motors of change, the leaders of their leaders, the shapers of history.

Bringing into being the SCLC, which after fits and starts surpassed the half-century old NAACP as the leading civil rights organization of the 1960s, was one of the crucial ways that the Montgomery bus boycott prepared the soil for the nationwide black freedom movement that transformed American politics, culture, and values over the next two decades. The bus boycott was "God's proving ground," manifesting the destiny of African Americans to achieve their own freedom and "to redeem the soul of America." It forged and tested the strategies and methodology, the support networks and alliances, the language and vision, the politics and spirituality that helped generate and came to fruition in the ensuing mass movement. The Montgomery experience showed the power, efficacy, and potential of mass nonviolent direct action in the American context. It set the standard for a profoundly democratic grass-roots movement in which leadership was ever more widely shared and creatively performed. It proved that ordinary people could behold the beloved community by building it, day by day, in the storm of heartfelt struggle.

NOTES

1. Discrepancies later found in the population figures of African Americans and other U.S. minorities, especially in urban areas, suggest that the official census figures cited here for Montgomery's black population might be under counted. U.S. Bureau of the Census, *Fourteenth Census of the United States*, vol. 2 (Washington, D.C.: Government Printing Office, 1920), p. 60; *Sixteenth Census of the United States*, vol. 2, pt. 1 (Washington, D.C.: Government Printing Office, 1940), p. 319; *Census of Population: 1950*, vol. 2, pt. 2, Alabama (Washington, D.C.: Government Printing Office, 1950), pp. 2–53.

2. *Census of Population: 1950*, pp. 2–62.

3. *Smith* v. *Allright*, 321 U.S. 649 (1944).

4. C. L. R. James to Martin and Jessie Glaberman, March 21, 25, 1957, Martin and Jessie Glaberman Collection, Walter P. Reuther Library, Wayne State University, Detroit, Mich.

5. The organizers utilized contacts with the white community to obtain quiet support or neutrality from a small but critical minority. A few whites were brave enough publicly to endorse the protest, such as Juliette Morgan, Will Sheehan, and Rev. Robert Graetz. Racially moderate governor James Folsom, who watched the walkers and vacant buses from his capitol office atop Dexter Avenue, met with boycott leaders there, seeking to mediate the dispute. He never publicly opposed the protest and may have privately backed its goals, though not its methods.

6. Quoted in David J. Garrow, *Bearing the Cross: Martin Luther King Jr. and the Southern Christian Leadership Conference* (New York: William Morrow, 1986), p. 625.

7. Nixon interview with Steven M. Millner, in *The Walking City: The Montgomery Bus Boycott, 1955–1956*, ed. David J. Garrow (Brooklyn: Carlson Publishing, 1989), p. 551.

8. Transcript of *Browder* v. *Gayle* federal court testimony, Montgomery, Ala., May 11,

1956, p. [23]. Plaintiff Aurelia Browder stated in the same hearing that it was the people, not King, who made the demands to white officials: "We employed him to be our mouth piece" (*Browder* v. *Gayle*, p. [5]).

9. Quoted in Lamont H. Yeakey, "The Montgomery, Alabama Bus Boycott, 1955–56" (Ph.D. dissertation, Columbia University, 1979), p. 234.

10. Transcript of *Browder* v. *Gayle*, May 11, 1956, SER-DNA. Quoted in Ellen Levine, ed., *Freedom's Children* (New York: G. P. Putnam's Sons, 1993), p. 24.

11. Mary Fair Burks, "Trailblazers: Women in the Montgomery Bus Boycott," in *Women in the Civil Rights Movement: Trailblazers and Torchbearers, 1941–1965*, ed. Vicki L. Crawford et al. (Brooklyn: Carlson Publishing, 1990), p. 82.

12. Jo Ann Gibson Robinson, *The Montgomery Bus Boycott and the Women Who Started It*, ed. David J. Garrow (Knoxville: University of Tennessee Press, 1987), p. 42.

13. Martin Luther King Jr., *Stride Toward Freedom: The Montgomery Story* (New York: Harper, 1958), p. 42.

14. Transcript of *Browder* v. *Gayle*, May 11, 1956.

15. Little known by posterity, Montgomery blacks had organized a two-year boycott of public transport half a century before. In August 1900, four years after the Supreme Court's *Plessy* v. *Ferguson* decision that sanctified racially segregated public conveyances, the city of Montgomery, like other southern cities at the time, enacted an ordinance requiring segregated seating on its electric trolley system, the first such system in the Americas. Responding to the new ordinance, many of the city's African American ministers urged their congregations to walk instead of ride. As much as segregation per se, boycott leaders opposed a provision giving police power to streetcar conductors. The *Montgomery Advertiser* reported that "they feared such power would lead to trouble for the negro race" (August 16, 1900). Ten days after streetcar segregation began, the *Atlanta Constitution* stated that "there has been a decided falling off in the travel of the negroes and the boycott is on" (August 16, 1900). Five weeks later the Atlanta daily commented that "Montgomery is experiencing the most unique boycott in its history" and that black riders "have kept it up with surprising persistency" (September 20). The streetcar company admitted that income had dropped 25 percent. In March 1901 a black visitor to Montgomery brought home news of the "universal boycott" he witnessed (*Cleveland Gazette*, March 16, 1901). Historians August Meier and Elliott Rudwick, who discovered streetcar boycotts in twenty-seven cities in every Deep South state during the century's first decade, claimed that the Montgomery protest forced the streetcar firm to suspend segregation, though Jim Crow seating resumed after the boycott died down (Meier and Rudwick, "The Boycott Movement against Jim Crow Streetcars in the South, 1900–1906," in *The Black Experience in America*, ed. James C. Curtis and Lewis L. Gould [Austin: University of Texas Press, 1970], pp. 97–98).

16. *Smith* v. *Allwright*, 321 U.S. 649.

17. A loyal New Deal–Fair Deal Democrat, he also led the Montgomery chapter of the Alabama Progressive Democratic Association, an alternative to the segregated state Democratic Party and a vehicle for blacks to influence it. A role model for black political leadership, Nixon ran a spirited but losing campaign for the Montgomery County Democratic Executive Committee in May 1954. The city's first black candidate in decades, probably since Reconstruction, he garnered 42 percent of the vote. Along with his outspoken NAACP activism, this insurgent campaign made him Montgomery's most visible black leader.

18. Quoted in Howell Raines, *My Soul Is Rested* (Harmondsworth, U.K.: Penguin Books, 1983), p. 44; Rosa Parks radio interview by Sidney Rogers, Montgomery, Ala., 1956 (cassette recording from Pacifica Radio Archive, Los Angeles, Calif.)

19. Transcript of interview with Rosa Parks by Marcia M. Greenlee, August 22–23, 1978, Detroit, Mich. (Black Women Oral History Project, Schlesinger Library, Radcliffe College), p. 9.

20. Raymond L. Parks, a barber at nearby Maxwell Field Air Force Base, had been an activist himself, a longtime member of the Montgomery NAACP who had served during the 1930s on the National Committee to Defend the Scottsboro Boys. Nevertheless, Virginia Durr recalled his panic over the prospect of his wife pursuing her case: "He kept saying over and over again, 'Rosa, the white folks will kill you'" (Virginia Foster Durr, *Outside the Magic Circle: The Autobiography of Virginia Foster Durr* [New York: Simon & Schuster/Touchstone, 1987], p. 280).

21. King, *Stride Toward Freedom*, p. 60; Transcript, First Mass Meeting of the Montgomery Improvement Association, December 5, 1955, reprinted in Clayborne Carson, Stewart Burns, and Susan Carson, eds., *Birth of a New Age: Papers of Martin Luther King Jr.*, vol. 3 (Berkeley: University of California Press, 1997), pp. 73–74.

22. MIA Resolution, December 5, 1955, MLKP-MBU: Box 1.

23. Rufus Lewis interview by Steven M. Millner, July 18, 1977, in Garrow, ed., *The Walking City*, p. 541.

24. Jo Ann Robinson interview by David J. Garrow, April 5, 1984, Los Angeles, Calif. (Interview transcript courtesy of David J. Garrow).

25. Martin Luther King Jr., "Our Struggle," *Liberation*, April 1956.

26. Martin Luther King Jr., "Recommendations to the Dexter Avenue Baptist Church for the Fiscal Year 1954–1955," September 5, 1954, reprinted in Clayborne Carson, Ralph E. Luker, Penny A. Russell, and Peter Holloran, eds., *Rediscovering Precious Values: Papers of Martin Luther King Jr.*, vol. 2 (Berkeley: University of California Press, 1994), p. 287.

27. B. J. Simms interview by Steven M. Millner, July 16, 1977, in Garrow, ed., *The Walking City*, pp. 577–78.

28. Quoted in Vernon Jarrett, "Ben Simms: Man Behind Bus Boycott," *Chicago Tribune*, December 3, 1975.

29. Recommendations of the MIA Strategy Committee, March 14, 1956, MLKP-MBU: Box 2. It continues: "Under no circumstance must that speaker hold a press conference. A copy of that speech may be given to the press but nothing more."

30. Jo Ann Robinson interview by David J. Garrow, April 5, 1984.

31. E. D. Nixon interview by Steven M. Millner, in Garrow, ed., *The Walking City*, p. 551.

32. King, *Stride Toward Freedom*, p. 78.

33. Although in retrospect Robinson felt some bitterness about her unrecognized leadership, particularly compared to the public acclaim bestowed upon Rosa Parks, she kept a low profile partly not to endanger her teaching position at Alabama State or the tacitly supportive college president, H. Councill Trenholm, to whom she reported regularly about the movement. Alabama State College was completely dependent on the white legislature, which did not look favorably upon the bus boycott and its supporters.

34. Erna Dungee Allen interview with Steven M. Millner, August 6, 1977, in Garrow, ed., *The Walking City*, p. 522.

35. Taylor Branch notes on interview with Rev. Robert Graetz (courtesy of Taylor Branch).

36. Vernon Jarrett, "'Nobodies' Paid Boycott's Way," *Chicago Tribune*, December 4, 1975.

37. King, *Stride Toward Freedom*, pp. 134–35.

38. Coretta Scott King interview by Stewart Burns, June 6, 1994, Atlanta.

39. Coretta Scott King interview, June 6, 1994.

40. Quoted in "Notes on MIA Mass Meeting," January 30, 1956, PV-ARC-LNT.

41. Notes on MIA Executive Board Meeting, by Donald T. Ferron, January 30, 1956, PV-ARC-LNT.

42. Gray and the NAACP lawyers had intended Rosa Parks to be the sole federal plaintiff, but because her case was already on appeal to the state court of appeals and because of her NAACP association, they decided to use less well known plaintiffs. The Alabama legislature had enacted the 1921 law, aimed at labor disputes, in the wake of a major strike that year by Birmingham coal miners; it rarely had been invoked.

43. Glenn Smiley interview by Stewart Burns, June 14, 1991, Los Angeles, Calif.

44. Glenn Smiley interview by David J. Garrow, April 6, 1984, North Hollywood, Calif. (courtesy of David J. Garrow). Smiley gave King several books on nonviolence, including Richard Gregg's *The Power of Nonviolence*, Joan Bondurant's *Conquest of Violence*, Krishnalal Shridharani's *War Without Violence*, and Aldous Huxley's *Ends and Means*. A few days later King told Smiley how impressed he was with these works and even quoted passages at a mass meeting.

45. Bayard Rustin, "Report on Montgomery, Alabama," March 21, 1956, ACLUA-NJP.

46. Glenn Smiley to John M. Swomley Jr. and Alfred Hassler, February 29, 1956, FORP-PSC-P.

47. King, *Stride Toward Freedom*, p. 85.

48. King interview by Glenn Smiley, February 28, 1956 (editor's italics), FORP-PSC-P.

49. Bayard Rustin, "Notes of a Conference: How Outsiders Can Strengthen the Montgomery Nonviolent Protest," March 7, 1956, BRP-DLC.

50. Ella J. Baker to King, February 24, 1956, MLKP-MBU: Box 14A.

51. King, "The Birth of a New Age," Address to the Institute on Nonviolence and Social Change, December 3, 1956, in Carson, Burns, and Carson, eds., *Birth of a New Age*, vol. 3, p. 458.

52. Rustin recalled that when he first arrived in Montgomery in February 1956 he suggested to Coretta Scott King the "need for a coordinating agency." Quoted in Eugene P. Walker, "A History of the Southern Christian Leadership Conference, 1955–1965" (Ph.D. dissertation, Duke University, 1978), p. 31. She wrote later that he then expressed his hope that the bus boycott would develop "into a nonviolent movement all over the country." Coretta Scott King, *My Life with Martin Luther King, Jr.* (New York: Holt, Rinehart and Winston, 1969), pp. 137–38.

53. Joseph Lowery interview with Aldon D. Morris, September 21, 1978, Atlanta, quoted in Aldon D. Morris, *The Origins of the Civil Rights Movement* (New York: Free Press, 1984), p. 82.

54. Bayard Rustin to King, December 23, 1956, BRP-DLC.

55. Seeking to evade the November Supreme Court decision applying to Montgomery, the Tallahassee City Commission enacted an ordinance later in January allowing bus

drivers to assign seats according to weight, health, and other ostensibly nonracial factors, which resulted in the arrest of black students contesting its constitutionality.

56. Coretta King recalled that she had participated in preliminary discussions at her home with her husband and other leaders. "When we were ready to go to Atlanta, Martin said 'you need to come with us,' because it wasn't a given that I was going to come, 'and you need to stay, come prepared to stay because the tensions are building, and I don't think you need to be here alone'" (Coretta Scott King interview, June 6, 1994).

57. Bayard Rustin, "Working Paper #1," January 10, 1957, in BRP-DLC.

58. Martin Luther King Jr. et al., "A Statement to the South and Nation," January 11, 1957, MLKP-MBU: Box 2, and Telegrams to Dwight D. Eisenhower, Richard Nixon, and Herbert Brownell Jr., January 11, 1957, DDEP-KAbE.

59. C. K. Steele, whom (according to one source) King handily defeated for president, was elected first vice president. Other officers were Davis, second vice president; Samuel Williams (Atlanta), third vice president; T. J. Jemison (Baton Rouge), secretary; Medgar W. Evers (Jackson), assistant secretary; and Ralph Abernathy, treasurer. Evers, the NAACP's Mississippi field secretary who was assassinated in June 1963, was the only nonminister among the officers; he soon resigned because of pressure from national NAACP leaders who saw his dual roles as a conflict of interest and a threat to NAACP's southern activities.

60. Smiley recalled that "my thought was to get particularly southerners white and black and not solely clergymen but college professors and so on and with a generous sprinkling of youth to come together and to form an organization" (Glenn Smiley interview by Stewart Burns, June 14, 1991). He organized a FOR-sponsored conference of 150 activists in Atlanta on January 8–10, attended by King, whom they elected chairman of the organization they formed. But this new group, intended either as a FOR affiliate or a southern-based Congress of Racial Equality (CORE), was preempted by the Ebenezer conference immediately following, and nothing came of it. Smiley remembered that he was not invited to and did not attend the second conference, although King asked him to come at the last minute.

61. Although King largely followed Rustin's design for the new organization, Rustin did not want the group to be so dominated by preachers or so overtly Christian. He feared it would exclude Jews, Muslims, and nonreligious people. He tried to recruit southern black labor leaders, for example, drawing several to the founding meetings, but they never played a major role in SCLC. The founders added "Christian" to the name partly for practical reasons: to distinguish it from the besieged NAACP and to provide cover against expected white supremacist attacks for leftist influence and "un-American" activities.

Chronology . . .

Spring 1949:   Mary Fair Burks, chair of English Department at Alabama State College, forms the Women's Political Council, a civic organization of African American women in Montgomery, Alabama.

February 9, 1950:   Launching his anticommunist witch-hunt, Republican senator Joseph R. McCarthy of Wisconsin, in a Wheeling, West Virginia, speech, accuses the Truman State Department of harboring 205 Communist Party members.

June 1950–July 1953:   War in Korea. Thousands of African American soldiers serve in integrated military units for the first time in war.

November 4, 1952:   Ending twenty years of Democratic rule, Dwight D. Eisenhower, Allied supreme commander in Europe during World War II, defeats Illinois governor Adlai Stevenson for the presidency. California Republican senator Richard M. Nixon is elected vice president.

June 1953:   Blacks in Baton Rouge, Louisiana, boycott segregated buses to protest drivers' refusal to obey the city ordinance permitting first come–first served bus seating.

May 4, 1954:   E. D. Nixon, the first local black candidate for elected office in decades, is defeated in the Democratic primary for Montgomery County Democratic Executive Committee.

May 7, 1954:	Vietnamese nationalists defeat the French at Dienbienphu, ending the eight-year French Indochina War financed by the United States. Geneva Agreements signed on July 20 divide Vietnam into Communist North and pro-Western South.
May 17, 1954:	In *Brown v. Board of Education of Topeka, Kansas*, the Supreme Court rules unanimously that racial segregation in public schools is unconstitutional.
May 21, 1954:	Jo Ann Robinson, president of the Women's Political Council in Montgomery, writes to Mayor W. A. Gayle, warning of a bus boycott.
July 11, 1954:	Segregationists in Indianola, Mississippi, form the first chapter of White Citizens Council (WCC) to resist desegregation of public schools and other institutions. Chapters of the WCC proliferate throughout the South.
September 1, 1954:	Martin Luther King Jr. assumes pastorate of Dexter Avenue Baptist Church in Montgomery.
February 23, 1955:	A political forum organized by E. D. Nixon's Progressive Democratic Association questions white candidates for the Montgomery city commission about their positions on the bus seating policy and other issues of concern to black citizens.
March 2, 1955:	Montgomery police arrest Claudette Colvin, fifteen, for allegedly violating bus segregation laws.
March 21, 1955:	Voters elect Clyde C. Sellers and Frank Parks to the Montgomery city commission and reelect Mayor W. A. Gayle to a second term.
April 18–24, 1955:	The first summit conference of Asian and African nations takes place in Bandung, Indonesia.
May 7, 1955:	Rev. George Lee is murdered in Belzoni, Mississippi, for civil rights involvement.
May 31, 1955:	The Supreme Court issues an order to implement *Brown v. Board of Education* decision—"with all deliberate speed."

July 14, 1955:	U.S. Court of Appeals, Fourth Circuit (Richmond, Virginia), rules in *Flemming* v. *South Carolina Electric and Gas Company* that intrastate bus segregation is unconstitutional.
August 28, 1955:	Emmett Till, fourteen, is murdered in Money, Mississippi, for allegedly insulting a white woman store clerk.
October 13, 1955:	Beat poet Allen Ginsberg reads "Howl, an indictment of American society" at Six Gallery in San Francisco.
October 21, 1955:	Montgomery police arrest Mary Louise Smith, eighteen, for allegedly violating bus segregation laws.
December 1955:	American Federation of Labor and Congress of Industrial Organizations merge to form the AFL-CIO.
December 1, 1955:	Montgomery police arrest Rosa Parks for alleged violation of bus segregation laws.
December 2, 1955:	Jo Ann Robinson and the Women's Political Council distribute flyers throughout the Montgomery black community calling for a one-day bus boycott on December 5 to protest Parks's arrest and the mistreatment of black bus riders. Black leaders meet to plan the bus boycott.
December 5, 1955:	Rosa Parks is convicted and fined in Montgomery Recorder's Court. The one-day boycott of city buses is a success. Black leaders create the Montgomery Improvement Association (MIA) and elect Martin Luther King Jr. president. Several thousand black citizens attend the first MIA mass meeting at Holt Street Baptist Church and decide to continue the bus boycott.
December 8, 1955:	The first negotiations between MIA leaders and city and bus company officials reach an impasse over the MIA proposal for more equitable bus seating.
December 10, 1955:	King announces that the bus company could accept the MIA's seating proposal without changing the law.

December 13, 1955:	The MIA car pool system begins operation and eventually includes more than 200 private automobiles.
December 16–17, 1955:	Kenneth E. Totten, vice president of National City Lines in Chicago (parent bus company), meets with city and local bus officials, then meets jointly with city officials and MIA leaders. Mayor W. A. Gayle forms a biracial negotiating committee with sixteen members; no progress is made.
December 19, 1955:	The biracial negotiating committee meets again and deadlocks. King is dismayed that a White Citizens Council leader joins the committee.
January 6, 1956:	At a White Citizens Council mass meeting in Montgomery, Police Commissioner Clyde Sellers announces he has joined the organization. Mayor W. A. Gayle and Commissioner Frank Parks join WCC on January 24.
January 9, 1956:	For the last time MIA leaders negotiate directly with city commissioners.
January 21, 1956:	After meeting with three black ministers, city commissioners announce the "settlement" of the bus dispute, which is denied by King and MIA leaders.
January 23, 1956:	Mayor W. A. Gayle announces the city's "get tough" policy in dealing with the bus boycott, including no further discussions with MIA leaders. An MIA mass meeting at Beulah Baptist Church reaffirms support of the bus boycott.
January 24, 1956:	The city commission extends the Montgomery bus company franchise for ten years. Governors of Virginia, South Carolina, Georgia, and Mississippi vow to resist the Supreme Court's *Brown* v. *Board of Education* decision through "interposition."
January 26, 1956:	Montgomery police arrest King for alleged speeding; he is jailed for the first time.

January 27, 1956:   After receiving threatening phone calls late at night, King sits at his kitchen table and, feeling despair, hears a divine voice urging him to "fight on" for justice and righteousness.

January 30, 1956:   The MIA Executive Board decides to file the *Browder* v. *Gayle* federal lawsuit challenging the constitutionality of city and state bus segregation laws. That night King's house is bombed; Coretta Scott King, their two-month-old daughter, Yolanda, and a friend escape injury. Standing on the damaged porch, King persuades an angry crowd to put away guns and go home.

February 1, 1956:   Fred D. Gray and Charles D. Langford file a petition, on behalf of four female plaintiffs, challenging the constitutionality of city and state bus segregation laws. E. D. Nixon's home is bombed, without injury.

February 2, 1956:   King and four other MIA leaders meet with Alabama governor James E. Folsom, seeking protection from violence.

February 6, 1956:   Following several days of protests, whites riot at the University of Alabama in Tuscaloosa against the court-ordered admission of the first black student, Autherine Lucy, on February 3. After initially admitting her, the board of trustees bars Lucy from attending classes "for her own safety" and later expels her.

February 10, 1956:   More than 10,000 whites attend a White Citizens Council rally in Montgomery featuring Mississippi senator James Eastland. The audience cheers the city commissioners for resisting bus desegregation.

February 13, 1956:   Montgomery Circuit Court judge Eugene Carter orders the Montgomery County grand jury to determine if bus boycott leaders are violating a 1921 Alabama boycott conspiracy law.

February 14, 1956:   At the Twentieth Soviet Communist Party Congress in Moscow, new Soviet leader Nikita Khrushchev denounces crimes of Stalin and calls for greater diversity in the Communist world. The speech disillusions many Communists worldwide and encourages democratization in Eastern Europe.

February 18, 1956: The Montgomery County grand jury charges attorney Fred Gray with "unlawful appearance as an attorney" for filing the *Browder* lawsuit on behalf of Jeanetta Reese. She had withdrawn as a plaintiff because of personal concerns; the charge is dismissed on March 2.

February 20, 1956: A MIA mass meeting almost unanimously rejects a bus settlement proposal by Men of Montgomery, a white businessmen's civic group.

February 21, 1956: The Montgomery County grand jury indicts eighty-nine bus boycott leaders for alleged violation of the 1921 Alabama statute barring boycotts without "just cause." New York activist Bayard Rustin arrives in Montgomery.

February 22, 1956: Most indicted leaders report for arrest and booking and are released on bond.

February 23, 1956: King, back from speaking trip to Nashville, Tennessee, reports for arrest and is released on bond.

February 24, 1956: The MIA leaders are arraigned in Montgomery Circuit Court and plead not guilty.

February 27–28, 1956: Glenn Smiley meets King in Montgomery and interviews him for a May 1956 *Fellowship* magazine article. Rustin leaves Montgomery after a black Birmingham newspaper editor threatens to expose his past leftist associations.

February 29, 1956: Attorneys for indicted leaders agree to waive jury trials. King is to be tried first, his case severed from the others.

March 1, 1956: The Alabama legislature convenes a special session to consider Governor James Folsom's proposal for a biracial commission to resolve racial conflict.

March 6, 1956: Alabama state legislators introduce strict new racial segregation bills, including one strengthening bus segregation.

March 12, 1956:   Nineteen U.S. senators and eighty-two House
                   members issue a "Southern Manifesto" ("Declaration
                   of Constitutional Principles") denouncing the
                   Supreme Court's *Brown* decision and other
                   desegregation actions.

March 19–22, 1956: King's boycott conspiracy trial takes place in
                   Montgomery Circuit Court. After four days of
                   testimony by sixty witnesses, Judge Eugene Carter
                   finds him guilty. King appeals, and his sentence (a
                   $500 fine or one year in jail) is suspended. A year later
                   he loses his state appeal on a technicality. He pays the
                   $500 fine in November 1957, and other indicted
                   leaders are never tried.

March 28, 1956:   A National Deliverance Day of Prayer to support the
                   bus boycott takes place in many cities. The
                   Massachusetts legislature halts work for an hour in
                   support.

April 16, 1956:   Students at South Carolina State College in Orange-
                   burg boycott classes after Governor George Timmer-
                   man sends police to halt a campus civil rights protest.

April 17, 1956:   Several thousand commence a boycott of buses in
                   Capetown, South Africa, protesting the imposition of
                   segregated seating.

April 23, 1956:   The Supreme Court dismisses an appeal of the July
                   1955 federal appeals court ruling in *Flemming* v. *South
                   Carolina Electric and Gas Company* outlawing bus
                   segregation in South Carolina. The decision is
                   interpreted erroneously by many as having declared
                   all intrastate bus segregation unconstitutional. The
                   Montgomery bus company decides to implement
                   desegregation.

April 24, 1956:   Bus companies in thirteen southern cities, including
                   Richmond and Dallas, end segregated seating in
                   response to the Supreme Court decision. Montgomery
                   mayor W. A. Gayle announces that city bus segrega-
                   tion will continue; Police Commissioner Clyde Sellers
                   threatens arrest of bus drivers who disobey segregation

laws. After the MIA Executive Board meets, King announces that the bus boycott will go on. Seventy-five black leaders hold a "State of the Race Conference" in Washington and form a committee headed by A. Philip Randolph to push school desegregation in the South.

May 1, 1956: Montgomery officials request an injunction from circuit court judge Walter B. Jones forcing the local bus company to comply with segregation laws.

May 9, 1956: Judge Jones orders the Montgomery bus company to continue to obey segregation laws.

May 11, 1956: A Montgomery federal court hearing on the *Browder* v. *Gayle* lawsuit challenging Alabama bus segregation laws takes place. Claudette Colvin, Mary Louise Smith, and two other plaintiffs testify before appeals judge Richard T. Rives and district judges Frank M. Johnson Jr. and Seybourn H. Lynne.

May 12, 1956: The Fellowship of Reconciliation holds an Atlanta conference of civil rights leaders, including King, Ralph Abernathy, A. J. Muste, and Glenn Smiley.

May 24, 1956: Eleanor Roosevelt, A. Philip Randolph, Roy Wilkins, and Autherine Lucy Foster speak at a civil rights rally in New York's Madison Square Garden. Rosa Parks and E. D. Nixon represent the bus boycott.

May 26, 1956: Two Florida A&M college students in Tallahassee are arrested for allegedly violating the bus segregation law. In response, students and supporters launch the Tallahassee bus boycott, which continues through 1956.

June 1, 1956: Alabama attorney general John Patterson secures a state court injunction barring NAACP operations in Alabama. In response Rev. Fred Shuttlesworth and other Birmingham leaders found the Alabama Christian Movement for Human Rights (ACMHR) to lead the city desegregation campaign.

June 5, 1956: In Montgomery federal court, judges Richard T. Rives and Frank M. Johnson Jr. rule Montgomery and Alabama bus segregation laws unconstitutional; Seybourn H. Lynne dissents.

June 11, 1956: While King is in California, Rev. U. J. Fields resigns as MIA recording secretary and charges fellow leaders with misusing funds. King returns to manage the crisis.

June 18, 1956: At an MIA mass meeting, Fields retracts allegations of financial malfeasance by MIA leaders and apologizes. King asks the audience to forgive him.

June 19, 1956: Following up on their June 5 decision, the federal judges in Montgomery issue a permanent injunction against segregation on Montgomery buses, then suspend the injunction pending an appeal to the Supreme Court.

June 28–29, 1956: The Alabama Public Service Commission and Montgomery city commission appeal the June 5 *Browder* ruling to the Supreme Court.

June 30, 1956: City buses in Tallahassee cease operation in response to the local bus boycott.

July 10, 1956: The ACMHR requests that Birmingham Transit Co. desegregate buses and hire black drivers.

July 20, 1956: King's lawyers submit an appeal of the March 22 boycott conspiracy conviction to Alabama Court of Appeals, which rejects it in April 1957 because of late filing.

July 26, 1956: The MIA Executive Board decides to wait for the full Supreme Court to rule on *Browder* v. *Gayle* rather than seek an immediate decision by Justice Hugo L. Black.

August 3, 1956: The Gold Coast League Assembly adopts Kwame Nkrumah's resolution for the national independence of Ghana.

August 11, 1956: King testifies in favor of a strong civil rights plank before the Platform Committee of the Democratic National Convention in Chicago; the committee approves a weaker civil rights stand. The convention renominates Adlai Stevenson to oppose President Eisenhower in the November election.

August 25, 1956: Lutheran minister Robert Graetz's home is bombed in Montgomery, without injury.

September 1, 1956:	Segregationists rally in Clinton, Tennessee, to protest admission of twelve black students to Clinton High School. A riot prompts the governor to send in the highway patrol and the National Guard; black students are enrolled. Riots opposing public school desegregation occur later that week in Oliver Springs, Tennessee.
September 9, 1956:	Elvis Presley (shown from the waist up) sings to an audience of 54 million Americans on the Ed Sullivan Show. His TV appearances, launching the era of rock and roll, thrilled teenagers and troubled many adults. Three Presley songs were number one hits for long periods during 1956.
September 18, 1956:	Britain grants independence to Ghana, the first African nation freed from colonial rule.
September 27, 1956:	On his way to speak in Hampton, Virginia, King is denied service at a segregated Atlanta airport restaurant.
October 1956:	Allen Ginsberg's *Howl and Other Poems* is published by Lawrence Ferlinghetti's City Lights Books in San Francisco. Police ban the book and arrest Ferlinghetti, whose obscenity trial draws national attention to Beat writers.
October 20, 1956:	A Tallahassee court convicts local bus boycott activists for illegal car pools.
October 29, 1956:	After Egypt nationalizes the Suez Canal, Israel attacks Egyptian forces. British and French troops intervene to seize the canal, but international pressure forces their withdrawal.
October 30–31, 1956:	In Hungary, after a week of anti-Soviet protest by students and workers, reformist leader Imre Nagy announces the nation's withdrawal from the Warsaw Pact. Khrushchev sends Soviet tanks to suppress the revolt. Fierce resistance in November leaves 30,000 Hungarians and 7,000 Soviet troops dead.

November 6, 1956:	President Eisenhower defeats Democrat Adlai Stevenson to win reelection.
November 13, 1956:	The Supreme Court, without dissent, upholds the Montgomery federal court's June 5 *Browder* v. *Gayle* decision striking down Alabama's bus segregation laws. Montgomery Circuit Court judge Eugene Carter enjoins operation of the MIA car pool system. Ku Klux Klan members drive through Montgomery black neighborhoods to harass residents.
November 14, 1956:	Mass meetings of the MIA vote unanimously to halt the bus boycott when the Supreme Court decision is implemented.
December 3–9, 1956:	The MIA celebrates the first anniversary of the bus boycott by organizing a week-long Institute on Nonviolence and Social Change, with guest speakers, seminars, and workshops.
December 5, 1956:	Coretta Scott King sings spirituals at a MIA benefit concert at Carnegie Hall in New York sponsored by In Friendship, also featuring Harry Belafonte and Duke Ellington.
December 17, 1956:	The Supreme Court rejects the Montgomery city commission's final appeal of the *Browder* decision.
December 20, 1956:	After delays, the Supreme Court's implementation of the *Browder* ruling takes effect. Mass meetings of the MIA reaffirm the decision to end the bus boycott.
December 21, 1956:	Led by King, Ralph Abernathy, and Glenn Smiley, black citizens desegregate Montgomery buses after the thirteen-month boycott. The bus company resumes full service. Minor resistance by segregationists includes a white teenager slapping a female passenger.
December 23, 1956:	A sniper fires a shotgun into King's home.
December 24, 1956:	Five white men assault a fifteen-year-old black girl at a Montgomery bus stop. The Tallahassee city

commission orders the local bus company to continue enforcing segregation laws after activists attempt to integrate buses.

December 26, 1956:   In Birmingham, Rev. Fred Shuttlesworth leads 200 activists seeking to desegregate city buses; police arrest twenty-one. On Christmas night, Shuttlesworth's house is destroyed in a bombing attack; no serious injury is inflicted. Birmingham activists vote to continue bus integration efforts. Snipers fire on two Montgomery buses.

December 28, 1956:   Rosa Jordan, who is pregnant, is shot in both legs while riding a Montgomery bus.

December 29, 1956:   Responding to bus shootings, the Montgomery city commission suspends evening bus service.

December 31, 1956:   A sniper fires on another city bus.

January 8–10, 1957:   In Atlanta, the Fellowship of Reconciliation holds a biracial conference of southern activists on nonviolent methods and future strategy.

January 10, 1957:   Sixty black movement leaders confer at Ebenezer Baptist Church in Atlanta. King and Ralph Abernathy return to Montgomery after four churches and two homes are bombed, including Abernathy's church and parsonage.

January 11, 1957:   The Southern Leaders Conference in Atlanta issues a "Statement to the South and Nation" condemning white violence and sends telegrams to the president, vice president, and attorney general urging federal intervention.

January 30, 1957:   Seven Ku Klux Klansmen are arrested for recent bombings and bus shootings. On May 30, the only two defendants tried are acquitted by an all-white jury of bombing a church on January 10. In November 1957, when King withdraws the appeal of his conspiracy conviction and pays a $500 fine, the county solicitor drops all pending boycott conspiracy prosecutions along with any further prosecution of alleged white bombers.

February 14, 1957: In New Orleans, the Southern Leaders Conference reconvenes, forms a permanent civil rights organization, and elects King president. At a third meeting, in August 1957, the organization changes its name to the Southern Christian Leadership Conference (SCLC).

February 18, 1957: King is on the cover of *Time* magazine, which features a favorable article on the bus boycott.

March 5, 1957: Martin and Coretta Scott King attend Ghana's independence celebration in Accra, invited by Prime Minister Kwame Nkrumah. King meets Vice President Richard Nixon in Ghana and urges him to visit Alabama.

May 17, 1957: The Prayer Pilgrimage, at which King is a featured speaker, brings thousands to Washington in the largest civil rights demonstration of the 1950s.

Editorial Practices . . .

The principle guiding the transcribing and editing of these historical documents from the Montgomery bus boycott was to reproduce the original primary source faithfully and accurately, but in readable form. Errors in spelling and punctuation are corrected except when they reveal information about the document or its creator. Typographical errors are corrected. Strikeouts are generally deleted. Spelling of certain frequently used terms or abbreviations is standardized.

Original titles of documents are placed in quotation marks. Authors' insertions are placed in curly brackets. Editor's insertions are in italics and enclosed in square brackets. The editor has standardized em dashes, ellipses, left-hand salutation and closing of correspondence, and paragraph indentation. Neither letterhead nor return address on correspondence has been reproduced. Ellipses in brackets indicate editor's deletion of text.

Nearly all documents were in typed or printed form in the original, occasionally including handwritten additions. The abbreviation at the bottom of each document indicates the location (usually collection and repository) in which it was found.

The editor's narrative linkages, indicated by a rule in the left margin, introduce and connect the original materials.

Abbreviations for
Collections and Archives . . .

ACLUA-NJP   American Civil Liberties Union Archives,
Public Policy Papers, Seeley G. Mudd
Manuscript Library, Department of Rare Books
and Special Collections, Princeton University

ASRC-GAU   Archives of the Southern Regional Council,
Woodruff Library, Atlanta University

BRP-DLC   Bayard Rustin Papers, Library of Congress,
Washington, D.C.

CJDP-A-Ar   Clifford J. Durr Papers, Alabama Department of
Archives and History, Montgomery, Ala.

CMCR-AMC   Circuit Court, Montgomery County Records,
Montgomery, Ala.

DABCC   Dexter Avenue King Memorial Baptist Church
Collection, Montgomery, Ala.

DDEP-KAbE   Dwight D. Eisenhower Papers, Dwight D.
Eisenhower Library, Abilene, Kans.

FORP-PSC-P   Fellowship of Reconciliation Papers,
Swarthmore College Peace Collection,
Swarthmore, Pa.

GESP   Glenn E. Smiley Collection, in private hands

HGP-GAMK	Hazel Gregory Papers, King Library and Archives, King Center for Nonviolent Social Change, Inc., Atlanta
HJP-GAMK	H. J. Palmer Papers, King Library and Archives, Atlanta
HRECR-WHi	Highlander Research and Education Center Records, State Historical Society of Wisconsin, Madison
MCDA-AMC	Montgomery County District Attorney's Files, Montgomery County Courthouse, Montgomery, Ala.
MLKJrP-GAMK	Martin Luther King Jr. Papers, King Library and Archives, King Center for Nonviolent Social Change, Inc., Atlanta
MLKP-MBU	Martin Luther King Jr. Papers, Mugar Library, Boston University
NAACPP-DLC	National Association for the Advancement of Colored People Papers, Library of Congress, Washington, D.C.
NTP-NN	Norman Thomas Papers, Rare Books and Manuscripts Division, New York Public Library, Astor, Lenox and Tilden Foundations
PACRADIO	Pacifica Radio Archive, Los Angeles
PV-ARC-LNT	Preston Valien Collection, Amistad Research Center, Tulane University, New Orleans
RGP	Robert Graetz Papers, in private hands
RWP-DLC	Roy Wilkins Papers, Library of Congress, Washington, D.C.
SBC	Stewart Burns Collection, Stanford University
SER-DNA	Southeast Region, National Archives, Washington, D.C.
VFDP-MCR-S	Virginia Foster Durr Papers, Schlesinger Library, Radcliffe College, Harvard University, Cambridge, Mass.

Prelude... 1 ...

For a generation, Charles Hamilton Houston, Thurgood Marshall, and other lawyers for the National Association for the Advancement of Colored People (NAACP) had pursued litigation through federal courts challenging racial segregation. Precedent upon precedent, the NAACP legal juggernaut won a succession of court battles in the 1940s that advanced black voting rights and desegregation of public postgraduate education. The NAACP legal reform strategy culminated in the *Brown* v. *Board of Education* decision of May 17, 1954, declaring public school segregation unconstitutional.

Four days after the unanimous Supreme Court ruling, an English professor at Alabama State College in Montgomery wrote a letter to the mayor urging him to accept minor reforms to improve the treatment of black passengers on the city's segregated buses. Jo Ann Gibson Robinson, president of the Women's Political Council, warned him that a number of black organizations were considering a boycott of buses if changes were not made. She had been directly lobbying the city commissioners to remedy bus inequities since she became head of the WPC four years before. Although she claimed to oppose such "forceful measures" as a bus boycott, she was a lightning rod for the community's rising sentiment for direct action. Indeed, that spring her own students at all-black Alabama State, including seventeen-year-old freshman Richard Nelson, had started their own bus boycott. Students had thrown bricks and bottles at buses and physically removed riders. According to Nelson, she had tried to discourage them from boycotting.[1]

May 21, 1954

Honorable Mayor W. A. Gayle
City Hall
Montgomery, Alabama

Dear Sir:

The Women's Political Council is very grateful to you and the City Commissioners for the hearing you allowed our representative during the month of March, 1954, when the "city-bus-fare-increase case" was being reviewed. There were several things the Council asked for:

1. A city law that would make it possible for Negroes to sit from back toward front, and whites from front toward back until all the seats are taken.

2. That Negroes not be asked or forced to pay fare at front and go to the rear of the bus to enter.

3. That busses stop at every corner in residential sections occupied by Negroes as they do in communities where whites reside.

We are happy to report that busses have begun stopping at more corners now in some sections where Negroes live than previously. However, the same practices in seating and boarding the bus continue.

Mayor Gayle, three-fourths of the riders of these public conveyances are Negroes. If Negroes did not patronize them, they could not possibly operate.

More and more of our people are already arranging with neighbors and friends to ride to keep from being insulted and humiliated by bus drivers.

There has been talk from twenty-five or more local organizations of planning a city-wide boycott of busses. We, sir, do not feel that forceful measures are necessary in bargaining for a convenience which is right for all bus passengers. We, the Council, believe that when this matter has been put before you and the Commissioners, that agreeable terms can be met in a quiet and unostensible manner to the satisfaction of all concerned.

Many of our Southern cities in neighboring states have practiced the policies we seek without incident whatsoever. Atlanta, Macon and Savannah in Georgia have done this for years. Even Mobile, in our own state, does this and all the passengers are satisfied.

Please consider this plea, and if possible, act favorably upon it, for even now plans are being made to ride less, or not at all, on our busses. We do not want this.

Respectfully yours,
The Women's Political Council
Jo Ann Robinson, President

MCDA-AMC.

1. "ASU Student Left Buses before Parks," *Montgomery Advertiser*, December 1, 1995; editor's interview with Richard Nelson, December 4, 1995, Montgomery, Ala.

Two years later, in the March 1956 conspiracy trial of Martin Luther King Jr., bus passengers testified under oath in Montgomery Circuit Court about their past mistreatment by white bus drivers and how they had challenged it in different ways.

Thelma Glass, a geography professor at Alabama State College, testified about activities of the Women's Political Council in regard to the bus situation and other issues of concern to black Montgomery.[1]

Thelma Glass, having been duly sworn, was examined and testified as follows:

DEFENSE LAWYER: State your name to the Court.

THELMA GLASS: Thelma Williams Glass.

DEFENSE: Do you live in Montgomery?

GLASS: Yes, I do.

DEFENSE: How long have you lived in Montgomery?

GLASS: Since 1947. Just recently I have been working around the college at Montgomery.

DEFENSE: Are you a member of the Women's Political Council?

GLASS: I am.

DEFENSE: Do you know when that council was first organized?

GLASS: Yes, I do. The Women's Political Council was organized in the spring of 1949.

DEFENSE: For what purpose or purposes was this council organized?

GLASS: Well, maybe the best overall purpose, I could say, would be to promote good citizenship. We have maybe one or two specific activities we have always listed in our prospectus under citizenship.

DEFENSE: What are those activities?

GLASS: The Women's Political Council naturally is concerned with women's activities. In the first place, we enter into political and civic problems, particularly those relating to Negroes. In the second place, we encourage women to become registered voters, to pay poll tax and vote. In the third place, to enter those women in a better national government as a result. Most activities are proposed and designed to acquaint women with current problems.

DEFENSE: As a member of this group, have they had any connection with the Montgomery bus situation?

GLASS: Well, that is one of our specific problems, particularly as relating to Negroes, and one of our current civic problems. Problems relating to the busses have recently been part of our program.

DEFENSE: What were some of those problems your group has considered?

PROSECUTOR: We object to what the group considered, what it did or didn't.

JUDGE: If it has to do with busses it would be admissible. What they considered wouldn't be.

DEFENSE: What particular problem has your organization taken up with the bus company, if any?

GLASS: We have been trying for the past six years, we have had various committees from the Women's Political Council who have made appeals to the City Commissioners. The things particularly that we had asked for—maybe there are four specific things as I can remember that we did send committees to ask for specifically.

DEFENSE: What are those things?

GLASS: Well, the very first thing we objected to mainly was Negroes have had to stand over empty seats.

PROSECUTOR: We object.

JUDGE: Testify to what you took up with the City Commission, what you told them. That would be admissible.

DEFENSE: Had this group had a meeting with the City officials of Montgomery?

GLASS: Oh, yes, sir, it has numerous meetings.

DEFENSE: You have called on the bus company?

GLASS: We have.

DEFENSE: Will you tell the court what happened?

PROSECUTOR: We object to that unless it is shown the time, the date it happened and where.

GLASS: In November, 1953, a committee from the Women's Political Council actually asked for seven specific things, I think. Not all pertaining to the busses, but I can tell you about six of the things.

PROSECUTOR: We object to anything unless it pertains to the busses.

JUDGE: Objection sustained.

GLASS: Negroes had to stand over empty seats when no whites were riding; requesting them not to occupy those seats where they are unoccupied; Negroes pay fares at the front door, get off and go to the rear door to board the bus; when fares are paid at the front passengers should get on at the front; there is a danger of a passenger being struck without the driver knowing it; and there have been instances where persons have paid their fares and the bus has driven off and left them standing; busses stop in sections occupied by white at every corner, but in sections occupied by Negroes they stop at every other block; since all pay the same fare the busses should stop at every corner in all communities. Those are the specific things that this committee asked for in November of 1953 that deal with busses.

DEFENSE: Have you had any other meetings with the City Commissioners on the bus situation?

GLASS: On the bus situation we have.

DEFENSE: Do you remember the dates?

GLASS: This meeting in March of 1954, the Women's Political Council, along with a large labor group, the Federation of Women's Clubs, the Citizens' Steering Committee, the Progressive Democrats, along with representatives of the Women's Political Council.

DEFENSE: Did you attend this particular meeting?

GLASS: This particular meeting in March, 1954, I did.

PROSECUTOR: We move to strike all that testimony.

JUDGE: If you were not there you wouldn't know what happened, you couldn't testify to that. Where you were present, you could.

DEFENSE: Will you testify as to what happened at this particular meeting in 1954?

GLASS: Well, we went before the Commission with a full program we later on developed with a re-statement of some of the same things the committee had worked on in November of 1953.

DEFENSE: Was that the Montgomery City Commission?

GLASS: That is the Montgomery City Commission. The usual seating arrangement, people were still complaining of standing over empty seats; let Negroes board the busses at the front where they paid their fares; many had been left on the sidewalk after paying their fares; busses should stop at every corner; people had to walk, and they had a right complaining, and names and dates, and names of busses, the bus lines, and specific experiences with Negroes, were turned over to the Commission from people who complained against the bus company. [. . .]

Georgia Gilmore, having been duly sworn, was examined and testified as follows: [. . .]

DEFENSE: How long have you been a resident of the City of Montgomery?

GEORGIA GILMORE: I don't know how long. I came here in 1920.

DEFENSE: During the time you have resided in the City of Montgomery, have you had opportunity to ride the busses owned by the Montgomery Bus Line?

GILMORE: Yes, sir, I have. At that time I did all my riding on the busses. They were my sole transportation because I didn't own any car or motor vehicle whatsoever.

DEFENSE: I believe you stated you did all your riding?

GILMORE: Did all my riding.

DEFENSE: When did you stop riding the busses?

GILMORE: October of 1955.

DEFENSE: For what purpose did you cease riding the busses?

GILMORE: The last of October, 1955, on a Friday afternoon between the hours of three and five o'clock I was on the corner of Court and Montgomery Street, and I usually rode Oak Park or South Jackson busses for both of them came up to that corner. This particular Oak Park bus came up to the corner. I don't know the driver's name. I would know him if I saw him. He is tall and has red skin. This bus driver is tall, hair red, and has freckles, and wears glasses. He is a very nasty bus driver. This particular time the bus was pretty near full of colored people, only two white people on the bus. I put my money in the cash box and then he told me to get off. He shouted I had to get on in back. I told him I was already on the bus and I couldn't see why I had to get off. A lot of colored people were in the middle aisle almost half way to the front, couldn't he let me stand there? Other people were down there, colored, not white passengers. He said, "I told you to get off and go around and get in the back door." I have a rather high temper and I figured, I have never been in any trouble whatsoever in my life. I was always taught that two wrongs don't make a right.

PROSECUTOR: We object to this.

JUDGE: All right.

GILMORE: I am just telling you. So I got off the front door and went around the side of the bus to get in the back door, and when I reached the back door and was about to get on he shut the back door and pulled off, and I didn't even ride the bus after paying my fare. So I decided right then and there I wasn't going to ride the busses any more, because of what happened in there. I was upset within myself, for I was so aggravated with the driver I didn't want to raise any fuss. And so I haven't missed the busses because I really don't have to ride them. The taxi takes me in the morning—I haven't returned to the busses—I walk, just to get a taxi in the morning and walk home. My children going to school—

PROSECUTOR: We object to what her children do.

DEFENSE: You are a member of the Negro race, are you?

GILMORE: I am.

DEFENSE: Believe you said the bus driver was nasty to you?

GILMORE: He was.

DEFENSE: What do you mean by the fact he was nasty to you?

GILMORE: Well, I didn't mean going around to the back door. What he said: "Nigger, get out that door and go around to the back door." I resented his tone because I had already paid my fare. When I paid my fare and they got the money they don't know Negro money from white money.

DEFENSE: Have you had any other unpleasant experiences riding busses prior to October?

GILMORE: Yes, sir, various. Many times I have been standing without any white people on the bus and have taken seats, and when the driver sees you he says, "You have to move because those seats aren't for you Negroes."

DEFENSE: During your experience riding busses in the City of Montgomery have you observed other bus drivers that have mistreated Negro passengers?

GILMORE: Lots of times I have seen people mistreated positively for nothing.

DEFENSE: What type of treatment have you generally received from these bus drivers? Have you ever heard any Negroes at all call the drivers any names?

GILMORE: No, never have.

DEFENSE: Have you heard the drivers call the Negroes any names?

GILMORE: I have.

DEFENSE: What are some names you heard?

GILMORE: "Black bastard," and "Back up, nigger, you ain't got no damn business up here, get back where you belong."

DEFENSE: You say this happened frequently?

GILMORE: Lots of times, because at that time I rode the bus daily.

DEFENSE: Can you give the name of another Negro citizen you observed being mistreated by them?

GILMORE: I cannot remember the names of anybody else except my mother, and she is deceased now.

DEFENSE: What happened in her case?

PROSECUTOR: We object unless she was present.

DEFENSE: Were you present?

GILMORE: Yes, sir, I was.

DEFENSE: What happened in her case?

GILMORE: She was an old person and it was hard for her to get in and out of the bus except the front door. The bus was crowded that evening with everybody coming home from work. She went to the front door to get on the bus, and this bus driver was mean and surly, and when she asked him if she could get in the front door he said she would have to go around and get in the back door, and she said she couldn't get in, the steps were too high. He said she couldn't go in the front door. He said: "You damn niggers are all alike. You don't want to do what you are told. If I had my way I would kill off every nigger person." And she always said, "You cannot ride, you are riding among maniacs," and she said—

PROSECUTOR: We object to what she said.

JUDGE: Sustain the objection.

GILMORE: Makes me mad to think about it. [. . .]

Martha K. Walker, having been duly sworn, was examined and testified as follows:

DEFENSE: During the time you were riding these busses did you have any unpleasant experiences with the bus driver?

MARTHA WALKER: Many of them.

DEFENSE: Do you recall specifically the last unpleasant experience?

WALKER: Yes, sir, I do recall.

DEFENSE: When was that?

WALKER: It was 1955.

DEFENSE: Tell us about that and when.

WALKER: Before Thanksgiving of 1955, I went out to get the bus on North Ripley Street, coming to town. I guess about four busses passed me up with about five or six colored people in the back. They had plenty of room up front to have gotten on them and sit back there on all of them. I had my husband with me, of course. He is blind and I was taking him down to the Veterans' Administration this particular day. So it took so long to get a bus, although the bus situation out that way is bad anyway. So I turned around and went back in my apartment and called the manager of the bus company. I got him on the phone, so I told him we had been passed up by four busses, and the fifth bus stopped and we got on the bus and rode to town. They had plenty of room in the front to sit in the back. We sat behind the back door on the little short seat there to the right.

DEFENSE: How far was that seat from the rear of the bus? How many seats between the seat in which you sat and the back of the bus?

WALKER: One long seat and the side.

DEFENSE: So you were just one seat from the rear of the bus?

WALKER: That is right.

DEFENSE: You were not in the middle, were you?

WALKER: No.

DEFENSE: You were not in the front of the bus?

WALKER: That is right.

DEFENSE: Go right ahead and tell us.

WALKER: He said when we got to Decatur Street and Columbus Street there, we had to get up, a couple of white girls got on the bus. And at that time my husband was blind. His condition is better now, but he is sightless though. And we still sat there. And that bus had two sets of empty seats, the front part was filled except two empties. And I was looking up toward the mirror and watching him because I was expecting some unruly words. He stopped. After he went another block he stopped. I think it was, I guess, in another block, in another street going up to Robinson's Corner Market, in that block, and I was still in a nervous strain there, and he looked back again, and then he pulled off and stopped within, you know, the middle of the block, and said, "Don't you niggers see that empty seat behind you?" I said, "Yes, I see it." He said, "Well, get up and get on back there." Well, that just tore my husband. We got up and got off the bus. Now, that is true, that experience.

DEFENSE: How far were you when you got off the bus, how far were you from your destination?

WALKER: It was near a feed store down there. I believe they call it the Alabama Feed Store, if I am not mistaken. We walked from there to the Veterans' Administration with me leading him. [. . .]

DEFENSE: Have you had other unpleasant experiences with the bus drivers or bus company?

WALKER: Yes, I have.

DEFENSE: Do you recall any specific incidence?

WALKER: Yes, I do.

DEFENSE: Will you tell us when it was and where it was?

WALKER: In 1954.

DEFENSE: Where was this?

WALKER: In Montgomery.

DEFENSE: On which line, which bus line?

WALKER: Maxwell Field bus line.

DEFENSE: Go ahead, tell us about that.

WALKER: My husband was coming back home again from the Veterans' hospital, from the Tuskegee Hospital, and he had his sight taken from him in Germany—

PROSECUTOR: We object to all these preliminaries. They wouldn't have anything to do with this specific incidence.

JUDGE: Yes. She said she was with him and he was blind. Tell what happened on the bus.

WALKER: Well, we were on this bus, we boarded the bus down town and our destination was to get off at Dickerson and Clay Street, we were living on Clay, and it was about 3:30 in the afternoon, and we pulled the cord. Different times I had to pull it to stop before it stopped. We pulled the cord in time for him to get stopped, and by the time he stopped, I thought he must have been stopping, I got ready to get my husband off the bus. Now, he noticed me when I left the bus, I was leading my husband. And when I got ready to get off he slowed down, he didn't stop, he slowed up. When he slowed up, I stepped down on the side of the step there, and he opened the door. I got out, ready for my husband to step down, and just as my husband put his left foot down, the driver started on out with his right foot still on the bus, and I screamed, and a white lady was in there and she said to wait a moment. Well, finally I jiggled his foot free, he couldn't get loose by himself, and with me helping him he did, and he got his foot out. I ran in a store at the corner of Dickerson and Clay and said—I was crying—I said, "I just had some trouble with a bus operator."

PROSECUTOR: We object to any hearsay testimony.

JUDGE: Objection sustained.

WALKER: I have to give that.

PROSECUTOR: Don't testify about that.

JUDGE: Tell what you know yourself.

WALKER: Anyway, I know it broke the skin on his right ankle.

DEFENSE: What did you do in that store, did you do something there?

WALKER: I got the manager of the bus company's name from the white lady that runs the store.

DEFENSE: What else did you do?

WALKER: When I left there I left my husband standing over there by her building and crossed the street on the other side. When the bus came back coming toward town, I knew, I recognized the bus. I waited for him. When he came back I stopped him. I said, "Look yourself what you just done to my husband." He said, "I don't remember seeing you niggers on the bus."

DEFENSE: I believe you said he used the word "niggers"?

WALKER: Yes.

DEFENSE: Spell that word for us.

WALKER: N-i-g-g-e-r-s, niggers.

DEFENSE: Go ahead.

WALKER: I said, "My husband and I got off that bus there." And I said, "He caught his foot in the door and broke the skin here on his ankle." He said, "I didn't do no such damn thing." That is the way he worded it. I said, "He is over there on the corner to prove it." I said, "If you cannot give me any consideration," I said, "I am afraid I will have to take further steps." It didn't do any good, of course.

DEFENSE: Did you report the accident to the bus company?

WALKER: I certainly did.

DEFENSE: Did you hear from them?

WALKER: They promised me I would, but I never did. [. . .]

Stella Brooks, having been duly sworn, was examined and testified as follows:

DEFENSE: I believe your name is Stella Brooks?
STELLA BROOKS: Estella Brooks.
DEFENSE: What is your address?
BROOKS: 633 Cleveland Avenue.
DEFENSE: That is located in the City of Montgomery?
BROOKS: That is right.
DEFENSE: How long have you been living there?
BROOKS: Two years.
DEFENSE: How long have you been a resident of the City of Montgomery?
BROOKS: All my life.
DEFENSE: You are over the age of twenty-one, are you not?
BROOKS: Twenty-six.
DEFENSE: You are also a member of the Negro race, are you not?
BROOKS: That is right.
DEFENSE: I ask you during your lifetime in the City of Montgomery whether or not you have had occasions to ride these busses in the City, operated by the Montgomery City Lines?
BROOKS: Yes, I have.
DEFENSE: Do you ride these busses frequently, or just sometime, or what manner?
BROOKS: I haven't rode the busses since they killed my husband, since 1950.
DEFENSE: What month?
BROOKS: 12th of August.
DEFENSE: For what reason did you stop riding the busses?
BROOKS: Because the bus driver was the cause of my husband's death.
PROSECUTOR: We object to that.
JUDGE: Tell what happened.
DEFENSE: Tell the Court what happened that caused you to stop riding the busses.
BROOKS: He just got on before the bus driver told him, the bus was crowded, he asked for his dime back and he wouldn't give his dime back.
DEFENSE: What happened then?
BROOKS: The police killed him.
DEFENSE: Did the bus driver call the police?
BROOKS: The bus driver called the police and the police came up and shot him.
DEFENSE: And shot him?
BROOKS: Yes, sir. [. . .]

Henrietta Brinson, having been duly sworn, was examined and testified as follows: [. . .]

DEFENSE: How long have you been a resident and citizen of Montgomery, Alabama?

HENRIETTA BRINSON: Ever since I married.

DEFENSE: During the time you have lived in Montgomery I presume you had occasion to ride the busses?

BRINSON: Yes, sir.

DEFENSE: Of Montgomery City Lines?

BRINSON: Yes, sir, I have.

DEFENSE: When was the last time you rode the busses?

BRINSON: I rode December the 4th.

DEFENSE: December the 4th, 1955?

BRINSON: That is right.

DEFENSE: Were you a frequent rider or just rode occasionally?

BRINSON: I rode all the time. I used to ride the trolley before the busses—twice a day. I ride in the morning and ride in the afternoon. I got two places I got to go a day.

DEFENSE: During the last ten years did you encounter unpleasant experiences with some or all of the bus drivers?

BRINSON: Oh, yes, I have.

DEFENSE: Will you relate the time and place of your first experience that you had?

BRINSON: I cannot tell you. I remember the time, but I don't know the date.

DEFENSE: Your best judgment?

BRINSON: It was 1953.

DEFENSE: What happened?

BRINSON: I ride the Court Street bus, and when I would go to get on the Court Street bus you had to push to get on the bus on account of the school children, so many white children going to Lanier School. I wasn't able to get in unless I pushed to get in with the white children. So I started in with the white children and left my transfer at the door and went on back and stood up in the aisle of the bus. And he stood up and said, "Who gave me this old transfer?" I cannot tell you the awful name he called me. He is the meanest man I ever saw in my life. I don't know his name, but I rode that bus all the time, and I rode to work in South Cloverdale. And why he had such a nasty way with the colored, I just don't know. He looked at me and said, "You gave me that transfer, I saw you give me that transfer." I said, "You just laid that transfer on top of the other transfers," and I said, "There it is." (Indicating) He said, "Who are you talking to?" I said, "I am talking to you. Every time I catch the South Cloverdale I always have to worry with you about something. I don't see why you always keep on griping about something. The other bus driver that carries me on the South Cloverdale bus, you don't have no trouble with him." So he looked at me like that and said, "Who do you think you are talking to? You are just getting off this bus, all you niggers behaving like a parcel of cows." I said, "Well, that is all right. Just as long as I get to work." And that is what I did. We have had a lot of trouble with bus drivers because they are all working together and they don't want to treat us the right way.

DEFENSE: Can you relate another circumstance and, if so, give us the time and place?

BRINSON: I cannot give you any time.

DEFENSE: Your best judgment?

BRINSON: I was on Day Street one afternoon coming in from work, and this bus came from Highland Avenue.

DEFENSE: When was this?

BRINSON: This was year before last now.

DEFENSE: 1953?

BRINSON: Yes, sir, that is right. I got on at Dexter. And when I got on at Dexter, well, I stood by the door, in front of the window, it was really hot, and I felt really bad that day, the day being hot and I was tired, I had worked two places. And I was standing up on the side as you come in the back door, I stood right there, I stood up in the back on this other side just as you enter into the door, and this white couple was sitting there until the bus got to the Square and they got off. And standing up I began to feel so bad so I sat down and hoisted the window. When I hoisted the window he looked at me, but I didn't look up. I just looked out the window. He said, "You, I am talking to you." So I had to look up. Finally I went on back, and he said, "I am talking to you, all you niggers know we got a law in Alabama." And this is what I would like to know, when they charge us dimes on the busses—

PROSECUTOR: We object to any argumental part by the witness.

BRINSON: Can I speak?

JUDGE: Just a moment. You are supposed to answer any question. Don't give us any discourse. Just answer any question.

BRINSON: Because we all feel we need the busses.

JUDGE: Just a moment. We are not going to hear any sermon from you. You are here as a witness. Just answer the question.

BRINSON: I believe you all feel like we ought to work together. Don't you want to hear what I have to say?

JUDGE: No.

DEFENSE: Just answer any question. You had numerous experiences?

BRINSON: Correct, I had. And I am just fed up with these bus drivers. I am just fed up to my neck.

JUDGE: Do you understand you are on the witness stand now and I have told you to answer the questions that are asked you. I will tell you what I can do if you won't do that.

BRINSON: All right.

DEFENSE: Don't volunteer any information. Answer the questions I am asking you.

BRINSON: All right.

DEFENSE: You have had numerous incidences, have you not?

BRINSON: Yes, I have.

DEFENSE: And you have observed other people have numerous incidences?

BRINSON: Yes, sir.

DEFENSE: Unpleasant experiences with bus drivers?

BRINSON: Sure, I have. [. . .]

Gladys Moore, having been duly sworn, was examined and testified as follows:

DEFENSE: Have you been on that bus during the ten years in which you rode the busses here in Montgomery when all of the Negro seats in back were crowded and you were standing up with empty seats in the front?

GLADYS MOORE: I have been on that bus.

DEFENSE: Were you ever at any time during that time allowed in those seats that were empty?

MOORE: Not any time.

DEFENSE: Did you all move when you were asked to move?

MOORE: Well, sometimes I don't think they could because they didn't have enough room, and the bus drivers wouldn't know anything about it unless you told them.

DEFENSE: Have you ever seen anybody or heard anybody complain at any time?

MOORE: No, I haven't because you are toward the rear of the bus and when the driver tells you to move you look the other way.

DEFENSE: How were you treated by the bus drivers on these two lines? Were you treated courteously? How were you treated generally?

MOORE: No, not courteously.

DEFENSE: Just tell us how you were treated.

MOORE: Just as rough as could be. I mean not like we are human, but like we was some kind of animal.

DEFENSE: The general manner was discourteous?

MOORE: That is right.

DEFENSE: During the whole course of those ten years?

MOORE: Yes, sir. Some drivers wasn't.

DEFENSE: Some of them?

MOORE: Some weren't as bad as others.

DEFENSE: Were not all bad?

MOORE: They wasn't good.

DEFENSE: Did they call Negroes names?

MOORE: Well, coming home on the bus, just getting on the Highland Avenue bus, and the driver—I don't know his name now—he said, "Don't you upset me with the racket." I stood still. There wasn't any disorder in the back of the bus whatever. And he said, "You niggers there."

DEFENSE: Will you state the whole thing you heard him say, begin at the beginning, tell what he said.

MOORE: He stopped the bus and looked back, they was just all regularly talking, and he said, "You niggers, come on and get your fare and get off." I guess he gave the fare to some. Because I wanted to get home I stayed on the bus.

DEFENSE: Will you spell that word he used for me?

MOORE: (spelling) N-i-g-g-e-r-s.

PROSECUTOR: We object to this testimony and move to exclude it until we know the time and place.

DEFENSE: She was indicating her experience.

JUDGE: About when was it, in your best judgment? What month was it, what year was it?

MOORE: This was about 1950. It has been a good long while.

DEFENSE: Have you had any other unpleasant experiences on either of these lines?

PROSECUTOR: We object unless we know the time.

JUDGE: Ask her to fix the time.

DEFENSE: Have you had any other unpleasant experiences while riding on any of these bus lines?

MOORE: I have.

DEFENSE: Can you tell us what routes and approximately when they happened?

MOORE: I could tell you what happened in 1952.

DEFENSE: Where?

MOORE: On a South Jackson bus going out.

DEFENSE: Tell us about it.

MOORE: This bus was the South Jackson bus going out, when I boarded it in town and rode that bus out. On the corner of South Jackson and Adams Street, the bus driver closed the door on my foot getting off the bus. And I had on a coat, it was a heavy coat, and landed on the highway. It throwed me clean off the bus when the door caught my foot. He said, "The next time you catch your foot I ought to drag you all the way up South Jackson Hill." He didn't wait long enough to see whether I am hurt, or not. I didn't report the injury because I didn't think it would do any good.

JUDGE: Why did you stop riding the busses on December the 5th?

MOORE: Why did I stop?

JUDGE: Yes.

MOORE: Well, no one told me to stop riding the busses.

JUDGE: I didn't ask you that.

MOORE: I am going to explain it to you. I didn't have anything to do with it.

JUDGE: I didn't ask you that.

MOORE: What is it you want me to answer?

JUDGE: I asked you why you stopped on December the 5th. I want to know for my own information why did you stop riding on December 5th?

MOORE: I stopped because we had been treated so bad down through the years that we decided we wouldn't ride the busses no more.

JUDGE: Who do you mean by "we"?

MOORE: All the fifty thousand Negroes in Montgomery.

JUDGE: When did you all decide?

MOORE: Well, after so many things happened. Wasn't no one man started it. We all started it overnight.

JUDGE: Where did you all decide it? You said you all decided it.

MOORE: Well, after that accident happened to Mrs. Parks, we all knowed it was unfair, and after they treated her like they did. So we just had an inward feeling, we just quit riding the busses.

JUDGE: Where did you all meet to decide that?

MOORE: We didn't meet nowhere to decide that.

JUDGE: Do you mean to tell the Court there was no meeting in which you decided? When did you decide to quit riding the buses, was it decided on December the 5th, the night of December the 5th?

MOORE: It wasn't decided that night. It came out in the paper. The bus company announced it in the paper that we stopped riding the busses.

JUDGE: Did it come out in the paper before December 5th or after December 5th?

MOORE: It came out before.

JUDGE: That you were not going to ride on December the 5th?

MOORE: That is right.

JUDGE: And that is what stopped you?

MOORE: No, not exactly. What stopped me was—

JUDGE: When did you make up your mind? That is what I am asking you. When did you make up your mind not to ride any more, since December the 5th?

MOORE: Because Mrs. Parks was mistreated on the bus, that is why.

JUDGE: You haven't answered my question. Why did you decide particularly on December the 5th, not December 6th or December 1st, or any other time?

MOORE: Mrs. Parks was riding the bus and we didn't think she was treated fairly, that is why. She wasn't justly treated.

JUDGE: You still haven't answered my question. Why you decided on December the 5th. That is what I was asking.

MOORE: I think I answered that clear enough.

JUDGE: What caused you to stop riding? Why did you decide not to do so on December 5th, that particular date?

DEFENSE: I think the witness has given an answer in reference to the question. I think her answers relate to the question. I think she said why.

JUDGE: She has given her reason for it. The only date I have asked her about particularly was December the 5th.

DEFENSE: I think she has answered it.

JUDGE: I don't think so.

MOORE: I think I have answered it in as clear words as I can.

JUDGE: I want you to tell me why you picked this particular date, December the 5th. You told me why you quit riding. Why December the 5th?

MOORE: Because that is the day of this Mrs. Parks' trial, and after they mistreated her the way they did and fined her. We didn't think she was guilty of what they accused her of. That is why we quit riding the busses. Is that clear enough?

JUDGE: That is clear enough. [. . .]

CMCR-AMC. *State of Alabama* v. *M. L. King, Jr.*, March 19–22, 1956.

On May 11, 1956, Claudette Colvin, one of four plaintiffs in the *Browder* v. *Gayle* lawsuit challenging bus segregation, testified in a Montgomery federal court hearing about her refusal to give up her seat to a white passenger in March 1955. She was then a fifteen-year-old junior at Booker T. Washington High School. "I thought segregation was horrible," Colvin later recalled. "My first anger I remember was when I wanted to go to the rodeo. Daddy bought my sister boots and bought us both cowboy hats. That's as much of the rodeo as we got. The show was at the Coliseum, and it was only for white kids. I was nine or ten.

"You could buy dry goods at the five-and-ten-cent stores, Kress's, H. L. Green, J. J. Newberry's," she continued, "but you couldn't sit down and eat there. When I realized that, I was really angry." Her mind "got pricked" by a ninth-grade history teacher, who impressed on her the importance of self-worth. Colvin wrote a class essay complaining about the indignities of segregation, especially for a teenage girl out shopping for clothes. She refused to straighten her hair, wearing it in little "kinky" braids—even though her friends ridiculed her and her boyfriend broke up with her. She wore her braids "until I proved to them that I wasn't crazy."[2]

Claudette Colvin, called as a witness, being duly sworn, testified as follows:

FRED GRAY, COUNSEL FOR PLAINTIFFS: State your name?
CLAUDETTE COLVIN: Claudette Colvin.
GRAY: What is your address, Miss Colvin?
COLVIN: 658 Dixie Drive.
GRAY: How old are you?
COLVIN: Sixteen.
GRAY: Who are your parents?
COLVIN: C. P. Colvin and Mary Ann Colvin.
GRAY: You are one of the plaintiffs in this lawsuit?
COLVIN: Yes.
GRAY: Prior to December 5, 1955, last year, did you ride the city buses?
COLVIN: Yes.
GRAY: How often did you ride?
COLVIN: Twice a day.
GRAY: Have you rode the busses since then?
COLVIN: No.
GRAY: Did you have an incident at any time while you were riding the buses?
COLVIN: Yes.
GRAY: When did this occur?
COLVIN: March 2, 1955.
GRAY: What bus did you ride?
COLVIN: Highland Gardens.
GRAY: About what time was it?
COLVIN: About 2:30 P.M..
GRAY: Where were you on the way to?
COLVIN: I was going home from school.

GRAY: Will you please tell the Court exactly what happened on March 2, 1955?
COLVIN: I rode the bus and it was turning in on Perry and Dexter Avenue, and me and some other school children, I sit on the seat on the left hand side, on the seat just above the emergency door, me and another girl beside me.
GRAY: You say another girl was sitting by you and another girl was sitting across from you, do you mean those two girls were Negroes?
COLVIN: Yes, sir. And he drove on down to the next block, and by the time all the people got in there, he seen there were no more vacant seats. He asked us to get up, and the big girl got up but I didn't. So he drove on down into the Square, and some more people boarded the bus. So, Mrs. Hamilton, she got on the bus, and she sat down beside me, and that leaves the other seat vacant.
GRAY: You mean that from across the aisle the other two girls had gotten up when the bus driver requested them to?
COLVIN: Yes, sir. So he looked back through the window and he saw us, and he was surprised to see she [*Hamilton*] was sitting down, too. He asked her to get up then and he asked both of us to get up. She said she was not going to get up, she didn't feel like it. He drove on down to the next corner or block, rather. And he got up and asked us to get up. So, he directly asked me to get up first. So I told him I was not going to get up. He said, "If you are not going to get up I will get a policeman." So, he went somewhere and got a policeman. He [*policeman*] said, "Why are you not going to get up?" He said, "It is against the law here." So I told him that I didn't know that it was a law that a colored person had to get up and give a white person a seat when there were not any more vacant seats and colored people were standing up. I said I was just as good as any white person and I wasn't going to get up. So he got off. And then two more policemen came in. He said, "Who is it?" And he was very angry about it. He said: "That is not new, I had trouble out of that thing before." So, he said: "Aren't you going to get up?" He didn't say anything to Mrs. Hamilton then. He just said it to me. He said: "Aren't you going to get up?" I said, "no." He saw Mrs. Hamilton but he was afraid to ask her to get up. He said, "If any of you are not gentlemen enough to give a lady a seat you should be put in jail, yourself." So, Mr. Harris, he got up and gave her a seat, and immediately got off the bus. He said, "You can have that seat, I am getting off." And so she taken his seat. So he asked me, if I was not going to get up. I said, "No, sir." I was crying then, I was very hurt because I didn't know that white people would act like that and I was crying. And he said, "I will have to take you off." So I didn't move. I didn't move at all. I just acted like a big baby. So he kicked me and one got on one side of me and one got the other arm and they just drug me out. And so I was very pitiful. It really hurt me to see that I have to give a person a seat, when all those colored people were standing and there were not

any more vacant seats. I had never seen nothing like that. Well, they take me down, they put me in a car and one of the motorcycle men, he says, "I am sorry to have to take you down like this." So they put handcuffs on me through the window.

GRAY: After that where did they take you?

COLVIN: They taken me to the City Hall.

GRAY: While you were at the City Hall, did anyone ask your age?

COLVIN: Yes, they asked my age and everything.

GRAY: Where did you go from the City Hall?

COLVIN: I went to the City Jail.

GRAY: Did they mention anything to you about taking you to the Detention Home? the Juvenile Court instead of the City Jail?

COLVIN: Yes, sir. One of the policemen.

GRAY: So they took you to the City Jail?

COLVIN: Yes, sir.

GRAY: How long were you there?

COLVIN: It was over an hour.

GRAY: What happened when you got to the City Jail?

COLVIN: Well, all the people were staring at me, and asked me what was wrong. One of the policemen said, "She didn't want to sit back there with the Negroes!" And so he said: "If any more of them act like that—she was the only one that didn't want to move back." So they put me in the cell and locked the door.

GRAY: And you stayed there until your parents came and made bond?

COLVIN: Yes, sir.

GRAY: What were you charged with?

COLVIN: I was charged with violating the City Code, or certain sections of the City Code.

GRAY: You were convicted?

COLVIN: Yes, I was.

WALTER KNABE, COUNSEL FOR DEFENDANTS: You have changed, that is, you and the other Negroes have changed your ideas since December 5, have you not?

COLVIN: No, sir. We haven't changed our ideas. It has been in me ever since I was born.

KNABE: But, the group stopped riding the busses for certain named things, that is correct, isn't it?

COLVIN: For what?

KNABE: For certain things that Reverend King said were the things you objected to?

COLVIN: No, sir. It was in the beginning when they arrested me, when they seen how dirty they treated the Negro girls here, that they had began to feel like that all the time, though some of us just didn't have the guts to stand up.

KNABE: Did you have a leader when you started this bus boycott?

COLVIN: Did we have a leader? Our leaders is just we ourself.

SER-DNA. Transcript of Record and Proceedings, *Browder v. Gayle*, May 11, 1956.

Although she was ably defended by Fred Gray and Charles Langford, the city's only African American attorneys, two weeks after her arrest the juvenile court judge (first cousin of Alabama senator J. Lister Hill) found Colvin guilty of violating the state, not city, bus segregation law and of assault and battery for resisting arrest. He gave her probation. Gray and Langford appealed to the Montgomery Circuit Court, where on May 6 Judge Eugene Carter affirmed the assault conviction while dismissing the segregation code violation. His ruling prevented the lawyers from using Colvin's arrest as a test case to challenge the bus segregation laws, which in any event her parents did not want.

The Colvin incident aroused the black community. The Citizens Coordinating Committee, led by businessman Rufus Lewis, issued an appeal to the "Friends of Justice and Human Rights." It denounced "certain legal and moral injustices incurred in the public transportation system" and offered the Colvin case as "an opportunity, in the spirit of democracy, and in the spirit of Christ, to deal courageously with these problems."[3] Robinson recalled that for several days "large numbers refused to ride the buses" in a spontaneous protest.[4] In a meeting of black delegates with city and bus company officials, Robinson reportedly threatened an organized boycott when the talk got heated.

Partly because of Colvin's arrest and the heightened tensions that resulted, bus segregation emerged for the first time as an issue in a Montgomery city election that same month. All three city commission seats, including the mayor's, were contested. In late February E. D. Nixon's Progressive Democratic Association had sponsored a candidates' forum at the Ben Moore Hotel, the city's sole black-owned hotel. In this unprecedented interracial meeting, African American activists cast aside their customary deference and interrogated the white candidates about their stands on the "Negroes' Most Urgent Needs." They began with the bus situation. Their mimeographed statement advocated the WPC seating proposal that would maintain bus segregation but on a more equitable basis.

Commission candidate Clyde Sellers, a former state representative and Alabama Highway Patrol head, exploited the black demands in a full-page newspaper advertisement, concluding that "I will not be intimidated for the sake of a block of negro votes." His overtly racial appeal enabled him narrowly to defeat the incumbent, racial moderate Dave Birmingham, forcing a runoff election. Sellers won the runoff after Birmingham withdrew abruptly for health reasons. Mayor Gayle, a commissioner for twenty years, was easily reelected. They were joined by newcomer Frank Parks, who had prevailed with the help of black voters.

1. This edited testimony is taken from the official trial transcript of *State of Alabama* v. *M. L. King, Jr.*, March 19–22, 1956, Montgomery County Circuit Court, CMCR-AMC. The judge was Eugene Carter. The chief defense attorneys were Fred D. Gray and Charles D. Langford.

2. Ellen Levine, *Freedom's Children* (New York: G. P. Putnam's Sons, 1993), pp. 20–22.

3. Quoted in Lamont H. Yeakey, "The Montgomery, Alabama, Bus Boycott, 1955–56" (Ph.D. dissertation, Columbia University, 1979), pp. 238–39.

4. Jo Ann Gibson Robinson, *The Montgomery Bus Boycott and the Women Who Started It*, ed. David J. Garrow (Knoxville: University of Tennessee Press, 1987), p. 42.

Campaign Advertisement, by Clyde C. Sellers

Here Is The Questionnaire Given Me By E. D. Nixon at a Meeting With All Candidates, and a Negro group at the Ben Moore Hotel

NEGROES' MOST URGENT NEEDS

Following are a few of the most urgent needs of our people. Immediate attention should be given each of these. What is your stand toward them?

1. The present bus situation. Negroes have to stand over empty seats of city buses, because the first ten seats are reserved for whites who sometime never ride. We wish to fill the bus from the back toward the front until *all* the seats are taken. This is done in Atlanta, Georgia, Mobile, Alabama and in most of our larger southern cities.

2. Negro Representation on the Parks and Recreation Board. Our parks are in a deplorable condition. We have protested, yet nothing has been done toward improving them. Juvenile delinquency continues to increase. In many instances these children are not responsible. The city is. Nobody knows better than Negroes what their needs are.

3. Sub-division for housing. Just recently a project for a sub-division for Negroes was presented before the City Commission for approval. Protests from whites and other objections prevented the development. There is no section wherein Negroes can expand to build decent homes. What of Lincoln Heights?

4. Jobs for qualified Negroes. Certain civil service jobs are not open to

Negroes, yet many are qualified. Negroes need jobs commensurate with their training. Everybody cannot teach.

5. Negro representation on all boards affecting Negroes. Negroes are taxpayers; they are property owners or renters. They constitute about forty-six percent of the city's population. Many boards determine their destinies without any kind of representation whatsoever. Only Negroes are qualified to represent themselves adequately and properly.

6. Congested areas, with inadequate or no fireplugs. Fire hazards are inviting.

7. Lack of sewerage disposals makes it necessary to resort to out-door privies, which is a health hazard.

8. Narrow streets, lack of curbing, unpaved streets in some sections. Immediate action should be taken on this traffic hazard.

Gentleman, what is your stand on these issues? What will you do to improve these undemocratic practices? Your stand on these issues will enable us to better decide on whom we shall cast our ballot in the March election.

Very truly yours,
Montgomery Negroes

Here Are My Answers:

In Answer To Question No. 1—

1—There is a state law which requires segregation of passengers on public conveyances. I feel that there should ALWAYS be seats available for BOTH races on our buses.

Questions Two and Five Are Inter-related and Here Is My Answer—

2–5—You have seen the candidates answers to these questions in the daily papers. Question No. 5 is just a follow up on question No. 2. If you appoint a negro to the parks and recreation board you have opened the way for negroes to be appointed on all of the other boards, which help govern our city. My answer was and is, "I would not recommend that the commission appoint a negro to the parks and recreation board, but I would gladly work with their representatives in an attempt to establish a negro park and expanded recreational facilities in Montgomery."

In Answer To Question No. Three—

3—I agree that the negroes of Montgomery do need a section of their own in which to build decent homes. But NOT in a section like Lincoln Heights, where they would be completely surrounded by housing developments occupied by white people. I am a firm believer in segregation as we now have it in Alabama, and the lack of adequate negro school facilities, in the Lincoln Heights area, would lead to dissatisfaction and dissention. I would be happy to try and help them locate a subdivision of their own, near more adequate negro school facilities—but NEVER in Lincoln Heights.

Answering Question No. Four—

4—If the commission were to comply with this request it would be only a short time before negroes would be working along side of whites and whites along side of negroes, under the merit system, in our city hall. Our fire department, the nation's finest, under the leadership of Chief Bob Lampley, would soon be filled with negroes. I have always felt that if a man wanted a job bad enough he could go where the job, for which he is qualified, is available. There ARE places in the nation where civil service jobs for negroes in cities are available, but not in Montgomery. I will expend every effort to keep it that way.

Questions Six, Seven and Eight Are All Inter-related and Here Is My Answer—

6–7–8—Montgomery has done and is doing an excellent job in the field of slum clearance and public housing for the negroes. As one of your commissioners I will cooperate with the other commissioners in an attempt to complete this job and eliminate these hazards.

I have answered these questions exactly the way I feel. I have many friends among the negroes of Montgomery and I will be fair and honest with them in all our contacts, yet I will not compromise my principles, not violate my Southern birthright to promise something I do not intend to do. I will not be intimidated for the sake of a block of negro votes.

I come to you not seeking your votes with wild promises, but with a positive and constructive program, based on my training and experience in the fields of business and law enforcement.

Montgomery Advertiser, March 20, 1955.

December . . . 2 . . .

If the *Brown* decision had made 1954 a somewhat hopeful year for African Americans, 1955 brought disappointment and outrage. In May the Supreme Court implemented its year-old decision with a decree requiring desegregation of public schools "with all deliberate speed," which meant gradually. Founded in the Mississippi Delta in July 1954, White Citizens Councils vowing to resist integration were mushrooming across the Deep South. In late August 1955 Emmett Till, a fourteen-year-old black boy from Chicago visiting his Mississippi cousins, was brutally murdered for allegedly saying "bye, baby" to a white female store clerk. The killers, who later confessed, were acquitted.

With renewed concern, civil rights activist Rosa L. Parks attended a two-week summer workshop on furthering school desegregation at Highlander Folk School in the Appalachian mountains of Tennessee. Started by Myles Horton in the early 1930s, Highlander served as a training center for community activists and labor organizers. Parks's friend Virginia Foster Durr, a white activist for whom she had worked as a seamstress, arranged a scholarship.

July 6, 1955
Montgomery, Ala.

Mrs. Henry F. Shipherd
Executive Secretary
Highlander Folk School
Monteagle, Tenn.

Dear Mrs. Shipherd:

This is to say that I accept with sincere appreciation the scholarship for the Desegregation Workshop. The registration card is enclosed. I am certainly most grateful to Mrs. Durr for recommending me to you. [. . .] The Highlander Folk School seems like a wonderful place. I am looking forward with eager anticipation to attending the workshop, hoping to make a contribution to the fulfillment of complete freedom for all people.

Sincerely yours,
Rosa L. Parks

HRECR-WHi: Box 22.

At the close of the August workshop, Horton asked participants what changes they hoped for in their far-flung southern communities. Parks said that she did not expect things to improve in Montgomery, where the Negroes were "timid and would not act" and "wouldn't stand together."[1] Still, she had been deeply stirred by her visit to the mountain retreat, experiencing Highlander as a microcosm of a racially integrated society: "I found out for the first time in my adult life that this could be a unified society, that there was such a thing as people of differing races and backgrounds meeting together in workshops and living together in peace and harmony. . . . I gained there strength to persevere in my work for freedom."[2]

Rosa Parks Radio Interview, by Sidney Rogers

April 1956

ROSA PARKS: [. . .] I left work on my way home December 1st, 1955. About six o'clock in the afternoon, I boarded the bus in downtown Montgomery on Court Square. As the bus proceeded out of town, on the third stop, the white passengers had filled the front of the bus. When I got on the bus the rear was filled with colored passengers, and they were beginning to stand. The seat I occupied was the first of the seats where the Negro passengers take on this route. The driver noted that the front of the bus was filled with white passengers, and there would be two or three men standing. He looked back and asked that the seats I had taken along with three other persons, one in the seat with me, and two across the aisle were seated. He demanded the seats that we were occupying. The other passengers very reluctantly gave up their seats, but I refused to do so. He then called the officers of the law. They came and placed me under arrest, and I was bond, bailed out shortly after the arrest. And the trial was held December 5th on the next Monday, and the protest began from that date. And it is still continuin'.

SIDNEY ROGERS: Mrs. Parks, what in the world ever made you decide to be the person who after all these years of Jim Crow and segregation, what made you at that particular moment decide you were going to keep that seat?

PARKS: I felt that I was not being treated right, and that I had a right to retain the seat that I had taken as a passenger on the bus.

ROGERS: But Mrs. Parks, you had been mistreated for many, many, many years. You've lived most of your life in Montgomery, Alabama. What made you decide at the first part of the month of December of 1955 that you had had enough?

PARKS: The time had just come when I had been pushed as far as I could stand to be pushed, I suppose.

ROGERS: Well, Mrs. Parks, had you planned this?

PARKS: No, I hadn't.

ROGERS: It just happened.

PARKS: Yes, it did.

ROGERS: Well, had there been many times before in your life when you thought that maybe you were going to do just that kind of thing?

PARKS: I hadn't thought that I would be the person to do this. It hadn't occurred to me.

ROGERS: But don't you suppose you and many others also thought one time or another you were going to do this thing, sooner or later?

PARKS: Well, we didn't know just what to expect. In our area we always tried to avoid trouble and be as careful as possible to stay out of trouble, along this line. I want to make very certain that it is understood that I had not taken a seat in the white section as has been reported in many cases. The seat where I occupied, we were in the custom of takin' this seat on the way home, even though at times on this same bus route, we occupied the same seat with white standing if their space had been taken up, the seat had been taken up. And I was very much surprised that the driver at this point demanded that I remove myself from the seat.

ROGERS: You have done something here that I didn't quite understand myself, namely this: You said that you did not take a seat in the white section. And there's no doubt that has been reported in that way. What happened then was that you were in what is normally a colored section, and because whites had to stand up at this point, the driver asked you to get up to allow someone else to sit down?

PARKS: Yes, white persons.

ROGERS: A white person to sit down. A person who may or may not have been as tired as you.

PARKS: Well, it's true.

ROGERS: But who had not paid any more than you had.

PARKS: No, he hadn't.

ROGERS: And then, what happened?

PARKS: The driver said that if I refused to leave the seat, he would have to call the police, and I told him, "just call the police." Which he did. And when they came they placed me under arrest.

ROGERS: Wasn't that a pretty frightening thing to be arrested in Montgomery, Alabama?

PARKS: No, I wasn't frightened at all.

ROGERS: You weren't frightened? Why weren't you frightened?

PARKS: I don't know why I wasn't, but I didn't feel afraid. I had decided that I would have to know once and for all what rights I had as a human being and a citizen, even in Montgomery, Alabama.

ROGERS: Because you considered yourself a citizen as well as a human being in Montgomery, Alabama. You say you weren't frightened, yet to be arrested in Montgomery, especially on a charge in which you are challenging the whole system of segregation could be a pretty frightening thing. It could even lead to a certain amount of physical brutality, couldn't it?

PARKS: That's possible, it could have.

ROGERS: But this didn't bother you?

PARKS: No, it didn't.

ROGERS: And a lot of people, of course, feel quite ashamed at the disgrace of being arrested. Apparently you didn't feel that there was any disgrace involved in this one?

PARKS: No, not in this one.

ROGERS: Well then, you were arrested, and what was the charge?

PARKS: Violation of the segregation law of the city and state of Alabama, transportation.

ROGERS: Yes, but you were sitting in the colored section. What law were you violating?

PARKS: I didn't think I was violating any.

ROGERS: Well, Mrs. Parks, at the recent trial of Reverend M. L. King, it was brought up by the defense that there had been over many, many years many brutalities and humiliations of Negro passengers on these buses. Can you give us some examples that you yourself have seen or experienced personally of some of these humiliations that took place day after day when you were riding the buses?

PARKS: Yes, I have been refused entrance on the buses because I would not pay my fare at the front and go around to the rear door to enter.

ROGERS: Let me have that again? Now, you mean you pay your fare at the front and then were forced to walk around and enter into the rear door?

PARKS: Yes, that was the custom, if the bus was crowded up to the point where the white passengers would start occupying.

ROGERS: And even if it was raining or anything of that sort, you might have to pay your fare at the front and walk back in the rain to the back of the bus and get in?

PARKS: Yes, that's true.

ROGERS: Well, Mrs. Parks, then you were arrested and you say you went to, you posted bond. Did you have a trial?

PARKS: Yes.

ROGERS: And you were found innocent or guilty?

PARKS: Guilty.

ROGERS: You were found guilty. And then what?

PARKS: The case was appealed.

ROGERS: How did this particular incident of your being arrested and convicted and appealing, how did this lead to this particular protest?

PARKS: From the time of the arrest on Thursday night and Friday and Saturday and Sunday, the word had gotten around over Montgomery of my arrest because of this incident. And people just began to decide that they wouldn't ride the bus on the day of my trial, which was Monday, December 5th. And Monday morning, when the buses were out on their regular run, they remained empty. People were walking, getting rides in cars of people who would pick them up as best they could. On Monday night the mass meeting at the Holt Street Baptist Church had been called and there were many thousand people there. They kept coming, and some people never did get in the church, there were so many. The first day of remaining off the bus had been so successful it was organized, and that we wouldn't ride the bus until our request had been granted.

ROGERS: Well, Mrs. Parks, how did word get around Montgomery, Alabama, so quickly, first of all that you were arrested and convicted, and second of all, how did the word get around so quickly that there would be a meeting and that people would refuse to ride?

PARKS: There were telephone calls from those who knew about it to others, and also an article came out in the newspaper on Friday morning about the Negro woman overlooking segregation. She was seated in the front seat in the white section of the bus and refused to take a seat in the rear of the bus. That was the first newspaper account.

ROGERS: They didn't ride on the day of the trial. They walked. And then how come they kept right on walking?

PARKS: I feel they kept on walking because I was not the only person who had been mistreated and humiliated. Others had gone through the same experience, some even worse experiences than mine. And they all felt that the time had come that they should decide that we would have to stop supporting the bus company until we were given better service. [. . .]

Pacifica Radio Archive, Los Angeles.

Parks was bailed out of jail that evening by veteran organizer E. D. Nixon, Virginia Durr, and her husband, attorney Clifford Durr. They drove her home, where Nixon persuaded her, over her husband's opposition, to use her arrest as the long-awaited test case to challenge the constitutionality of bus segregation. Having worked with her closely in the NAACP for a decade, Nixon was certain that she was the right person to serve as a public symbol. She was well known and respected in the black community as an activist and church worker, her character was above reproach, she was well educated and articulate. It helped, too, that she had light complexion. "If ever there was a woman who was dedicated to the cause," Nixon later recalled, "it was Rosa Parks."[3]

That night attorney Fred Gray informed Jo Ann Robinson about Parks's arrest and they concluded that if they were ever going to boycott the buses, this was the time—as long as they could get support from the ministers. She then talked with Nixon on the telephone. They concurred that pursuing the legal test case should be reinforced by a boycott, initially intended for just one day, that the Women's Political Council had long been considering and that others had tried to start more than once. She quickly drafted a leaflet and around midnight drove over to Alabama State College, where she and a business professor stayed up all night mimeographing thousands of copies. The next day, between classes and into the evening, she and two trusted students distributed bundles of flyers all over black Montgomery.

A bus driver found the flyer stuck to an advertisement in the rear of his bus and turned it in to a supervisor. "All drivers should check their busses at end of route" for the flyers and remove them, a bus official had scrawled on it; this "would keep lots of passengers from reading it."

This is for Monday, December 5, 1955

Another Negro woman has been arrested and thrown into jail because she refused to get up out of her seat on the bus for a white person to sit down.

It is the second time since the Claudette Colbert [*Colvin*] case that a Negro woman has been arrested for the same thing. This has to be stopped.

Negroes have rights, too, for if Negroes did not ride the buses, they could not operate. Three-fourths of the riders are Negroes, yet we are arrested, or have to stand over empty seats. If we do not do something to stop these arrests, they will continue. The next time it may be you, or your daughter, or mother.

This woman's case will come up on Monday. We are, therefore, asking every Negro to stay off the buses Monday in protest of the arrest and trial. Don't ride the buses to work, to town, to school, or anywhere on Monday.

You can afford to stay out of school for one day if you have no other way to go except by bus.

You can also afford to stay out of town for one day. If you work, take a cab, or walk. But please, children and grown-ups, don't ride the bus at all on Monday. Please stay off of all buses Monday.

MCDA-AMC: Complaint File.

On Friday morning, December 2, before he left on his regular Pullman train to Chicago, Nixon called Montgomery's black ministers, asking them to back a one-day boycott and to attend a planning meeting that evening with other community leaders at Martin Luther King Jr.'s downtown Dexter Avenue Baptist Church. Over the weekend volunteers handed out a revised version of Robinson's flyer (drafted by King and Rev. Ralph Abernathy) that concluded: "Come to a mass meeting, Monday at 7:00 P.M. at the Holt Street Baptist Church for further instruction." The preachers pushed participation in the protest from their pulpits Sunday morning. The best publicity came from a front-page article about it in the Sunday *Montgomery Advertiser* by city editor Joe Azbell, who had been called by Nixon, his longtime news source in the black community.

Awed by the boycott's stunning success, the leaders met on Monday afternoon to plan the evening mass meeting, which would decide whether to continue the protest. They created a new organization called the Montgomery Improvement Association (the name suggested by Abernathy) and elected King president unopposed. In Recorder's Court that morning, Rosa Parks had been convicted and fined for violating the state bus segregation law. Gray, her lawyer, appealed the conviction to Montgomery Circuit Court and later to the state court of appeal.

1. "Mrs. Rosa Parks Reports on Montgomery, Ala., Bus Protest," March 4, 1956, Highlander Folk School, Monteagle, Tenn., ACLUA-NJP.

2. Quoted in Frank Adams, *Unearthing Seeds of Fire: The Idea of Highlander* (Winston-Salem, N.C.: John F. Blair, 1975), p. 122.

3. Quoted in "Eyes on the Prize: America's Civil Rights Years," PBS television documentary (1987), segment 1, "Awakenings (1954–1956)."

Minutes of the Montgomery Improvement Association Founding Meeting

A group of 18 persons met at the Mt. Zion A.M.E. Zion Church at 3 P.M. Officers were elected:
Chairman—Rev. M. L. King
Vice Chairman—Rev. Roy Bennett
Recording Sec.—Rev. U. J. Fields
Corresponding Sec.—Rev. E. N. French
Financial Sec.—Mrs. Erna Dungee
Treasurer—E. D. Nixon

Name
    The Montgomery Improvement Association
    Moved and second that the 16 persons here and a suggestion that 9 names be brought in making 25 which constitute the Executive Committee

Agenda
    1. Opening Hymn Onward Christian Soldier
    2. Prayer—Rev. Alford
    3. Scripture Rev. Fields
    4. Occasion—Rev. King
    Presentation of Mrs. Parks, Fred Daniels—Rev. French
    5. Resolutions—Rev. Abernathy
    Vote on Recommendations
    6. Offering—Rev. Bonner
    7. Closing Hymn—My Country Tis of Thee
    8. Benediction—Rev. Roy Bennett

It was recommended that resolutions would be drawned up.
Resolution Committee & Recommendations
    Rev. Abernathy Chairman
    Rev. Alford
    Mr. Gray
    Mr. Nixon
    Rev. Glasco

The president, Rev. M. L. King, attorney Gray and attorney Langford is on the committee. The program would be tape recorded at its Holt Street Baptist Church.

It was agreed that the protest be continued until conditions are improved.
Transportation Committee
Finance
It was passed that the recommendations from the committee be given to the citizens at the night meeting.

MLKP-MBU: Box 1.

"At Holt Street Baptist Church: Deeply Stirred Throng of Colored Citizens Protests Bus Segregation," by Joe Azbell

As I drove along Cleveland Avenue en route to the Holt Street Baptist Church Monday night, I could see Negroes by the dozens forming a file, almost soldierly, on the sidewalk. They were going to the Rosa Parks protest meeting at the church.

They were silent people, bundled in overcoats, performing what appeared to be a ritual. I parked my automobile a block from the church and noted the time was 6:45. Already cars were strung out for six or seven blocks in each direction.

In fact, the area around the church looked like Cramton Bowl at an Alabama State-Tuskegee football game. Except for one thing: these people were stony silent.

The Negroes eyed me and one inquired if I was a policeman. He turned to his three companions: "He says he ain't the law." I walked up to the steps of the church and two Negro policemen were standing there chatting. Both were courteous when I introduced myself and one went inside and found out about the seating arrangement for the press. Chairs were placed down front for the reporters. The TV cameraman from WSFA-TV and the United Press reporter later took these seats. I stood in the rear of the church during the meeting while Reporter Steve Lesher anchored himself in a chair near the church's pulpit.

The inside of the church is impressive because of its simplicity. The church has the ordinary equipment of the upper middle class white church and there's a large mirror across the back wall.

I observed police squad cars parked two blocks away in each direction from the church and occasionally a police sergeant would drive by and check with the four Negro policemen who were handling the traffic at the church.

'FURTHER INSTRUCTIONS'

I went inside the church and stood at the front for a few minutes. The two rear doors were jammed with people and a long aisle was crammed with human forms like a frozen food package. I went to the rear of the church and it was the same. The Negro policemen pleaded with the Negroes to keep the aisles free so people could get out. In the end the policemen gave up in despair of correcting the safety hazard. Bodies at the front were packed one against the other. It required five minutes for a photographer to move eight feet among these people in trying to leave the building.

The purpose of this meeting was to give "further instructions" on the boy-cott of city buses which had been started as a protest of the Negroes against the arrest, trial and conviction of Rosa Parks, 42-year-old seamstress, on a charge of violating segregation laws by refusing to give up her seat to a white person and move to the rear of a city bus.

There were four white reporters or photographers at the meeting. Only one other white person attended. He appeared to be a young college student or airman and he came with a Negro and left with a Negro. He sat in the group of Negroes in the balcony.

SPEAKERS UNIDENTIFIED

The meeting was started in a most unusual fashion. A Negro speaker—appar-ently a minister—came to the microphone. He did not introduce himself but apparently most of the Negroes knew him. He said there were microphones on the outside and in the basement, and there were three times as many people outside as on the inside. There was an anonymity throughout the meeting of the speakers. None of the white reporters could identify the speak-ers. Most of the Negroes did. The introduction of Fred Daniels and Rosa Parks were clear and brief. Daniels was arrested in the boycott Monday.

WHITES LISTEN

The passion that fired the meeting was seen as the thousands of voices joined in singing *Onward, Christian Soldier*. Another hymn followed. The voices thundered through the church.

Then there followed a prayer by a minister. It was a prayer interrupted a hundred times by "yeas" and "uh-huhs" and "that's right." The minister spoke of God as the Master and the brotherhood of man. He repeated in a different way that God would protect the righteous.

As the other speakers came on the platform urging "freedom and equality" for Negroes "who are Americans and proud of this democracy," the frenzy of the audience mounted. There was a volume of clapping that seemed to boom through the walls. Outside the loudspeakers were blaring the message for blocks. White people stopped blocks away and listened to the loudspeakers' messages.

THE HAT IS PASSED

The newspapers were criticized for quoting police authorities on reports of intimidation of Negroes who attempted to ride buses and for comparing the Negro boycott with the economic reprisals of White Citizens groups.

The remark which drew the most applause was: "We will not retreat one inch in our fight to secure and hold our American citizenship." Second was a statement: "And the history book will write of us as a race of people who in Montgomery County, State of Alabama, Country of the United States, stood up for and fought for their rights as American citizens, as citizens of democracy."

Outside the audience listened as more and more cars continued to arrive. Streets became Dexter traffic snarls. There was hymn singing between speeches. In the end there was the passing of the hats and Negroes dropped in dollar bills, $5 bills and $10 bills. It was not passive giving but active giving. Negroes called to the hat passers outside—"Here, let me give."

PEACEFUL MEANS

When the resolution on continuing the boycott of the bus was read, there came a wild whoop of delight. Many said they would never ride the bus again. Negroes turned to each other and compared past incidents on the buses.

At several points there was an emotionalism that the ministers on the platform recognized could get out of control and at various intervals they repeated again and again what "we are seeking is by peaceful means."

"There will be no violence or intimidation. We are seeking things in a democratic way and we are using the weapon of protest," the speakers declared.

MORE HYMNS

I left as the meeting was breaking up. The Negroes made a path for me through the crowd as I went to my car, but the packed group found it uncomfortable to move. A cry of "fire" would have caused a panic that could have resulted in scores of deaths. Negroes on the outside recognized this danger but these people wanted to see and hear what was going on.

There was hymn singing as I drove away. At the first corner where I turned, I nodded at the policemen in a squad car. At the next corner I saw another squad car. And at the next corner where I stopped for a signal light, the driver of another squad car asked if the meeting had ended.

The meeting was much like an old-fashioned revival with loud applause added. It proved beyond any doubt there was a discipline among Negroes that many whites had doubted. It was almost a military discipline combined with emotion.

Montgomery Advertiser, December 7, 1955.

Ralph Abernathy, pastor of Montgomery's First Baptist Church, read the resolution to the mass meeting. The several thousand participants, inside and outside the church, approved it by cheering acclamation.

WHEREAS, there are thousands of negroes in the city and county of Montgomery who ride busses owned and operated by the Montgomery City Lines, Incorporated, and

WHEREAS, said citizens have been riding busses owned and operated by said company over a number of years, and

WHEREAS, said citizens, over a number of years, and on many occasions, have been insulted, embarrassed, and have been made to suffer great fear of bodily harm by drivers of busses owned and operated by said bus company, and

WHEREAS, the drivers of said busses have never requested a white passenger riding on any of its busses to relinquish his seat and stand so that a Negro may take his seat; however, said drivers have on many occasions, too numerous to mention, requested Negro passengers on said busses to relinquish their seats and stand so that white passengers may take their seats, and

WHEREAS, said citizens of Montgomery city and county pay their fares just as all other persons who are passengers on said busses, and are entitled to fair and equal treatment, and

WHEREAS, there has been any number of arrests of Negroes caused by drivers of said busses and they are constantly put in jail for refusing to give white passengers their seats and stand.

WHEREAS, in March of 1955, a committee of citizens did have a conference with one of the officials of said bus line; at which time said official arranged a meeting between attorneys representing the Montgomery City Lines, Incorporated and the city of Montgomery, and

WHEREAS, the official of the bus line promised that as a result of the meeting between said attorneys, he would issue a statement of policy clarifying the law with reference to the seating of Negro Passengers on the bus, and

WHEREAS, said attorneys did have a meeting and did discuss the matter of clarifying the law, however, the official of said bus lines did not make public statement as to its policy with reference to the seating of passengers on its busses, and

WHEREAS, since that time, at least two ladies have been arrested for an alleged violation of the city segregation law with reference to bus travel, and

WHEREAS, said citizens of Montgomery city and county believe that they have been grossly mistreated as passengers on the busses owned and operated by said bus company in spite of the fact that they are in the majority with reference to the number of passengers riding on said busses,

BE IT THEREFORE RESOLVED AS FOLLOWS:

1. That the citizens of Montgomery are requesting that every citizen in Montgomery, regardless of race, color or creed, to refrain from riding busses owned and operated in the city of Montgomery by the Montgomery City Lines, Incorporated until some arrangement has been worked out between said citizens and the Montgomery City Lines, Incorporated.

2. That every person owning or who has access to automobiles will use their automobiles in assisting other persons to get to work without charge.

3. That the employers of persons whose employees live a great distance from them, as much as possible afford transportation for own employees.

4. That the Negro Citizens of Montgomery are ready and willing to send a delegation of citizens to the Montgomery City Lines to discuss their grievances and to work out a solution for the same.

Be it further resolved that we have not, are not, and have no intentions of using any unlawful means or any intimidation to persuade persons not to ride the Montgomery City Lines Busses. However, we call upon your conscience, both moral and spiritual, to give your whole-hearted support to this undertaking. We believe we have a just complaint and we are willing to discuss this matter with the proper officials.

MLKP-MBU: Box 5.

Recollection of First MIA Mass Meeting, by Ralph D. Abernathy

We, M. L. King, and I, went to the meeting together. It was drizzling rain; I had been working up until the last minute on the resolutions. I was given instructions: one, to call off the protest, or two, if indicated, to continue the protest until the grievances were granted. We had had a successful "one-day protest," but we feared that if we extended it beyond the first day, we might fail; it might be better after all to call the protest off, and then we could hold this "one-day boycott" as a threat for future negotiations. However, we were to determine whether to continue the protest by the size of the crowds. If we found a large number of persons at the church this would indicate that Negroes would be interested in continuing the protest. But, if there were only a few, we felt that Negroes were not sufficiently interested, and that they might return to the buses the next day even in spite of our wishes.

When we got about twenty blocks from the church we saw cars parked solid; we wondered if there was a funeral or a death in the community. But as we got closer to the church we saw a great mass of people. The *Montgomery Advertiser* estimated the crowd at approximately seven thousand persons all trying to get in a church that will accommodate less than a thousand. It took us about fifteen minutes to work our way through the crowd by pleading: "Please let us through—we are Reverend King and Reverend Abernathy. Please permit us to get through."

Once we broke through the crowd there was another ten minutes of picture-taking coupled with flashing lights, cheering and hand-clapping. Those inside applauded for at least ten minutes.

It was apparent to us that the people were with us. It was then that all of the ministers who had previously refused to take part in the program came up to Reverend King and me to offer their services. This expression of togetherness on the part of the masses was obviously an inspiration to the leadership and helped to rid it of the cowardly, submissive, over timidity.

We began the meeting by singing *Onward Christian Soldiers, Marching as to War*. Then Reverend Alford, who later resigned from our movement because he felt that the bus boycott should be halted, and that Negroes should, for the sake of peace, accept segregated seating again, offered a prayer which was soul-stirring. Next Reverend U. J. Fields, who likewise eventually broke with our movement but for other reasons (he believed we had misappropriated funds)—read a scripture from the thirteenth chapter of First Corinthians. After which Reverend King made one of his now famous statements:

> There comes a time when people get tired of being trampled over by the iron feet of oppression. There comes a time when people get tired of being pushed out of the glittering sunlight of life's July and left standing in the piercing chills of an Alpine November.

He has said this many times since, but we heard it on that evening for the first time; it was beautiful.

Mrs. Rosa Parks was presented to the mass meeting because we wanted her to become symbolic of our protest movement. Following her we presented Mr. Daniels, who happily for our meeting had been arrested on that day. The policemen alleged that he tried to prevent a Negro woman from riding the bus, while he claimed he was only assisting her across the street. The appearance of these persons created enthusiasm, thereby giving added momentum to the movement.

We then heard the resolutions calling for the continuation of the boycott [. . .] unanimously and enthusiastically adopted by the 7,000 individuals both in and outside the church. We closed the meeting by taking an offering with people marching down the aisles giving their nickels, dimes, quarters, and dollars for freedom. The *Montgomery Advertiser* described the movement the next morning under the heading—"Hymn Singing Negroes of Montgomery, Alabama."

Ralph D. Abernathy, "The Natural History of a Social Movement" (M.A. Thesis, Atlanta University, 1958).

Virginia Foster Durr (1903–) reported on Montgomery events to her close friend Clark Howell Foreman. Like her husband, Clifford Durr, Foreman had been an official in President Roosevelt's New Deal. He and Virginia Durr, civil rights activists since the 1930s, were founders of the Southern Conference for Human Welfare (SCHW) and the Southern Conference Educational Fund (SCEF). Durr, a leader in abolishing the discriminatory poll tax (a constitutional amendment was finally approved in 1964), worked with her husband in his Montgomery law office. They had moved to the city in 1951, after Clifford Durr had resigned from the Federal Communications Commission in protest of the Truman administration's anticommunist loyalty oath.

December 7, 1955

Dearest Clark:

Well it always seems darkest just before some break comes your way and while our personal fortunes are still precarious still the most wonderful thing has happened right here in Montgomery, Ala.

It may have been in the papers up there, but in any case what has happened is that the Negroes here have organized a boycott of the busses in protest against the arrest of Mrs. Parks and it is almost 100 per cent effective and they are carrying it on in the most orderly and disciplined way and with the utmost determination.

The custom here in the busses is that the Negroes fill up from the back and the whites from the front and if there are no whites then the Negroes can sit as far forward as there are seats, but if any white person gets on they are ordered to get up and give them their seats. Of course as you can see this creates endless difficulties and irritations and bad feeling, as no whites are ever ordered to get up and give up their seats.

Last Spring a little fourteen year old Negro girl got arrested because she refused to move and the local NAACP was going to make a test case out of it, BUT [. . .] her Mama made her drop the case because she didn't want her to be shamed by going into court. So the local head of the Youth Branch of the NAACP—Mrs. Parks—refused to move last Friday [*Thursday*] night and she got arrested and was fined and found guilty and the NAACP is going to take up her case as a test case and as a measure of protest the entire Negro community is boycotting the busses, at I don't know what cost to themselves in terms of difficulties and trouble. While only a few of us are in sympathy with it, still the whole population has been very much impressed by their determination and courage. It is still going on and has been so far absolutely orderly and disciplined.

They called us to get her out of jail, which Cliff did, but then the local NAACP attorney took over for the test case, a young and very intelligent Negro, Fred Gray, who adores Cliff and consults him on every move he makes and uses our library. The Heroine of the occasion—Mrs. Parks—has sewed for me ever since I have been here and we have become fast friends and last summer I got her a scholarship to Highlander and she was thrilled by it as for the first time in her life she was treated as an equal. She is a lovely person and very intelligent and brave. She asked me to speak at the meeting on Sunday afternoon which I did, and I must admit rather trembled at the thought of it being in the papers the next morning but it wasn't. Aubrey [*Williams*] is out at four in the morning taking passengers I think—and he is so is thrilled to death as it seems to be a vindication of all his work and faith in the Negroes. It has really been astonishing. [. . .]

Of course the "best people" here explain it all away by saying that the Negroes are so intimidated that is why they are not riding the busses—and when "Poor Cora" doesn't run to work until ten o'clock they say it is because she is so frightened. But the whole town is impressed and they know after this that they have a united group to deal with.

Well that is about all the news around here that I know of. It is mighty interesting down here just now if we can just hang on. [. . .]

Lots of love and do write.

VA

VFDP-MCR-S: Box 2.

The biracial Alabama Council on Human Relations (ACHR), state affiliate of the Atlanta-based Southern Regional Council, worked to improve race relations. The ACHR arranged the first negotiating session between the MIA and city and bus company officials on December 8.

Minutes, Alabama Council on Human Relations, December 7, 1955

Several board members of the Alabama Council and staff discussed the possibility of offering "the good offices" of the Alabama Council to bring together the opposing factors in the Montgomery, Alabama bus boycott. Agreement was reached that this should be done. The Rev. Thomas Thrasher, Episcopal minister, representing the Alabama Council talked with the leadership of the Negro group who are protesting the treatment of Negro passengers on Montgomery buses and who proposed that a policy of seating by the rule of "first come first served" be followed and that Negro bus drivers be employed for those routes that serve the Negro district. This group agreed to sit down and discuss with the bus company and city officials their grievances and their proposals for rectifying the same.

Contact was made with the management of the bus company. The management expressed regret about the situation as it then existed but held they were merely "obeying the law." They further said there was no sense in negotiating unless the city was willing to interpret the law in a manner other than the bus companies' attorneys then understood it. The Secretary of the Mayor of Montgomery was then contacted (the Mayor being inaccessible) and it was proposed that the city government call together the opposing factions to work out like grownups a solution to the problem. The Mayor's secretary promised to fully inform the mayor of this proposal and of the offer of the "good offices" of the Alabama Council.

ASRC-GAU: 01-67-13.

On Thursday morning December 8, the opposing sides met at Montgomery City Hall. King, Ralph Abernathy, Jo Ann Robinson, Fred Gray, and eight others negotiated for the MIA. Mayor W. A. ("Tacky") Gayle and commissioners Clyde Sellers and Frank Parks represented the city; manager J. H. Bagley and counsel Jack Crenshaw spoke for Montgomery City Lines.

"4-Hour Huddle: Bus Boycott Conference Fails to Find Solution," by Tom Johnson

Montgomery Negroes will continue to boycott city buses until a "satisfactory" seating arrangement is devised, a spokesman told officials of City Bus Lines yesterday. The Rev. M. L. King, speaking for a delegation that conferred with bus lines officials four hours, proposed that bus patrons be seated on a "first come—first served" basis with no sections reserved for either race. Negroes would continue to seat from the rear and whites from the front, he said, but there would be no reassignment of seats once the buses were loaded.

TWO OTHER CONDITIONS

He laid down two other conditions sought by Negroes: More courteous treatment and the hiring of Negro drivers on routes "predominantly" Negro.

On all but the "courtesy" proposal, Atty. Jack Crenshaw, counsel for the bus lines, demurred. [(*From Minutes:*) He said we have courtesy, and the record shows that. He said what are you going to do about white passengers who get on the bus if it is filled with Negroes. The only alternative is to reserve seats for whites.[1]]

He said it would be impossible to accept the proposed seating arrangement "in view of the segregation law" and, he added, the company has no intentions of hiring Negro drivers. "We do not contemplate and have no intentions of hiring Negro drivers," said Crenshaw. "The time is not right in Montgomery, but who can say what will happen in 10 years."

One of the delegation replied: "We don't mean ten years, we mean this year." King, who is pastor of the Dexter Avenue Baptist Church, emphasized the group was not trying to change the segregation law.

BETTER ACCOMMODATIONS

"We are merely trying to peacefully obtain better accommodations for Negroes," he said. Commenting on reports of violence, King said most of his race deplores such acts as much as anyone and promised to report "anyone we know to be guilty." But, he added, the boycott will continue "until something is done."

J. H. Bagley, manager of the bus line, was asked if this statement would cause the company to reduce its service immediately. He replied: "We will continue to provide service adequate to the public needs." He added that service has already been curtailed on some routes but declined to name them.

A Negro attorney, Fred D. Gray, questioned whether the state law applied to city bus lines and urged that a ruling be obtained from the attorney general. Mayor W. A. Gayle later said the City Commission had not yet decided whether to seek the ruling. Crenshaw told the protesting delegation the bus company would do everything possible to serve its passengers but could not "change the law." [. . .]

Several instances of violence have been reported. Four city buses have been fired on. But Police Chief G. J. Ruppenthal said there was "no evidence to date" of any connection between the incidents and the boycott. Two Negro houses including the home of Policeman A. G. Worthy were hit by shotgun blasts Wednesday night but no one was reported hurt.

Montgomery Advertiser, December 9, 1955.

With the meeting at an impasse, to which press coverage might have contributed, Mayor Gayle asked a smaller group (King, Gray, Sellers, Parks, Bagley, Crenshaw) to talk further in private, but the four whites in the group were unyielding. According to King's account, Crenshaw, "our most stubborn opponent," admitted at the smaller meeting: "If we granted the Negroes these demands, they would go about boasting of a victory that they had won over the white people; and this we will not stand for."[2] The white officials' rigid stance surprised the MIA leaders and dashed their expectations that the protest would take only a few days to win their moderate demands. Later that day they wired Chicago-based National City Lines, owner of bus firms in three dozen cities including Montgomery, and asked the parent company to "send a representative to Montgomery to arbitrate."[3]

1. Minutes of Meeting in Montgomery Mayor's Office, December 8, 1955, State's Exhibit 45, *State of Alabama* v. *M. L. King, Jr.*, CMCR-AMC.

2. Martin Luther King Jr., *Stride Toward Freedom: The Montgomery Story* (New York: Harper & Row, 1958), pp. 111, 112.

3. MIA to National City Lines, Inc., December 8, 1955, MLKP-MBU: Box 6.

Two days after the deadlocked talks, King and the MIA submitted a statement to the press, which the *Montgomery Advertiser* quoted from in a front-page article the next day.[1] Contesting the bus company stance that altering its seating policy would be unlawful, they interpreted the Alabama statute as not making segregation mandatory. They also pointed out that the Montgomery City Code did not require a person to relinquish a seat unless another was available (thus, Rosa Parks was charged only with violating the state law). The MIA argued that the state and local laws were flexible enough to permit its proposed seating arrangement, which would not eliminate bus segregation.

"Statement of Negro Citizens on Bus Situation"

December 10, 1955

We have heretofore stated the position of the Negro Citizens of Montgomery with reference to the local bus situation. As good citizens we want to comply with the law until the law is changed or is over-ruled. However, we feel that we have the right to insist that the law be fairly administered.

In answer to our request that the Montgomery City Lines adopt a policy of loading busses from rear to front with colored passengers and from front to rear with white passengers and that all passengers be permitted to retain their seats on a "first come—first served" basis, without reservation of seats for any particular race, the bus company contends that such an arrangement would be in violation of the law and particularly the Act of July 18, 1947 (General Acts of Alabama, 1947, #130, Page 40).

In answer to this contention we would like to call attention to the pertinent provision of Section 1, of this Act, which reads as follows:

> Section 1. All passenger stations in this state operated by or for the use of any motor transportation company *shall be authorized* to provide separate waiting rooms, facilities, or space, or separate ticket windows, for the white and colored races but such accommodations for the races shall be equal. All motor transportation companies and operators of vehicles, carrying passengers for hire in this state, whether intrastate or interstate passengers, *are authorized and empowered* to provide separate accommodations on each vehicle for the white and colored races. Any officer or agent of such motor transportation company or operator, in charge of any vehicle, *is authorized* to assign or reassign each passenger or person to a division, section or seat on the vehicle designated by such company or operator or by such officer or agent for the race to which the passenger or person belongs . . . (italics supplied).

We believe that this Act was not intended to apply to busses operating within a single municipality, but only to those under the jurisdiction of the Alabama Public Service Commission. However, it should be noted that under the provisions quoted the method of handling the seating of passengers is left entirely to the transportation companies themselves. They are *authorized* and *empowered* to provide separate accommodations but are not *directed* or *required* to take any action whatsoever.

The Legislature, it seems clear, wisely left it up to the transportation companies to work out the seating problem in a reasonable and practical way, subject to the limitations of reasonableness and equality of treatment to all passengers, regardless of race.

It should be further noted that even under the City Code of Montgomery (Chapter 6, Section 10 and 11) no person, white or colored, can be required to give up a seat unless there is a vacant seat in the portion of the bus to which the passenger is assigned.

We feel that there is no issue between the Negro citizens and the Montgomery City Lines that cannot be solved by negotiations between people of good will and we submit that there is no legal barrier to such negotiations.

Respectfully submitted,
The Montgomery Improvement Association
M. L. King, President

RGP.

1. "Bus Service at Standstill in Negro Area," *Montgomery Advertiser*, December 11, 1955.

Montgomery native Juliette Morgan, librarian at the Montgomery Public Library, wrote the following letter to the *Advertiser*, one of several from white sympathizers during the first weeks of the protest. A 1935 University of Alabama alumna, she was the fifth generation of female college graduates in her family; her great-great-grandmother had graduated from college in 1822. Morgan's first letter to the Montgomery daily criticizing segregation, entitled " 'White Supremacy' Is Evil," appeared on June 9, 1952. For months after the December 1955 letter was published, whites harassed her, which was probably a cause of her suicide a year and a half later.

"Lesson From Gandhi," by Juliette Morgan

Editor, *The Advertiser*—Not since the First Battle of the Marne [*September 1914*] has the taxi been put to as good use as it has this last week in Montgomery. However, the spirit animating our Negro citizens as they ride these taxis or walk from the heart of Cloverdale to Mobile Road has been more like that of Gandhi than of the "taxicab army" that saved Paris.

As you remember, Gandhi set out on his "Salt March" from Sabarmati to the sea—about 150 miles—as a boycott against the government's salt monopoly. He took with him only a loin cloth, a bamboo walking stick, and a consuming idea. He vowed that he would not return until India was independent. Depending on their point of view, people laughed, sneered, or shook their heads, but 17 years later India was free. Passive resistance combined with freedom from hate is a power to be reckoned with.

The Negroes of Montgomery seem to have taken a lesson from Gandhi—and our own Thoreau, who influenced Gandhi. Their own task is greater than Gandhi's, however, for they have greater prejudice to overcome.

One feels that history is being made in Montgomery these days, the most important in her career. It is hard to imagine a soul so dead, a heart so hard, a vision so blinded and provincial as not to be moved with admiration at the quiet dignity, discipline, and dedication with which the Negroes have conducted their boycott. Yes, there have been "incidents," but the actual damage inflicted has been rather less than that done by the Lanier students in their protests against the abolition of sororities and fraternities. And a great deal less than in most strikes.

Of course, the fewer "incidents," the stronger the case for the Negroes. Their cause and their conduct have filled me with great sympathy, pride, humility and envy. I envy their unity, their good humor, their fortitude, and their willingness to suffer for great Christian and democratic principles, or just plain decent treatment. The other side is willing to fight all right, say cruel things, and to make others suffer, but the case is such that it calls for no suffering or sacrifice on their parts. That weakens their case.

It is sad indeed that the most reasonable and moderate requests presented to the bus company and City Commission by the Rev. M. L. King were met with such a "Ye rebels! Disperse!" attitude as voiced by their attorney and others. No, the law must be enforced with all pharisaical zeal and inflexibility. Well, I say the law ought to be changed. And I recommend to those in authority Edmund Burke's Speech on Conciliation with the Colonies.

I am all for law and order, the protection of person and property against violence, but I believe the Constitution and Supreme Court of the United States constitute the supreme law of the land. I find it ironical to hear men in authority who are openly flouting this law speak piously of law enforcement.

I also find it hard to work up sympathy for the bus company. I have ridden the buses of Montgomery ever since they have been running. I have ridden them from once to four times a day for the past 14 years until this October. Personally I have received courteous and friendly treatment. I consider many of the drivers my good friends. With no exception I have never seen any human being give such excellent service to the public as Mr. Alton Courtney. Mr. Eliot I. Newman and others are fine too. On the other hand, I have heard some bus drivers use the tone and manners of mule drivers in their treatment of Negro passengers. (Incidentally Negroes pay full fare for fourth class treatment.) Three times I've gotten off the bus because I could not countenance treatment of Negroes. I should have gotten off on several other occasions. Twice I have heard a certain driver with high seniority mutter quite audibly "black ape." I could not tell whether the Negro heard or not, but I did and felt insulted.

It is interesting to read editorials on the legality of this boycott. They make me think of that famous one that turned America from a tea to a coffee drinking nation. Come to think of it, one might say that this nation was founded upon a boycott.

The likening of the bus boycott to those of the White Citizens Councils is misleading. The difference in the causes and in the spirit behind each is vast. Just compare the speeches delivered at Selma and here in the City Hall with those at the Holt Street Baptist Monday night. Read them side by side as reported in *The Advertiser*—and blush. Joe Azbell's account of the Holt Street meeting is the best reporting I have ever read.

Instead of acting like sullen adolescents whose attitude is "Make me," we ought to be working out plans to span the gap between segregation and integration to extend public services—schools, libraries, parks—and transportation to Negro citizens. Ralph McGill's [Atlanta Constitution *editor*] is the best advice I've heard: "Segregation is on its way out, and he who tries to tell the people otherwise does them great disservice. The problem of the future is how to live with the change."

This may be a minority report, but a number of Montgomerians not entirely inconsequential agree with my point of view.

Montgomery Advertiser, December 12, 1955.

To provide alternative transportation, most of Montgomery's 108 black taxicab drivers agreed to cut rates to ten cents per person, the bus fare. At the first negotiating session on December 8, Police Commissioner Sellers mentioned that a city ordinance required cab drivers to charge a minimum fare of forty-five cents. This prompted King and the MIA Transportation Committee to organize a car pool system modeled on the one used during a brief bus boycott in Baton Rouge, Louisiana, in June 1953. Montgomery cab drivers offered the low fare until they received warnings from a city official. In response, one of the eighteen black taxicab companies passed a resolution on December 14, affirming the minimum fare but allowing each passenger in a group to ride for a fraction of it.

Be it Resolved:

We the Cab Company of the City of Montgomery agree to charge during the hours of 5:00 to 9:00 A.M. and 3:00 to 6:00 P.M. as follows:

A flat charge of 45¢ for each trip within the City limits, a distance of not more than one mile, an additional charge of 5¢ for each additional one half mile. On groups of two or more passengers from the same origin and the same destination, we agree to charge the said group the same as one passenger.

MLKP-MBU: Box 6.

Lutheran minister Robert Graetz sent a letter to *Time* magazine on December 22 in an effort to get national press coverage to counter what he calls "one-sided stories" in local newspapers. *Time*'s first report on the bus boycott appeared on January 16, 1956. Its generally positive treatment of the Montgomery protest culminated in a cover story on King in February 1957.

National News Editor
TIME Magazine
TIME & LIFE Building
9 Rockefeller Plaza
New York 20, New York

Subject: Bus protest in Montgomery, Alabama

Dear Sir:

I am writing this letter to you, because I have long been impressed with the fair and unbiased treatment you give in your news stories. (I am a regular cover-to-cover TIME reader.) I have been particularly impressed with the bold and courageous way in which you have handled the extremely touchy subject of race relations.

There is a story in the making here in Montgomery, Alabama, that may be just as explosive as the [*Emmett*] Till case, before it is over and done. I am referring to the protest which the Negroes (and many whites) of Montgomery are making against the local bus company. Undoubtedly you have received some reports about this over the AP and UP wires.

What you may not know is that only part of the story is actually reaching the public through the normal channels of communication. The local newspapers have consistently printed one-sided stories about the developments in this protest. They have at times (purposely, or otherwise) omitted pertinent facts that would have put a much more favorable light on what the Negroes are asking for.

In addition, all of the "law-enforcement" agencies in the city and county have been doing everything possible to break the back of our campaign. Laws that have rarely been enforced are now being pulled put of the books and being used against the Negroes (but, we hear, not against the whites). For example, hundreds of people double-park on the downtown streets while waiting for parking places or while waiting for a passenger to get out, do some quick shopping and return. Recently, however, many people have been charged and fined for blocking traffic, if they happened to be picking up or letting out Negroes.

I am a white Lutheran minister, serving a Negro congregation. I cannot even give my own members a ride in my car without fear of being stopped by the police and accused of running a taxi. On last Monday Sheriff Butler himself watched me put several Negroes in my car, while parked in a legal parking zone. Then he stopped me, accused me of running a taxi, took me in for questioning, searched my car (without showing me a warrant or indicating that he had one), and finally released me. The same thing is being done over and over in this city every day.

If you want a good look at the way a one-race press and a one-race police force band together to discredit fifty thousand people who are tired of being treated like animals on the city busses, and who are registering their feelings by refraining from riding those busses, then I urge you to send a reporter to Montgomery as soon as possible.

There are many more discriminatory factors that have been introduced into this whole picture, in some cases by rather high officials. But the worst factor of all is that it has become almost impossible to tell our story to the people of the city without having it distorted and turned against us. [. . .]

I respectfully request that the contents of this letter be kept confidential until such time as they have been verified by you. Please advise me as to your reaction to my request that you have this story covered by your own staff member.

Sincerely yours,
Robert Graetz

Copies: Dr. King, Atty. Gray, Rev. Hughes

MLKP-MBU: Box 107.

After MIA leaders held two further fruitless meetings with officials, they published a half-page paid advertisement in the Sunday *Advertiser* and *Alabama Journal* on Christmas Day.

"To the Montgomery Public"

We, the Negro citizens of Montgomery, feel that the public has a right to know our complaints and grievances which have resulted in the protest against the Montgomery City Lines and our refusal to ride city busses. We, therefore, set forth here some of the many bitter experiences of our people, who have, at various times, been pushed around, embarrassed, threatened, intimidated and abused in a manner that has caused the meekest to rise in resentment:

COMPLAINTS:

1. *Courtesy:*
The use of abusive language, name calling and threats have been the common practices among many of the bus operators. We are ordered to move from seats to standing space under the threat of arrest, or other serious consequences. No regard for sex or age is considered in exercising this authority by the bus operator.

2. *Seating:*
The bus operators have not been fair in this respect. Negroes, old, young, men and women, mothers with babes in their arms, sick, afflicted, pregnant women, must relinquish their seats, even to school children, if the bus is crowded. On lines serving predominantly Negro sections, the ten front seats must remain vacant, even though no white passenger boards the bus. At all times the Negro is asked to give up his seat, though there is not standing room in the back. One white person, desiring a seat, will cause nine Negroes to relinquish their seats for the accommodation of this one person.

3. *Arrests:*
Numerous arrests have been made even though the person arrested is observing the policy as given us. This year the following persons have been arrested and convicted, although they were seated according to the policy given us by the bus company. They are Claudette Colvin, [*Mary Louise*] Smith, and Mrs. Rosa Parks. Among others arrested at other times are Mrs. Viola White, Miss Mary Wingfield, two children from New Jersey, and a Mr. Brooks, who was killed by the policeman.

4. *Two fares:*
Many house-servants are required to pay an additional fare if the bus is late getting to town, causing them to miss a bus going to Cloverdale or other

distant points. Some of these have complained that on returning from work similar incidents have occurred necessitating the payment of double fares.

5. *Making change:*
We understand that correct change should be given the operator, but there are times that such is not possible. Several bus operators have refused to make change for passengers and threatened to put them off for not having the exact amount. On one occasion a fellow-passenger paid the fare of one such passenger to prevent her from being put off.

6. *Passing up passengers:*
In many instances the bus operators have passed up passengers standing at the stop to board the bus. They have also collected fares at the front door and, after commanding Negro passengers to enter from the back door, they have driven off, leaving them standing.

7. *Physical torture:*
One Negro mother, with two small children in her arm, put them on the front seat while she opened her purse for her fare. The driver ordered her to take the children from the seat, and without giving her the chance to place the children elsewhere, lunged the vehicle forward, causing the small children to be thrown into the aisle of the bus.

8. *Acknowledgement:*
Not all operators are guilty of these accusations. There are some who are most cordial and tolerant. They will go to the extent of their authority to see that justice and fair play prevail. To those we are grateful and sympathetic.

9. *Adjudication:*
Every effort has been used to get the bus company to remove the causes of these complaints. Time and time again complaints have been registered with the bus company, the City Commission and the manager of the bus company. Committees of both sexes have been conferred but to no avail. Protests have been filed with the mayor, but no improvement has been made.

In March we held a conference with the Manager of the Montgomery City Lines and made a very modest request: (1) that the bus company attorney meet with our attorneys and give an interpretation to laws regulating passengers and (2) that the policy of the bus on seating be published so that all bus riders would be well-informed on the policy of the bus. To this date this has not been done.

The manager read to us the city code and informed us that this is in the hands of every bus driver. At this meeting, the arresting officers of the Claudette Colvin case were there along with the Police Commissioner. The bus operator, who caused the arrest of Claudette Colvin, was requested to be present. But did not come.

A committee met with the Mayor and Associate Commissioner when the bus company requested a raise in fare. No protest was made against the raise, but only against seating and courteous treatment of passengers. Nothing came of this and Negroes were treated worse after the increase in bus fare than before.

10. The great decision:

The bus protest is not merely in protest of the arrest of Mrs. Rosa Parks, but is the culmination of a series of unpleasant incidents over a period of years. It is an upsurging of a ground swell which has been going on for a long time. Our cup of tolerance has run over. Thousands of our people, who have had unhappy experiences, prefer to walk rather than endure more. No better evidence can be given than the fact that a large percent of the Negro bus riders are now walking or getting a ride whenever and wherever they can.

11. Our proposal:

The duly elected representatives of the people have the approval of the bus riders to present three proposals:

1. That assurance of more courtesy be extended the bus riders. That the bus operators refrain from name calling, abusive language and threats.

2. That the seating of passengers will be on a "First-come, First-Served" basis. This means that the Negro passengers will begin seating from the rear of the bus toward the front and white passengers from the front toward the rear, until all seats are taken. Once seated, no passenger will be compelled to relinquish his seat to a member of another race when there is no available seat. When seats become vacant in the rear Negro passengers will voluntarily move to these vacant seats and by the same token white passengers will move to vacant seats in the front of the bus. This will eliminate the problem of passengers being compelled to stand when there are unoccupied seats. At no time, on the basis of this proposal, will both races occupy the same seat. We are convinced by the opinions of competent legal authorities that this proposal does not necessitate a change in the city, or state laws. This proposal is not new in Alabama, for it has worked for a number of years in Mobile and many other Southern cities.

3. That Negro bus drivers be employed on the bus lines serving predominantly Negro areas. This is a fair request and we believe that men of good will, will readily accept it and admit that it is fair.

12. *Nature of movement:*

1. Non violence—At no time have the participants of this movement advocated or anticipated violence. We stand willing and ready to report and give any assistance in exposing persons who resort to violence. This is a movement of passive resistance, depending on moral and spiritual forces. We, the oppressed, have no hate in our hearts for the oppressors, but we are, nevertheless, determined to resist until the cause of justice triumphs.

2. Coercion—There has not been any coercion on the part of any leader to force any one to stay off the busses. The rising tide of resentment has come to fruition. This resentment has resulted in a vast majority of the people staying off the busses willingly and voluntarily.

3. Arbitration—We are willing to arbitrate. We feel that this can be done with men and women of good will. However, we find it rather difficult to arbitrate in good faith with those whose public pronouncements are anti-Negro and whose only desire seems to be that of maintaining the status quo. We call upon men of good-will, who will be willing to treat this issue in the spirit of HIM whose birth we celebrate at this season, to meet with us. We stand for Christian teachings and the concepts of democracy for which men and women of all races have fought and died.

The Negro Ministers of Montgomery and Their Congregations

The Methodist Ministerial Alliance,
The Rev. J. W. Hayes, President

The Baptist Ministers' Conference
The Rev. H. H. Hubbard, President
The Rev R. D. Abernathy, Secretary

The Inter-Denominational Ministerial Alliance
The Rev. L. Roy Bennett, President
The Rev. J. C. Parker, Secretary

The Montgomery Improvement Association
Dr. M. L. King Jr., President
The Rev. U. J. Fields, Secretary

MLKP-MBU: Box 2.

Roy Wilkins (1901–81) was chosen NAACP executive secretary in April 1955 upon the death of Walter White, who was NAACP chief for a quarter century. On December 27 Wilkins responded to a detailed memorandum about Montgomery from the organization's Alabama field secretary. In his December 19 report, W. C. Patton stated that he had interviewed King, Rosa Parks, and Fred Gray and had arranged a board meeting of the Montgomery NAACP branch, which, according to Gray, had taken "no positive action" on the protest. King assured him, Patton wrote, that the MIA's "ultimate goals are the same as those of the NAACP, but that they were working to solve some immediate crisis." Gray told him that the MIA seating proposal was only a "tentative arrangement" and "expressed a willingness to handle the legal aspects with the direction of the National Legal Staff of NAACP."[1]

Mr. W. C. Patton
1630 Fourth Avenue, North
Birmingham, Alabama

Dear Mr. Patton:

Thank you for your memorandum on the Montgomery, Alabama, movement protesting segregation on the buses. Mr. [*Thurgood*] Marshall is away, but I shall consult with Mr. [*Robert L.*] Carter on the legal angle and our cooperation thereon.

In the meantime I think it should be understood that the NAACP will not officially enter the case or use its legal staff on any other basis than the abolition of segregated seating on the city buses. We now have a city bus case [Flemming] on appeal from South Carolina, having won in the lower court. Obviously, when our national program calls for abolishing segregation and our lawyers are fighting on that basis in South Carolina, we could not enter an Alabama case asking merely for more polite segregation.

Please keep me advised. I will write you or have Mr. Carter write you shortly.

Best wishes for the Holiday Season.

Very sincerely yours,
Roy Wilkins
Executive Secretary

NAACPP-DLC.

1. Patton to Wilkins and Gloster B. Current, December 19, 1955, NAACPP-DLC.

January . . . 3 . . .

Befitting its namesake Janus, the Roman god of gates and doorways, January 1956 opened a critical new phase of the bus boycott. The month began with heated public debate in the pages of the *Montgomery Advertiser*, on the street, and in meeting rooms about whether a compromise settlement was feasible, of what it might consist, and whether the protest was justified. January ended with a "get tough" policy by city officials, a historic decision by MIA leaders and lawyers to challenge the constitutionality of bus segregation—stepping beyond their demand for "separate but equal" treatment—and the bombing of King's parsonage. Meanwhile, day in and day out through the winter cold and rain, thousands of black citizens trod miles to work or school or rode in hundreds of hymn-singing car pools that crisscrossed the city every morning and afternoon.

"Let's End the Boycott," by Mrs. Myron C. Lobman

Editor, *The Advertiser*: Montgomery has always had the reputation as a city of "good will, pleasant living, and cordial relations between the races." I, for one, think the vast majority of its people still believe this to be true, and cannot understand why the bus boycott has dragged on and on, and hasn't been settled long ere this. There is so much basis for compromise, without violating either city or state laws on segregation, if only men will meet together with "open minds and good will in their hearts."

There is no reason not to take in good faith the statements and advertise-

ments of the Negro Improvement Association, that they are willing to compromise, and are not asking a violation of the segregation laws. The threatening ads of the Central Alabama Citizens Council, that bus fares will be increased or buses will be discontinued if the boycott is not called off, certainly
do not help the situation nor tend to solve it. Threats have never solved any
problem.

The committee which Mayor Gayle appointed have twice met and failed to
get together on a single issue. It's up to Mayor Gayle, or the other members of
our city commission, to now take the initiative, appoint entirely new committees, with no pre-conceived opinions, to meet together in "good will," and
settle this issue. Every day that it drags on not only hurts the reputation of our
fair city, but its economy as well. It must be settled with dignity on both sides,
and there is no reason why it cannot be done. Let's re-establish Montgomery
once again, as a city of "good will, pleasant living, and cordial relations between the races." Mr. Editor, perhaps you, too, can help to bring this about.

Montgomery Advertiser, January 2, 1956.

"Why Is It a Sin to Ride the Bus?" by Julie Seale Harris

Editor, *The Advertiser*: Can you help some of us cooks? The folks tell us that
they pass a law against the colored folks riding any bus.

I don't have enough money to ride the taxicab. Last week it took $3.80 for
taxicabs. The bus company has been mighty nice to me and so has our bus
driver. He helps the old white folks and the old colored folks and is nice to all
alike. I wanted to ride the bus and the bus driver said I could, but some folks
told me I would get myself in trouble.

Mr. Advertiser, can you please help us, so we can ride the bus. The preacher
at our church told us not to ride—maybe a year or more, and that it would be
a sin, but I don't see how it is a sin for colored folks to ride a bus.

The bus is more convenient for us. I get to my job late every morning since
the boycott. The white lady I been working for is mighty nice to me and I want
to stay on, but this boycott is hurting a lot of us colored folks. Please help us
if you can and tell the mayor we want to ride the bus like we been doing all
the time.

"Overbearing Bus Drivers," by Will T. Sheehan

Editor, *The Advertiser*: As the magnificent and successful bus boycott continues I would like to make it a matter of record that there are white bus riders

in Montgomery who are honoring the request of our colored friends by refraining from patronizing the City Lines in an effort to express our sympathy.

The plaintive plea of Mayor Gayle, calling for public support of bus service has a futile and hollow ring, coming from a man who has callously ignored the appeals of delegations who have called upon him repeatedly in the past for redress. Someone should scrawl across his office wall, "It is later than you think."

The demands of the Negro populace are extremely moderate and within the law. I challenge any legal light in the state to show how these modest requests are outside of the law, though city hall politicians, City Lines counsel, and curbstone lawyers continue to prattle about the sacrosanct inviolateness of state statutes.

Man and boy, I have ridden street cars and buses in Montgomery for over 40 years. Seamy and sordid have been the scenes I have witnessed. The charges brought by the Negro protestants in their paid advertisement of Dec. 25, are confirmed by personal observation many times over. Has the bus company ever conducted a training program among its drivers stressing courtesy and consideration to its customers?

There are bus drivers who are courteous to both races, but has any effort been made to weed out the belligerent, overbearing and profane drivers who have caused most of the trouble? Would any responsible businessman permit his employees to insult his customers in such ways and expect to remain in business? Are our city fathers less aware of their responsibility than the leaders of Mobile and Houston, Texas? Are our newspapers less capable of keeping citizens abreast of the changing times than the publications of those two cities? Are those of us who sympathize too timid to make our views known? There is ample blame to share among all of us.

Answering the mayor's appeal to save the franchise by patronizing the bus lines, here is one white ex-bus rider who would like to declare that as long as the bus boycott is on, it will be a dreary, rainy day, when I have a sprained ankle, and less than 45c cab fare, before I board one of those yellow rolling cell blocks again.

Montgomery Advertiser, January 4, 1956.

"Negroes Cannot Compromise," by U. J. Fields

Editor, *The Advertiser*: I have noticed that since the protest began there has been an avalanche of letters appearing in the *Grandma* column urging that a compromise be reached. Some of these letters and suggestions came from people who are quite optimistic in their thinking; a few came from people who are realistic in their reasoning; but the majority of them came from people who are pessimistic in their belief.

Be it known, now, henceforth and forever, that the Negroes of Montgomery have no desire to compromise in this "bus situation." I have moved through the streets, and have been convinced beyond a shadow of a doubt that Negroes prefer walking rather than to go back to riding the busses. [. . .]

On our side there can be no compromise with this principle involved. In the first place this is a compromise to begin with. We should have demanded complete integration which does away with Jim Crow, and what our constitutional rights guarantee to all American citizens. It then seems to me that those who cry "compromise," should be courageously seeking ways to supplement these proposals.

The type of segregation, Jim Crow and discrimination being practiced here in the South is on its deathbed. There are some who are trying to keep it alive. But internal coercion and external pressure is sure to cause this personality to have an early funeral.

The Negro ministers have been charged by some as misusing religion and the Church. If there is any group of people who have come in personal contact with Jesus it certainly must be the Negro ministers. We don't teach people however, that the Bible teaches separation of the races. We teach them to believe in and live the life applicable to one who practices the brotherhood of man and the fatherhood of God. To underestimate the Negro ministers is uncalled-for, unjustifiable and absurd at the least. We believe in "good race relations" or as Mrs. Myron C. Lobman calls it "cordial relations between the races." However, I am quite sure we do not define the term alike. We believe that good race relations exist only when everyone is treated as an equal. This cannot be as long as there are laws preventing men of one race from enjoying the privileges and rights enjoyed by another race.

We shall never cease our struggle for equality until we gain first-class citizenship, and take it from me this is from a reliable source of Negro citizens of Montgomery. We have no intention of compromising. Such unwarranted delay in granting our request may very well result in a demand for the annihilation of segregation which will result in complete integration.

(The Rev.) U. J. Fields
Minister, Bell Street Baptist Church
Secretary of the Montgomery Improvement Association

Montgomery Advertiser, January 5, 1956.

"Negroes, Look Around You," by Hill Lindsay

Editor, *The Advertiser*: The white people of Montgomery are typical of the other white people of America, slow to anger and slow to make up their minds. But once they do they have always come out victorious.

The bus fare has already been raised 50%. Should you continue the bus boycott six months the loss would be repaid in 18 months and you will keep on paying and paying as long as you live. So what have you gained?

Where is your appreciation, your sense of duty? Look around your home. Who furnished the "know how" to build your homes and furnish them? Who furnished the "know how" to prepare your foods and medicines, give you electricity, make your clothes, design and build your cars and every other convenience you so richly enjoy, that goes with civilization. Now what have you done for yourself?

You are indebted to the white people of Montgomery for life itself. As the white doctor brought most of you into the world. The white man paid about 95 percent for your education, furnished you jobs and a place to live, etc. Now suppose the white people of Montgomery would not hire you any longer or give you a place to live, where would you go or do?

Montgomery Advertiser, January 13, 1956.

January 5, 1956

Hon. W. A. Gayle, Mayor,
City of Montgomery,
Montgomery, Alabama.

Dear Tacky:

I feel that I can call you Tacky, because I have known you a mighty long time and have always voted for you and expect I always will, especially as long as you keep the same attitude you have maintained during the present bus boycott.

No doubt you read the item in the Old Grandma column by Will T. Sheehan. Well, in spite of the awfully fancy and big words used by him, I think that his little piece in the Montgomery Advertiser was the "Masterpiece of Stupidity" of the year. He mentions our colored friends. I expect that is about the only kind of friends he has as I have never seen him on Montgomery streets with any one worth mentioning, and it may be that if it were known where he lurks out at night, in some dark alley probably, the reason for his taking the stand he has would be perfectly clear.

Also, in spite of the fancy words he uses if he is the Sheehan I think he is, then you should see the kind of job he holds, the kind of menial tasks he has to perform, and he is too fat, lazy and stupid to do that with any kind of satisfaction, and in order for him to get lower in his position he would have to roll one of the janitors for his job. If he is the son of the Mr. W. T. Sheehan that I used to know that was with the Advertiser, I know that he must have been the bane of their existence. He and his big words. Phooey!

Also in regard to that U. J. Fields' statement in yesterday's paper about the negroes couldn't compromise, I think that they had better compromise for as long as we have men like yourself and Mr. Jack Crenshaw and the Manager of the Bus Company fighting this bunch that is controlled by that Communist front, the NAACP, we will be in pretty good hands.

You noticed what he said about walking among the colored people and that they would rather walk than to ride the buses under the present conditions. Well, how about that piece in the Advertiser by the colored woman who asked the Editor of the Advertiser to do something to help the cooks so they could ride the buses; and that her preacher had told his congregation that it would be a sin to ride the buses? Do all of the "nigger" preachers get up in their pulpits and lie to their congregations about such things; trying to stir up hatred?

They get sore if you call the NAACP a Communist front. Well aren't they using the same "Big Lie" that the Communists have used to try and rule the World? Even old [Adam Clayton] Powell, who is a preacher, came down here from Harlem, N.Y. and told lies about what Governor Folsom had said and done and what Governor Clements had said, and Governor Clements denied that he had ever seen him or talked to him.

Of course, Mayor, I can't sign this, as I happen to hold a position where there are one or two other stupid oafs like Sheehan, but just wanted to let you know that I have expressed the consensus of opinion of most of the decent white Southern people in Montgomery, and to let you know that we are behind you and hope you and Mr. Crenshaw, etc. will hold out to the end.

Sincerely,
    G. R. E.

Copy to The Bus Co., Mr. Jack Crenshaw, Mr. Grover Hall, Mr. W. T. Sheehan, U. J. Fields, M. L. King.

MLKP-MBU: Box 107.

January 6, 1956

Dear Rev. King,

I am sorry I must be so hasty in writing this letter as I am attempting to write to each of the presidents of the negro ministerial Alliances in Montgomery. If I do not finish today, I shall attempt to later, but will you please pass the word along.

First, please tell your people, to keep on with the boycott. You can win. Tell them to be kinder and politer than ever to all with whom they come in contact, but stay off the bus! Now I have absolutely nothing against the bus company, as a company, but I know what it can mean to both races if you can win on this one point. I sincerely believe that if the bus company had voluntarily established the "first come, first served" policy with politeness and without fanfare, everything would be over with by now. They would be making more money, and everybody would have been happier. Why they wouldn't, I'll never be able to understand.

Tell your people, that we, the white people, of Montgomery, (I am white, by the way) have never seen the negro population organize and discipline themselves, to carry something out to a finish. And that we need to see. It will be good for you and us too. I believe they know it, but stress this fact—that violence of any kind would knock the boycott into a "cocked hat." It just must not happen. The White Citizens Council is meeting to-night. I don't know what they are planning, but I do know they can't do anything as long as you just stay off the bus. They can't make you ride and you are not breaking any law, so continue in the spirit of Christ. He is your real leader. Don't forget Him!

Again let me apologize for haste. My thoughts are not very coherent, I know, but tell the negroes to cease telling white people that you like things as they are. The words will be given them I believe, if they pray, but tell them somehow to get it over to white people, that though they love and appreciate America very much, there are other things they need very much—good schools, recreational facilities, better jobs and the vote when they can qualify. If you can just get enough votes these politicians will begin making promises and keeping them.

By the way, had you thought of this. When white people write letters to the Advertiser, criticizing the boycott, why don't you get about ten or fifteen of your best educated and most christian people to call them immediately. Don't tell them who you are, they might call the wcc's, just keep your voice calm & smooth and if they will let you, tell them just what you believe. This will be difficult, and you'll need experts, but you have them, and I believe it would [*do*] a world of good. I saw a woman won over last summer, just by hearing some negroes speak. The WCC's have about twenty or thirty people, who call every white person who writes to the Advertiser. They won't tell who they are but they use vile language, I am told. So, in God's name, don't let anybody stoop to that, unless you want to pull things backward.

Too, I have been thinking, you might begin some goodwill projects among your people. There are hundreds of things you might do to win the white race over by kindness, like carrying their suitcases or bundles at bus stations for nothing. Anything to let them know you have Christian hearts, and want nothing so much as a place in American life, as a citizen and servant of Christ and democracy.

I must close. God bless you and your people. You may read this any where to your congregations.

A white friend

MLKP-MBU: Box 106.

"Housewife Counter-Boycott," by Mrs. George L. Foster

Editor, *The Advertiser*: All conversations now seem to eventually get on the subject of the bus boycott but as Mark Twain remarked about the weather, "no one seems to do anything about it."

Although I've never had a maid to complain about any mistreatment by a bus driver I have heard of many cases of rudeness of the drivers towards Negro passengers.

Noticing since the boycott how most of the Negroes have become sullen and indolent I feel perhaps the bus drivers dealing with these people collectively have seen a side of them that we dealing with them singly have not seen and evidently the patience of the most tactful drivers has been tried. There are many Negroes like Julie Seale Harris (*Grandma*, January 4th) that want to ride the busses but are afraid to. *Where* are these people getting this fear and *who* is putting this fear into them that they cannot ride to work or to town without being afraid of bodily harm?

I think those people who want to ride the bus should band together and ride the bus. There is safety in numbers. On the other hand, most of us housewives have been patient through this past month, allowing our household servants to be late and to leave early when a ride is available (most of the servants taking advantage of us).

The time has come when we housewives must quit being so lazy, get together and tell the help to either ride the busses and get to work on time or quit. We white people have tried to be understanding of our servants for years and I feel we were understanding until some outside influence put fear in them.

We have been good to our Negroes but now is the time to make them understand a few things. We should quit paying taxi fare, quit going for them or taking them home, quit paying their social security tax, quit lending them money for debts contracted for unnecessary items, etc.

Montgomery Advertiser, January 9, 1956.

Norman Thomas (1884–1968), American Socialist Party leader and six-time presidential candidate, wrote on January 12 to several northern civil rights leaders about whether to create a new support committee for southern civil rights work.

TO Roy Wilkins, Rev. Allan Knight Chalmers, A. Philip Randolph, Ben Mc-Laurin, Rowland Watts, Ray Bennett, Phil Heller, Rev. Oscar Lee, Curtis McClane, Dr. Frank Graham, Patrick M. Malin

I am sending this memo as if it were a personal letter. I very much want your advice.

It has been suggested to me that I take an initiative in forming an ad hoc committee, or at least in getting the right people together to discuss a committee, on what might be called broadly the political aspects of the whole complex struggle for integration and human rights against the forces typified by Senator Eastland's Federation for Constitutional Government.

This committee might also theoretically serve as a clearing house for the local relief committees which I am glad to say are springing up. There is danger in purely local collections for relief from New York, Chicago, Philadelphia, and so forth. For instance, after some of us had arranged to protect Amzie Moore [*Mississippi voting rights organizer*], Chicago friends seem to have sent him $4,500. We cannot afford to endow individuals in the struggle. I can imagine certain valuable things that an ad hoc committee might do, providing that it could get leading people in important walks of life. The question is, do we need another committee, or can existing committees broaden and integrate their work without the cost and difficulty of forming a new committee? For instance, can the NAACP and ACLU make arrangements to cover what could be done by the sort of committee that has been suggested.

I do think that there may be advantages in adding a group, independent of the NAACP, which to some extent can supplement it and defend it against the

Mississippi charge that it is the communist devil. I very much want your opinion on this whole matter on the question of procedure. Should we even explore further the setting up of a committee; whom should we approach for membership; and how can we make administrative machinery simple, efficient and economical? We might start by a luncheon or dinner discussion if we decide to start at all. Who, then, in your opinion should be invited?

Initiative should be taken by more than one person in sending out invitations if they are to be sent out at all. I will be glad to help and to use to a limited extent my office to get things started, but I am not anxious to add to my work unless it is clearly very valuable. One last word: It is possible that if we get the right people on a non-partisan committee, it could exert the right sort of pressure not only on government but on the course of political campaign.

Please give me your best thought promptly.

Sincerely,
Norman Thomas

NAACPP-DLC.

Around 9 P.M. on Saturday, January 21, *Minneapolis Tribune* reporter Carl T. Rowan telephoned King long-distance to ask about a wire service report he had just received announcing that the bus boycott had been settled. That afternoon Montgomery city commissioners had met with three black ministers, none associated with the MIA. Ostensibly conferring about an insurance matter, the commissioners told the preachers that they could not discuss insurance until the bus boycott ended. There is no evidence that the ministers agreed to a proposed compromise preserving reserved seating sections, but the officials told the press that black leaders had accepted their terms and that the protest was over.

Rowan recalled that King "was startled to hear of the phony announcement of a boycott settlement. He came to the same conclusion that I did: the whites had bought, cajoled, or threatened three blacks into acting as though they had authority to end the boycott, the assumption being that if the mass of blacks could be tricked into going back aboard the buses, it would be almost impossible to get the boycott going again." King and other MIA leaders frantically called dozens of volunteers, who ran all over town crying out, "No matter what you hear or read, the boycott is not over. Please do not go back onto the buses."[1] Late into the cold night King and Abernathy visited bars, poolrooms, and nightclubs to deny the bogus settlement, and on Sunday morning the ministers informed their congregants. The boycott did not lose a beat.

At the next MIA Executive Board meeting on January 23, King explained the false settlement, defended himself against scurrilous white accusations, and received a vote of confidence from fellow leaders. The following notes on the meeting were taken by Donald T. Ferron, a Fisk University researcher.

Monday, Jan. 23, 1956
11:00 A.M.–2:45 P.M.
Baptist Center
Meeting of the Executive Board
Rev. M. L. King (Presiding)
Mrs. [Erna] Dungee (Secretary)

Rev. King describing his first knowledge that the protest had "ended." Carl Rowan is doing a series of articles for the "Minneapolis Tribune" on the protest here. His first article was to have appeared on Sunday morning, Jan. 22. Mr. Rowan in the interim before publishing his article received an Assoc. press dispatch stating that the protest had ended. He immediately phoned (Rev. King) because he was disturbed over this, for he didn't want a compromise. He was told that this was the first that he (Rev. King) had known about it, and that none of the members of the MIA had been to any meeting with the city commissioners. Rowan called Commissioner Sellers, and while Sellers wouldn't give the names of the men, he did say that they were three Negro ministers and gave their denominations. In the mean time, Rev. King called Mr. Brennan of the A.P. to have the release modified by stating that none of the members of the MIA were present at the meeting. This was done in order that the public wouldn't get the impression that the protest had ended, so that money (contributions) wouldn't be blocked. Rowan called Rev. K. and gave him the information that he had received from Sellers. Att. Gray, through a process of elimination, found the men to have been Rev. Mosely, Bishop Rice, and Rev. Kynes.

In giving the possible reasons for the newspaper article, Rev. King suggested that the Mayor wanted it to appear that there are two factions within the Negro Community; that we're split up; divided; to confuse the people into thinking that the leader did this.

Rev. King describes a talk which he later had with Rev. Kynes: Kynes said that the Mayor called (phoned—at least the person said he was the Mayor) him to come to the Chamber of Commerce Bldg. to discuss an insurance plan that was trying to be adopted in the city. When he entered the room the only person he recognized was Bishop Rice. The group talked for about 3 min. about insurance, and then the Mayor said that they couldn't arrive at suitable arrangements until the bus situation is straightened out first. Whereupon Rev. Kynes asked why the members of the MIA weren't called. The Mayor answered by saying that they wouldn't compromise, and the commissioners just couldn't work with them; wanted people with sense. The meeting ended with no agreement. Rev. Kynes said he didn't know why the Mayor called him. (Rev. King told the Exec. Board that he didn't know how true Rev. Kynes' statement was).

At this point there resulted general disorder for about two minutes, with on the one hand, most if not all of those present (there were approx. 22 members there) voicing disapproval and resentment over the fact that the 3 ministers had even attended the meeting, and, on the other hand, the President trying to achieve order. He said, in effect, that there are some violent Negroes (smiling) who would like nothing better than to get their hands on those ministers (their names had not officially been made known to the public), and he stated further that at one of the night clubs where it was announced that the newspapers on the following day would carry the story that a compromise had been reached, while in reality the protest was still on, someone shouted: "Just let us know who they were, we'll hang 'em." Rev. King smiled as he said it. Then quickly changing to a serious, solemn, and determined attitude, he said that we cannot overestimate the importance of non-violence. We must be sane and unemotional. We must not be accused of intimidation. "We can't hurt Uncle Tom's by violence, but only by mass action."

All agreed that this must be the policy.[. . .]

The truth of the editorial by [Tom] Johnson in the "Montgomery Advertiser" [January 19] concerning Rev. King was then refuted. This was in the form of what amounted to a "pep talk" [by King], aimed at preventing a "split within the ranks." It was denied that there was any discussion of Deacons in his church, or that his was a "professional church." It was further denied that he knew anything about the transferal of $5,017 to the Citizens Trust bank of Atlanta, as he was out of the city at the time (at Conference of Baptist Ministers in Hot Springs, Arkansas). It was verified that the transferal was made without his knowledge, that it (then only) was drawn in a check made to "cash," and sent in the form of money orders to the Atlanta bank; it was denied that he has a Cadillac car and his wife a new station wagon. Rev. King had been interviewed by Johnson but when he was asked about the policy of the NAACP, Rev. King said that all he said was that "the policy of the NAACP doesn't allow compromise on segregation," and that if he wanted more information to see the Pres. of the local branch, Mr. [Robert] Matthews. All of the above statements were printed in order that there would be a split in the ranks. Rev. King emphasized the importance of unity, that he was made pres. of the MIA by a unanimous vote. Rev. Young asked for a vote of confidence—there was loud approval and a unanimous rising vote of confidence.

Next on the Agenda was a report from the Strategy Committee:

I. Action Relating to Franchise

Recommendation: We will immediately (today) file application for [*transportation*] franchise. If our franchise is not granted and a franchise is granted to another co., or the Montgomery franchise is renewed with a reduction in service, the MIA will get a court injunction and attack the segregation law itself.

II. Some members be present from the MIA just to sit in and not as representing the organization, at discussion of franchise at Chamber of Commerce, room 204, tomorrow at 11:00 A.M.

III. Transportation (nothing to report)

Rev. Glasco suggested (sarcastically) that the Chairman of the Program Comm. (Rev. Abernathy) before leaving town pass his responsibilities to someone within the committee in order that a good, efficient job be done. It seems that Rev. Bennett took over the responsibility and in turn it was given to someone else not on the committee. This concerned the mimeographing and distribution of the programs for simultaneous mass meetings. Rev. Abernathy retorted that if you look around you will see inefficiency in all of the Committees, *including* the finance committee and the transportation committee.

IV. The President at his discretion may make releases to the press. All other releases must be approved by the exec. comm., and such releases must be in writing with the newspaper having a copy and copy (duplicate) kept by the committee as a protective measure.

V. Simultaneous Mass Meetings are worthwhile. Did somewhat better financially than was true in one large mass meeting. More important it reached more people.

VI. Contributions by those individuals or organizations which prefer anonymity should not be revealed at mass meetings. [. . .]

It was at this point that the question was raised concerning the wisdom of transfering funds from the city. It was explained that there was talk about the legality of boycotts and that the money might be "tied up" if the boycott was proven illegal. On the advice of the attorneys, the money was sent to the Citizens Bank in Atlanta (a Negro Bank).

Dr. Saye [*Solomon S. Seay Sr.*] reminded the Exec. Comm. that there had been so far no definite understanding about the lawyers fee and that it should be settled. On the one hand, he indicated, one of the main reasons Negroes in

Montgomery haven't been able to get together in a movement like this has been because Negro lawyers haven't stayed here long enough because they can't make any money; people are looking for something for nothing. "I believe in paying for services rendered." He indicates that he doesn't believe that either of the lawyers question his honesty in believing first of all that they are capable men, but that the "figures" are too high. For example, they have had the job of getting the franchise written up and presented to the Commissioners for almost a month, but now they have to finish them and get them in today. He reiterates that he doesn't mind paying for services rendered. Exec. Comm. refers adjustment of fees to lawyers to come to conclusion at a later date. Lawyers talk among themselves for approx. a minute and announce retainers fee of $100 or $50/lawyer/week. Decision refused on the grounds that the proposal stated "at a future date." (next meeting)

At this time it was announced that buses were running in the Negro areas, that it was raining and that this might cause Negroes to ride buses. Meeting adjourned with prayer, and with the suggestion that all available cars and personnel assist in covering the various bus routes.

PV-ARC-LNT.

1. Carl T. Rowan, *Breaking Barriers* (New York: Harper Perennial, 1992), p. 140.

Virginia Foster Durr to Myles and Zilphia Horton

January 30, 1956

Dear Myles and Zilphia:

I just received a communication from there giving a summary of the past year's activities and I think you should add how much you had to do with the Montgomery Bus Boycott which is really making history and is of the deepest significance. LIFE, TIME, CBS, NBC, and countless other papers have been down here covering it and also Fisk is doing a Social Science research on it. I think it is the first time that a whole Negro community has ever stuck together this way and for so long and I think they are going to win it.

But how your part comes in is through the effect the school had on Mrs. Parks. When she came back she was so happy and felt so liberated and then as time went on she said the discrimination got worse and worse to bear AFTER having, for the first time in her life, been free of it at Highlander. I am sure that had a lot to do with her daring to risk arrest as she is naturally a very quiet and retiring person although she has a fierce sense of pride and is, in my opinion, a really noble woman. But you and Zilphia should certainly take pride in what you did for her and what she is doing.

All OK here, I think things look good although Aubrey [*Williams*] doesn't. Lots of love to all, come and see for yourself.

VA

HRECR-WHi: Box 11.

City officials' "get tough" policy included stepped up harassment of car pool drivers, who were stopped by police for trivial or contrived offenses. On January 26 police arrested King for alleged speeding (30 MPH in a 25 MPH zone) and jailed him for the first time. On his way to the city jail, the handcuffed minister feared that police might deliver him instead to a waiting lynch mob. That night the MIA conducted several mass meetings because of concern about King's arrest.

The next day, a Fisk University researcher interviewed a bus protester, who was giving her a ride home.

Interview with Store Maid, by Willie M. Lee

Time: Afternoon [*January 27*]
Place: Street
Age: 30–35

[*Maid*]: I'm so mad I don't know what to do. Do you know those bastards put Rev. King in jail last night, and this morning they all parked on the corners and asking folks how come they didn't ride the bus. They think they bad 'cause they got guns, but I sho hope they know how to use 'em, cause if they don't, I'll eat 'em up wid my razor. If they can use 'em, they bet not come up on me and hit me 'cause he'll never use it then 'cause he'll be in pieces so fast he won't know what hit 'em.
[*Lee*]: Before the people stopped riding the buses, did you ever have to get up and stand so white people could sit down?
[*Maid*]: Yea, that happen almost every day. But let me tell you 'bout this. One morning I got on the bus and I had a nickel and five pennies. I put the nickel in and showed him the five pennies. You know how they do you. You put five pennies in there, and they say you didn't. And do you know that bastard cussed me out. He called me bastards, whores, and when he called me motherfucker, I got mad and I put my hand on my razor. I looked at him and told him "Your mammy was a son-of-a-bitch, that's why she had you a bitch. And if you so bad,

git up outta that seat." I rode four blocks, then I went to the front door and backed off the bus, and I was jest hoping he'd git up. I was going to cut his head slamp off, but he didn't sey nothing. Dey started this thang, and now they can't finish it. They didn't have a bitter need to 'rest Miss Park. All they had to do was talk to 'er lack she was a lady, but they had to be so big and take her to jail. Dey bit the lump off and us making 'em chew it. I know ole Sellers, ole dog, wish he could spit. But God fix 'em all colored folks ain't like they use to be. They ain't scared no more. Guns don't scare us. These white folks jest keep messing up. Dey gona have a war if they keep on. We be jest forced to kill 'em all 'cause if they hurt Rev. King, I don't mine dying, but I sho Lord am taking a white bastard with 'em. If I don't have my razor with me, I'll use a stick.

[*Lee*]: You know, I was reading in the paper a couple of days ago that the commissioner wanted to settle by giving ten seats to whites and ten to colored. What do you think about that?

[*Maid*]: That ain't nothin'. That's the same thang we had all the time. They jest want to make fools outta us. But 'fo we get on the buses, they going to let us keep our seats when we get 'em, they going to be courteous and give us colored drivers. You can do anything for 'em, but jest don't set beside 'em. Now you know it ain't no harm in that. I don't wont they no good men 'cause a white man can't do nothing fur me. Give me a black man any day. And I never worry 'bout any no good white bitch taking a man o' mine. She ain't woman 'nough to take 'em.

You know I'm going to New York when this is over and git me a job and work up there.

[*Lee*]: Speaking of working, do the people you work for ever say anything about your riding the bus?

[*Maid*]: See, I work in a store. Now the man who own the store is nice, but there one ole cracker who lack to boss people 'round. So the other day when I got to work she asked did I ride the bus, and I told her that that wasn't the worst of it. I ain't going to ride it. So she tried to be smart all that day. Every time I dust, she sey I half dust. She kept it up 'til most 2 o'clock. I told her if she didn't lack the way I did it to do it herself. She didn't hire me and, she sure couldn't fire me. She bristled all up lack she wanted to hit me. I said, "Look, my ma was black and she's resting (deceased) and the white woman ain't been born dat would hit me and live. They'll (policeman) git me but when they do, you'll be three D: Dead, Damned, and Delivered." And you know that huzzy ain't did nothing but spoke to me since den. When they fine you ain't scared of 'em, they leave you lone. Son-of-a-bitches.

[*Lee*]: By the way, how did you get word that the people would not ride the buses?

[*Maid*]: I found a slip of paper in my door, then I read it in the newspaper. You see, I'm off on Monday, so that Tuesday I started walking early. I'm on time now more'n I use to be 'cause I leave home in time to walk and it jest about a mile, but I ketch a ride most times. If they start back running, I'm gona walk that mile still. If they git another dime from me, I won't know it. Well this is my stop. Let's hold out and pray, and I know we'll get what we wont.

Interviewer: [*The maid*] was clean and neatly dressed with tendencies in dress slightly toward the masculine side with cap and jacket. She was of dark complexion with smooth skin, of medium build and height, very expressive with face and hands, forceful personality.

PV-ARC-LNT.

On the same day, Lee recorded similar angry sentiments at a car pool dispatch station where protesters were waiting for rides to work.

DOMESTIC 1: I'll crawl on my knees 'fo I git back on dem buses. Look at dem red bastards over der watching us. Ain't nobody skered of dem. Dey jest jealous. Dey ain't gittin no money now. Did you hear what ole Sellers said last night on television? He said he's tired of des niggers pussy footing around. Dat wuz a pretty big word to be saying on television.
DOMESTIC 2: You know I heard 'em. But I ain't 'bout to get on dem buses. Des white folks gona mess right 'round here and git killed. I don't mind dying but I sho take one of dem with me. God done got fed up wid des white folks. We kin stand hard time betterin dey kin 'cause us use to it and dey ain't. Der wuz a girl living by me and her boss told her dat if she didn't ride de bus she wuz gona fire her and evy morning she rides dat bus.
DOMESTIC 1: She sho is a fool. I wush dat son-of-a-bitch I work fur would tell me dat. I beat her skinny ass and tell 'er keep de money 'cause I ain't hongry. [. . .] Did you see 'em when dey put dat boy [*King*] in jail?
DOMESTIC 2: Dey jest trying to skere us back on dem buses, but I'll be damn if I get on one. I'll walk 20 miles 'fo I ride 'em. Dey trying to be smart, but if dey beat dat boy dere is going to be hell to pay.

Moving around among the people I heard statements like: "Dey got dem guns but us ain't skered"; "Dey bet not come in our neighborhood by de self"; "Some of 'em gona mess right 'round here and get killed"; "I ain't got but one time to die and I may as well die fur somethin'." [. . .]

PV-ARC-LNT (January 27, 1956).

At a specially called meeting of the MIA Executive Board (recorded by Fisk researcher Donald Ferron), King and other leaders discussed two important matters: whether the MIA should agree to a bus-seating compromise falling short of their proposal, and the filing of the *Browder* v. *Gayle* lawsuit challenging the constitutionality of the city and state bus segregation laws. The four plaintiffs in the federal lawsuit were Aurelia S. Browder, Claudette Colvin, Susie McDonald, and Mary Louise Smith. A fifth plaintiff, Jeanetta Reese, withdrew because of apparent intimidation by white authorities. Despite King's urging, none of the ministers present at this meeting was willing to serve as a plaintiff.

Executive Board "Call" Meeting
Monday, January 30, 1956
11:00 A.M.–2:35 P.M.
Rev. M. L. King, presiding

Prayer

This meeting was called because there are some "important issues to discuss rather than to hold off until Thursday."

Rev. Alford—Said that he had been pondering over a proposal which was made to Rev. Binion by some of his "white friends" some weeks back. (apparently the exec. board rejected it then). Rev. Alford feels that it is "worthy of our studying it. I think we should go back under those conditions."

Rev. [R. B.] Binion—to the question of the nature of the proposal:

Mr. Nacrosie (his "white friend") explained the proposal to him before the three N. [*Negro*] ministers had been "hoodwinked" into a "compromise." The City had decided that if N. would give W. [*White*] the first two seats on the Jackson, Day and Cleveland St. routes [*predominantly used by blacks*], and on the rest of the routes give the first six seats to the W., an agreement could be reached.

Mr. E. D. Nixon—Did the proposal of two seats mean the long seat plus the next two seats?

Mr. Binion—"I don't know."

Mr. Nixon—If you talk about the first two seats, then that's the same as before. We would be returning to the same conditions, and if we accept it we are "going to run into trouble" with the people who had been riding the bus. "If that's what you're going to do, I don't want to be here when you tell the people."

Mr. White—"This morning was the test." The rain was pouring and "they still walked." "If they don't want to go back, I don't see why we should decide otherwise. Folk just made too much sacrifice. I hold that we should go on to the end. I think we should stay just where we're at."

Rev. King—"I've seen along the way where some of the ministers are getting weary." Says he won't call names. "If you have that impression (that N. should go back under same conditions to the buses), we won't ostracize you. We should iron it out here (exec. meetings) and show wherein we shouldn't go back."

Rev. Alford—"There's a time in the life of any crisis when you ought to be reasonable. The parties concerned ought to give and take. If we can get two out of the three demands (Alford called them 'concessions'), I think we ought to accept. We have no protection to give those people—our wives and daughters* are not out there. We can arrive at some type of agreement that is pleasing even to us." {*Rev. Bennett has referred to the masses of Negroes, those who had once ridden the buses, but who are now walking, as "those in the gutter."}

Rev. King—"From my limited contact, if we went tonight and asked the people to get back on the bus, we would be ostracized. They wouldn't get back. We shouldn't give people the illusion that there are no sacrifices involved, that it could be ended soon. My intimidations are a small price to pay if victory can be won. We shouldn't make the illusion that they won't have to walk. I believe to the bottom of my heart that the majority of Negroes would ostracize us. They are willing to walk."

Rev. King—(changing the subject), "I think this is a basic point."

[*King:*] We agreed that in the event the Chicago franchise was renewed and ours [*for the MIA jitney service*] was rejected, we would go to court. Attorney Gray went to New York last week for a few days to discuss this whole problem with Thurgood Marshall and another lawyer. Att. Gray has drawn up two suits: 1) demanding that the segregation law of the City is null and void because it is unconstitutional; 2) in the process of litigation, all intimidation be outlawed. This joint suit is to be filed in the Federal Court this afternoon or tomorrow. We are in the process of drawing up a list of plaintiffs (those who can stand up under intimidation and who are not susceptible to losing their jobs). So far we have Miss Colvin, Miss Smith, Mrs. Reese, Mrs. Hamilton, and Mrs. McDonald. This suit on the City of Montgomery would go directly to the federal courts, but it would not be filed in the name of the NAACP.

Rev. King—What are we to do for the people in the process of litigation? The court has 20 days to answer—don't know how long the litigation would take.

Mr. Seay—Number 1, "issue an ultimatum—giving a time limit (leaving out goal 3) to the Commission stating our position to see what they would do; 2, we need to do that to have a point from which to prepare people to return to the buses. We need to train people to go back to the bus. We would disgrace ourselves before the world if we give up now."

Mr. Nixon—Hold people off the bus for the end of the 20 days, instructing them about going back to the bus. At least for the first 20 days from tomorrow keep them off the bus.

Rev. King—It is very important that this information does not leak out about the NAACP and the court action until it's printed in the newspaper. We want to surprise the whites. Don't mention the 20 days. Some liberal whites say that because of the stigma that has been put on the NAACP, its part in this should not be mentioned because of its effect on public sentiment. We should use the "legal structure of the NAACP," but refer to the participants as "legal citizenry."

Dr. Seay—Because we can't settle this within the framework of the law, we should state publicly that we're taking it to the federal court.

Rev. King—By the way, I've found out that the N. lady who was beat up by a N. man a few days ago is the cook for the Mayor; she attends the mass meetings and tells the mayor what happened the next morning. We also found out that Sellers has let 3 N. prisoners attend the mass meetings so that they can tell him what has happened.

Att. Gray—about selection of plaintiffs: I think it's good strategy to have at least one minister, people of different ages, and people with different griev-ances. It's not good strategy to have Rev. King because he's too much in the limelight.

Rev. King—I think its very important in throwing sentiment our way if we have a minister as a plaintiff. Who (of 25 present) will volunteer? After discus-sion of about 10 minutes in which Rev. King said that he knew of many in the meeting who had been fined and otherwise intimidated, still no one would volunteer. Rev. King reiterated their stand on a policy of non-violence. It was suggested in this connection that we go "on record not to come to the rescue of people arrested for carrying concealed weapons." [. . .]

Meeting ends with prayer.

PV-ARC-LNT.

That evening, King, Rufus Lewis, Rev. Ralph Abernathy, and Rev. Solo-mon S. Seay Sr. spoke to a mass meeting at Abernathy's First Baptist Church, responding to the city commission's "get tough" policy. (Notes were taken by Willie M. Lee.)

Hymn—"Onward Christian Soldiers"
Prayer

Scripture

Hymn—"Plant My Feet on Higher Ground"

Speaker #1—Presiding Officer

"It's time for the white man to realize that he is not dealing with a child. Even the 'Uncle Toms' are tired of being 'Uncle Toms,' and this reminds me of something which was supposed to have happened in Mississippi a couple of years ago.

"The whites in Mississippi wanted to show to the world that they were not as bad as they were said to be. So they went all over Mississippi searching for 'Uncle Toms.' Finally, they dug up the best one they had in the state and told him that he would be put on television, that the whole nation would see him, and he must tell them what wonderful relations existed between white and colored folks of Mississippi. Finally the day came, and he was on television. He looked at the white folks all around and said,

'Did you say I'll be heard in Boston, New York, Chicago, Philadelphia and all over the world?'

'Yes, now tell the people how wonderful it is here.'

'You really mean I'm on all over the country and that's the God sent truth?'

'Yes.'

'HELP!!!'

"So you see 'Uncle Tom' is fed up too."

Speaker #2—Rev. M. L. King

"Some of our good white citizens told me today that the relationships between white and colored used to be good, that the whites have never let us down and that the outsiders came in and upset this relationship. But I want you to know that if M. L. King had never been born this movement would have taken place. I just happened to be here. There comes a time when time itself is ready for change. That time has come in Montgomery and I had nothing to do with it.

"Our opponents, I hate to think of our governmental officers as opponents, but they are, have tried all sorts of things to break us, but we still hold steadfast. Their first strategy was to negotiate into a compromise and that failed. Secondly, they tried to conquer by dividing and that failed. Now they are trying to intimidate us by a get-tough policy and that's going to fail too because a man's language is courage when his back is against the wall.

"We don't advocate violence. We will stay within the law. When we are right, we DON'T MIND GOING TO JAIL! (The applause rang out like a great clap of thunder). If all I have to pay is going to jail a few times and getting about 20 threatening calls a day, I think that is a very small price to pay for what we are fighting for (applause very loud).

"We are a chain. We are linked together and I cannot be what I ought to unless you are what you ought to be.

"This good white citizen I was talking to said that I should devote more time to preaching the gospel and leave other things alone. I told him that it's not enough to stand in the pulpit on Sundays and preach about honesty, to tell the people to be honest and don't think about their economic conditions which might make them dishonest. It's not enough to tell them to be trustful and forget about the social environment which may necessitate their telling untruths. All of these are a minister's job. You see God didn't make us with just souls alone so we could float about in space without care or worry. He made a body to put around a soul. When the body was made in flesh, there became a material connection between man and his environment and this connection means a material well being of the body as well as the spiritual well being of the soul is to be sought. And it is my job as a minister to aid in both of these (roaring applause).

Speaker #3—Mr. Rufus Lewis
"The 'Get-Tough Policy' will not stop us. (No's and Amen's rang out). I want you to know that there is one sure fire way to deal with Mr. Sellers—by the vote. He was put in by the lack of your vote. So pay your poll tax now and get ready to vote."

Speaker #4—Rev. Abernathy
"The next mass meeting will be held at the Day Street Baptist Church and if I can't see you there, I'll see you in the city jail. (loud laughs & applause).

"You know they have on the car tags 'Heart of Dixie.' Well, let's walk until Dixie has a heart (roaring applause)."

Speaker #5—Minister from Mobile
"We have for you $500.43. That .43 is to let you know that some more is coming. Just fight on and with God on our side we cannot lose. And no matter what the other side does, one thing it cannot do—They Cannot Pick You Up And Put You Back On the Buses (thundering applause)."

Pep Talk—Rev. Seay
"When I was a boy, my mother use to take a string and tie it around her waist to hold her dress up so that it would not get wet in the morning dew when she trudged her way into the cotton fields. But more than that I remember what she use to sing. I haven't heard it in over 30 years, but I think it's time

to sing it again in our hearts. She use to sing 'Oh freedom, Oh freedom over me. Before I'd be a slave, I'd be buried in my grave and go home to my Lord and be free.' That is how I feel. And we can be free.

"You know, if a man doesn't want to sit besides me because I'm dirty, that's my fault, if he doesn't want to sit besides me because I'm loud, that's my fault too, but if he doesn't want to sit besides me because I'm BLACK, That's not my fault because God made me black and my white brother is discriminating against God and His will. But even though they are, we must love them. We must love Mr. Sellers and Mr. Gayle for God said that we must love our enemies as ourselves. Let's not hate them for with love in our hearts and God on our side, there are no forces in hell or on earth that can mow us down.

"I had a book which was so interesting that I gave it to the city officials to read. It's a book on great powers, the stories of men who ruled and conquered by force only to lose. Men like Alexander the Great, Napoleon and Hitler were discussed, men who lived by the sword. Their empires are no longer, but have perished. But there was a man who was passive, who taught that love and faith could move mountains and more mountains. And unto this day that empire which was built by a man who said while dying on the cross, 'Forgive them O Lord, for they know not what they do.' That is the empire of Jesus Christ! He was asking forgiveness for the men who crucified him, drove nails through his hands and put thorns on his head. So we forgive Sellers and Gayle, but we do not give up.

"There were two armies once and they both gave out of ammunition. The soldiers said to the general in one army, 'What are we going to do?' The general replied 'Retreat.' In the other army the soldiers asked 'What are we going to do?' The general, 'Forward March!' They won the battle. So we are going to 'Forward March' to a victory. And if any of you are scared, Keep your fears to yourself. Get your flat shoes and Walk. Heaven knows how much it will help."

There was thundering applause throughout the talk.

Collection from the mass meeting the week before: $2046.26.

PV-ARC-LNT.

While King was supervising the collection at the mass meeting, Abernathy told him that his house had been bombed. Not knowing right away whether his wife and two-month-old daughter, Yolanda, were injured, he calmly told the meeting why he had to leave. "Let us keep moving," he said, "with the faith that what we are doing is right, and with the even greater faith that God is with us in the struggle."[1] Returning to the parsonage at 309 South Jackson Street, he passed hundreds of blacks who had quickly gathered, many armed. He was greeted by Mayor Gayle, Police Commissioner Sellers, police officers, and reporters inside his modest, six-room house. Coretta Scott King and a friend, Dexter member Mary Lucy Williams, had been watching television when they heard an object land on the front porch. They rushed to the back room where Yolanda was sleeping just as a dynamite bomb exploded, denting the porch floor, shattering four front windows, and damaging a porch column. Finding his wife and baby unharmed, King walked out on the porch. His impromptu speech persuaded the angry crowd to put away their guns and go home.

We believe in law and order. Don't get panicky. Don't do anything panicky at all. Don't get your weapons. He who lives by the sword will perish by the sword. Remember that is what God said. We are not advocating violence. We want to love our enemies. I want you to love our enemies. Be good to them. Love them and let them know you love them. I did not start this boycott. I was asked by you to serve as your spokesman. I want it to be known the length and breadth of this land that if I am stopped this movement will not stop. If I am stopped our work will not stop. For what we are doing is right. What we are doing is just. And God is with us.

Montgomery Advertiser, January 31, 1956.

1. Quoted in Martin Luther King Jr., *Stride Toward Freedom: The Montgomery Story* (New York: Harper, 1958), pp. 135–36.

"The Bombing Episode," by Willie M. Lee, January 31, 1956

Approximately five minutes after the bombing of the Kings' residence, a crowd has assembled, policeman, detectives, reporters, photographers, the Mayor and the Commissioner were swarming the place. Lights were flashing in all directions, but the people stood silent.

While the city officials and employees were busy taking pictures and searching for evidence, the crowd became denser and began to close in around the house. The policemen counteracted by yelling and walking around the edge of the group, but the people only moved back an inch or so. In the process a policeman said to an elderly man,

"Move back, boy. What's the matter, you can't understand plain English?" The man never answered, he just stood silent with the crowd.

Soon following this the policemen were told to order the people to go home and were told to tell them that everything was fine on the inside, that the Kings were not harmed. The crowd did not disperse, the people only moved off the walks for a couple of minutes. Seeing that a gun and a badge were of little importance if any, Commissioner Sellers was at a loss. Rev. King at this time had the power to cause great damage in Montgomery. He chose to keep the resistance passive. Only he could control the crowd.

Rev. King walked onto his porch and the people let out with cheers that could be heard blocks away. With the raising of his hand they became quiet to hear what he had to say. He spoke with dignity and reserve. He told the people to be calm and quiet like he and his wife, that they were not harmed and everything would be fine. He said,

"With love in our hearts, with faith and with God in front we cannot lose." He urged that there be no violence and that the people must stay within the law. Commissioner Sellers and Mayor Gayle looked very much like the members of the beet family.

Sellers was asked to speak after King. There was excessive mumbling during most of Sellers talk, but he was applauded when he offered police protection for the Kings. Following this they dispersed a bit only to come back about 15 minutes later. They stood like the rock of Gibraltar and sang 'My Country tis of Thee.' At times they were out of tune, but they kept singing and hummed when they did not know the words. After this they sang 'I once was blind but now I see' ["*Amazing Grace*"] and finally they drifted away.

On the inside the phone rang constantly. Most times they were persons who wanted information on the Kings' welfare. Other times no one was on the other end when the phone was answered. One white woman called, and said that she was sorry it happened, but the Negroes were responsible. Because of their action they had made the white people lose all respect for them, a respect which the Negroes could never hope to regain. When she was asked by a friend of the Kings', couldn't that analysis be reversed, she hung up. Another white woman called and said that she threw the bomb and that she was sorry that she did such a poor job, but what she did do was teach Rev. King a lesson. She hung up before the detective could get to the extension. After this the Kings were photographed for television news with statements.

Mrs. King was extremely calm throughout the night under the circumstances. She can be admired for her strength and patience throughout the movement. The phone calls alone, when you answer no one is on the other end, are enough to drive a person insane and then there are the threatening calls too. She surely has been taking it on the chin.

PV-ARC-LNT.

January 31, 1956

Dear Rev. King,

For years, we Negro Mothers of the Southland have prayed that God would send us a leader such as you are. Now that the Almighty has regarded our lowly estate and has raised *you* up among us, I am indeed grateful. Be assured that day and night without ceasing I shall be praying for your safety and that of your family's. The Arm of God is everlastingly strong and Sufficient to keep you and yours. There shall no harm come to you, and the Comforting Spirit of God shall guide you.

A fellow Suffer
(Mrs.) Pinkie S. Franklin of the Sixteenth Street Baptist Church [*Birmingham, Ala.*]

MLKP-MBU: Box 17.

Claudette Colvin (Photograph from *Freedom's Children*, by Ellen Levine; used by permission of Claudette Colvin)

Rosa Parks, 1975 (Photograph by Bob Fitch)

Empire Theater on Montgomery Street, site of Rosa Parks's arrest on December 1, 1955 (Photograph by Stewart Burns)

First mass meeting of Montgomery Improvement Association, Holt Street Baptist
Church, December 5, 1955 (Courtesy of *Montgomery Advertiser*)

Rev. Martin Luther King Jr. speaks at an MIA mass meeting, 1956. (Courtesy of *Montgomery Advertiser*)

Rev. Ralph Abernathy hugs a supporter at Montgomery County Courthouse upon his indictment for boycott conspiracy, February 22, 1956. (AP/Wide World Photos)

Boycott leaders arraigned: Ralph Abernathy, King, and adviser Bayard Rustin walk away from Montgomery County Courthouse after the arraignment of eighty-nine bus boycott leaders for conspiracy, February 24, 1956. Thousands of blacks walked that day in protest of the mass indictments and arrests. (AP/Wide World Photos)

King at his conspiracy trial, Montgomery County Courthouse, March 19, 1956 (AP/Wide World Photos)

E. D. Nixon (*left*) and Rosa Parks arrive at Montgomery County Courthouse for King's trial, March 19, 1956. (AP/Wide World Photos)

Montgomery Improvement Association car pool station, June 12, 1956 (Courtesy of *Montgomery Advertiser*)

Lutheran minister Robert Graetz speaks at an MIA mass meeting, 1956. (Courtesy of *Montgomery Advertiser*)

First day of desegregating buses, Court Square in Montgomery, December 21, 1956 (AP/ Wide World Photos)

King, Glenn Smiley, Ralph Abernathy, and an unidentified woman sit at front of Montgomery bus, December 21, 1956. (AP/Wide World Photos)

Mrs. Jeanne Graetz in her bombed kitchen, January 10, 1957 (Courtesy of *Montgomery Advertiser*)

Facing page: Bombed Bell Street Baptist Church and Mount Olive Baptist Church, Montgomery, January 10, 1957 (Courtesy of *Montgomery Advertiser*)

Police defuse dynamite bomb on King's front porch, January 28, 1957. (Courtesy of *Montgomery Advertiser*)

Which way for the South? Montgomery, December 1995. (Photograph by Stewart Burns)

Interlude . . . 4 . . .

Interview with Rufus A. Lewis, by Donald T. Ferron

Date: Friday, January 20, 1956
Time: 11:00 A.M. to 2:15 P.M.
Place: Respondent's home, 801 Bolivar Street, Montgomery, Alabama

[*Ferron*]: [. . .] What is your relation to the Montgomery Improvement Association?
[*Lewis*]: I belong to the executive committee as a result of being co-chairman of the transportation committee. The executive committee is composed of the transportation committee, the committee for strategy, committee for public relations, and the finance committee.
[*Ferron*]: Who is the other chairman?
[*Lewis*]: Reverend [W. J.] Powell. Initially he was elected to contact taxis to see about hauling people at a reduced fare. I was elected to contact private car owners to see if they would furnish their cars for a pool and drive riders where they want to go. After two weeks, we combined our efforts.
[*Ferron*]: What is your job as co-chairman?
[*Lewis*]: I try to get private cars, and adequate amount of service out of the system, designate gas out to those who need help with gas, to get dispatch and pick-up stations, and persons to organize the riding public. A *dispatching* place is where people congregate in the morning to go to work. These dispatch places are mostly churches and voter's clubs. *Pick-up* stations are places where people congregate to come home from work. Police are active in giving

tickets for minor things like over loading, improper turns, donations, blocking traffic, etc. Things they had up to now not noticed. *Transfer* stations are places to put people off who are not going where the majority of people are going. They get off and transfer to a car going in their area.

[*Ferron*]: How effective is the movement?

[*Lewis*]: About 90% effective. There are a very few Negroes who ride the buses now. I don't know who they are. They hide themselves on the bus by sitting very low in the seats. They may be those who come from rural areas and don't know about what's happening.

[*Ferron*]: To what do you attribute the success of the movement?

[*Lewis*]: I would say that there are three reasons: 1) The most important is the attitude of the people—so many have been mistreated that they're just tired of the situation. 2) Pamphlets suggesting not to ride the buses. 3) The complete cooperation of the Protestant ministers in the city. The white press helped by printing a copy of the pamphlet on the front page. I would call this an indirect aid. And the police driving behind buses in the morning (to prevent Negroes from trying to intimidate or prevent other Negroes from riding the buses). People didn't know why they followed the buses, but they thought it was for the purpose of preventing people (Negroes) from riding. Five days later the buses were taken off the streets in predominantly Negro areas. This was interpreted to mean that buses didn't want to carry Negro passengers any more. The reason given for taking buses off the street was that one was fired into by Negroes at Holcombe and Jeff Davis Streets. This is a white neighborhood and the shot is reported to have been fired from an upstairs apartment. And then we've financial aid from New York, Pennsylvania, Florida, New Orleans, and places in Alabama, without any particular appeal. We also receive donations from whites who refuse to leave their names. [. . .]

[*Ferron*]: What's the reaction of whites now toward Negroes?

[*Lewis*]: Whites are afraid that the boycott will become a weapon, so now white businesses are treating Negroes with more courtesy. [. . .] There is talk of retaliation by whites, but they are not those who do business with Negroes; they are the *politicians*. The boycott has helped Negro business. We buy all of our gas from eight Negro filling stations. There is an appeal in mass meetings to trade with Negroes. This whole thing has brought about closer cooperation between Negroes. [. . .] Whites can't help but have high regard for Negroes now, since there has been no violence. There have been a number of good articles written by whites about the unity of Negroes. On the other hand, it has frightened them because they can see the results of mass action. They probably feel that it may lead to future demands.

[*Ferron*]: What do you think the reaction is of Negroes to whites?

[*Lewis*]: They are very nice, but you always wonder whether they are for or against you. They lean over backwards to be nice, but even there you wonder if he's on the White Citizens Council side. A Negro fellow was fired by Schlitz beer. It was reported that he had been unfair to the fellow with his wages. I stopped buying his beer. They always feel we hold a hammer over their heads.

[*Ferron*]: What will be the relationship between the two groups if the demands are met?

[*Lewis*]: If demands are met in a month or so things will go on in a normal way. I don't think there will be more hate. It may help because further back when there was less integration, there was more friction. It used to be that Negroes were shot, and beat up. Since we have four Negroes in the Police Department things are better—this happened about two or three years ago. [. . .]

Interviewer's note: I get the impression that insofar as this respondent has answered some of the questions, the answers are basically true. However, I sense that in addition to Reverend King, there is another leader, tho unknown to the public, of perhaps equal significance. The public recognizes Reverend King as *the* leader, but I wonder if Mrs. Robinson may be of equal importance. The organizational process is being kept secret, as well as the organizers. Superficially it appears to be a spontaneous move, but listening and talking with different leaders, after a time you receive an altogether different impression.

PV-ARC-LNT.

Interview with Will T. Sheehan, by Anna Holden

Place: Veterans' Administration
Date: January 31, 1956, 12 noon

Mr. Sheehan is 45, was born and grew up in Montgomery area, is married, has three children—one married, one boy 19 and one boy 9. His wife works in the bookstore at A. Nachman's Dept. store. He spoke of it as though the bookshop were her business or partly hers—said she had a "book business" in Nachman's. They are friends of the Durrs and Aubrey Williams—he mentioned having been out at Aubrey Williams' house recently and the Durrs mentioned that he was a friend of theirs. Mrs. Durr said Sheehan came from an "old Montgomery family."

I went by the VA office in the morning before the City Commissioner meeting and we arranged to meet at a nearby cafe for lunch. I mentioned that I was going to the City Commission and might be a little late. Mr. Sheehan seemed rather nervous and upset when I talked with him in the VA office—he acted like someone being hunted down—he was jumpy and shaky then and also during lunch, he kept looking around like he was watching for someone. I go to the restaurant first and waited for him to arrive.

[*Sheehan*]: I see you found the place. What happened at the Commission meeting?

[*Holden*]: Nothing. That is, nothing on the boycott. They turned down the application for the jitney service as soon as it was introduced and that was that.

[*Sheehan*]: Was there any discussion?

[*Holden*]: None at all. The city clerk read the application and the Mayor asked if it were an application for a franchise or for a hearing for a franchise—like he had never heard of it before. The clerk said he had read an application for a franchise and then Commissioner Parks moved that it be denied. The Mayor seconded the motion and all three voted to deny the franchise. No one spoke for it or against it. I was surprised there weren't any of the applicants there to speak for it.

[*Sheehan*]: (Shakes his head sadly)

[*Holden*]: I don't suppose they really thought they could get it—not after the stand the Commission has taken.

[*Sheehan*]: Didn't Sellers say anything?

[*Holden*]: Not this morning.

[*Sheehan*]: I guess you know about him joining the Citizens Council. Sellers is the one that's causing all the trouble on the Commission. I have known him a long time and he's been like that since he was in high school. He's always been belligerent and a dictator—what he would really like to have is a police state.

[*Holden*]: I have been trying to find out about Sellers—is he the Sellers that has a termite business? I notice a Sellers' termite company in the phone book.

[*Sheehan*]: I think he has something like that on the side—I'm not sure. He comes from Alex City, up in Tallapoosa County. My brother played football against him when he was a student at Auburn and he was as mean as he could be then. Clyde never did finish Auburn. I don't know whether he was kicked out or he quit, but he didn't go but about two years. Then he went back home and was assistant deputy to his father. His father was sheriff of Tallapoosa County and Clyde worked for his dad until it was time for him to run again. He had been so mean to everybody—whites and Nigras both, beating them with rubber hoses and stuff like that—that folks told his dad they wouldn't back him again unless he signed a statement he wouldn't appoint Clyde again. That was the only way his old man could get back in office. Then he was in the legislature for a while. [. . .] I said, "Clyde, how do you stand on reapportionment?" He said he was against it. Then I asked him, "How do you stand on the poll tax? Are you for getting rid of it or keeping it?" He said he wanted to keep it. So I told him I was sorry, but he'd never get a vote of mine. He was mad as the devil.

[*Holden*]: Is this police commissioner's office his first city office or has he been in local politics before?

[*Sheehan*]: He ran for the legislature from this county, but this is his first city office. He was in the state highway police for a long time, worked his way up to the top, but they kicked him out on account of his conduct. I don't know what job he had in the state police, but he was way up when they threw him out. He would have fit in fine in Nazi Germany—he is that type.

[*Holden*]: That's interesting. You are the first person I have talked to that knew much about him. Let me get off Sellers and ask you about your letter [*to the* Montgomery Advertiser, *January* 4]. I read it in one of the back issues of the newspapers and Mrs. Durr told me you had had lots of calls. I wondered if you could tell me how many calls and some of the things that were said and what people have said to you about the letter?

[*Sheehan*]: Well, I don't think I could tell you how many calls. That phone rang for about four days solid—it nearly jumped out of the wall, it rang so much. What they said was mostly cursing and profanity—I have never heard so much profanity in all my life. Most of them wanted to know if I had "nigger" blood in me or how much "nigger" blood I had. Some of them asked me what side my grandfather was on during the Civil War. I told them he was on the Confederate side which he was. They would ask where I came from and I would tell them I was born right in this county, about 15 miles from here, and so was my father and my grandfather before me. I would usually say too, that my grandfather had about 90 slaves, but that I thought it was time in 1955 to end slavery. One man said he bet I didn't get along with my grandfather—I said, "No, I never had the chance to. He died in 1894 and I wasn't born until 1910."

[*Holden*]: Did any of the callers identify themselves?

[*Sheehan*]: No, most of them were saying things they'd be ashamed to put their names to. I did notice this, they didn't all come from uneducated and ignorant people, like you might think they would. Some of them sounded like educated, well-spoken people. Another thing. They would want to know where I worked and when I told them I had a civil service job, that made most of them mad. I guess they wanted to have me fired if they could.

[*Holden*]: What else would they say?

[*Sheehan*]: Oh, said they bet I was sleeping with a "nigger" woman or they would ask me if I had any children and when I said three, they wanted to know if I wanted them going to school and sleeping with "niggers." I've never been called an s.o.b. so many times in my life. One man said, "You know what you are, you are a son of a bitch, aren't you?" I laughed and I answered him, "I guess maybe I am. Everybody else seems to think so, so maybe I had better admit it."

[*Holden*]: Did you get any favorable calls or comments?

[*Sheehan*]: I got one sweet and comforting letter from Rev. Bond (not sure of the name) and a few favorable comments from friends. Most of them were unfavorable. I would say they were favorable comments from friends. Most unfavorable. I have gotten a lot of ragging about it down at the office. Now some of those fellows feel like I do—they are boys from outside the South who were out at Maxwell [*Air Force Base*] and married Montgomery girls or they just decided to stay here. Those fellows feel like I do, but they don't say anything. I guess maybe they don't want to be going against everyone else, so they just smile and don't open their mouths. The rest of them kid me a lot and they bring me messages from the bus drivers. One of them came in this morning and said one of the drivers told him he was going to slip up on me and run a knife through me. You may have seen him—he's a big old 260 pound fellow—I sure wouldn't want to have any trouble with him. He [*bus driver*] keeps telling them to tell me things. They were kidding me this morning when I came in—they said when I went home tonight I wouldn't have any porch to walk on to—it would be blown off. (This was day after King's home was bombed.) By the way, what have you heard about King's bombing? Has anybody said anything to you about that?

[*Holden*]: I really haven't talked to anyone this morning. There was a man buying a paper at the news rack where I picked up mine and he seemed very upset about it—he said King used to come in his store a lot and that he was a smart fellow.

[*Sheehan*]: You know what they're saying? The taxi driver told me this morning when I came in that the Nigras had done it themselves to get sympathy— what they won't think of next! They can explain away everything. Then he said in the next breath that he wished they'd done a good job and finished King off. [. . .]

[*Holden*]: Have your neighbors or your friends said anything about the letter?

[*Sheehan*]: It depends. We have friends that don't agree with us on this and they haven't said anything. The ones that feel like we do have said nothing. I'll tell you this, the people in this cafe are as bad as the Citizens Council. I have been eating here for three years and have a running account here and after the letter was published one of the waitresses told my boss I was in here drunk. She's never seen me drunk in my life, but she reported that to my boss.

[*Holden*]: What about your wife—have people said anything to her?

[*Sheehan*]: My wife says her book business has fallen off and she thinks maybe the letter has something to do with that. I think I told you Rev. Bond wrote me a letter. Well, he called me and asked me if I needed any help. He didn't know where I worked and he thought maybe I had been fired and might need help. I told him that we were OK, but that Jane mentioned her business falling off. I said maybe we could ask him to pass the word around that she was at the bookstore and we would appreciate their business. Jane didn't think we ought to do that—she said this was too idealistic a cause to get it mixed up with business—that she didn't think anybody ought to take advantage of a situation like this to make money. So we never did call on him. I'll tell you, this cab fare is about to break us. Neither one of us use the bus anymore and that cab fare twice a day eats up the money.

[*Holden*]: Aren't there any car pools at the office? I haven't heard about any boycott car pools for whites.

[*Sheehan*]: They're lots of pools at the office, but I can't seem to get in on one.

[*Holden*]: Because of the letter?

[*Sheehan*]: You see, I live way out and there aren't many people who go out that far. I've gotten some rides with one man out my way who does some farming and he goes right by my place, but I never know what time I'll get home. He stops by to get seed and fence posts and all kinds of things and sometimes it takes him two hours to get home. I tried that a while, but I figured the time wasn't worth it. There's another fellow at the office I used to ride with some—we have been arguing about this whole thing for years—and I hadn't said anything about riding with him till the other day. He said something about my not riding the buses and I said I hadn't asked him for a ride because I figured he didn't want to be seen with me. He kind of laughed and said he guess he didn't. I was broke the other day and asked one of the men upstairs to loan me a dollar. He's as tight as the paper on the wall and when he gave it to me he said, "Now don't use that for cab fare." This man I used to ride with sometimes. He said he was surprised to see my letter. I told him I didn't know why he was, we had been on opposite sides of the fence about this for years and he knew how I felt.

[*Holden*]: What about your children? Have they been kidded or singled out at school?

[*Sheehan*]: I just have the one boy in school—he goes to Cloverdale and it's a nice school. No one has said anything to him about it. If he were out at Cottage Hill or some other school like that, they probably would have made it tough on him, but Cloverdale is different—they wouldn't say anything out there. An unfortunate thing did happen to my wife in the bookstore the other day. She was waiting on a Nigra customer, showing her some bridge tallies. A white woman came in while the Nigra woman was looking at the selection and my wife asked the white lady if she could help her. The woman wanted a book she named and Jane left the Nigra woman to show the white woman the book. When she came back, the woman wanted to know why she had left her and asked for the other lady who works there. Jane told her the other lady was out to lunch and that was why she had left her for a minute. The woman was real mad and said she didn't want to buy in a store where people went off and left her while they were waiting on her. Jane was upset about it and I told her not to take it like that—that they had been pushed around so much and mistreated and you couldn't blame them for being touchy.

[*Holden*]: I think everybody is more or less touchy right now. Tell me this, do many white people think Negroes were mistreated on the bus? Would many feel like that complaint is justified?

[*Sheehan*]: Most of the boys at the office don't think so. They say all the things Nigras were saying aren't true, but I know from riding the bus that they are. Here is the kind of thing they would do. Some of the drivers would take the Nigras' money at the front and tell them to walk around to the back door to get on. Then they would go off and leave them while they were walking to the back. They did all kinds of things like that.

[*Holden*]: Do people seem awfully tense to you? This past week I felt that almost anything might touch off a really bad situation.

[*Sheehan*]: Well, I'll tell you. I'm opposed to violence, but if it comes to that, we'll just have to fight it out. I think we're in for a long hard pull. It may take a thousand years to straighten this thing out, people are that set against any change. I got interested in this thing during the Depression when things were pretty bad. I could see that everything was stacked against the Nigras and they didn't have a chance. We've come a long way since then, but we've still got a mighty long way to go and most white people are just as set against change now as they were then. I'm a moderate. I'm not like Aubrey Williams and some of those that think we're ready for integration right now. I'm for it, but I know you have to do it gradually in a place like Montgomery. If you did it all at once you'd have violence sure enough. You take the schools—the first time you had a white child and a Nigra child fighting on the playground they'd go home and tell their parents and then the trouble would start. I don't see how it can come any way but slowly, bit by bit. [. . .]

PV-ARC-LNT.

Interview with Cab Driver, by Anna Holden

Date: February 9, 1956, 8:00 P.M.
Place: Montgomery, Alabama
General Statement: Cab driver; Red Cabs; age 25–27; southern accent.

[*Driver*]: (as we crossed the street on which King lives)—Look at that spotlight. Wonder what he's up to now?
[*Holden:*] What who's up to?
[*Driver*]: That nigger preacher King. That's his house down there with the spotlight.
[*Holden*]: I didn't know that he lived over here.
[*Driver*]: Right down that street.
[*Holden*]: Maybe he's afraid—maybe that's why the light is on.
[*Driver*]: Afraid of what?
[*Holden*]: Some more dynamite?
[*Driver*]: Then he must be afraid of his-self. (Laughs)
[*Holden*]: Afraid of himself?
[*Driver*]: Most people thinks they done it to theirselves.
[*Holden*]: I hadn't thought about that.
[*Driver*]: Didn't you see in the paper how it happened? His wife was in the front of the house and she said she heard a noise on the porch and then run to the back. Now that ain't what somebody'd do unless he know what it was. When you hear a noise on the porch you naturally go and see what it is. You don't run to the back of the house. Don't worry, they done it.
[*Holden*]: I just took it for granted that a white person did it. They haven't caught anybody yet have they?
[*Driver*]: No, but when they do, it'll be a nigger. I'll tell you now, lady, I feel sorry for them poor niggers that's walking. The ringleaders like that preacher ain't walking—they're riding in their cars feeling like big shots. It ain't hard on them. But the rest of 'em are having it hard and all along, it costing 'em to keep the big shots going.
[*Holden*]: What do you mean, it's costing them to keep the big shots going?
[*Driver*]: They're paying for it, these niggers that are walking. Lady, there's one thing about niggers, they don't have nothing theirselves, but they pay their preachers and they pay their lodge dues. If they don't do nothing else, they pay those dues so the big shots can put on a good show. That's what they're doing right now—these poor folks that are walking are paying for the big shots to ride.

(Reached our destination about here.)

PV-ARC-LNT.

February ... 5 ...

Black Montgomerians hated segregation for many reasons. One was the conviction, reaffirmed almost daily, that it could never be equitable or fair. In December and January they experienced publicly, as a unified community, what many had known privately all along: that legalized segregation could never be anything but white supremacy, naked or veiled. It could not be palliated by cosmetic reforms.

The authorities "did not do what we wanted done," Fred Gray later reflected. "When that became apparent, then the question is, 'how long are we gonna stay off the buses?' People have to look forward to something. And the logical thing is to stay off the buses until we can return to them on an integrated basis. Because they wouldn't give us the smaller things, we go for the larger and the only way we could go for that, and I knew that, was a federal suit."[1]

The dynamics of the mass protest taught participants that they had no recourse but to challenge the constitutionality of bus segregation. Officials had delegitimized their own segregation laws when they refused to implement them fairly, yet hid behind and manipulated them to preserve the unsustainable status quo. The movement spawned an efficient car pool system that might have developed into an independent system of public transport. But the city commission's denial of the MIA proposal for a jitney service closed off the last possibility of a "separate but equal" solution and made bus desegregation inescapable.

When the protesters shifted course suddenly to change the law, the city moved to shut down the bus boycott by prosecuting eighty-nine of its leaders.

Although counterproductive for the segregationists by making King a national hero and the bus boycott a cause célèbre, the legal crackdown seemed at the time the only recourse for the white officeholders.

Gloster Current, NAACP director of branches, sent a February 2 memorandum to executive secretary Roy Wilkins reporting on the filing of the federal lawsuit.

Mr. Patton called today to report injunctive proceedings have been filed in the Montgomery Bus situation. Mrs. Motley gave me the following report on this.

A suit was filed in the Federal District Court in Montgomery, February 1, by NAACP attorneys Fred Gray and Robert L. Carter seeking a decree that the Alabama Statute requiring racial segregation on the public buses is unconstitutional and enjoining the Mayor, W. A. Gayle; Frank Parks and other members of the Board of City Commissioners; Clyde Sellers, Police Commissioner, and Goodwin J. Ruppenthal, Chief of Police; as well as other city officials from interfering with the plaintiffs, Claudette Colvin, a minor represented by her father, Q. P. Colvin, and other Negro citizens of Montgomery in their exercise of their constitutional right to ride the public buses without state imposed racial segregation.

NAACPP-DLC: Group 3A-273.

1. Fred Gray interview by David J. Garrow, August 20, 1985, Tuskegee, Ala. (courtesy of David J. Garrow).

Executive Board Meeting
Baptist Center—Rev. King presiding
2-2-56, 11:00 A.M.—2:00 P.M.

Prayer—Rev. [H. J.] Palmer

REV. KING—"We got to decide how the suit will be handled." There has been an "increase in the amount of violence in recent days." "Fortunately no one was injured; that was very fortunate. I don't know the motives, whether along line of fear tactics, or attempts at bodily harm. They may become more desperate with the suit on. We need right now a committee of 50 people who will volunteer to patrol all of the churches where mass meetings are being held (before and during). Look for time bombs and the like. Now this mustn't get to the people, because it may panic them and they may not come. I'm not saying that these things will happen, but it's well to take precautionary measures. The minute that it was announced that the commissioners had joined the White Citizens Council, we received 20–25–30 threatening calls each day. We're not going to give up. They can drop bombs in my house every day. I'm firmer now than ever. I went to the sheriff to get a [gun] permit for those people who are guarding me. Couldn't get one. In substance he was saying 'you are at the disposal of the hoodlums.'

"Mrs. Reese agreed to be plaintiff last night, but I heard that she had been to the mayor's office and withdrew. How will that affect the case?"

ATTY. GRAY—"It won't affect the case, but the whites will use it as a propaganda technique."

MR. BINION—"Her husband received a call this morning from a man with a rough voice who asked for Julia Reese." He said she was "not home."

" 'Is she in town?'

" 'Yes.'

" 'Better tell her not to be in town tonight.' "

REV. SEAY—"I don't pose to be a wise man, but there's one thing I'm dead sure of—you had better turn over every leaf. Make sure you know the husband, for God's sake. We have to use precautions every step of the way."

REV. KING—suggestion that two committees be formed immediately:

1. "To talk with plaintiffs"—to give them "assurance," let them know "we're behind them." Chairman—Rev. Seay [. . .]

REV. PALMER—"This is a convincing person"—referring to Rev. Seay.

REV. SEAY—"I think I should say that I'm the most vulnerable, living in the country—all those woods and fields. They can get to me easily."

REV. FIELDS—"That'll give you plenty of running room"—laughter.

2. To see that the churches are patrolled

REV. SEAY—"Let ministers of the various churches appoint men; if necessary—pay them." Chairman—Rev. Hilson [. . .]

REV. KING—"You are to contact the ministers, keep secret, they are not to let anybody know that they are doing this. We don't want it to get out because it will hurt our mass meetings. You should start out immediately." [. . .]

REV. KING—"As you know the suit is before us. So the question is, what is our role now? Whether or not the name of the NAACP might create emotional disturbance, tension (on part of whites), if not otherwise mentioned."

MR. [Robert] MATTHEWS [local NAACP president]—"Dr. Berry called me and asked for a meeting. He advanced this thought—whether the local branch will take the responsibility, or Mrs. [Ruby] Hurley—Regional Director of the seven states."

REV. BENNETT—"Would the NAACP stay in the background?"

MR. MATTHEWS—"I firmly believe this—that if it remains local, they would. I'm not saying they would. When the case is appealed to a higher court, I'm sure that the national NAACP would step in then. If the NAACP takes over the case, Atty. Gray would have the assistance of the staff of the national NAACP. Any pay would go to lawyer Gray, and not to anyone else."

ATTY. LANGFORD—"If the case goes to a higher court there will be another lawyer."

REV. HUBBARD—"All of us belong to the NAACP, or should. I say bring the whole thing out in the open. Turn over the whole thing to the NAACP, and let the Ass'n support the NAACP financially."

REV. KING—"What about transportation?"

ATTY. LANGFORD—"Continue the protest until the hearing of the [federal] district court. They must answer the charges within 20 days or we win by default."

REV. PALMER—"Will we be able to make enough money to support the NAACP and the protest at the same time? The NAACP says it won't work in the background. Would we get any help from the state office?"

REV. KING—"I understand that they've been raising money for the Rosa Parks case."

MR. MATTHEWS—"The only expenses you have are the expenses of the two lawyers, if the NAACP takes the case."

REV. SEAY—"To me it doesn't matter who handles this case, this is still {N. of Montgomery} our case. I don't think we should go out for saying we're raising money in the name of the NAACP."

REV. PALMER—"Since Mrs. Hurley will be here at 5:30, I move that we table the discussion until then." Motion carried.

Moved that Ass'n. assume the responsibility for paying fees for night watchmen out of Sunday offerings for the movement—homes of key individuals (leaders).

MRS. PARKS—"Some strange men have been coming in my neighborhood inquiring about the woman who caused all of this trouble. I'm not worried about myself, but it does upset my mother quite a bit."

Motion (by Rev. Bennett) carried that the Ass'n assume the responsibility for giving Mrs. P. protection at night.

PV-ARC-LNT.

Later that day MIA leaders met jointly with Montgomery NAACP officers, southeastern regional secretary Ruby Hurley, and Alabama field secretary W. C. Patton.

MIA-NAACP Meeting, Baptist Center
2-2-56, 6:15–7:55 P.M.
Rev. King Presiding

MRS. HURLEY—"I am very much concerned about the two bombings in two days. The chips are down, but this is just the beginning. The worst is yet to come."

MR. PATTON—"We know where we are now. The question is—where do we go from here? That's the main objective."

REV. KING—"We need the NAACP in an advisory capacity, the machinery they have set up over a period of years."

MRS. HURLEY—"This is no longer a local problem, but the end of segregation in intrastate travel. The import goes far beyond the scope of Montgomery, or Alabama. It affects the entire nation."

REV. SEAY—"This is our baby, and we (MIA) want to go along with it all the way up. We want to develop good, strong lawyers right here on this ground."

REV. PALMER—"If we turn it over to the NAACP, it means that we would have no more to do with it, except to raise funds. Wouldn't the NAACP have the opportunity to solicit funds?"

MRS. HURLEY—"When the NAACP takes over, it takes over from a legal point of view. This is so broad that you will be able to call upon people beyond the confines of Montgomery. Keep on with the mass meetings. They will aid psychologically, educationally, and financially."

MR. PATTON—"Keep the mass meetings for financing the transportation and part for the NAACP. After the protest is it your intention to divert the money from the mass meetings to the NAACP?"—not answered by the MIA.

MRS. HURLEY—"The case must go through the local and state NAACP before it goes to the national. The local branch has the responsibility of notifying the state and national. If you don't take it to the local and you go directly to the national, you have to foot the full financial responsibility."

DR. [Moses] JONES—"I'm concerned about the people who walk long distances. We need to keep the protest going, and if the NAACP takes the case, and they need $10,000, we can get it quicker than they can."

Motion that "the case be turned over to the local branch of the NAACP." Motion carried.

Motion "that we continue our mass meetings and the funds be collected in the name of the Ass'n. (for anonymity), and necessary contributions be made to the NAACP." Motion carried. The local branch will agree on a fee with the lawyers. The Ass'n. will send money to the NAACP for their fees.

PV-ARC-LNT.

February 2, 1956

Mr. Nathan David, Attorney at Law
Pennsylvania Building
Washington, D.C.

Dear Nate:

[. . .] The situation here in the Confederacy is getting rough. The local Legislature has already adopted an "ordinance of secession" from the jurisdiction of the United States Supreme Court, but at least the Governor [*James E. Folsom*] refuses to sign it. He seems to be about the only "Union" man in Alabama, at least among the local politicos. Our old pal, Jim Eastland, is coming down for a big rally of the White Citizens Council on February 9th and I would not be surprised to see him take the oath of office as the second President of the Confederacy. After all, the first President of the Confederacy came from Mississippi also, so tradition favors him for the high office.

The "Negro Boycott" of the busses has been going on for two months and is apparently as effective as ever. Few people believe that they would stick together as they have done. To meet the situation all three members of the City Commission have publicly announced their membership in and their adherence to the principles of the White Citizens Councils and at the same time they announced that the police had been instructed to break up the Negro car pools by diligent enforcement against them of all traffic regulations, however minor and also that Negroes assembled for car pool or taxi service would be charged with "loitering." The announcement of the Commissioners was quite naturally taken by the denizens of the woodwork and the under side of rocks to be a signal to come out and do their worst, so bombings have been added to the threats by telephone etc. On Monday, a bomb was thrown against the home of Rev. King, a Baptist preacher who has been the main spokesman for the Negroes and last night another was thrown against the home of E. D. Nixon, a pullman car porter who heads the Negro Democratic organization. A few crosses have been burned to add to the display. The Commissioners and the White Citizens Councils, of course, deplore the whole thing and have even offered rewards for the arrest and conviction of the hoodlums, who they continue to egg on with their public statements.

The moths got my Grandpa's Confederate uniform a long time ago, so I don't know exactly what to do about it. The last time we seceded, as I recall, it did not work out so well, but maybe you Damned Yankees will be more reasonable now and more of a pushover for us.

Sincerely yours,
Clifford J. Durr

Dear Nate:

Do you think from your knowledge of them that there would be any chance to get the Hennings [*Senate Judiciary*] Committee to come down this way and investigate any of these outrages? Things are really getting rough and it looks as though it might develop into a real sort of race war. Even the more or less decent white people say that all white people have to stand together whether the cause is right or wrong, but the solidarity of the white race must be preserved. I still think most Southern people are amenable to reason if it comes in the form of something concrete. Of course if the big Federal military installations would have the guts to declare all these seething southern towns out of bounds for the military, then they would calm down in a minute as the towns draw their life blood from these installations. To show you how silly this whole thing really is, Maxwell Field [*Air Force Base*] is now completely integrated, and thousands of white people from here work out there and accept Negroes in the Library, Cafeteria, work by them, and even in some cases, go swimming with them, BUT let them get back to Montgomery and they go nuts. It is not a fear of the Negroes but a fear of each other, what people will think about them. They all have a sort of schizophrenia.

Love, VA [*Virginia Durr*]

CJDP-A-Ar.

White extremists passed out the following racist handbill at a huge Montgomery rally organized by the Central Alabama Citizens Council on Friday evening, February 10. Reporter Joe Azbell described the event as a mix of pep rally, political convention, and old-fashioned revival. About 12,000 whites packed the state coliseum—the "largest segregation gathering in recent history of the South," one speaker said—to hear Mississippi's senior senator James Eastland and other segregation leaders defend "the Southern way of life." The crowd cheered wildly when Mayor W. A. Gayle and commissioners Clyde Sellers and Frank Parks promised to "hold the line against Negro integration." Eastland, a founder of the Citizens Council movement, declared: "There is only one course open for the South to take, and that is stern resistance. . . .

We must fight them with every legal weapon at every step of the way. Southern people are right both legally and morally" and in order to win must "organize and be militant." Condemning the Supreme Court's 1954 *Brown* decision as "illegal, immoral, dishonest, and a disgrace," he warned that the South now faced an "era of judicial tyranny." But, he said, "the Anglo-Saxon people have held steadfast to the belief that resistance to tyranny is obedience to God."[1]

"Preview of the 'Declaration of Segregation' "

When in the course of human events it becomes necessary to abolish the Negro race, proper methods should be used. Among these are guns, bows and arrows, sling shots and knives.

We hold these truths to be self evident that all whites are created equal with certain rights; among these are life, liberty and the pursuit of dead niggers.

In every stage of the bus boycott we have been oppressed and degraded because of black slimy, juicy, unbearably stinking niggers. The conduct should not be dwelt upon because behind them they have an ancestral background of Pigmies, head hunters and snot suckers.

My friends it is time we wised up to these black devils. I tell you they are a group of two legged agitators who persist in walking up and down our streets protruding their black lips. If we don't stop helping these African flesh eaters, we will soon wake up and find Rev. King in the White House.

LET'S GET ON THE BALL WHITE CITIZENS

The Book "Declaration of Segregation" will appear April, 1956. If this appeals to you be sure to read the book.

HGP-GAMK.

1. *Montgomery Advertiser*, February 11, 1956.

Virginia Foster Durr to Myles Horton

February 18, 1956

Dear Myles,

I do wish we could come up on March 3rd and 4th and if I see any chance I will let you know, but we are terribly busy right now and I doubt if we can get away.

I will try and encourage Mrs. Parks to come as she would be a wonderful inspiration to such a meeting. She has lost her job and had her rent raised and I am at the moment trying to raise some money for her to live on. It is fine to be a heroine but the price is high.

It looks as though the bus boycott might get settled. The Men of Montgomery which is a group that is trying to bring industry to the city has stepped into the picture as they think this is all giving Montgomery a bad name. Also the Negroes have now filed suit in Federal Court to declare the bus segregation laws unconstitutional, but at the same time the Grand Jury has convened and it looks as though they were going to try and get indictments for criminal conspiracy against the leaders but the report has not yet come out. [. . .]

Lots of love, VA

HRECR-WHi: Box 11.

On February 20, Horton wrote Parks inviting her to the planning conference in early March for Highlander's summer workshops on public school integration. He mentioned telling people "how proud we were of your courageous role in the boycott. I was very sorry to learn from a letter from Virginia Durr today that you had lost your job. Doing what's right is not always the easy thing to do. But all of us together should be able to manage somehow. Perhaps we can help."[1]

February 24, 1956

Dear Myles and Zilphia:

Your letter came yesterday and I saw Mrs. Parks yesterday afternoon. She had just received your telegram and was delighted to get it. She wants very much to come up to Highlander and the only thing that stands in her way as far as I can see is money. She is having a very hard time. Both her husband and her Mother are sick and she has lost her job and had her rent raised and with all the demands on her time she finds it very hard to sew enough to make anything. You would be amazed at the number of pictures, interviews etc. that she had taken and all of that takes up time, and then too all the meetings and then having to walk nearly everywhere she goes takes time too. I have been able to get her $35.00 from various people but that is not very much. I keep trying and think some more will come in but most people want to contribute to the Boycott itself rather than to an individual, but that particular individual is to my mind very important and I think she should certainly be helped. She would like to go on to the NAACP meeting in Washington if it were possible in terms of money and time and it would be wonderful to have her there.

As for us coming, I really don't see how right now. Only one of us could come in any case on account of the children and our old jeep is just about done for, and Baggett has not paid off YET. I hope you can manage to raise a little money for Rosa as she really needs it and she would love to come if she could. Highlander is the promised land for her and I truly think her experience there had a great deal to do with her bravery and determination to resist here. It was the contrast with her life there that made the Jim Crow here completely unbearable and it was the first time she had ever lived in a free society. Well all of us who stuck in the South or who came back (willy nilly) can at least feel that in our various ways and in spite of all the freezing out, that we have done something in this crucial struggle. Certainly Highlander can feel proud of itself and maybe one of these days it will be given the credit due it. [. . .]

Lots of love to all, VA

HRECR-WHi: Box 11.

1. Myles Horton to Rosa L. Parks, February 20, 1956, HRECR-WHi.

February 25, 1956

Mr. Myles Horton
Highlander Folk School
Monteagle, Tennessee

Dear Myles:

I was very happy to receive your letter of February 20 inviting me to the planning conference on March 3–4, and would like so much to be present.

You may know that I was also included in the mass indictment and arrest of 89 bus protest leaders. I was also found guilty in Circuit Court of the charge resulting from my arrest on the bus December 1, 1955. The case is appealed. My job was terminated January 7. Mrs. Durr is very concerned about our welfare. I appreciate her friendship, especially at this trying time.

Anne Lockwood wrote some time ago, asking if my arrest was planned. It was not at all planned by any individual or organization.

I do not know at present if any one else from here will come to the meeting. You will hear from me immediately if there will be some one else. I would like to drive up with some one with a car.

Your telegram was very much appreciated by all of us. We have received many messages of encouragement and contributions from all parts of the country.

My best regards to all the Highlander staff.

Sincerely yours,
Rosa L. Parks

HRECR-WHi: Box 22.

On February 20 the Men of Montgomery, a group of white businessmen, presented to Abernathy a proposal that the city and bus company had just accepted. That evening at the St. John AME Church, four thousand bus boycott participants voted it down almost unanimously. The new terms did not differ from concessions the MIA had rejected before. Rev. L. Roy Bennett and his assistant pastor apparently cast the only votes in favor.

The Men of Montgomery

The proposals submitted by your organization approved by the City Commission and City Bus Line and with the fare conveyed to me by telephone were presented at the mass meeting of the Montgomery Improvement Association tonight at the St. John AME Church. Sorry to report the proposals were not approved having received only two affirmative votes with three Thousand Nine Hundred Ninety Eight voting against acceptance. However, the audience gave your organization a rising vote of thanks for the very fine exemplification of good will and its willingness to see justice prevail in our city for all citizens.

Rev. Ralph D. Abernathy

MCDA-AMC.

In a press statement following the mass meeting, which had been closed to reporters, Abernathy explained that blacks would gain little by accepting the proposal and "would have to return to the buses with increased rates besides. . . . We have walked for 11 weeks in the cold and rain. Now the weather is warming up. Therefore, we will walk on until some better proposals are forthcoming from our city fathers."[1]

1. *Montgomery Advertiser*, February 21, 1956.

Clifford J. Durr to George Eddy

February 21, 1956

Mr. George Eddy
5151 Polk Avenue
Alexandria, Virginia

Dear George:

[. . .] The local situation appears to be getting back to where it was about one hundred years ago, what with the "nullification" and the "interposition" etc. and other ringing statements repudiating the United States Supreme Court. I suppose you have read in the WASHINGTON POST of the happenings at the University of Alabama and also of the "boycott" of the busses by the Negroes here in Montgomery. The local Grand Jury is busy working up indictments against various and sundry of the local Negro leaders on any grounds they can find and also seeking to put out of action one of the two local Negro lawyers, by alleging that he filed a suit in the Federal Court attacking the constitutionality of the bus segregation laws without the consent of one of the persons named in the suit as a plaintiff. As she, along with all the other plaintiffs, had signed a written authorization for the suit before it was filed and the newspapers themselves have carried stories of the pressure put on her by the Mayor as well as anonymous telephone calls, I don't see how the charge will hold up but in the present temper almost anything might happen.

It is rather difficult right now to take a stand in favor of the preservation of the Union. Our old pal, Eastland, has become the leader of the crusade for righteousness and racial purity and as he got an audience of between ten and fifteen thousand to hear him when he spoke here last week, I don't think he can be laughed off, as irresponsible as he has proved himself to be.

Black rather than red seems to be the incendiary color here, but they are rapidly beginning to identify them as one in the Southern Spectrum. The problem, however, becomes a little bit more difficult in view of the fact that there are considerably more Blacks than reds, and that the Blacks admit their blackness and also that they are standing together in a way that the pure Whites had not anticipated.

Things are getting pretty rough, but we shall see what we shall see. [. . .]

Sincerely yours,
By Sec. VFD.

CJDP-A-Ar.

Civil rights leader Bayard Rustin (1912–87) remembered that it was Lillian Smith, controversial Georgia novelist and nonviolent activist, who sparked his involvement with the bus boycott. They had worked together during the 1940s when he was race relations director of the Fellowship of Reconciliation and she served as an FOR board member. "She had also been closely associated with my work with CORE," he recalled, "and she had traveled around the country in some of the interracial workshops which I had put on. Therefore, she considered me to be a kind of minor authority on nonviolence. It was she who brought me to King." Knowing that King was inexperienced in nonviolent methods, she felt that Rustin's work with the Gandhian independence movement in India would especially benefit the bus boycott. "She wrote a telegram to King saying that she was going to telegraph me asking me to go, to see if I could be of help to him. As a result of her telegram, I in fact did go. But something happened in the process of my going, which created great divisiveness in the black community."[1] He obtained approval for his mission from New York colleagues, including his mentor A. Philip Randolph, and he got a leave of absence from his position as executive secretary of War Resisters League. Randolph raised funds for Rustin's Montgomery visits.

John M. Swomley Jr., executive secretary of the Fellowship of Reconciliation, wrote to FOR's southwestern regional secretary on February 21 expressing concern about Rustin's decision to visit Montgomery because of baggage from his past. A democratic socialist, Rustin had served as a Communist youth organizer during the 1930s, had done prison time during World War II for resisting the draft, and in 1953 had been arrested for homosexual activity in Los Angeles, which forced his resignation from FOR.

Wilson Riles
1205 W. Jefferson Blvd.
Los Angeles, California

Dear Wilson:

Thanks for your letter. There have been complications re. work in the South. Bayard Rustin has decided to fly to Montgomery with the idea of getting the bus boycott temporarily called off while he organizes a workshop or school for non-violence with a goal of 100 young Negro men who will then promote it not only in Montgomery but elsewhere in the South. He has made overtures to AFSC [*American Friends Service Committee*] to have them release Bob Gilmore, their New York College Secretary, to be a contact with white people for him in Montgomery.

Charles Lawrence [FOR *chairman*] feels strongly that it were better if Bayard did not go South, that it would be easy for the police to frame him with his record in L.A. and New York, and set back the whole cause there. He mentions frame-up though there could be an actual incident or dramatic effort in which he becomes the focal point. Bayard has indicated to Al [*Hassler*] that he does not plan to work with NAACP but try to organize an independent show.

Charles Lawrence, Al, Glenn [*Smiley*] and I met Monday and agreed 1) not to compete with or collaborate with Bayard, 2) Glenn should go to Orangeburg, Atlanta, Montgomery, and Tuscaloosa to find out what is happening and what the possibilities are; 3) Explore possibility in Atlanta, Orangeburg and elsewhere of two one-week workshops on non-violence etc. in connection with a college, theological seminary, etc. to be run by you and Glenn during the two-week period preceding staff meetings here.

4) Explore possibility of two or three four-day institutes in the South in June.

5) If Bayard is unsuccessful with his plans for a workshop in Montgomery something might be done there. If he is successful it is all to the good and the South is a big area needing work at other points as well as what you or Glenn might add in Montgomery.

All of the above about Bayard is confidential, but you ought to know about it. [. . .]

Always cordially,
John M. Swomley Jr.

FORP-PSC-P.

1. Bayard Rustin, "The Reminiscences of Bayard Rustin" (Oral History Research Office, Columbia University, 1988), p. 135; see also pp. 136–42.

An important link between Montgomery's black leaders and national African American leadership was the long association between trade unionist and political activist E. D. Nixon and Randolph, the preeminent leader of black labor. Nixon, a Pullman porter since the 1920s, joined Randolph's Brotherhood of Sleeping Car Porters a year after he founded it in 1925. At the start of World War II Nixon helped Randolph organize the March on Washington that was called off when President Roosevelt agreed to ban racial discrimination in the nation's defense industry. For many years Nixon headed the Alabama sleeping car porters' local in Montgomery. Just as Randolph used his union leadership to promote black advancement, Nixon had agitated for black rights in Montgomery and statewide, concentrating on voter registration. Randolph sent him a telegram of support on February 23.

ED NIXON
647 CLINTON AVE MONTGOMERY ALA

HAVE FOLLOWED WITH GREAT PRIDE AND INSPIRATION THE GREAT FIGHT FOR
RESPECT AND HUMAN DIGNITY YOU AND YOUR FELLOW CITIZENS ARE WAGING IN
SEEKING TO WIPE OUT STIGMA AND DISGRACE OF JIM CROW BUS SERVICES. BE
ASSURED THAT JUSTICE AND RIGHT ARE ON YOUR SIDE AND THE MORAL CON-
SCIENCE OF NEGRO AND WHITE AMERICANS IS WITH YOU AS WELL AS THE GOOD
WHITE PEOPLE OF MONTGOMERY WHO BELIEVE IN GOD AND HIS RIGHTEOUS-
NESS. SUFFER AND SACRIFICE IF NEED BE BUT NEVER GIVE UP FOR IF YOU
REMAIN STEADFAST YOU ARE BOUND TO WIN. THE BROTHERHOOD OF SLEEPING
CAR PORTERS AND ALL THE NEGRO AND WHITE PEOPLE WHO LOVE JUSTICE AND
HUMAN LIBERTY WILL NEVER FORSAKE YOU

A PHILIP RANDOLPH

MLKP-MBU: Box 91.

King learned of the grand jury indictments of eighty-nine leaders while he was on a speaking trip in Nashville, Tennessee. On his way home he stopped in Atlanta, where his father gathered influential friends, including Morehouse College president Benjamin Mays and *Atlanta Daily World* editor C. A. Scott, to dissuade him from returning to Montgomery. Although he respected their advice, King told them, "I would rather be in jail ten years than desert my people now. I have begun the struggle, and I can't turn back."[1] As did most of the indicted leaders the day before, he voluntarily reported to the county courthouse on February 23, accompanied by his father and Abernathy; like the others he was released on bond. That night he spoke to a prayer meeting of several thousand at First Baptist Church. This *New York Times* report on the meeting was its first front-page article on the bus boycott.

"Negroes Pledge to Keep Boycott," by Wayne Phillips

One after another, indicted Negro leaders took the rostrum in a crowded Baptist church tonight to urge their followers to shun the city's buses and "walk with God." More than 2,000 Negroes filled the church from basement to balcony and overflowed into the street. They chanted and sang; they shouted and prayed; they collapsed in the aisles and they sweltered in an 85-degree heat. They pledged themselves again and again to "passive resistance."

It is under this banner that they have carried on for eighty days a stubborn boycott of the city's buses. The boycott has brought criminal charges against Negro leaders. Eighty-nine of them, including twenty-four Protestant ministers, were arrested yesterday and today and charged with carrying on an illegal boycott. More arrests are to be made under eleven indictments handed up Tuesday. Tomorrow those arrested are to be arraigned in Circuit Court. The Negroes have been called on to stage at that time a "prayer pilgrimage day"— to give up the use of automobiles and taxis and walk the streets in protest.

"It is not expected that a single race-loving Negro will turn the key in his ignition or turn the crank of his automobile or ride a taxicab," the Rev. Ralph D. Abernathy told tonight's meeting. "And we know," he added, "that nobody will ride the buses." Mr. Abernathy, 29 years old, is the pastor of the First Baptist Church, where the meeting was held. He headed the negotiating committee that tried unsuccessfully to settle the boycott that was organized Dec. 5. The boycott was a protest against the arrest of a Negro woman who refused to give up a seat in the white section of a bus.

"We're not trying to impress anybody with our strength," Mr. Abernathy said. "We just plan to demonstrate to the people who do not have cars that we're willing to walk with them." Sixty-five per cent of the city's bus passengers before the boycott were Negroes. Since the boycott buses have plied the streets almost empty, while Negroes make their way to and from work in taxis, with the aid of a 300-car auto pool, or on foot.

As the Negroes waited for the meeting to start they sang, picking up the hymns that sprang to mind. When the leaders appeared at the rear of the church the audience stood and shouted and whistled and waved and cheered.

The program opened with a hymn—"Onward Christian Soldiers"—and a prayer to God "not to leave us in this hour." The scripture was from Corinthians I—"If I have no love I count for nothing." And then they sang "O lift me up and let me stand on higher ground."

Rev. Martin Luther King Jr., head of the Montgomery Improvement Association, which has directed the eighty-day boycott, told the gathering that the protest was not against a single incident but over things that "go deep down into the archives of history."

"We have known humiliation, we have known abusive language, we have been plunged into the abyss of oppression," he told them. "And we decided to rise up only with the weapon of protest. It is one of the greatest glories of America that we have the right of protest."

"There are those who would try to make of this a hate campaign," the

Atlanta-born, Boston-educated Baptist minister said. "This is not war between the white and the Negro but a conflict between justice and injustice. This is bigger than the Negro race revolting against the white. We are seeking to improve not the Negro of Montgomery but the whole of Montgomery.

"If we are arrested every day, if we are exploited every day, if we are trampled over every day, don't ever let anyone pull you so low as to hate them. We must use the weapon of love. We must have compassion and understanding for those who hate us. We must realize so many people are taught to hate us that they are not totally responsible for their hate. But we stand in life at midnight, and we are always on the threshold of a new dawn."

His talk was followed by a prayer by the Rev. S. S. Seay, former executive secretary of the African Methodist Episcopal Church—"A prayer for those who oppose us." The Rev. A. W. Wilson, vice president of the Negro Alabama Baptist convention, brought greetings to the meeting from Negro Baptists throughout the state. "No other race but the Negro race," he said, "could smile as we have smiled tonight, and sing as we sang tonight and get happy and shout as we have shouted tonight."

New York Times, February 24, 1956.

1. Quoted in Martin Luther King Jr., *Stride Toward Freedom: The Montgomery Story* (New York: Harper, 1958), p. 145.

Shortly after his arrival in Montgomery, Glenn Smiley, FOR's national field secretary, met with King. The next day, February 29, he reported on his meeting to FOR colleagues around the country, especially fellow clergy.

Neil Salinger
Nashville, Tenn.

Dear Neil:

I have just had one of the most glorious, yet tragic interviews I have ever had. I spent a half hour with Martin Luther King, 27-year-old pastor of the great Dexter Ave. Baptist Church in Montgomery, Alabama, and spiritual leader of the now famous "Non-violent Protest" in this capitol city. This is the young man who said last week to 5,000 people in Montgomery: "Let no man drive you so low as to make you hate him" and "This is not a struggle between white and black people, but between darkness and light, justice and injustice."

The die has been cast, there is a crisis of terrifying intensity, and I believe that God has called Martin Luther King to lead a great movement here and in the South. But why does God lay such a burden on one so young, so inex-perienced, so good? King can be a Negro Gandhi, or he can be made into an unfortunate demagogue destined to swing from a lynch mob's tree. *That is why I am writing more than two dozen people of prayer across the nation, asking that they hold Martin Luther King in the light.*

Of his own free will, he has sought counsel from some of us older. May he burst, like fruit out of season, into the type of leader required for this hour.

Sincerely,
Glenn E. Smiley

FORP-PSC-P.

"Montgomery Diary," by Bayard Rustin

FEBRUARY 21

I ARRIVED in Montgomery this morning and had an interview with Reverend Abernathy, one of the leaders of the non-violent protest. The situation is so tense that men in shifts watch his home while he and his family sleep. I am warned that I will be watched while in town and that it is important that I have the bolts tightly drawn on the windows in my hotel. As one person put it, "This is like war. You can't trust anyone, black or white, unless you know him."

This afternoon I talked with E. D. Nixon, whose home was bombed on February 1st. For years he has been a fearless fighter for Negro rights. He suspects that his home will be bombed again, but says: "They can bomb us out and they can kill us, but we are not going to give in."

Later, I sat in on a conference with a committee of the Montgomery Im-provement Association, which coordinates the protest activities. Three recom-mendations were accepted:

1) The movement will always be called a *non-violent protest* rather than a boycott in order to keep its fundamental character uppermost.

2) A pin should be designed for all those who do not ride the busses to wear as a symbol of unity, encouragement, and mutual support.

3) The slogan for the movement will be "Victory without Violence."

Tonight I walked past Reverend King's house. Lights are strung all around the house, and it is being carefully guarded by Negro volunteers. White police patrol the Negro section of town, two by two. A hotel employee advised me not to go into the streets alone after dark. "If you find it necessary to do so, by all means leave in the hotel everything that identifies you as an outsider. They are trying to make out that Communist agitators and New Yorkers are running our protest."

Abernathy put Rustin to work right away. Folksinging and songwriting were among Rustin's many talents. Years before he had sung in a quartet with Josh White and Leadbelly to support his schooling at New York's City College. Abernathy asked him to compose a song for that day's mass meeting and to draft a leaflet. The indicted leaders accepted his tactical suggestion that in Gandhian fashion they voluntarily report to the courthouse for arrest and booking. Subsequently Rustin wrote more songs and led singing, helped plan strategy, organized support from around the country, wrote speeches and articles for King, and held nonviolent training workshops.

FEBRUARY 22

ONE HUNDRED leaders of the protest received word that they had been indicted. Many of them did not wait for the police to come but walked to the police station and surrendered. Nixon was the first. He walked into the station and said, "You are looking for me? Here I am." This procedure had a startling effect in both the Negro and the white communities. White community leaders, politicians, and police were flabbergasted. Negroes were thrilled to see their leaders surrender without being hunted down. Soon hundreds of Negroes gathered outside the police station and applauded the leaders as they entered, one by one. Later, those who had been arrested were released on $300 bail. They gathered at the Dexter Avenue Baptist Church for a prayer meeting and sang for the first time a song which had been adopted that morning as the theme song for the movement. The four stanzas proclaim the essential elements of a passive resistance struggle—protest, unity, non-violence and equality. Sung to the tune of the spiritual, *Give Me That Old-Time Religion*, the text is:

> We are moving on to vict'ry
> With hope and dignity.
> We shall all stand together
> 'Til every one is free.
> We know love is the watchword
> For peace and liberty.
> Black and white all are brothers
> To live in harmony.
> We are moving on to vict'ry
> With hope and dignity.

After the prayer meeting I went to the home of Mrs. Jeanetta Reese, a Negro woman who had informed the police that she had not known what she was doing when she signed legal papers to challenge bus discrimination in the courts. A few days earlier her attorney, one of the two Negro lawyers in Montgomery, had been arrested for fraud, because of Mrs. Reese's retraction. Although the police had provided no protection for King and Nixon after their houses had been bombed, I found two squad cars parked before Mrs. Reese's home. In addition, a policeman was patrolling the area with a machine gun. After ten minutes of negotiation, the police finally permitted me to see Mrs. Reese; her only comment was: "I had to do what I did or I wouldn't be alive today." I felt sorry for her.

FEBRUARY 23

THIS MORNING Reverend King invited me to attend a meeting of the protest committee. The committee decided not to hold any more mass meetings but only prayer meetings. This was to emphasize the moral nature of the struggle. The meetings will center around five prayers:
  1) A prayer for the success of the meeting.
  2) A prayer for strength of spirit to carry on non-violently.
  3) A prayer for strength of body to walk for freedom.
  4) A prayer for those who oppose us.
  5) A prayer that all men may become brothers to live in justice and equality.
  This afternoon at 3:30 the Negroes began to fill the church for the 7 o'clock prayer meeting. From 4 o'clock on, without leadership, they sang and prayed. Exactly at 7 the one hundred who had been arrested worked their way to the pulpit through 5,000 cheering men, women and children. Overnight these leaders had become symbols of courage. Women held their babies to touch them. The people stood in ovation. Television cameras ground away, as King was finally able to open the meeting. He began: "We are not struggling merely for the rights of Negroes but for all the people of Montgomery, black and white. We are determined to make America a better place for all people. Ours is a non-violent protest. We pray God that no man shall use arms."

FEBRUARY 24

42,000 NEGROES have not ridden the busses since December 5. On December 6, the police began to harass, intimidate, and arrest Negro taxi drivers who were helping get these people to work. It thus became necessary for the Negro leaders to find an alternative—the car pool. They set up 23 dispatch centers where people gather to wait for free transportation.

This morning Rufus Lewis, director of the pool, invited me to attend the meeting of the drivers. On the way, he explained that there are three methods, in addition to the car pool, for moving the Negro population:

1) Hitch-hiking.

2) The transportation of servants by white housewives.

3) Walking.

Later he introduced me to two men, one of whom has walked 7 miles and the other 14 miles, every day since December 5.

"The success of the car pool is at the heart of the movement," Lewis said at the meeting. "It must not be stopped."

I wondered what the response of the drivers would be, since 28 of them had just been arrested on charges of conspiring to destroy the bus company. One by one, they pledged that, if necessary, they would be arrested again and again.

This afternoon the coordinating committee rejected a proposal that people be asked to stop work for one hour on March 28. I was impressed with the leaders' response, which adhered to the Gandhian principle of consideration for one's opponents. As King put it, "We do not want to place too much of a burden upon white housewives nor to give them the impression that we are pushing them against the wall."

This evening a few of the leaders got together to consider a constructive program for inculcating the philosophy of non-violence in the community. After hours of serious discussion, several proposals were accepted. The following impressed me as being particularly significant:

An essay contest for high-school students on the subject, "Why We Should Use Non-violence in Our Struggle."

The distribution of a pamphlet on non-violence.

The importance of preaching non-violence in the churches.

The possibility of a workshop on the theory and practice of non-violence.

This meeting concluded with agreement that the committee should do everything possible to negotiate the issues. The Montgomery Improvement Association is asking for these assurances:

Greater courtesy on the part of drivers.

Accepting first come, first served seating within the pattern of segregation while the question of intra-state segregation is being decided in the courts.

The employment of some Negro drivers on predominantly Negro routes.

THIS MORNING I had a long talk with Reverend [*Robert*] Hughes, a white Southerner who is executive secretary of the Alabama Interracial Council with offices in Montgomery. Hughes indicated that his association with an interracial group has always tied his hands in dealing with the conservative whites, who distrust anything interracial. Now the liberals, to whom his group normally appeals, are also alienated because of the psychological confusion in the changed situation.

For generations the status quo has been based on violence with the Negro as victim. A few whites have managed to be liberal without feeling a direct threat to their social position. Now, as the Negroes reach the stage where they make specific, if minimum, demands, a new and revolutionary situation has developed. There is little middle ground on which to maneuver and few compromises that are possible. For the first time, the white liberals are forced to stand for racial justice, or to repudiate the liberal principles which they have always wanted to believe in.

The one definite principle they can cling to is to condemn overt violence. Even the non-violence of the Negroes has not counterbalanced their horror of the violence which they fear will break out sooner or later. The result is that they are immobilized by confusion and fear. [. . .]

FEBRUARY 26 (SUNDAY)

TOGETHER WITH a number of Negro and white reporters, I attended King's packed church. He spoke simply, emphasizing the non-violent nature of the struggle, and told his congregation, "We are concerned not merely to win justice in the busses but rather to behave in a new and different way—to be non-violent so that we may remove injustice itself, both from society and from ourselves. This is a struggle which we cannot lose, no matter what the apparent outcome, if we ourselves succeed in becoming better and more loving people."

This afternoon I received word that the white community has learned that I am in Montgomery, that I am being watched, and that efforts will be made to get me out of town. I was warned under no circumstances to go into the white areas of the city.

Tonight I spent discussing the protest campaign with Reverend and Mrs. King over coffee in their kitchen. I asked King if he felt that the activities of the White Citizens Council would lead to further bombings and other violence and whether he felt some elements in the Negro community would return violence with violence. He said that he felt the behavior of the White Citizens Council could very easily lead to serious violence and that the results might be catastrophic. "But," he added, "give us six weeks. The spirit of non-violence may so have permeated our community by that time that the whole Negro community will react non-violently."

When Abernathy first took him to meet the Kings, Rustin discovered that he knew Coretta Scott King from when he once lectured at her rural Alabama high school and later at Antioch College, her alma mater. He and Rev. King "hit it off immediately," he later recalled, "particularly in terms of the whole concept of nonviolence, because . . . when I got to Montgomery, Dr. King had very limited notions about how a nonviolent protest should be carried out. For example, when I first got there, the leadership were carrying guns; when I first got there, the leadership had Dr. King's home and the homes of others, protected day and night by men, not only with shotguns, but with pistols. In fact two days after I got down there, CORE activist Bill Worthy, a young black who became quite famous because he had gone to China—at the time he was a newspaper reporter for the *Afro-American* newspaper, and he had gone to China, against the will of the United States government. . . . Bill walked into Dr. King's house, and was about to sit down, and I'd say, 'Oh, Bill, wait, wait, Bill; couple of guns in that chair. You don't want to shoot yourself.' . . . I do not believe that one does honor to Dr. King by assuming that, somehow, he had been prepared for this job. He had not been prepared for it: either tactically, strategically, or his understanding of nonviolence. The glorious thing is that he came to a profoundly deep understanding of nonviolence through the struggle itself, and through reading and discussions which he had in the process of carrying on the protest. . . .

"It was as he began to discuss nonviolence, it was as the newspapers throughout the country began to describe him as one who believed in nonviolence, he automatically took himself seriously because other people were taking him seriously. I can remember one of the most fascinating things in that early period was the number of quiet discussions Dr. King and I had about nonviolence, about my experience after I got to India, with the followers of Gandhi, in regard to what they thought about strategy and tactics, and the like. I remember, in particular, one very important discussion in which I pointed out to King, in discussing my thoughts on the Indian Revolution: that the great masses of Indians who were followers of Gandhi did not believe in nonviolence. They believed in nonviolence as a tactic: the British can, in fact, be won over without violence . . . But it was precisely what I discussed with Dr. King that, because the followers will seldom, in the mass, be dedicated to nonviolence in principle, that the leadership must be dedicated to it in principle, to keep those who believe in it as a tactic operating correctly. But if, in the flow and the heat of battle, a leader's house is bombed, and he shoots back, that is an encouragement to his followers to pick up guns. If, on the other hand, he has no guns around him, and they all know it, they will rise to the nonviolent occasion of a situation. Well, we had many, many chats like that."[1]

FEBRUARY 27

I LEARNED this morning from reliable sources that there is some indication that the bombing of the King and Nixon homes was not the work of irresponsible youth or cranks, but had the support of powerful vested interests in the community. There is some evidence that even the dynamite used passed through the hands of some people in the community who should be responsible for the maintenance of order.

This afternoon I attended another meeting of the working committee, which has been up against great problems because the protest, originally planned for one day, is now running into the twelfth week. I am impressed with the seriousness and determination of these people. They are handling their money very carefully and anyone who contributes can be certain that the funds will be spent carefully.

Reverend Abernathy concluded the meeting with a statement which was unanimously adopted:

1) We have all worked hard to make our protest known around the world.

2) We have kept our struggle Christian and non-violent and intend to keep it so.

3) Although many have been arrested, we continue our protest, for none of our actions has been illegal.

4) The car pool continues.

5) All who were arrested are out on bail thanks to our community's fine spirit.

6) We have received moral support and encouragement from all over the United States.

7) The NAACP will help us carry on the legal aspects of the struggle.

8) We shall have occasional days of prayer and pilgrimage.

9) We pray God for strength to carry on non-violently.

As I watched the people walk away, I had a feeling that no force on earth can stop this movement. It has all the elements to touch the hearts of men.

Liberation, April 1956.

1. Bayard Rustin, "Reminiscences of Bayard Rustin" (Oral History Research Office, Columbia University, 1988), pp. 137–40.

February 29, 1956

Glenn E. Smiley
Gen. Del.
Montgomery, Ala.

Dear Glenn:

I have just come from a meeting of twenty or so people, including Norman Thomas, A. Philip Randolph, Charles Lawrence and others, and it was the feeling of this group that Bayard should be urged to leave Alabama and return to New York. They felt that there were very serious elements of danger to the movement there for Bayard to present. The letters that were received from Bayard indicated that he had been responsible for many of the things that have happened down there. However, Philip Randolph reported that just the night before the meeting, influential leaders down there had phoned him to find out whether Bayard was the genuine article, and whether they should cooperate with him. There is some danger that Bayard is indicating that he has had more to do with what is happening, than he actually has. My own feeling is that you should be wary of him, as to getting in touch with him, for he is obviously being watched, in view of the fact that he has been accused of being a Communist and coming down from the North. The group that met here is thinking of a further meeting later on, but has decided not to form a definite committee. Instead, Jim Farmer has been asked to talk with Adam Clayton Powell in an effort to get him to meet with Oscar Lee of the National Council of Churches and other responsible church leaders, to see whether there can be a genuine prayer meeting organized on a date other than March 28th, so that there can be the maximum organization in advance. I shall keep you posted on any other developments.

Cordially yours,
John M. Swomley Jr.

FORP-PSC-P.

Dear Glenn:

You may have seen the enclosed clipping in which Rev. Joseph Jackson, President of the National Baptist Convention (federation of Negro churches), rejected proposals by Adam Clayton Powell for a work stoppage and hour of prayer on March 28, asking instead for a day of mourning, fasting, and prayer on March 17. This was considered by the meeting in Philip Randolph's office yesterday and an approach was to be made to Powell to see if he would work with Mr. Jackson and National Council of Churches and A.M.E. Zion people to get a really large prayer observance or demonstration nationally.

It was the conviction yesterday that we should not try from the North to train or otherwise run the non-violent campaign in Montgomery, as Bayard had hoped to do, but rather to expect them to indicate ways in which we could be of help. Only Bayard's roommate argued for his staying in the South. Phil Randolph indicated that the Montgomery leaders had managed thus far [*more*] successfully than "any of our so-called non-violence experts" a mass resistance campaign and we should learn from them rather than assume that we know it all.

The meeting decided not to organize a committee. Even if it had this would not alter our plans. They felt that one of the most useful jobs to be done in Montgomery was getting whites who are prepared to negotiate with Negro leaders to have some understanding of the situation and perhaps a meeting. This might well be a major contribution you could make. For example, some white merchants are losing a considerable volume of business because Negroes will not shop downtown and carry packages all the way home on foot. Thus there are economic reasons for a softening of the white attitude.

There were about thirty persons present at the meeting, which was called by Jim Farmer, who is working for a labor union now, by Bob Gilmore of AFSC whom Bayard wanted to be his co-worker in the South, and by A. Philip Randolph.

This is in somewhat more detail than I had time for in my hasty note yesterday. [. . .]

Sincerely,
[*John M. Swomley Jr.*]

FORP-PSC-P (February 29, 1956).

In the wake of the mass arrests King, Abernathy, Rufus Lewis, and other leaders massaged morale at a February 27 mass meeting at Holt Street Baptist Church.

Report on MIA Mass Meeting, by Donald T. Ferron

Hal and I arrived at the church at 4:55 p.m. to find the street (Holt) for several blocks in either direction traveled by Negroes heading toward the direction of the church. The closer we came to our destination the more compact became the collectivity of brown humanity, so that by the time we reached the steps it became apparent that so early in the day no seats were available. We managed somehow to get in the main auditorium and discovered that the balcony, too, was filled, except for a few remaining seats in the choir chamber which extended over and above the pulpit. We decided that while we could see the speakers only as they entered, the congestion would be too great to permit writing. So, to the choir "loft" we ran and finally became seated.

Across the main auditorium, directly ahead of us, was a large rectangular mirror which was centered in front of the balcony and just below its guard rail. Under ordinary circumstances we would have been able to see the reflections of the speakers, but the church was packed and the temperature (climatic as well as emotional) was high. As a result, many members of the congregation removed their coats, jackets, sweaters, etc., and hung them over the guard rail, which therefore obstructed the vision of those who were seated over the speakers' platform.

From the time we arrived until the mass meeting officially began, there was an informal, unplanned, undirected, yet cooperative, concerted singing and humming of hymns and spirituals, and sporadic individual prayers. At exactly 7:02 (there was a clock just below the mirror) Rev. King entered, followed by Rev. Abernathy, Rev. Hubbard, and several other men whom I was unable to identify as they quickly became lost in the crowd. {Hymn—"Guide Me O'er My Great Jehovah"} As presiding officer, Rev. Bennett opened the meeting by asking Rev. J. W. Barnes "to give a brief prayer asking for non-violence" and to "give us strength to continue" with the protest.

Rev. Barnes gave the prayer asking that the Lord "direct us, tell us what you want us to do. We know that no harm can come over us with your hand over us. We don't hate anybody, we're neighbors to all."

Spiritual—"Lay Down My Burdens." It may be interesting to note that during the singing of each hymn or spiritual, Rev. Abernathy would stand and lead the singing the way a musical director or conductor would do.

Rev. M. L. King—"Presiding officer, platform associates, and friends, good evening. We have new zeal, new stamina to carry on. When we saw this protest many, many weeks ago, we thought it would last but a short time. It has reached out beyond Montgomery; it has become an international problem. We have the prayer and support of men and women all over the nation. They're saying <u>one</u> thing—'you've gone too far; you can't turn back now.' Although confronted with splinters, we're going to keep going. Wherever there's progress, there is the pulling back force of retrogression; where there's burden there is pain. Therefore we're using Christian principles. Out of progress may come damaging revolution as set forth by Karl Marx and communism, or passive resistance with love as ammunition and a breast plate of righteousness. Negroes have suffered economic reprisal, have been segregated, and have suffered humility," Rev. King concluded, but if in spite of these obstacles we continue to carry on with a policy of non-violence, a "voice from high heaven will say, 'Well done.' This is the way we'll carry on. God bless you."

Transportation Observations—Mr. Rufus Lewis (Chairman of Transportation Committee)

"During the mass arrests our transportation system has deteriorated. We need you now more than ever. Register your cars in the pools. We need more cars . . . now. The spirit of the group is what has kept the transportation going. We need more dispatchers, more people who can use their cars all day. Don't now lose faith, the hard part is just beginning. You who can use your cars we need them. Let us keep our faith with those who are walking. Show more courtesy to those who drive. Be concerned with those who own cars. Stick with us and we'll stick with you."

Rev. Bennett—"You have noticed the gravity of this meeting, no laughing, no jokes. But I'll tell you—I started to hold the Interdenominational Ministerial Alliance meeting in jail last Wednesday, there were so many ministers there. It is your prayers that has kept this thing going. That's what we're going to do now. Brother Palmer will give a prayer on strength, guidance, and non-violence."

Rev. Palmer—"We will continue to use the weapon of love and non-violence. This is not a fight of black against white, but justice against injustice."

Hymn—"Sweet Hour of Prayer"

Introduction by Reverend Abernathy

Spiritual—"Steal Away"

Rev. Abernathy—"Even those who oppose us must agree that this is a spiritual movement. It gives us just room for giving thanks to God. We are not trying to put any firm out of business. This is not a matter of economic reprisal. The buses can run the streets as long as they please, but we're going to continue to walk. Thanks must go to 50,000 Montgomery Negroes. This is your movement; we don't have any leaders in the movement; you are the leaders. Someone asked me yesterday—'Who are the leaders?'" (Before Rev. Abernathy could answer, the congregation answered for him, saying at one time—"We are"; or "There ain't no leaders," etc.) Rev. Abernathy continued: "There are too many people to talk at once. We tell Rev. King what to say and he says what we want him to say. We're going to have one big prayer meeting on Thursday evening. So, if you want to be sure to get a seat be there (Hutchinson St. Church) at 3:00. Let us not get tired and weary, but let us walk, and walk together. It's your dime. If you choose not to give it to the mass meeting, then keep it in your pocket."

Prayer—Rev. S. H. Smith—"Makes us strong to walk the sea of time."

Spiritual

Pep Talk—Rev. [*speaker not identified*]

"For the past 84 days many of us have sacrificed, suffered, and have been put in jail. In spite of our previous experiences, the fact remains, the end is not here yet. The novelty has worn away, and we're down to the deep roots of the situation we find ourselves in. We've emptied ourselves of pent-up emotions. Something will fill that vacuum—what it is remains up to you. This is not local. It did not begin in Montgomery. But it was in Montgomery that God chose us to play this all-important role. We must accomplish the will of God. The white church does not practice what it preaches—the Brotherhood of man and the Fatherhood of God. We must grab the whites with a spiritual hand and tell them we love you as though you were our very own. We must not fail God in this hour.

"It used to be that the white man could toe us along. The white man has discovered that Negroes are no longer afraid to go to jail. I spent Wednesday night in jail. Remember this day, the year of our lord, 1956. I stayed home all day waiting on them. They tried to finger-print me and were all thumbs. When they finished they couldn't tell what it was. They tried to do it again and I said 'Don't bother, Mr., I'll do it myself.' We don't mind going to jail, giving our lives. All we want is to make this contribution for you and yours."

Introduction of Rev. Hubbard by Rev. Bennett, followed by the former's brief appeal.

Announcements by Rev. King.

1. "Keep your sense of dignity."

2. Vote to stop protest—"Rev. Bennett was exercising his democratic right to vote the way he did. We should admire him for his courage. He is as much with us as he was in the beginning."

3. "Continue your policy of non-violence."

4. Mrs. Reese withdrew her name as a plaintiff. "Stop bothering her with phone calls, threats."

PV-ARC-LNT.

Interlude . . . 6 . . .

Interview with Bus Drivers, by Anna Holden

While I was waiting for a bus to leave the garage, I talked with a couple of the drivers who were sitting around waiting for their buses. The first one I talked to looked about in his late 30's, told me he had been driving 19 years—did not attempt to identify him as far as name was concerned. I started out by asking him whether business was picking up on the lines. He said Saturday used to be one of their best days but that this one had been pretty bad. Went into lengthy discussion of how everybody had cars now and wanted to drive them in town no matter how long they had had to look for a place to park and how many times they had to send their kids back to put money in the parking meters. He wouldn't be bothered with all that worry about the meters but people didn't seem to mind. They were car crazy and were going to drive their own cars no matter how much it cost them or how much trouble it was.

HOLDEN: This boycott has hurt a lot, hasn't it?
DRIVER: Sure has and I don't know what they're going to do about the fares when the Nigras start riding again. They can't pay that much but I don't think the company will want to come down.
HOLDEN: I guess nobody ever thought it would last this long.
DRIVER: No. When I heard about it, I said well, it'll only be a day or two and they'll be riding again. But you'll have to hand it to 'em. They've done a good job with it.
HOLDEN: It's been way over a month now and they still seem to be going strong.

DRIVER: They'll come back though and I'll tell you what'll do it, lady. There are two things about Nigras. First, they don't trust each other—none of 'em—and they'll be fighting pretty soon. You see lots of the money for this has been coming in from the outside and lots of it has been misappropriated. Well, people get tired of giving and they'll quit and then they'll begin getting in trouble in these misappropriated funds. And the second thing about Nigras, they love their cars. They take good care of them and they're proud of them. You notice how they keep their cars shined and polished? Well, they won't keep this up when their cars begin to depreciate. They're running their own cars like taxis now and not getting anything for it and when their cars begin to get worn, they'll quit. When you have all kinds of people using your car like a taxi, they wear out the seat covers and get it dirty and they won't stand for that.

HOLDEN: Where is all this outside money coming from?

DRIVER: From all over—this NAACP is what started it. Now don't get me wrong, lady. I'm for right and I think they have kicks, but they went about it wrong. They should have come to the bus company and told them what they didn't like first.

HOLDEN: They didn't try to talk things over first?

DRIVER: No, they just quit riding the buses. Now I think that's o.k. if they had to do it that way, but they should have threatened the company first. If they had come down and threatened the company with a boycott, put it on the line that they would quit if they didn't get a better deal, the company would have come through, but they quit first and that's not right.

HOLDEN: This has been hard on the drivers. How many have been laid off?

DRIVER: I don't know, but lots. They've done pretty well with jobs. Some of the construction people have taken some on. Now they aren't busy this time of year, they didn't have enough work to keep their own people busy till around March 1, when building picks up, but they've taken them on to help out. Lots of people are helping out. Surprised me how many have gotten jobs with business so bad.

HOLDEN: Is business bad now?

DRIVER: Things are slow this time of year but people are helping out [. . .] (Mentioned a teacher who sometimes rides the bus but usually gets ride with friends who have car pool. Cites this as instance of people who used to ride buses and are now paying more for cars and making the bus company suffer.)

HOLDEN: That sounds almost like the car pools in the boycott.

DRIVER: The Nigras will be back though. They'll have to come back. I think they have their rights, but this isn't doing them any good. You know, the old diehards that didn't want them to have anything are dying off, and the younger people coming along are getting educated and we're beginning to see they are human too and they have their rights, but then they go and do something like this and it sets everything back. When they get something they act so important—the young ones especially. I was in a store the other day and a young Nigra just pushed me aside, wouldn't give me room. Now they shouldn't be so important, it ruins everything.

About this time, a driver who was going off duty asked me if I wanted a ride to town in his "old Wreck." He spoke with a southern accent, looked about 37 or 38 (Note: saw him Feb. 10 at White Citizens Council rally).

HOLDEN: You mean you would deprive the bus company of 15 cents?
SECOND DRIVER: Oh, it won't hurt them. Well on second thought, maybe it will. Maybe this will be the straw that breaks the camel's back.
HOLDEN: Are they still losing money, even with the new fares?
DRIVER: They're not in as bad shape as they were, but you see how many buses are laid up.

At this point, walking from the lot to the bus, we passed two drivers coming in thru the gates. He asked them how much money they brought in and I think one said $27 and another said he was "up a few dollars that day" but still "under." They all shook their heads indicating things were bad. [. . .]

DRIVER: Now lady, I'll tell you the whole thing in a nutshell. They are just trying to cram this down the people's throats and do it in a hurry, and they won't swallow it. You look at all the progress they have made in the last 20 years by going slow. They could get somewhere but they won't to do it fast.
HOLDEN: I am thinking about the different places in the South where I have ridden the buses and what they do about seating. I know that in Atlanta where I lived several years they used this 1st come 1st served plan like they are asking for here.
DRIVER: It might work some places but I don't know about here. Now they say they do it down in Mobile and it worked there, but the reason they say it works is that they have a real tough judge on the bench and when there's trouble he really throws the book at them.
HOLDEN: You don't think it could work here?
DRIVER: I just don't know. They are going to have to do something to get 'em back on the buses. Those buses are my bread and butter, lady, and I want this thing settled. I have been driving 15 years and I don't want to start looking for another job. I want to keep on driving the buses. (Let me off on corner at this point)

PV-ARC-LNT (January 21, 1956).

Interview with W. A. Gayle, by Anna Holden

DATE: February 10, 1956
TIME: 11:15 A.M.
PLACE: Mayor's Office

General Statement: The Mayor is probably in his late 50's, has been Mayor for 6 years, on the commission for a total of 21 years. According to other sources, he is a native of the Montgomery area, owes his success in life to his marriage to the Anderson family, an old family that has been prominent since before the Civil War. Everybody agrees that "Tacky" (as he is called by his friends) is not too bright. The morning I talked with him he looked completely worn out; he answered my questions in a dull, absent kind of way relating the "line" mechanically. His exhaustion and tiredness with the situation stands in sharp contrast to Sellers' bright-eyed interest and brisk, businesslike approach.

I made no appointment with the Mayor, but dropped in and waited until he was free. His secretary asked if I were a newspaper reporter and when I said "No," remarked that the Mayor had already had enough press conferences for the day and was seeing no more reporters. "With all these reporters," she said, "he doesn't have the time to run the city any more." Presented myself to the Mayor as from Fisk, working on a study of Montgomery and interested in the bus situation. He said that he didn't have time to talk to me, for me to go and read the papers, everything was in the papers. I went ahead and began asking questions, which he answered to get rid of me.

HOLDEN: I saw the stand which the commission took several weeks ago, closing the door to further negotiations, and I want to know if there has been any change in the policy since that stand?
GAYLE: There has been no change in the commission's stand. The only way to stop it is for them to start riding the buses.
HOLDEN: I noticed King's statement in the paper this week that they might reopen negotiations for a settlement. Have they approached the commission?
GAYLE: There is nothing to negotiate. We offered them what they could have under the law and they refused to accept it. They can keep on walking until they decide to ride. The buses are there and they only cost 15 cents. If they will go back, the company will reduce it to 10 cents when this is over.
HOLDEN: Then the commission has definitely not reopened negotiations?
GAYLE: That's right. We have not and we do not intend to.
HOLDEN: As I understand it, the franchise renewal is still not final. Would you

be willing to lose the bus company rather than offer a compromise that the boycott leaders would accept?

GAYLE: There is no chance of losing the bus company. I just had a letter from the bus company this week and there is no chance of the franchise falling through. The transportation will be there when they want to use it. [. . .]

HOLDEN: Are there any circumstances under which you would reopen the negotiation with the boycott leaders?

GAYLE: None. We don't care if they never ride the buses again. They can keep on walking until they are ready to ride them under the terms we offered.

HOLDEN: We were interested in the background of the boycott, any incidents that led to it and anything else that might indicate something like this was coming.

GAYLE: We had no indication that it was coming. We didn't expect the boycott.

HOLDEN: There wasn't any trouble on the buses before, you hadn't had complaints that would lead you to expect something?

GAYLE: It started when the Parks woman refused to move. We had no indications that it was coming.

HOLDEN: Has anything like this ever happened before in Montgomery? You have been on the commission a long time, haven't you? You would know about it, if it had.

GAYLE: I have been on the commission 21 years and nothing of this type has ever happened before.

HOLDEN: How long have you been Mayor?

GAYLE: Six years.

HOLDEN: We were also interested in the leadership in the boycott—in knowing whether the leaders are recognized leaders who usually work on matters concerning the Negro community.

GAYLE: King never came to the commission before the bus strike. Some of the others had been there before in connection with the schools and the parks.

HOLDEN: What is the basic issue involved in the bus situation?

GAYLE: Segregation. They want to destroy our whole social fabric. We have laws that they want to ignore.

HOLDEN: When you said that statement publicly, the papers reported that you got a number of letters in response. At the time the papers reported, they said that the response was overwhelmingly favorable. Have letters or calls continued to come in, and has the trend remained favorable?

GAYLE: The response has been 100 to 1 favoring my stand.

HOLDEN: Could you tell me approximately how many letters, telegrams and calls you have received and where they come from?

GAYLE: I don't have time to get into that. There is a whole tableful of letters and wires—I don't know how many—more than I can keep up with.

HOLDEN: Where do they come from?

GAYLE: Most of them are local, but there are some from all over Alabama and from other parts of the country. There are some from California, some from Oregon and Illinois—from all over the country.

HOLDEN: Do you know how many are from local sources, and from outside the South?

GAYLE: No, we haven't counted them. It's all we can do to try to keep up with them as they come in.

HOLDEN: I saw in the paper where you joined the Citizens Council. Would you say that you have their full support in the bus situation?

GAYLE: What is it that you are asking me?

HOLDEN: I said that I noticed you have joined the Citizens Council and I assume that from that you are supporting them. I wonder if they are supporting you and the Commission fully. Are they 100% behind you?

GAYLE: Yes, we have the full support of the Citizens Council in this. They are working closely with us on it. You may have seen that they offered a reward along with the city commission in the bombings. They advocate peaceful, legal means of maintaining segregation and they are cooperating fully with the commission.

HOLDEN: In what way are they working on the situation?

GAYLE: They have offered a reward, as I mentioned.

HOLDEN: I wondered if they were doing anything else, perhaps through their membership?

GAYLE: I think you had better talk to them. I really don't know much about it.

HOLDEN: Do you think that there will be violence before this is settled? Do you think there is any danger of that?

GAYLE: No. I don't think so, I don't think there is any danger.

HOLDEN: Of course, there have already been the two bombings, and I have had the impression that people are very tense and afraid of what might happen. People seem to fear there is a great possibility there will be outbursts of violence.

GAYLE: We are working to keep calm and collected.

HOLDEN: How are you working?

GAYLE: Through civic groups, such as the Men of Montgomery.

HOLDEN: In what way are you working through them? What is your approach?

GAYLE: They are helping us try to stop rumors and check teen-age vandalism—things like that.

HOLDEN: Is the Men of Montgomery the only civic group that you are working with?

GAYLE: We are also working with the Ministerial Association and other civic groups.

HOLDEN: Have any of these civic groups discussed your stand with you—have any of them expressed an interest in reopening negotiations?

GAYLE: No.

HOLDEN: I thought perhaps the two bombings might have caused enough fear that people would want to settle it, even if it meant concessions.

(No comment from Gayle)

HOLDEN: Let me ask you about this. Has it had any effect on business?

GAYLE: We had one of the best Christmases we have ever had. Retail sales have been up.

HOLDEN: Was January a good month also?

GAYLE: January sales were low, but not appreciably lower than usual. January is always an off month for retail sales.

HOLDEN: I have talked with individual merchants who feel like the boycott has made their sales go down lower than usual.

GAYLE: They might tell you that, but business has been as good as usual and December was certainly a record month.

HOLDEN: I want to ask you about Maxwell Field. I understand that the setup at Maxwell is integrated, and I wondered if that has any effects on the situation in Montgomery, as far as segregation is concerned?

GAYLE: We don't have any trouble with boys from Maxwell. Montgomery enjoys the best relations with an army post than any city in the country. The people out at Maxwell say that quite frequently—(named Officer) made that statement at a dinner at the Chamber of Commerce just a few days ago.

HOLDEN: It looks to me like there would be some conflict there, with an integrated post and a segregated town. Don't the boys who make friends with Negroes on the base want to come into town with them and to do things together? When they come in on the bus, for example, do they want to sit together?

GAYLE: Of course, you have boys out there from all parts of the country, and some of them pal around with the niggers on the base. They are orientated to conform to the segregation laws in town and we don't have any trouble about that.

HOLDEN: It occurred to me that you might have trouble. One more thing, I get the impression people are surprised this has gone on as long as it has. How do you think it has lasted this long?

GAYLE: The money they are getting from the outside. They are getting enough money to furnish the niggers with free rides, and they like that.

HOLDEN: Where is the money coming from?

GAYLE: I don't know where it is coming from, but there's a lot of it coming from the outside. Why don't you ask them?

HOLDEN: Just one more question. What effect do you think that this will have on the city of Montgomery as far as business and industry locating here?

GAYLE: It won't have any. Business continues as usual and building is stable. There is no damage being done.

HOLDEN: It looks to me like this would give Montgomery a bad name and prospective business and industrial investors might not want to get into Montgomery because of this.

GAYLE: The publicity hasn't helped any, but I wouldn't say it has hurt us. You can check the records—sales, building, everything is goin' on at the usual pace.

PV-ARC-LNT.

Interview with a Prominent Local Attorney and White Citizens Council Leader and Sam Englehardt, by Anna Holden

DATE: February 8, 1956, 2:15 P.M.
OCCUPATION: Attorney
PLACE: Office, 21 S. Perry

General Statement: [*The attorney*] is about 38–40, comes from an established family in Montgomery. Everyone I mentioned him to said that he is a person who is considered respectable and that he commands prestige in the community. He is the general counsel for the Central Alabama White Citizens Council and on the board of directors of that organization. According to Bob Hughes, he is the chief organizer for Montgomery and was responsible for starting the ball rolling there. He was the temporary president before the organization got under way and [*Sam*] Englehardt was elected president. (Bob thought that the Central Alabama organization had been set up, rather than a county chapter, so that Englehardt could be pulled into the Montgomery organization. According to Bob, Macon County was not responding to the WCC ("the white people over there are scared of it"). Bob also said that [*the attorney*] is a one-time state senator and that he does a great deal of collection work among Negroes. Someone else said that he is a member of Rev. Thrasher's church.

I talked to [*the attorney*] in his office two days before the Eastland rally. Sen.

Englehardt was in his office when I arrived and was in and out while we talked. Both, in fact, were in and out, as they were receiving and making phone calls about the WCC rally, going over details as they came up. A young man introduced as "Griffin" came in toward the end of the interview, and I saw him again at the rally, doing the leg work or carrying messages to the band, the press men and the TV camera men. Englehardt had very little to say during my interview with [the attorney] to me, except to ask me questions about myself and Fisk, though [the attorney] invited him to join our conversation several times. [The attorney] took my interviewing him as a joke, more or less, and seemed to get a kick out of the fact that someone like myself, from Fisk, would come and get his views. Englehardt did not share [his] sporting spirit and looked on me as the enemy invading his camp. Englehardt's presence had a restraining effect on [the attorney], and at several points [he] quieted down or dropped a point at a look from Englehardt.

In comparing the two men, I would guess that Englehardt is much more serious about the fight for white supremacy than [the attorney]—in any case, I think they would be fighting in a different spirit. Englehardt impressed me as a much soberer personality, with a deeper concern. He is an older man, probably about his mid or late 50's. He was dressed in a conservative gray business suit. I think this is all too sacred for Englehardt to joke about. [The attorney], on the other hand, seemed to take it in a lighter spirit. I would guess that the excitement, the publicity, and the empire would appeal to him. [The attorney] is, apparently, a sportier type than Englehardt. He was dressed in a tweed sport coat and slacks that blended with his coat, believe he had on some kind of gabardine sport shirt, without a tie, had a crew cut.

[The attorney] is in law practice alone, has a nicely furnished, carpeted inside office, and two outside rooms that look kind of beat up and far removed from decorating and redoing. There was an old man at one of the desks in the first outside office when I first went in—he seemed to be working there. No secretary around. Presented myself as a member of the staff of Fisk University, working on a study on Montgomery. Said we were interested in the bus situation and that I understood he had served on the Mayor's committee; that we wanted to get as good an understanding as we could.

[Attorney]: Come on inside the office and we can talk there. Senator Englehardt is in my office now and you can talk to him, too. (Ushers me into his office; Englehardt is seated at his desk, getting ready to make a phone call.) Sam, there is a young lady here from Fisk University in Nashville who wants to talk to me and I told her she could come in here and talk to both of us. Miss Holman, this is Senator Englehardt.

ENGLEHARDT: Fisk University? That's a colored school, isn't it?

HOLDEN: Yes, it is. I am on staff there.

ENGLEHARDT: You take white students there now, don't you?

HOLDEN: Yes. It has been opened to white students since the Supreme Court decision.

ENGLEHARDT: How many do you have?

HOLDEN: I don't know the exact number, but I think about five or six.

ENGLEHARDT: Is the president a white man?

HOLDEN: Dr. [*Charles*] Johnson is the president. He is a Negro. (Laughing) I don't mind telling you about Fisk, but I did come here to ask you some questions.

[*Attorney*]: You said you wanted to ask me about the bus boycott. What did you want to know?

HOLDEN: Well, we are interested in some general information about how it started and how it is affecting the community, but I wanted to talk to you particularly about the Mayor's committee. I was not here at the time the committee had its meeting and I thought that if I talked to various members of the committee it would help me to understand the problem that the committee faces and the thinking behind their recommendations.

[*Attorney*]: (Laughs) Well, you aren't going to like anything I am going to say but I don't really mind talking to you.

HOLDEN: It doesn't really seem to matter, does it? Say what you please and I will write it down. That's what I'm here for, to get everybody's view.

[*Attorney*]: Who have you talked to so far?

HOLDEN: On the [*mayor's*] committee, I have talked with Dr. [*Henry*] Parker and Dr. [*G. Stanley*] Frazer.

[*Attorney*]: They have already told you what I would tell you.

HOLDEN: You will probably bring in points that they overlooked. Different people remember different things.

[*Attorney*]: Well, you probably know by now that it was started by NAACP agitators. Ninety-five per cent of the Nigras here were happy with things the way they were and are now the victims of their exploitation—they didn't want this. NAACP leadership forced it on them. The Mayor's committee was picked to meet with them and work out a compromise, but we couldn't get anywhere. I wasted seven hours of my time in those meetings. They came into them with a mimeographed sheet with their stand printed on it and they never departed from it. We came into it willing to compromise, but they wouldn't give an inch. They wanted first come, first serve without any regard to the state segregation law and that was it. We offered them the whole bus except for one seat in the back and one in the front, but they wouldn't take that. So that's what the committee did—wasted a lot of time. Has anybody called the statute making a boycott illegal to your attention? Have you seen that law?

HOLDEN: I have heard it mentioned several times, but I haven't read the law, if that's what you mean.

[*Attorney*]: Wait a minute, I'll show it to you. (Gets down volume of Alabama Code and turns to section.) Here it is. Do you want the reference?

HOLDEN: Yes, while you have it there, I might as well get it.

[*Attorney*]: (hands me book) You'd better know what that means.

HOLDEN: 1940 Code of Ala., Title 14, Ch. 20, Section 54. "Misdemeanor for two or more persons to enter into any conspiracy to deprive. . . ." I knew there was such a law, but I hadn't heard anything about anyone trying to enforce it.

[*Attorney*]: You'll hear plenty about it when Monday rolls around. The grand jury goes in session Monday and you'll hear plenty about it then. They will be indicting all the Nigras who are pulling the thing.

HOLDEN: They are a little slow about it, aren't they? I would think they would have done this long before now.

[*Attorney*]: They haven't been in session. That's why this thing was timed like it was. (Gets calendar) The grand jury met on Nov. 7th and it hasn't been in session since then.

HOLDEN: The November session was over before the boycott started?

[*Attorney*]: Oh, yes. It only meets for about two weeks and it was over when they started. They knew they would be Scot free until February 13. They probably thought it would be over by then.

HOLDEN: That's interesting. I didn't realize there was that much time between sessions. Now, getting back to the committee. There were other demands besides the seating arrangements, weren't there?

[*Attorney*]: Two others—courtesy and Nigra drivers. The committee held no brief on courtesy—all races are entitled to that. (Laughs) We don't hate the Nigras or want to be mean to them or anything like that. Certainly drivers should be polite to them, and the bus company wanted them to be. After all, they are in business.

HOLDEN: I wondered if there was any evidence that the drivers had been discourteous to them? Were people aware that anything was wrong on the buses, that they were being mistreated?

[*Attorney*]: I don't ride the bus myself, but I hadn't heard anything about it. Our own girl never said anything about being treated discourteously. She did come to work late all the time and when I said something to her about it, she told me that the bus wouldn't stop and pick her up—that it would go on by and leave her. I went down to the bus company to find about it and they said that they couldn't run so many buses during peak hours and that the buses would only hold so many people. What they said sounded logical to me and I took their word that that was the reason they would pass people by sometimes and not stop. Of course that didn't help her get to work on time. I don't know what she's doing about getting to work now, I haven't even asked her, but she has been on time since the boycott started.

HOLDEN: I thought perhaps there was discussion of that point at the meeting.

[*Attorney*]: The bus company did state that more whites than Nigras were arrested by the drivers for misconduct on the buses. I don't doubt that some of the drivers were rude at times, but I don't think they were any ruder to the Nigras than to the whites.

HOLDEN: The other request was for drivers, wasn't it?

[*Attorney*]: They wanted forty percent Nigra drivers—to match the population ratio. That was out of the question. The bus company is a private business and you can't tell them who they can hire.

HOLDEN: I want to be clear on the seating demand. Did the first come, first serve basis they asked for mean they would want that on a non-segregated basis?

[*Attorney*]: They said that they wanted it on a front to back, back to front basis, but what they are out for is full integration. Hell, we don't care whether they have two seats or ten seats—this bus boycott is piddling stuff. Everybody knows what the NAACP is after—complete integration, even to intermarriage. [. . .]

HOLDEN: I am interested in how this whole thing started. I mean, this probably isn't the first time the driver asked a Negro to move on the bus.

[*Attorney*]: It was a plant to get a case. The Parks woman tried five or six times to create an incident before they finally arrested her—I got that from the drivers. You know she used the white toilet at Montgomery Fair [*department store*]—she worked there and they rehired her. Then she used the white toilets. You can see what she is after.

HOLDEN: Let me ask you this. I know you have already told me that the first come, first serve seating they asked for is illegal under the present law. But suppose it weren't, do you think it would work? I mean on the front to back, back to front basis that they asked for.

[*Attorney*]: It would create riot and havoc. White people are afraid of integration, and they have said time and time again that integration is what they want. King himself said that in a statement in the newspaper. He said they would not stop fighting until they got it and they made a mistake not to ask for integration at the beginning of the boycott. Complete integration—intermarriage and all—is what the NAACP wants.

HOLDEN: How do most white people feel about this?

[*Attorney*]: They are scared to death. Most of them are afraid there will be violence if this thing keeps on. They feel sorry for the Nigras who are walking and suffering and are afraid to do anything to end it. You know how they have kept them off the buses, don't you? They have goon squads take them out and work them over. I don't mean they work everybody over—most of them can be kept in line by threats and intimidation. But I know of two cases where they worked on two of them—beat them up. One was the cook of a personal friend of mine. Those are exceptions, of course. But that keeps the rest of them afraid.

HOLDEN: Has anybody been able to do anything about the intimidation, anything to stop it?

[Attorney]: What could you do? You are fighting a phantom. You can't find out who is doing it or anything to work with. When you can't find out anything about it, there is nothing that you can do.

HOLDEN: What about your organization, the Citizens Council? Are you doing anything on the bus boycott?

[Attorney]: We ran some ads, that's all we've done. We ran some ads beginning about December 20, asking all citizens to ride the buses. We asked Nigras as well as whites to support the buses.

HOLDEN: Have you done anything else?

[Attorney]: No, that's all. We have been building up our membership.

HOLDEN: What is your membership—how many people are members?

[Attorney]: Nearly 10,000.

HOLDEN: Is that Montgomery membership?

[Attorney]: The Central Alabama Council. But most of them are in Montgomery. We only had about 165 in November—less than 200.

HOLDEN: And you haven't done anything about the bus situation except publish the ads?

[Attorney]: That's all.

HOLDEN: I have heard that you are doing some other things. I heard, for one thing, you have tried to get people to take economic sanctions against Negroes who are taking part in the boycott.

ENGLEHARDT: (who came in just before we started talking about the Citizens Council) The White Citizens Council doesn't work through economic sanctions.

HOLDEN: I had the impression that you did. I don't know anything about the organization except what I have read in the papers, and I had the impression from the papers that you worked that way.

ENGLEHARDT: Well, we don't. The papers have given people a false picture of the Citizens Council. Don't believe anything about the Citizens Council you read in the newspaper.

HOLDEN: That is the only way I had of knowing anything about it so far, but I believe in checking things at the source and while I am talking with you I would like to find out how you do work.

ENGLEHARDT: We definitely don't use economic sanctions. ([*The attorney*] gets a copy of the constitution and gives it to me.)

HOLDEN: Well, how do you work? This is rather general.

[*Attorney*]: (after look from Englehardt) Did you come here to talk about the Citizens Council or the bus boycott?

HOLDEN: I am interested in the relationship between the two. I am assuming that you would work on this bus situation in the same way you would approach other situations. So if I know your general approach, it will give me an idea of how you would be handling the bus boycott.

[*Attorney*]: We are an educational organization—you might say an eleemosynary [*charitable*] organization. (Laughs) We are non-political, too.

HOLDEN: I suppose you would have to be chartered as an eleemosynary organization—that's the way that you would be classified under a state charter, isn't it?

[*Attorney*]: We aren't chartered.

HOLDEN: You're not? I was going by Georgia law. I lived there before I moved to Nashville and I know that organizations like the Klan had to be chartered.

[*Attorney*]: You don't have to in Alabama.

HOLDEN: I didn't mean to get off on that. You were saying that the Citizens Council is an educational organization. How do you carry out your educational program?

[*Attorney*]: Well, on this local thing, we published the ads and I have tried to point out the importance of supporting the bus company. Individual members try to persuade people in talking to them personally. I have talked it over with my yardman, for instance. I haven't discussed it with our girl yet, but I did talk to the yardman and told him why he should ride the bus. He said he is afraid to ride and I can't talk him into riding it. But we work like that—other people are talking to them, too.

HOLDEN: I heard that you are asking people to fire their maids or suspend them until they went back to the buses.

[*Attorney*]: Hell, you can't get people to do anything like that. I told you, I haven't even discussed this with our girl. I'm still paying her the same salary and I gave her a better Christmas present than I gave my wife. She couldn't see to look up numbers in the phone book and I kept telling her she should get some new glasses—she would hold the book way out from her. I finally told her I would get her a pair for a Christmas present, thinking that they would cost around $15. She got a new pair of bifocals and I ended up paying over $30 for them. (Laughs). You see how bad we treat them? I haven't even asked her how she comes and goes.

HOLDEN: Does the WCC have any plans to take any further action in the boycott?

[*Attorney*]: No.

HOLDEN: Do you think you will be doing anything?

[*Attorney*]: I don't know. I couldn't say. We have a board of directors and it's up to them to decide what we will do.

HOLDEN: Would you tell me this. Is this the sort of problem that your organization would be interested in taking action on? Is this the sort of problem your group would be interested in tackling?

[*Attorney*]: I really couldn't say. Your guess is as good as mine. We have a good cross-section of manufacturers, businessmen, lawyers, and working men and I don't have the slightest idea what they will decide about anything.

(About this time [*the attorney*] either started talking on the phone for a few minutes or went out of the room.)

ENGLEHARDT: Where is your home, Miss Holman? (They started calling me that at first and I didn't correct them.)

HOLDEN: Ocala, Florida. It's in the central part of the state. My father farms there.

ENGLEHARDT: Where did you do your college work?

HOLDEN: At one of the state universities—Florida State University in Tallahassee.

ENGLEHARDT: Have you always lived in the South?

HOLDEN: Yes. I worked in Atlanta before I moved to Nashville.

ENGLEHARDT: Do you mind telling me how you happened to take a job at a place like Fisk University?

HOLDEN: Not at all. I don't know if you know very much about Fisk, but it has a very good social science department. That is the reason I was interested in working there.

([*Attorney*] is back on the job now.)

[*Attorney*]: Well, is there anything else? I told you I could give you some time, but I can't spend the whole afternoon on this.

HOLDEN: I think I have covered everything I wanted to. You have been very generous with your time, and I appreciate it.

[*Attorney*]: Have I been courteous to you? Have I been kind?

HOLDEN: Oh, yes, indeed. No complaints on that score.

[*Attorney*]: I don't want you to go away from here saying that you weren't well received. Well, if you are through asking me questions, there are some that I would like to ask you. (Pulls out a mimeographed or typewritten sheet with one full page of single spaced questions and some more on the other side.) The first group were all aimed at creating the impression that the white race had discovered and invented everything that is important to modern life. The second group was designed to create the impression that Negroes had *not* discovered and invented anything. The third group was to establish the impression that the Negro in America is a great financial and social burden for whites. He rushed through the questions rapidly, not expecting me to answer, and I smiled in response to his pauses.) What race invented the steam engine? What race invented electricity? What race invented the airplane? What race discovered the laws of gravity? Why is it that the Nigra race has not developed its own culture? Why is it that the Nigra race has made no contribution to civilization? Why is it that Nigras commit — percent of the crimes committed in this country? — percent of the rapes? — percent of the school funds? — percent of the welfare funds? Why is it that they pay only — percent of the taxes and spend — percent of the public funds? (The percentages, except for the tax percentage, were very high—in the 60's, 70's and 80's. I don't remember the exact figures, didn't get them down at the time.) That is something for you to think about. There's one more question I want to ask you. Would you marry a Nigra?

HOLDEN: (Laughing) I haven't married anybody so far, white or black.

[*Attorney*]: That's not what I asked you. Would you be willing to marry a Nigra?

HOLDEN: Why don't you ask me whether I would be willing to marry a soldier or a farmer? I am not under the impression that people marry on the basis of these large categories.

[*Attorney*]: Now, you still aren't answering my question. Would you marry a Nigra?

HOLDEN: I am answering you by saying that is not the kind of question a person can answer "Yes" or "No." How do you know who you would marry and who you wouldn't until the situation comes up? People marry individuals, they don't marry because a person is a teacher or a member of some large group like that. [. . .]

[*Attorney*]: All other things being equal, would you? [. . .] You're young, honey, but you're off on the wrong road, and you'd better think about this. Here you are working in a Nigra college. You'd better ask yourself that question and answer it. If you can't answer it now, you'd better hurry and make up your mind, because intermarriage is what is at the heart of the whole thing. Tell me this. If you let your children go to school with Nigras and eat with them and play with them and go to the same social functions and work with them, how can you teach them that it's wrong to marry them? (Smiled at him, didn't answer)

[*Attorney*]: Well I see you aren't going to answer any of my questions, so you might as well be on your way. Now I meant that. You'd better think about whether you'd marry a Nigra, because that is the whole thing in a nutshell.

PV-ARC-LNT.

March ... 7 ...

Unlike most of his fellow leaders and followers, King joined the bus boycott committed to a qualified understanding of Christian nonviolence. If his interpretation of it had been rooted mainly in the New Testament, it might have looked, from the outset, more like the Gandhian nonviolence espoused by Bayard Rustin and Glenn Smiley. But King's faith-based nonviolence was anchored in the Hebrew Scriptures and had been tempered by Reinhold Niebuhr's persuasive conception of evil. The young preacher's tentative nonviolent philosophy differed from that of Gandhi and his radical pacifist disciples in that he faced sin squarely, without illusion, like the Hebrew prophets. He grasped that love could not endure without power to defeat the evil that revolts against love—and that this power of justice and righteousness required coercion as well as suasion.

In his mind King was not being inconsistent when to Rustin he defended keeping guns in his house and asserted that his concept of nonviolence might not preclude use of violence in self-defense as a last resort. The gun might be needed still as an instrument of justice, if it was the only way to keep love alive. Largely through Rustin's and Smiley's tutoring (and from others like Lillian Smith and Harris Wofford), King came to reject all use of violence, and he refashioned the love and justice dialectic, replacing armed force with "soul force." Nevertheless, throughout the bus boycott and beyond, his nonviolent philosophy changed inflection depending on his audience. To black mass meetings, for example, he kept the Old Testament stress on the ubiquity of evil (white supremacy as the devil), while to largely white, northern audiences he more often evoked faith in white redemption.

King's March trial on conspiracy charges reflected his ambivalence. While Gandhi used his court trials to extend his nonviolent ethic and asked judges for the maximum sentence, King and colleagues answered questions evasively and kept nonviolent principles out of the courtroom. This legal realpolitik owed partly to the training and mindset of his NAACP lawyers, partly to his realistic fear of southern jails.

Galvanized by the conspiracy trial, mass meetings fired up the movement's energy. The weekly or semiweekly church gatherings shared news, information, and personal testimonies of forbearance and small victory; raised money; praised people's contributions and sacrifice; debated strategy and tactics; determined policy; fortified courage, morale, and hope. For participants mass meetings manifested the holy spirit. They conjured the beloved community. They transubstantiated democracy from "thin paper" to "thick action," revealing its grace and glory inside the steepled places of black Montgomery.

Report on MIA Mass Meeting, March 1, by Donald T. Ferron

I arrived at the Church at 5:07 and although it was comparatively crowded, the number of people who were there then and who subsequently arrived was far less, approx. 1500, than at the mass meeting at Holt St. Baptist Church on Monday (Feb. 27). (I tried to locate Rev. Wilson, Pastor of Holt St. Church to find the seating capacity of his church, but unfortunately he was out of town. The consensus was that there were between 3500 and 4000 people present, and a collection of over $8000.) It might be interesting to note that this marked the first time that I had observed any commercializing going on at any of the mass meetings. At least two persons were present who were selling "Jet" and the "Pittsburgh Courier," on the steps of the church. As I entered the main auditorium I recognized that Hal had already arrived, so I proceeded to the balcony where the atmosphere appeared less formal, where I might hear something of value. Another occurrence which might be worth mentioning was the prayer given by a young boy who was close to 8 or 9 years of age. It was the type of prayer that is typical among, what appears to me to be, the less articulate ministers. It was following that incident that another prayer was given and emotionalism, hysterics captivated a woman of about 40 years of age who was seated not more than ten feet from me. It was at 7:03, during the singing of "When the Saints Go Marching In," that Rev. King, followed by Rev. Abernathy, entered the main auditorium; Rev. King presided during the meeting.

Hymn: "Leaning on the Everlasting Arm" (with Rev. Abernathy standing and facing the audience, and directing the singing as might a choir director)

3rd Psalm

Scripture: Rev. U. J. Fields—"Remember that God is our Shepherd. Our Shepherd will never lead us astray."

Hymn: "Jesus Keep Me Near the Cross"

Prayer: Rev. B. D. Lambert. It was during the prayer that two interesting developments took place. Rev. Lambert impresses me as one who resorts to emotionalism to capture his congregation. This was evinced by his manner-isms, his shouting presentation which later flowed into a type of "singing prayer." It was at this point that the audience began to complain (but not so loudly) by making such comments as "oh! oh!," "oh, my!," "Not again!," and "Why doesn't he shut up?" The second development was what appeared to me to be a state of discomfort, uneasiness, restlessness on the part of Rev. King. I was in the balcony facing Rev. King and observed him crossing and uncross-ing his legs, placing first one and then the other hand over his face. Unless I'm greatly mistaken, he mustered all of his resources to prevent his smiles from leading to open laughter. It was comical to me to see him "fighting" with himself and to note his definite relief once the prayer had ended.

Hymn: "What A Friend We Have in Jesus"

Rev. King: "We have among us tonight a number of distinguished guests. I must decrease that they might increase. God is using Montgomery as a prov-ing ground. He will cause democratic conditions to stand where they should stand. We have now new dignity and awareness. We are God's children. We're walking because we're tired of being suppressed politically. We're walking because we're tired of being suppressed economically. We're walking because we're tired of having [been] segregated and discriminated. Freedom is the just claim of all men. As we walk we're going to walk with love in our hearts. Somebody has to have sense enough to cut off the hate. The power of love is very strong; love your enemies. The whole armour of God is the weapon of love and the breastplate of righteousness. There is something about love that transforms; we're going to keep on in the same spirit."

Rev. [R. J.] Glasco: Observations from the Transportation Committee

"We're interested in seeing more drivers; we need more cars." Rev. Glasco asked "those who own cars raise your hands," and "those who drive for the pool raise your hands." More than three times the number of hands were raised in response to the former question than to the latter. "Some people are going to the dispatch stations who have only a few blocks to go. Cooperate to the extent that if you have only a few blocks there are those who go way on the other side of town. Those who go a short distance, please walk!" On Saturday at 7:00 P.M. there will be a "meeting for the drivers at the Citizens Club." There will be a meeting with the drivers after this meeting; "some stations aren't being covered."

Rev. King: Briefly reiterates the importance of cooperating with the transportation system, announces that membership cards to the Montgomery Improvement Ass'n. are being issued free of charge in the balcony.

Rev. Abernathy—Announcements:

"Are you tired" [*Response:*] "No-o-o!" "Are you weary?" R. "No-o-o!" "Do you feel like turning around?" R. "No-ooo!" "Are you still with the movement?" R. "Yes-s-s-s!!" "If all the cars break down and go to the garage, what are you going to do?" R. "Walk!" "Are you still praying?" R. "Yes-s-s-s!" "We must keep God at the forefront. It takes strength to walk to and from work, and only God can give us that strength. We aren't going to leave Montgomery; we're going to enjoy freedom, and right here in Montgomery." Rev. Abernathy relates a joke someone had told him. Commenting on the "Heart of Dixie" on Alabama license plates somebody said, "I didn't know Alabama had a heart," to which the other party responded, "It does, but it has heart trouble." To which the answer was given, we have a "heart specialist, the Supreme Court. For the past 10, 15, 20 years, Negroes in Montgomery have been pushed around; we're just tired. We're just going to keep our dime in our pocket."— Laughter, applause. Rev. Abernathy makes notice of the appeal through March to join NAACP, with a goal of at least 8000 new members.

Spiritual: "Nobody Knows the Trouble I've Seen"

Pep Talk and Inspirational Address from "one of the most militant men we know, a man who loves people," who just returned from N. Carolina—

Rev. S. S. Seay: "Dr. King, fellow ministers, distinguished visitors, friends— this is a weary night for me. I planned to stay at home. I allowed these young men to push me around because I believe in them. I don't stick with people I don't believe in." Speaking of Rev. King, Dr. Seay said, "He's a Ph.D. with common sense and humility," and not many people have both. "One thing we've learned is that you need a leader. You have to make your leader; a young man with potentiality." We must "share the responsibilities of our objectives." Dr. Seay relates at this point a story he had read in which there were several children of a poor family which had but a glass of milk for all. The first person to drink asked "How deep shall I drink?" So the mother marked on the glass where he should stop. The boy didn't drink past the line although he knew that he could before he would be stopped; his conscience was at work. Dr. Seay said he wondered sometimes, "should I go out and drive not knowing whether I would be arrested or not? I had my truck downtown today and was in a hurry, when I saw a lady walking when the question came to my mind, 'How deep shall I drink?' If you're riding when you could walk, ask yourself three times, 'How deep?'" Double applause, series of handshakes, congratulations until each person (there were approx. 20) on the platform had shaken his hand.

Spiritual: "Steal Away"

Rev. King: Introduction of Guests [. . .]

PV-ARC-LNT.

Rev. M. L. King Jr.
Dexter Ave. Baptist Church

Dear Sir.

I'm a reader of The [*Pittsburgh*] Courier and get it also. Seeing where you were asking for help in order to keep up the fight. Sorry I can't send no money I were hurt year before last and haven't been able to work since. But I'm sending 2 pairs of Shoes some of my better ones to two of the ladies who can wear them and tell them may God bless all of you and I'm with you even if I'm so far off. The prayers of the ones who are pure in heart are heard by the lord.

I've been able to send money each time the Naacp ask for it but once. And maybe I'll be able to send some later on. I do pray So.

May God bless all of you and what ever you do keep up the fight, and let them know God is Mightier than Man.

Please let me know when you get them.

From one of the race
Mrs Earline Browning
502 So. 14th St.
Boise Idaho.

MLKP-MBU: Box 91 (March 6, 1956).

After abruptly leaving Montgomery at the end of February, Rustin continued to aid and abet the bus boycott from a distance. On March 7, King met with him and an associate, journalist and CORE activist William Worthy, in Birmingham. Rustin sent a report on the meeting to his New York colleagues, including Randolph, James Farmer, and A. J. Muste.

Notes of a Conference: How Outsiders Can Strengthen the Montgomery Nonviolent Protest

The Rev. Mr. King is very happy to receive outside help. However, he is sensitive to the effort on the part of white people in general in the South and the newspapers and vested interests in particular to give evidence to their feeling that New Yorkers, northern agitators and communists are in reality leading the fight. It was his view therefore that all communications, ideas, and programs that can be developed, as they directly pertain to activities in Montgomery, come through him or Mr. Nixon rather than directly to the Improvement Association. *It was agreed that this was a wise and necessary procedure.* The Rev. Mr. King is aware that the struggle for equality is an American and not a sectional problem. However, strategically the Improvement Association must give the appearance of developing all of the ideas and strategies used in the struggle.

There are three different kinds of services that those of us who believe in nonviolence can offer. They are:

a. Suggestions and plans for nonviolent education functionally applied to the bus protest.

b. Techniques for fortifying the will to resist in Montgomery by nonviolent means.

c. Overall education to spread the idea of nonviolent resistance.

Specifically, to deal with each in turn, there was agreement to proceed with the following:

a. 1. Encourage visitors to Montgomery for short stays. Such people as Amiya Chakravarty, Jim Robinson, A. J. Muste, could observe the situation and write reports for us to pass on to King.

2. Younger people like Pauli Murray, Wilson Head, Dick Starhouse, Jim Farmer, etc., who could go in for short visits and make suggestions on technique.

3. Raising of funds for specific nonviolent literature in Montgomery. (AJ has a pamphlet that might be helpful.)

4. Ghostwriters for King who cannot find time at present to write articles, speeches, etc., himself.

b. 1. Keeping an eye on their news coverage and suggesting ideas on what is important and when to emphasize certain elements in the struggle.

2. Developing in other parts of the country sympathetic protest action by many kinds of groups. (Chicago ministers in relation to the bus company is one such idea: A White House demonstration is another.)

3. Funds and ideas for reaching various segments of the population with

the importance of nonviolence. Two ideas have emerged: one, a poster contest, and two, a high-school essay contest on the Importance of Non-Violence in the Negro's Struggle for Equality.

4. The project to collect 50 bicycles from all over the country to relieve the car pool.
5. Responsibility to order the pin-symbol in New York.
6. Responsibility for printing 30,000 copies of the song, with a short statement on nonviolence on the back of it.
7. Responsibility for a revolving bail fund if it becomes necessary.
8. The preparation of a pamphlet to be published by the MIA.

c. The establishment of a Workshop on nonviolent resistance to be held in June or July in Atlanta to which would be invited *leaders* from many areas of tension in the deep South. The purpose would be to explore the *Philosophy, Theory and Practice of Nonviolence*. The staff would include some five or six leaders in various fields mentioned. Nixon and King will participate and bring several younger leaders. Their sharing in the seminar on *Practice* could have a very important effect on other groups exploring method. Perhaps King's father, one of the most important ministers in Atlanta, or Benjamin Mays could act as host. At any rate, King is all for bringing this off.

These are just a few ideas that were discussed on March 7. But I jot them down because I believe they reveal that an *ad hoc* committee is essential if these and other ideas are to be carried out with any semblance of order and efficiency.

BRP-DLC.

Lillian Smith (1897–1966) was a novelist, essayist, educator, and civil rights activist from southern Georgia. Her controversial 1944 novel, *Strange Fruit*, about an interracial love affair in the Deep South, had been banned in Boston and Detroit; it sold three million copies and was translated into fifteen languages. Committed to nonviolent racial reform, she had been active in CORE since the 1940s.

March 10, 1956

Dear Dr. King:

I have with a profound sense of fellowship and admiration been watching your work in Montgomery. I cannot begin to tell you how effective it seems to me, although I must confess I have watched it only at long distance.

It is the right way. Only through persuasion, love, goodwill, and firm nonviolent resistance can the change take place in our South. Perhaps in a northern city this kind of nonviolent, persuasive resistance would either be totally misinterpreted or else find nothing in the whites which could be appealed to. But in our South, the whites, too, share the profoundly religious symbols you are using and respond to them on a deep level of their hearts and minds. Their imaginations are stirred: the waters are troubled.

You seem to be going at it in such a wise way. I want to come down as soon as I can and talk quietly with you about it. For I have nothing to go on except television reports and newspaper reports. But these have been surprisingly sympathetic to the 40,000 Negroes in Montgomery who are taking part in this resistance movement. But I have been in India twice; I followed the Gandhian movement long before it became popular in this country. I, myself, being a Deep South white, reared in a religious home and the Methodist church realize the deep ties of common songs, common prayer, common symbols that bind our two races together on a religio-mystical level, even as another brutally mythic idea, the concept of White Supremacy, tears our two people apart.

Ten years ago, I wrote Dr. Benjamin Mays in Atlanta suggesting that the Negroes begin a non-violent religious movement. But the time had not come for it, I suppose. Now it is here; now it has found you and others perhaps, too, in Montgomery who seem to be steering it wisely and well.

I want to help you with money just as soon as I can; I cannot, just now; I have had cancer for three years and have been unable to make much of a living during this time; also have found it an expensive illness. My home, also, was burned this winter by two young white boys; and this fire destroyed all my writings, manuscripts, work in progress, books, records, 7000 letters on race relations etc. etc. But I will have a turn of luck soon, I hope, and just as soon as I do I shall send your group some money.

In lieu of money, I send my encouragement and just a spoonful of advice: don't let outsiders come in and ruin your movement. This kind of thing has to be indigenous; it has to be kept within the boundaries of the local situation. You know the fury a northern accent arouses in the confused South—especially if that accent goes along with a white face. Keep the northern do-gooders, sincere and honest as they may be, out; tell them to help you with their publicity in the North, giving you a sympathetic and honest press; tell them to send money if they are able to do so; tell them to try to use some of these methods in their northern communities. But don't, please, my friend, let them come down and ruin what you are doing so well. It will then seem to the country a "conspiracy" instead of a spontaneous religio-social movement. It has had a tremendous effect on the conscience of the people everywhere. But it won't have, if these people come in.

Dr. Homer Jack has written a most sympathetic news-letter about his visit. I was glad he wrote it. But I think his advice for northern "experts" in non-violence to go down and help is unwise. You can't be an expert in non-violence; it is like being a saint or an artist: each person grows his own skill and expertness. I think Howard Thurman could be of help, perhaps, to you. He is truly a great man; warm, deeply religious. Bayard Rustin is a fine man, too. Whoever comes should come only on invitation and should give only quiet advice. Except Howard Thurman. Mr Thurman, as I said, is a truly great religious leader. Your congregation and that of other ministers in Montgomery would respond to him. He would encourage them in numerous ways and his advice would be wise and skilled. I think, instead of coming, if these leaders of CORE (with whom I have worked for years) would write you letters; send messages of encouragement to your group that would in the end help more than anything else. You have the awe and respect of many southern whites at present; they are genuinely touched and amazed at the discipline, the self-control, the dignity, the sweetness and goodness and courage and firmness of your group. It would break my heart were so-called "outsiders" to ruin it all. The white South is irrational about this business of "outsiders."

But please give your group a message from me: Tell them that Lillian Smith respects and admires what they are doing. Tell them, please, that I am deeply humbled by the goodwill, the self-discipline, the courage, the wisdom of this group of Montgomery Negroes. Tell them that I, too, am working as hard as I can to bring insight to the white group; to try to open their hearts to the great harm that segregation inflicts not only on Negroes but on white people too. Tell them, that I hope and pray that they will keep their resistance on a high spiritual level of love and quiet courage; for these are the only way that a real change of heart and mind can come to our South.

Sincerely,
Lillian Smith

MLKP-MBU: Box 65.

Human rights leader and former First Lady Eleanor Roosevelt commended the bus boycott in her widely syndicated newspaper column.

"My Day," by Eleanor Roosevelt

NEW YORK, MARCH 12—I think everyone must be impressed by the dignity and calmness with which the boycott of the bus companies in Montgomery, Alabama, has been carried on by the Negroes. Gandhi's theory of nonviolence seems to have been learned very well. [. . .]

Eleanor Roosevelt's My Day, vol. 3 (Mahwah, N.J.: Pharos Books, 1991), p. 87.

March 12, 1956

Rev. Homer Jack
Unitarian Church of Evanston
1405 Chicago Avenue
Evanston, Illinois

Dear Homer:

Thanks for your report of Montgomery. It confirms what I had understood. I cannot help, however, disagreeing with one of your suggestions.

I do not think it good from all I have heard to send Northerners into that Montgomery situation especially as on your own showing the Southern Negroes are handling it so well. I doubt if I should urge those Negroes to invite Northerners and they ought to use mighty good judgment if they are to invite any. It would, for instance, in my judgment, be a great mistake for them to invite Chakravarty, a Hindu, in view of the temper of the white population.

This, by the way, was the unanimous opinion, before your letter came, of a numerously attended conference at Phil Randolph's office. I think the use of field workers for organizations such as you mention in the South generally would have to be very carefully managed but I can see some use for them if they are the right people and go about their job well.

The Powell idea [*national day of support for the bus boycott*] is excellent, as we agreed, and we asked Jim Farmer to correlate activity. Powell blows off on his own without consultation too much. Especially I want to caution against the use of Bayard Rustin. He is entirely too vulnerable on his record—and I do not mean his record as a c.o. [*conscientious objector*]—if any trouble should arise and would, therefore, greatly handicap Southern Negroes who would use him in a critical situation.

Sincerely yours,
Norman Thomas

NTP-NN.

March 15, 1956

Mr. Norman Thomas
112 East 19th Street
New York 3, New York

Dear Norman Thomas,

Thank you for your letter. Yes, northerners must be careful about what they do in the South, but if southern Negroes invite Northerners, I think it is appropriate that they make themselves available to go. For the southern Negroes will be criticized mightily in any case.

For all the problems of Bayard Rustin, I can attest that he did a very competent job with the Negro leadership in Montgomery. In fact, he did a necessary job which nobody else apparently had the foresight to do: to help indoctrinate the Negro leadership into some of the techniques of Gandhism. [. . .]

Cordially,
[*signed*] Homer
Homer A. Jack

NTP-NN.

As King's trial approached, with its anticipated windfall of publicity, the Strategy Committee urged the executive board to exercise tighter control over public speakers and press statements to ensure that the leadership would speak with a unified voice.

Recommendations of MIA Strategy Committee, March 14

It was agreed by common consent in a called meeting of the Strategy Committee that a recommendation be made to the Executive Committee that each speaker who goes away to represent the Montgomery Improvement Association will follow a given pattern prepared by a committee for such specific speeches or submit his speech in writing to the speakers' bureau.

Under no circumstance must that speaker hold a press conference. A copy of that speech may be given to the press, but nothing more.

This committee also agreed to recommend that the presiding and participation at mass meetings be rotated so that others may be given a chance.

This committee further recommends that all indicted persons let the lawyers handle the legal cases coming up Monday.

2. The lawyers know the score and are prepared to defend the indicted group.

[3.] What we should accept to go back to the bus was discussed and the committee recommends

1. That our proposals are met.
2. That we renew our request for a [*jitney*] franchise.
3. That the fare be reduced to the pre-boycott price, except transfers.
4. That we make no move until the mass arrests trials are over in the first court.
5. That, in stating our position in going back to the bus, that the first and second proposals be accepted in totality, and that number three should get some promise for future consideration.
6. It was recommended that the Public Relations Committee release a news bulletin every week or every two weeks.
7. It was recommended that some statement from the police be given in protecting the masses that will gather in town for the trial.
8. That if the bus boycott continues station wagons be purchased.

4. Things that need attention:

1. Have bondsmen present in case of convictions.
2. At mass meetings get all persons who are willing to testify to mistreatment on busses.

MLKP-MBU: Box 2.

March 15, 1956

John P. Frank, Esq.
Lewis, Roca, Scoville and Beauchamp
919 Title and Trust Building
Phoenix, Arizona

Dear John:

[. . .] As you have doubtless seen in the papers, things in the Capitol of the Confederacy are lively to say the least. The Negroes stand together and it looks like infighting is going on between the various segments of the Citizens Councils for control, which is all to the good. The *Respectable* people want so much to be respectable and to disobey the law in a nice lawful way and are beginning to get quite embarrassed over the *Uncouth* elements who come right out with what the polite and the uncouth are both thinking and trying to do.

The lid is tight on all rational discussion for the moment and I imagine in some ways conditions are very similar to those in the 1850s, but the last time we seceded, it did not turn out so well and I don't believe we will try it again. There is, of course, potential violence in the situation, but somehow, you don't feel it in the atmosphere. The Negro Church has proven itself to be the source of power and unity and all emphasis on that side is on non-violence and Christian charity.

Maybe cussin' the Courts will provide a sufficient outlet for the frustrations and I am hoping that will prove to be the case.

The local Press is devoting itself to the effort to prove that the Yankees discriminate worse than we do. There is some justice in the charge, but it seems rather irrelevant to the issue. However it seems to make us feel better and this provides another escape for the passions. We shall see what we shall see. [. . .]

Sincerely yours,
Clifford J. Durr

CJDP-A-Ar.

Roy Finch, chairman of War Resisters League, introduced Rustin's March 21 report on his Montgomery visit, which the WRL disseminated:

On February 20 the League's Executive Committee learned that a request had been received for Bayard Rustin to go to Montgomery, Alabama, to consult with certain leaders of the bus boycott. A one-day protest demonstration had unexpectedly developed into a major experiment with non-violent resistance and was entering its eleventh week. Because tension was mounting, and because there is grave danger of violent racial conflict, the Executive Committee felt the League should do all in its power to help strengthen those forces in the Negro community which are exploring non-violence. Furthermore, the kind of potentially violent conflict we are faced with in the South today is one of the important factors which creates the atmosphere in which international war takes place. The Committee voted unanimously to send Bayard, since he has had considerable experience with non-violent resistance in both the North and South. A report issued on March 9, by Dr. Homer Jack, who visited Montgomery, indicates the value of Bayard's work. Dr. Jack says: "He seemed especially effective in counseling with the leaders of the protest during the crucial two weeks after the mass arrests for the boycott. His contribution to interpreting the Gandhian approach to the leadership cannot be overestimated."

Report on Montgomery, Alabama, by Bayard Rustin

I. Tension in the South today has been caused by many factors:
   a. *A Rapid Industrial Revolution* has disrupted the old social and economic patterns in the South. Intense social confusion has been created. Poor White and poor Negro people, over 50% of whom have become urbanized in the last few years, are faced with making radically new adjustments. In such a time as this, if this were the only factor, a certain amount of tension would be inevitable.
   b. *The Supreme Court Decision of May, 1954* is viewed by many white Southerners as federal intervention designed to destroy their way of life. There is a determined effort to frustrate this and any other court decision indicating increased justice for Negroes. In fact, every effort for justice is considered to be related to this major Supreme Court decision.
   c. *The New Negro Attitude:* All over the South the Negro has reached the position where he no longer is prepared to accept injustice and indignity. He is determined to have justice *now*. He has a new sense of dignity and destiny. He is united as never before.
   d. *The Emergence of The White Citizens Councils* and the use of propaganda, threats, arson, mass arrests, bombing and murder to obstruct the progress of Negroes at every point—in schools, in transportation and in voting. Economic boycotts against Negroes are increasingly being used.
   e. *The Decline of White Liberalism*: In Alabama the white liberals, the white church leadership and the so-called middle-of-the-road race relations groups have literally been immobilized by fear of violence and fear of ostracism. They do not speak out. They do not act. The fields of comment and action have been left to white extremists, on the one hand, and to Negroes who demand justice now, on the other. For example, in Montgomery no white minister except one who has a Negro congregation has spoken out. At the University in Tuscaloosa, the American Association of University Professors has not met nor made a statement on the Autherine Lucy case. In Birmingham the Interracial Council announced that they were neither for nor against integration. The recent remarks by novelist William Faulkner [*for slower change*] indicate that this decline of white liberalism is not limited to Alabama.
II. The Montgomery Boycott:
   a. The leadership in general is exploring the principles and tactics of

non-violence. All the leaders are clear that they will have no part in starting violence. There is, however, considerable confusion on the question as to whether violence is justified in retaliation to violence directed against the Negro community. At present there is no careful, non-violent preparation for any such extreme situation.

b. The Reverend Martin Luther King Jr., leader of the Montgomery Improvement Association, which is organizing the non-violent protest, is developing a decidedly Gandhi-like view and recognizes there is a tremendous educational job to be done within the Negro community. He is eagerly learning all that he can about non-violence and evidence indicates that he is emerging as a regional symbol of non-violent resistance in the deep South.

c. Until recently the Montgomery Improvement Association had no constructive program. Now, however, such an educational and work program is underway. Huge prayer meetings and symbols, including slogans, discussions and songs, are designed to keep the movement going. The car pool, substitute transportation for the Negro community, is efficiently operated and utilizes constructively the energies of many scores of the secondary leadership.

d. The leadership, comprising about one hundred Negro men and women, from all classes, is courageous. Many have been arrested and are prepared to go to jail. Their trials began March 19.

e. The Negro community of approximately 45,000 people is almost to the man behind the protest, refuses to use the buses, contributes over $2,000 weekly to help with the car pool and will not return to the buses until their minimal demands are met. The movement is strong because it is religious as well as political. It has been built upon the most stable institution of the southern Negro community—the Church. There is no evidence of Communist infiltration.

f. The protest is a rank and file movement. No particular person or persons began it. It arose from a very general response to the arrest of a respectable Negro woman who refused to move to the rear of a bus. The community resented her treatment; the community began to act. Later the ministers began to give guidance to a movement which they had [not] created.

III. The Importance of the Montgomery Protest:

a. Through the non-violent action in Montgomery, Negroes, North and South, have come to see that many of the stereotypes they have held about themselves are not necessarily true. The protest has given them a sense of pride and dignity and they now believe,

1. that they can "stick together"
2. that their leaders do not necessarily "sell out"
3. that violence, such as the bombing of the leaders' homes, does not necessarily "any longer intimidate"
4. that their church and ministers "are now militant" . . . 25 of those arrested are ministers
5. that they have found a new direct-action method that is bound "to spread over the deep South"

b. Montgomery has convinced many southern Negroes that certain elements in the white southern community do not intend to see them make any progress. The Negroes see evidence of this in the fact that their prerequisites for returning to the buses are merely conditions prevailing in other southern cities already. The protest leaders seek
1. courteous treatment on the buses
2. first-come-first-served seating *within the segregation pattern* while the courts determine the legality of intra-state segregation
3. *some* Negro drivers on buses serving predominantly Negro areas.

Why, the Negroes ask, are white people unwilling to grant these simple requests? The answer, they believe, is that a line has now been drawn against any final abolition of segregation. This has led the Negro in Montgomery to redouble his effort since his treatment on the buses is a long-standing grievance and has caused Negroes in other areas of the South to believe all is lost unless they vigorously struggle for justice now.

IV. Our Peculiar Role: Those of us who are interested to see progress toward a peaceful interracial society in the South, and who are convinced that to a considerable degree such a society depends on a non-violent response by the Negro community, have something to do in addition to supporting the Montgomery Improvement Association. More specifically, we must use our resources to strengthen the forces of non-violent resistance in the Montgomery situation. This means, among other things, helping to prepare literature, helping to plan workshops on non-violence in theory and practice, helping to construct functional work programs and raising funds to carry on other programs related to non-violent education.

V. Two Important Considerations:
a. We in the North should bear in mind that the most important thing we can do to help the Montgomery situation is to *press now for total integration in the North*. Montgomery is important if it stimulates us to greater action where we are.
b. Montgomery is also significant because it reveals to a world sick with violence that non-violent resistance has relevance today in the United

States against forces that are prepared to use extreme measures to crush it. This is a very real educational factor for all people to utilize who are working for world peace. [. . .]

ACLUA-NJP.

JUDGMENT AND SENTENCE OF THE COURT
THURSDAY, MARCH 22ND, A.D. 1956
COURT MET PURSUANT TO ADJOURNMENT
PRESENT THE HONORABLE EUGENE W. CARTER, JUDGE PRESIDING.
THE STATE, #7399
M. L. KING, JUNIOR
INDICTMENT FOR VIO. SECTION 54 TITLE 14 CODE OF ALABAMA 1940.

This day came the State by its Solicitor and came also the defendant in his own proper person and by attorney; and the said defendant being duly arraigned upon the indictment for his plea thereto says he is not guilty.

And after taking of testimony on behalf of the State and after the State had rested its case; the defendant filed a motion to exclude all of the evidence introduced by the State; and said motion being argued by counsel and understood by the Court, it is considered and ordered by the Court that said motion to exclude be and the same is hereby overruled.

And after the completion of all testimony in said cause; and after hearing said testimony, and after hearing arguments of counsel, the Court being of opinion, it is considered and ordered by the Court, and it is the judgment of the Court that the said defendant is guilty as charged in the complaint and a fine of five hundred ($500.00) dollars was assessed against him by the Court.

And said fine and cost not being paid; and the said defendant being asked by the Court if he had anything to say why the sentence of the law should not now be pronounced upon him says nothing. It is therefore considered and adjudged by the Court that the said defendant perform hard labor for Montgomery County for one hundred forty days for the fine; and the cost of this prosecution not being presently paid or otherwise secured, and the same being now ascertained and amount to $184.00, it is further considered and adjudged by the Court, and it is the judgment and sentence of the Court that the said defendant perform hard labor for Montgomery County for an additional term of 246 days in payment of said costs at the rate of 75 cents per diem, making in all 386 days during which said defendant is to perform hard labor for Montgomery County beginning from this day and ending on the 12 day of April, 1957.

And questions of law arising in this case for the decision of the Court of

Appeals of Alabama, the defendant gives notice of appeal and requests a suspension of sentence pending said appeal; it is therefore considered and ordered by the Court that pending said appeal to said Court of Alabama this sentence be and the same is hereby suspended and that pending said appeal the defendant may be admitted to bail in the sum of $1,000.00 to be made and approved as required by law.

CMCR-AMC: File 9399.

Report on MIA Mass Meeting, March 22, by Anna Holden

Only one mass meeting was held the Thursday night after King's trial ended, and it took place in the Holt Street Church, where the first meeting was held. As the lady sitting next to me explained, "We all wanted to be together tonight and we wanted to be here, because this is where we started."

When I arrived about 6:20 or 6:25 all seats in the upstairs part of the church and balcony were taken and there were standees in the front part of the church and in the aisles in the back. I stood in the doorway between the main part of the church and the vestibule, in view of the speakers platform. There were a number of people sitting on and around the speakers' platform by that time, though there were vacant seats on the platform reserved for persons on the program, press, visitors. The white audience that night consisted of several "outside" newspaper reporters in Montgomery for the trial (*Boston Globe*, two *New York Post* artists, *France Soir*, NBC-TV), a young man, very much ill-at-ease, who I took to be a student, a social psychologist from the Air University at Maxwell and myself. Didn't see any local press upstairs.

The crowd gathered in the church was singing when I arrived and continued to sing and pray alternately until about 7:15 when the formal portion of the meeting started. Hymns included "I'll Not be Moved," "I'll Go, Send Me, Oh Lord," and "Climbing Jacob's Ladder." Two persons, a man and a woman, prayed for about 15 minutes each, with a great deal of response from the audience throughout their prayers. Both stressed a need for God and for His help, and faith that He would respond, as he had in the past. There were few specific references to the current situation in either prayer, both running somewhat along this line: "We need You now, Oh Lord, we need You. We need You in our hearts, we need you in our homes, we need You. You always come to us when we called. You come to us in our darkest hours, You come to us when we need light. Now we're callin' on You again. We need You now." In reciting the instances when God had previously answered their call for help, the woman included a reference to the court. "We needed You in the court room and You were there." She also pleaded that "They," meaning the white people, don't know what they're doing. "They don't know what they're doing. They are your children. We are your children. We are all your children."

There was some conversation among the standees during the singing and I asked a lady near me how early you had to get in to get a seat. She answered about two or three o'clock and said that next time she was going to bring her lunch and get there about two. (Observer) "I guess people who work never can get here early enough to sit down." (Lady)—"It ain't hardly fair. Folks who works and needs to sit down can't be coming in time to get a seat. Those that don't work and don't need to sit gets here and takes up all the seats."

About 7:15 a man whom the [Alabama] *Journal* identified as W. C. Lee stepped up on the speakers platform and motioned to the crowd to stop singing. "He who was nailed to the cross for us this afternoon approaches. Let us give him the best ovation we have ever given him. Let him know that we appreciate what he has done for us." King then entered amid a thunderous burst of applause and cheering. Remarks in my vicinity ran like this: "He's next to Jesus himself," "We are sure with him," "He's my darling," "He's right there by God." A woman in the front row of the upper left balcony broke out into hysterical high-pitched cries, throwing her head back and then bending down, putting her head on the railing. If she was saying anything, I couldn't understand any of it. Comment in my area indicated disapproval: "There's — again," "She does that every time," "Emotional outburst, that's all it is," "Can't control herself."

Dr. [*Moses*] Jones (M.D.), who presided during the evening, permitted a second round of applause for King, then started the program with two hymns, "I Need You," and "I Want to be Near the Cross Where They Crucified My Lord." Following the singing Dr. Jones stated. "It would be a discourtesy to introduce Dr. King. We all know him. He is a part of us. He is our leader, our president. Whatever happens to him, happens to us. Today he was crucified in the courts. I now turn the meeting over to Dr. King."

After a lengthy applause, King finally quieted the crowd and began to speak:

"Tonight I stand before you, a convicted minister. Several weeks ago, I stood before you an indicted minister. Now I have been both indicted and convicted.

"I seem to have committed three sins. I have done three things that are 'wrong.' First of all, being born a Negro. That is my first sin. Second, being tired of segregation. I have committed the sin of being tired of the injustices and discriminations heaped upon Negroes. Third, having the moral courage to sit up and express our tiredness. That is my third sin.

"Thank God we are no longer content to accept second class citizenship. Thank God we are determined to struggle for justice until we receive it.

"I guess you know that I have been in court for four days. I never worked so hard in all my life—I was there every day from nine till six. Today the judge handed down the verdict. He said I am guilty of disobeying the anti-boycott law. There are 90 others accused of the same crime, but there will be no trials for them right now. Their cases will be continued until the appeal goes out. The judge fined me $500. The penalty could have been 6 months and $1,000 but the judge said he was lenient because I had enough religion to preach nonviolence.

"I think we were aware of the consequences before the cases came up. I think we knew when we started that this might happen. I was enough of an optimist to expect the best, but enough of a realist to also expect the worst. We are not to condemn Judge Carter. He was in a tragic dilemma. Maybe he did the best he could have in his position, in the expedient position.

"We are not bitter. We will still protest nonviolently, using the method of love, the method of passive resistance.

"I feel confident that as the case moves on up the courts, the decision will be reversed. Let us not lose faith in democracy. With all its weaknesses, that is the base of democracy: our constitutional right to struggle for change by peaceful means. We must transform democracy from thin paper to thick action.

"Democracy gives us this right to protest and that is all we're doing. We have never and never intended to practice violence. There was no evidence in the court that we had. The court did not prove that any acts of violence were carried out by Negroes. We can say honestly that we have not advocated violence, have not practiced it and have gone courageously on with a Christian movement. Ours is a spiritual movement depending on moral and spiritual fortitude. The protest is still going on. (Great deal of applause here)

"I want you to know that for the last two months I have had a great rendezvous with the jail house. I was arrested for driving 35 miles an hour and put in a cell. I went to court and was convicted and fined. I go to jail again with some of the finest citizens of Montgomery when we are arrested for breaking the anti-boycott law. I had to go to court this week and now I will have to go again. I might have to go four or five times more.

"This past conviction, the one before it, and all they can heap upon us will not diminish our determination one iota. (two rounds of applause) I'm going to stand in the morning, stand in the afternoon, and stand in the evening. I want it to be known through the length and breadth of the nation and to take wings and go to the far corners of the world, to Asia, to China, and to all parts of the world. (Lots of applause) I am standing, and we will not retreat until we receive justice.

"We don't mind the cross, because we know that beyond the tragedy of Good Friday is the breathlessness of Easter. We know that Easter is coming through the suffering of Good Friday. Easter is coming to Montgomery. Almost since the beginning of his existence, man has recognized the struggle between the forces of good and evil. Men have called these forces by different names, but what they have said about them and about the struggle is much the same. A philosopher named Plato saw it, and later on, a man called Thoreau. Christianity has always insisted that in the persistent struggle between good and evil, in the long battle between dark and light, the forces of light emerge as victor. This is our hope, that we will know the day God will stand supreme over the forces of evil, when the forces of light will blot out the forces of dark, when God will stand before the universe and say, 'I am God.'

"In ancient times, God stood before the forces of evil and said, 'Don't play with me, Babylon.' God said, 'Don't play with me. I'll break the backbone of your power. Don't play with me. I'm going to be God in this universe.'

"God controls the destiny of the universe, and evil cannot conquer. This keeps us going in all our trying experiences.

"Freedom doesn't come on a silver platter. With every great movement toward freedom there will inevitably be trials. Somebody will have to have the courage to sacrifice. You don't get to the Promised Land without going through the Wilderness. You don't get there without crossing over hills and mountains, but if you keep on keeping on, you can't help but reach it. We won't all see it, but it's coming and it's coming because God is for it. When God is for a thing it will survive. Don't worry about some things we have to go through. Some of them are a necessary part of the great movement we are making toward freedom. There can never be growth without growing pains. There is no birth without birth pains. Like the mother suffering when she gives birth to new life, we know there is glory beyond the pain.

"We won't back down. We are going on with our movement.

"Let us continue with the same spirit, with the same orderliness, with the same discipline, with the same Christian approach. I believe that God is using Montgomery as his proving ground. It may be that here in the capital of the Confederacy, the birth of the ideal of freedom in America and in the Southland can be born. God be praised for you, for your loyalty, for your determination. God bless you and keep you, and may God be with us as we go on."[1]

As King finished, people in my vicinity were commenting, "Gone too far," "Can't quit now."

Following King's talk the congregation sang, "I'll Not Be Moved."

Dr. Jones then called on one person to state why he was with the protest. A young woman who had testified at the trial got up and stated that she was with the protest because she had been called a "nigger" on the bus. "I've been called a 'nigger' and I said so at the trial and the judge asked me if I heard the driver call anybody else a 'nigger.' What the driver said to *me* didn't count, but I been called a 'nigger' and I told 'em so. I was asked to give a white *man* a seat and I told them about that too. I am filled up to my bones in this, it's way down in my bones and when there ain't no protest, I'm still gonna' have it. I'm still gonna' have my protest."

Dr. Jones called for one more statement and a man who must be Claudette Colvin's father got up. "I am with the protest because they put my daughter in jail. They put her in jail and kept her all night and they didn't even tell her mother where she was. And I'm with the protest because they put Mrs. Parks off the bus. Mrs. Parks is one of our fine citizens and they put her off the bus."

Dr. Jones commented that he wished there were time for more statements, but that would have to be all for that night. At this point Rev. King, who had taken a seat on the platform after he finished speaking, got up and came to the microphone. King: "I want to ask you all a question. I want to ask you because they said in court that I started the protest. They said that a selfish, power-seeking group who wanted to get publicity started it. Who started the protest?" Audience: "We did." "The bus drivers." "The bus company." King: "I heard that you are tired of it. Are you tired?" Audience: "No, No." "We're going to keep on."

Dr. Jones remarked that he noticed how anxious all the people who appeared in court were to tell their stories and that the judge wouldn't let them finish. "I even saw one lady come out of court crying because she couldn't tell her story like she wanted to."

Audience sang "Nobody Knows" next and then Dr. Jones introduced Rev. [R. W.] Hilson, St. John's AME Church. In introducing Rev. Hilson, Dr. Jones commented that he recently entertained a visitor who went to five churches while he was in the city. The visitor told him when he got ready to leave that usually a town has one outstanding minister, but that he had never seen a city with as many outstanding ministers as Montgomery. Dr. Jones: "Our Movement is a Christian movement because our ministers are outstanding ministers."

Rev. Hilson: "I can feel the strength and courage of 50,000 Negroes who are standing with me. If I grow weak, you are standing with us and others throughout the world. I feel the strength and courage of 16 million Negroes standing up for this same thing. This is a growing movement. It is impossible for one man to bring such a movement into being by himself. This is not a one-man show. We all know what one-man shows are and we know that they come and go. A one-man show can't last this long.

"It is too big to stop now. The commission found out they couldn't stop it. They call it a boycott. We are not carrying out a boycott. They themselves have turned our protest into a boycott.

"To us it has become a spiritual movement. We had our first meeting here in Holt Street Church. It was opened by the best people God has and the protest is something. You have the bone disease. It gets in the bones and in your heart and after you become a part of it, you get the 'can't-help-it.' (Lots of applause here) You can't quit. It's not something someone got up, but something we can't set down. It is a spiritual movement because it involves a corporation of three: man, our fellow man, and God. That corporation is an unbeatable corporation.

"They say if Rev. King were put out of the way, we would be ended. If Rev. King were put out of the way, the only thing it would do would be to take the 3 or 4 persons who are left on the buses off. (Someone shouts, "Send the buses back to Chicago.")

"I want to interrogate you. I want to ask you, 'Where do we go from here?' We could go to jail. When Mrs. Parks was put in jail, every Negro went to jail with her. A court ruling won't hold us. Neither will jail. Where do we go from here? Attorney Gray stated our case in a way you couldn't afford to be ashamed. He is a great representative of our people. But where do we go from here? Do we go on protesting? Wherever we go, let's go together.

"I want to tell you a story about some rabbits and a hound. Both lived near a river and the hound was always catching and eating the rabbits. He was bigger than they were and he had a terrible bark and they were all afraid of him. One day one of the rabbits decided that since they couldn't win against the hound, and they were all being killed one by one, it would be best for them to all go down to the river and drown themselves together. They talked it over and decided that that was the best thing for them to do, and on the appointed day, formed a double line and began marching down to the river together. The rabbits had hardly begun their march when they heard the hound baying in the distance. One rabbit was frightened and wanted to run, but the rest of them said, 'We are going to die anyway and we all want to die together, one-thousand strong.' And when the hound approached and saw them he became afraid and turned and ran away. The rabbits saw, then, that something happened when they all stuck together, and they decided not to jump in the river after all.

"We have learned something has happened in Montgomery. We need to keep on sticking together. A sentence was passed, but this is not the time to give up. This is the time to stick together.

"We have learned a precious secret about Christian life. We have learned how to love. It is easy to love folk when they love you. That is not hard. But when folk dagger you in the back when they love you as an individual and hate you as a race and you can step over the boundary and love them, you have learned something. The Negroes of Montgomery have learned to be courteous and to love. Keep on. In the end you will kill hate, prejudice, everything else, because you will kill them with love.

"At the end of his argument Attorney Shores quoted a passage from Micah that is written on a plaque on the courtroom wall: 'And what doth the Lord require of thee but to do justly, to love mercy and to walk humbly with thy God.' [*Micah* 6:8] If the world wants to know what we're going to do in Montgomery, we're going to do just that—do justly to every man, love mercy and walk, walk, walk, walk. (Burst of cheering and applause from audience)

"We have disease of the bone and the only cure for it is the end of injustice."

Dr. Jones decided to substitute "Walk Together Children" for the hymn they had planned to sing.

Rev. Abernathy introduced next, in his capacity as program chairman.

Abernathy: "I have taken on new courage. I am not tired, I have taken on new strength. Are you tired? I want to hear you say. I want to hear you say loud so Mayor Gayle can hear you. Are you tired? (No, no no, from audience.) Let me hear you again. I like to hear you good and loud. Are you tired? (Thunderous 'NO' in response)

"It's been rough so far, but not as rough as it's going to get. We must be ready to go all the way and it will get rougher. We don't know how the transportation will hold up. Are you going back if anything happens on the way? ('NO, NO, Gone too far') We may have to walk. ('WE'LL WALK') We may have to walk and walk 'til we can't walk any more. If we can't walk, then we'll crawl.

"This is a great movement. The eyes of the world are on us here. We are determined to keep on 'til justice prevails. If they give us what we ask for, we'll go back. We have no malice in our hearts. We're not trying to put the bus company out of business. Kill as many of us as they may, they will never be able to pick us up and put us back on the buses until justice is done.

"I wonder how those who went back on us feel? I wonder how those three who testified against us must feel tonight. Pray for them. Share their sorrow and their grief. I feel sorry for them not having the courage to stick with us, with their race.

"I have been invited to go out to California next week, and I have a message to carry to the people of Los Angeles. I will tell them the 50,000 Negroes of Montgomery have been walking 110 days and are not tired. I will also tell them that we are going to stay here in Alabama but we are not going to be pushed around. People want to know why we stay here. In the next few years we are going to speed things up. We are going to learn to walk a little faster. We may even get a proper brogue so you can't tell us from Philadelphia. But we are going to stay here and get our rights here in Alabama." [. . .]

Next item—"Pass Me Not, Oh Gentle Savior."

Rev. [*William H.*] Anderson of Philadelphia brought a contribution of $900, commented: "There is a change in the South. Judge Carter stood in the world court and his decision condemned him. Prayer will march you on to glory."

Rev. [*Jesse Jai*] McNeil brought a contribution of $4,553.55 collected by the Baptist Ministers Conference of Detroit, said he would be back again with another contribution. "I have never seen such emancipated people as the Negroes of Montgomery."

Loeb of the National Negro Publishers Association brought a contribution of over $3,200 raised in Cleveland. He stated: "Judge Carter bought time today for the ones who want to put off the simple proposition of saying that a man is a man. Fortunately time and the scared Negro are both running out."

The representative of the National Funeral Directors Association brought a contribution of $1,000.

Don't believe Patterson brought any money from Selma, but he stated: "Selma is behind you, on the side of you, with you. We thank you for standing together and holding your hope. If you lose in Montgomery, we have lost in America. If you win, Seattle, Boston, and Chicago have won. Hold your hope."

After the guests were introduced, Dr. Jones or someone on the platform made several announcements. [. . .] He then commented that "The fellowship is like an electric charge to us. We can't give it up."

E. D. Nixon called for the offering.

Rev. U. J. Fields asked the Thanksgiving.

Meeting closed with hymn, "God Be with Us." [. . .]

PV-ARC-LNT.

1. This concluding paragraph of King's speech is taken from King, Address to MIA Mass Meeting, March 22, 1956, MLKP-MBU: Box 80.

Interlude . . . 8 . . .

Interview with Domestic Worker, by Willie M. Lee

Date: January 18, 1956
Time: Morning
Place: Female interviewed in pool car
Occupation: Domestic in white rental area
Age: about 40

[*Lee*]: Would you tell me what's going on around here? You see I just came into town, and I've been reading in the newspapers something about the people not riding the buses, and I don't quite understand really what's happening. So I'd appreciate it if you would tell me.
[*Domestic*]: You mean 'bout us boycottin' the buses?
[*Lee*]: Yes.
[*Domestic*]: Well, you know, dis is a Jim Crow town, and us is boycottin' the buses 'cause dey put one of our 'spectable ladies in jail and we didn't lack it. You know, child, you can jest take so much and soon you git full. Dat's what happen here. Dey jest put us in jail and put us in jail, and Lord knows we tied of it.
[*Lee*]: Why did they put the people in jail?
[*Domestic*]: Dey jest don't want to treat us right, and ef us didn't move back, they put us in jail. Twuz her last year dey put some school chillen in jail, but dat soon died down. But 'bout 2, 3 months ago Miss Rosa Park, one of our nice 'spectable ladies wuz put in jail, and the folks got full and jest wouldn't take no

more. My sister called me and seyed that she heard dat we wouldn't ride the buses fur a day causer what they did to Miss Park. We didn't ride 'em neither. We shor fixed 'em.

[*Lee*]: Well, tell me this, what are you doing in this thing?

[*Domestic*]: Honey, I jest do like the leaders sey. I go to the rally, pay my money and don't worry bout nothin'. I tell dat woman I wuk fur dat I gets dare when I kin and ef dat won't do, nothin' twill. Some of dem fired the workers but dey went right on an got other jobs so dey stopped firing 'em.

[*Lee*]: When do you think this thing will end?

[*Domestic*]: I don't care. I get to wuk an I ain't hungry, so it don't matter wid me. It ain't hurtin' us, it's hurtin' dem. I heard dat they had lost $32 million since we stopped ridin' the buses. Well dis is my stop, see y'all later.

PV-ARC-LNT.

Interview with Maid, by Willie M. Lee

Date: January 20, 1956
Time: 9:00 A.M.
Place: 650 South Decatur Street
Age: 45
Sex: Female

[*Maid*]: [. . .] I had heard about Rosa Parks getting put in jail because she would not get up and stand so a white man could sit down. Well, I got a little mad, you know how it is when you hear how white folks treat us. And after that day it just sort of slipped my mind. So things rocked on 'til that Sunday night (the Sunday following Mrs. Parks' arrest), and the man next door who is a Mason went down to the Tijuana Club. When he came back, he came by my house and showed me these slips of paper that somebody gave out at the club. It said that one of our ladies had been arrested and the next time it may be you, so don't ride the buses Monday.

I felt good. I said this is what we should do. I got on the phone and called all my friends and told them, and they said they wouldn't ride.

I didn't have to work the next day and my insurance lady come by, and I asked her did she ride the bus and she said yes. Then I showed her the slip of paper. She said she hadn't seen one and asked me if she could have it so she could pass it along to her friends. That's why I don't have it. If I did, I'd let you see it.

[*Lee*]: Thank you very much for what you've told me, but now tell me this. Had anything like this ever happened before Mrs. Parks was arrested?

[*Maid*]: Oh yes, honey, this stuff has been going on for a long time. To tell you the truth, it's been happening ever since I came here before the war (World War II). But here in the last few years they've been getting worse and worse. When you get on the bus they yell: "*Get on back there*" (very empathetic and expressive person), and half of the time they wouldn't take your transfer, then they make you get up so white men could sit down where there were no seats in the back. And you know about a year ago they put one of the high school girls in jail 'cause she wouldn't move. They should have boycotted the buses then. But we are sure fixing 'em now and I hope we don't ever start back riding. It'll teach them how to treat us. We people, we are not dogs or cats.

[*Lee*]: Speaking of the way they treat you, exactly what do you want them to do before you will ride the buses again?

[*Maid*]: All we want 'em to do is treat us right. They shouldn't make me get up for some white person when I paid the same fare and I got on first. And they should stop being so nasty 'cause after all they are not doing us no favors. We pay just like the white folks. And too, we want them to put Negro bus drivers in the sections where Negroes live.

[*Lee*]: Do you think the bus company will agree to give these things?

[*Maid*]: Well, they are the ones losing the money and our preachers say we will not ride unless they give us what we want.

[*Lee*]: Speaking of money, have you been down town to shop any since this protest started?

[*Maid*]: I've been there plenty times, but it's only when I have to.

[*Lee*]: I see. Well, tell me, did the clerks in the stores treat you any different than they did before this thing started?

[*Maid*]: No, they were just as nice as they could be. Some of them even call you 'Miss.' You see the business men are losing money too, because people only go to town when they have to.

[*Lee*]: How do the people you work for feel about it?

[*Maid*]: I almost forgot about them, I'm glad you brought it up. You see I work out in Cloverdale (elite section of town) for Mrs. Prentiss, and she hates it, but it sure ain't nothing she can do about it.

She said to me when I went to work that Wednesday, "Beatrice, you ride the bus, don't you?"

I said, "I sure didn't."

She said, "Why Beatrice, they haven't done anything to you."

I said, "Listen, Mrs. Prentiss, you don't ride the bus, you don't know how those ole nasty drivers treat us, and further when you do something to my people you do it to me too. If you kick one, if you can get around to me you'll kick me too. My mother taught me, Mrs. Prentiss, to 'treat thy neighbor as thy self,' but I don't have anything in my heart but hatred for those bus drivers."

"Beatrice, don't feel that way. I've always been nice to you."

"That true, Mrs. Prentiss. If I get sick for a couple of days, you come by to see me, pray [for] me, and bring me food, but if I stayed sick 2 or 3 weeks would you do it?"

"'Course I would Beatrice, but I just can't see white and colored riding together on the buses. It just wouldn't come to a good end."

"You people started it way back in slavery. If you hadn't wanted segregation, you shouldn't got us all mixed up in color."

"Beatrice, you don't know anything about that, and it's not happening now."

"That's what you say. I read about it and my aunt told me about it, and right now I can sit on my porch, and when it starts getting dark I can look down the street by those trees and see colored women get in the cars with policemen. And what about that colored boy who had to leave town 'cause that white woman out here was going crazy about him. So you can't tell me that it's over."

"You know Beatrice, Clyde Sellers (City Commissioner) is a very good friend of mine."

"You sure have a poor friend."

"I'm going to tell you this, Beatrice, because I know you can keep your mouth shut. In the White Citizen Council meeting, they discussed starving the maids for a month. They asked me to lay our maid off for a month, that they'll be glad to ride the buses again. If they do it I still want you to come one day a week."

"Well, Mrs., I just won't come at all and I sure won't starve. You see, my husband is a railroad man, my son and daughter have good jobs, and my daddy keep plenty of food on his farm. So I'm not worried at all, 'cause I was eating before I started working for you."

"Beatrice, that ole Rev. King and Ole Graetz should be run out of town. They keep this mess going. You know I heard that Rev. King is going to take all your money and go buy a Cadillac with it. He's going from door to door asking for $2. Beatrice, don't you give him $2."

"Whoever told you that, told you a lie, but if he did it ain't no more for me to pay $2 than it is for you to pay $3.50 for that White Citizen thing."

"And you know, Beatrice, ole Rev. King want people to go to church together and I just can't see it."

"I didn't ask you to come to my church and I ain't particular about going to yours, but a church is a house of worship and the doors should be open to everybody. You don't want to go to church with us when down in the 5th ward until a couple of years ago, you couldn't go in or leave after dark 'cause all those white men and women were down there after those colored people." (intimate racial mixing) She stood there looking at me like a sick chicken, then hurried off, talking about she had to go to town. She didn't say anything more after that. I came right home and called Rev. Abernathy, my pastor, and told him about them talking about firing the maids. You know our pastors tells us what to do. They lead us in a Christian way. We just act nice and quiet. [. . .]

[*Lee*]: Are there any colored people against this thing?

[*Maid*]: Oh yes, there is Rev. Wright's wife. She talks about "these niggers don't know what they are doing, they are going to get in trouble." She's with the white folks. All she needs is for someone to fix her back end up with a nice board so she can't sit for a while and she'll be alright. I'm going to give you her address so you can talk to her. You'll have to be sneaky to get the truth out of her though.

[*Lee*]: Tell me, how do you think things will be between whites and colored when the colored start back riding the buses?

[*Maid*]: I tell you the truth, I think for a while they'll be very nice 'cause they'll be getting out of the hole, but after that they'll probably get worse than before, 'cause they are building up hatred in their hearts right now. That's why I go to all the meetings and pay what I can so we can stay off the buses. I didn't ride but a little when they were running. Most times except one or two my boss picks me up. [. . .]

General Statement: [*The maid*] keeps all Negro papers and magazines in order to keep up with what the presses say about Montgomery. She sends clippings to her children in California. She also subscribes to one of the Montgomery dailies. She is a tall stately woman, expressions are very impressive; appearance neat, complexion dark-brown.

PV-ARC-LNT.

Interview with Music Instructor, by Willie M. Lee

Place: 1405 Marguerite Street
Age: 55–60
Sex: Female

[*Music Instructor*]: I know very little about it except what I've read in the papers, however, I can tell you how I feel about it. I don't think the people know what they are doing. They went about this thing in the wrong way and secondly, they asked for too much. They know the southern tradition and they should have asked for one thing instead of being like the dog with a bone and his shadow. He was so greedy that he tried to get the bone his shadow had and he ended up without a bone. I said that to say, Miss, asking for three things they are not going to get anything. [. . .]

[*Lee*]: Which do you think they should have asked for?

[*Instructor*]: I think first come, first serve is all they should have asked for. I'm for that if they do it in the right way. I was embarrassed once on the bus. Two white men asked me to get up, and I didn't move, then the bus driver asked me up. I got off the bus, went down to the bus company and reported the driver, and I asked the manager where were colored people suppose to sit. He was very nice and that driver was taken off the Jackson Street line. And since this mess started, I started through Oak Park and the policeman yelled "Good Lord, don't come through here." If my daughters had not pleaded so, I would have kept on through. When I got home I called Sellers and his secretary told me that he did not handle that information, so she gave me the name of the person to see. When he first started talking he said:

"Yes ma'm, no ma'm." But when I said, I'm a colored citizen, his tone became very indignant. I told him I was a good citizen. I owned almost a block out here, have been living here all my life and have been going through Oak Park. I pay taxes just like white citizens, and I wanted to know why I couldn't go through that park.

He said: "Niggers can go through that park." I asked him to repeat what he said, and he said the same thing again. I was really angry by then, so I told him that I am not a nigger and that he was acting more like a nigger. Then he apologized, saying he said "Negro," and I must have misunderstood him. I haven't had any more trouble coming through the park since then.

[*Lee*]: You have mentioned several times that the people did not go about this thing in the right way. What do you suggest they should have done?

[*Instructor*]: Well, in the first place, the ministers have no business in this and turning the church into a political organization. Some academic building over on the campus (Alabama State Teachers College) should be used for meetings and the white and colored intelligentsia should decide this thing. These poor folks and some of these ministers don't know what they are doing. The principals and teachers should run it. They should get together, discuss it, then vote on it and do whatever the majority says. I sure wish it would end. I'm tired of it. I've lost about half of my music students. And other business people I've talked to are losing too. I bet the ministers wouldn't want the members of their churches to do to them what they are doing to the bus company. I wonder how they would feel if their members refuse to come to church and to pay dues. They wouldn't like it at all. And the people are only holding themselves down by not riding the buses. They should go on and end this thing. I'm sick of it. I'm losing money every day.

These ministers should stop telling people what to do. They should let the buses run and let those ride who want to. The first day they struck, my boy was fixing to get on a bus and a lady dared him to get on, she said that she would cut him if he did. Way out on the outskirts of town, I have heard that quite a few folks have been beaten up, but I don't know how true it is. I just don't believe in telling people what to do. I think for myself, and if I want to ride a bus, I ride. That's why I don't go to any of the meetings, because I'll speak my mind. You know, I'm a member of Rev. King's church. I play the organ. One of my friends told me that if I went to a meeting and told them how I felt, that they would throw me out. So I take no part in it. This is a democratic country and I have a right to say what I want to. If the people could hear me now, I know they'd crucify me, but I've always thought for myself and I teach my children to think for themselves. My daughters came home one day and said:

"Mother, I'm never going to buy from the Fair (Montgomery Fair Department Store) again. The people are going to boycott it because they fired Mrs. Parks."

I told her not to be a fool, that if she wanted something, don't let a group of people tell you where to buy it. It's more to buy from the Fair than it is to sit in the back of shoe stores and drink water out of segregated fountains in other stores. I'm no "Uncle Tom" woman, but I believe there is a way to do anything. I've had people tell me that I'm thinking antebellum time.

[Lee]: Do you think this is favorable to the Colored people at all?

[Instructor]: Well, yes, it is. For one thing it show that they can stick together. Whatever they want I'm for them because it's my race; however, like I said, I would have done things differently. My church, Dexter Avenue Baptist, and most of the clubs play big parts and I don't agree with them. They can do just what they want to, but I'm losing money and I sure wish they'd start the buses back.

[Lee]: What do you think the accomplishments will be?

[Instructor]: There won't be any. Sellers hates Negroes and he'll never give in. What the Negroes in Montgomery should do is vote. About 45,000 people here are colored and only 2 or 3 thousands, or not that many, vote. A man in office don't have to worry about colored votes, because there are not enough voting. If they use their voting power, they can get almost anything.

[Lee]: I see. Well tell me this, how do whites in stores and various places treat you since this thing started?

[*Instructor*]: They all treat me very nice, same as they always did. I haven't been downtown very many times, but those few times I did go, the clerks treated me the same. [. . .]

PV-ARC-LNT (January 23, 1956).

Interview with Domestic, by Willie M. Lee

Time: afternoon
Place: street
Age: approx. 40

[*Lee*]: How are you, Ma'm?
[*Domestic*]: I'm fine. Jest a bit tied, thank you.
[*Lee*]: How far have you walked?
[*Domestic*]: I walked from town t'day. My lady brang me home most times, but I had to stop in town t'day.
[*Lee*]: How nice of her. What does she say about the people not riding the buses?
[*Domestic*]: She never seyed anythang but once, and dat wuz right after we stopped ridin' 'em. One day she seys to me, "Dealy, why don't you ride the bus? Dat Rev. King is jest making a fool outta you people." I seyed back to her, "don't you sey nothin' 'bout Rev. King. You kin sey anythang else you wont to, but don't you sey nothin' 'bout Rev. King. Dat's us man and I declare he's a fine un'. He went to school and made somethin' out of hisself, and now he's tryin' to help us. Y'all white folks done kept us bline long enough. We got our eyes open and now us sho ain't gona let you close 'em back. I don't mean to be sassy, but when you talk bout Rev. King I gits mad. Y'all white folks wuk us to death and don't pay nothin'—"

"But Dealy, I pay you."

"What do you pay, jest tell me? I'm shame to tell folks what I wuk fur."

"Dealy, I didn't mean to make you mad, I was just talking."

"Well, talk about Sellers and ole no good Gayle. I walked to wuk the fust day and I kin walk now. If you don't wanna bring me, I ain't begging, and I sho ain't gettin' back on da bus and don't you never sey nothin' 'bout Rev. King." I ain't gona get back on the bus 'til Rev. King sey so, and he seys we ain't going back 'til they treat us right. [. . .] I don't reckon you ride de bus, but us is tied of these white folks making us stand so white folks kin set down. So us ain't going to get back on de buses 'til they treat us the same as dey treat white folks. I won't be particular 'bout ridin' then. I don't care if they don't ever start back.

We got these white folks where we want 'em, and dere ain't nothing dey can do but try to scare us. But we ain't rabbit no more, we done turned coon. My daddy use to tell me 'bout coon huntin'. If he's in a tree and you shake him down, he'll kill three dogs, and if he's in the water, he'll drown evvy dog dats come in de water. It's jest as many of us as the white folks and dey better watch out what they do.

[Lee]: There are still one or two people riding the buses. What do you think about them?

[Domestic]: Honey, let any of 'em ride who want to. Dey conscious [conscience] will whip 'em. But I ain't gitten back on. I go to the meetin', pay my money and be satisfied.

Interviewer: [The domestic] was very neat; is of medium height and build. She appeared rather timid, but while relating her experiences with her employer about Rev. King, she appeared very forceful from facial expressions and tone of voice.

PV-ARC-LNT (January 24, 1956).

Interview with Cook, by Willie M. Lee

Place: 666 S. Elwood street
Age: 45–50
Sex: Female

[Cook]: Child, I'm glad to see you, it's good that somebody came to see what's going on. I tell you, it's like dis, dey tole me to git up once and that was 'nough for me. Dey been makin' us git up long 'nough, but dey bit off more'n dey can chew when dey put one our fine ladies in jail. God git tired of ugly and as long as we put him first, he'll lead us like he did the children of Israel. I'm countin' on him too.

[Lee]: Well, tell me, how did you first hear about this thing?

[Cook]: I found a note on my porch and it said dey had put Mrs. Parks in jail and next time it may be me and it said fur us not to ride de buses. I felt good, I felt like shoutin' 'cause de time done come for dem to stop treating us like dogs.

[Lee]: How did you get to work the next day?

[Cook]: I got dem flat shoes back der, put my foot in de road and walked.

[Lee]: Did the people you work for have anything to say about it?

[Cook]: She asked me how did I get to work and I told her I walked and she ain't said nothing to me since. She git in dat car and bring me home dough.

[*Lee*]: Do you think the buses will start back running soon?

[*Cook*]: Honey, I don't care if dey don't ever run again. I ain't gonna let my foots touch them and I ain't gonna ride or touch my foots. I go to de meetin', I pay my money and listen to what us man says (Rev. King). He is sho 'nough a God sent man. Did you hear him last night, ain't he somethin', I declare wid his little self. He sho got some sense in his head. We ain't gonna git on dem buses 'til he sez so, den I doubt whether I ride it agin.

[*Lee*]: What is it you want the bus company to do before you start back riding the buses?

[*Cook*]: All us want is for dem to treat us right, stop making us give white folks our seats and to put colored drivers where colored folks stay. Excuse what I say, child, but ole Sellers got too much hell in him to do anything, but he might as well give up 'cause we ain't gonna be pushed down no more. Our eyes is open and dey gonna stay open. [. . .] Dem bus folks gonna take dese buses out of here if Sellers keep acting like a fool. Now he's running round telling lies about us man (Rev. King) but he manga well shet his mouth 'cause he ain't doing nothin' but lying. And if us did buy Rev. King a Cadillac, it sho wus us money and he ain't got nothin' to do with it.

[*Lee*]: Are there any people still riding the buses?

[*Cook*]: Yes, der some and I know dey conscious is beatin' 'em.

[*Lee*]: I heard that there were goon squads beating people up who ride the buses now. Is that true?

[*Cook*]: Naw, ain't no sech thing as no goon squad, dat's another one of Sellers' lies. [. . .]

PV-ARC-LNT (January 24, 1956).

Interview with Cook/Maid, by Willie M. Lee

Time: Morning
Place: 328 North Jackson St.
Age: 35–40

[*Cook/Maid*]: Girl, I sho know a heap I kin tell you, and I sho wont to tell 'bout dem white folks I wuk fur. But fust let me tell ya how it started. One day me and a girl wuz waitin' fur a bus and der wuz plenty folks there, white and collud. I said to dis girl, "You know us keep dese buses running. If dey didn't have us dey'd stop running and dey'll stop treatin' us like us ain't human. You know dey don't treat us like human!" I wuz jest talking down at the bus stop and all the folks heard. My friend hunched me to be quiet cause a white man had tipped up 'hind me and wuz trying to hear what I wuz saying, but I had seyd it and I didn't care. And child when I got home, Junior came runnin' with the paper, "Momma, they say don't ride the buses." I said, "Lord you sho answered my prayer." Honey, I coulda shouted. Jest what I'd been talkin' 'bout and it had happen. Evyday dey kept tellin' us not to ride de next day. If it wuz left to me dey wouldn't ride nare day. But you know, girl, der is some good bus drivers. I ain't gon lie. I been ridin' dese buses for nigh 15 years and you know dey change routes with de drivers and I sho seed some good uns. But most of 'em ain't good. Dey say nasty thangs and dey talk under folks' clothes lack dat ole Sellers did on television dat night. Did ya hear him? He knowed he aught to been shame. I ain't gon never git back on dem ole buses.

[*Lee*]: How did you get to work the first day the people stopped riding the buses?

[*Cook/Maid*]: The lady cross de street, her husband got a taxi and us work in de same neighborhood, so us and some more girls pay him to take us to work.

[*Lee*]: What about the time, are you ever late?

[*Cook/Maid*]: I git to work better now den I did when de buses wuz running. Um spose to be dere at a quarter to nine, but I gits dere every day 'tween 8:00 and 8:30. Dis girl's husband comes back fur us.

[*Lee*]: In the beginning you said something about the people you work for.

[*Cook/Maid*]: Oh, I 'most forgot dat. You see I work fur two families, and dey stay next doe to each other. Let me tell you 'bout one fust, den I tell you 'bout the other.

The fust one, her husband is a bus driver. Fur a week nothing happen. Den one evening I wuz 'bout to leave the other lady's house and the other'n came to the fence and told me to come by her house when I finish, she had somethin' fur me. Said she had some bacon grease. She told me don't let her husband see it 'cause he told her don't gimme nothin' else. I told 'er if her husband seyd don't gimme nothin' else, den don't gimme nothin' else. Den she said, "Irene, what happen at the meeting last night?" I told 'er we sung and prayed. She looked at me and told me I wuz telling a damn lie. I seyed back to 'er, "Now listen, I know we did sung and prayed, and if you don't b'lieve me, YOU go to de meetin' fur yoself." And girl, I seyd to myself, she must take me fur a fool—thank I'll come back here and puke everything my folks seys to her, and then for some little ole stinking bakin' grease at dat.

She seyd den, "Irene, I didn't know you wuz so damn stupid." By dat time I wuz over 'er house and I wuz mad as I could be. Den she lied out, "I didn't know you were skered to ride the bus?" I wuz so mad by den, girl, 'fore I relize what I wuz doing, I had done told the 'omen off. I told her dat I wuz not skered to ride de bus, I'd ride if I wont to, but her husband never would git a dime fom me no more. I told her I wuz wid de crowd 'cause I wonted to be. I don't have to stay down here, I could go up north where my peoples is, but um going to stay right here and help out. And do you know what dat ole 'omen said den? She seyd Rev. King come here 'cause he wuz runned outer Atlanta. I told her he wuzn't runned outer Atlanta, and don't she stand dere and sey he wuz. Dat man come here 'cause he wuz called. And one sho thang he ain't got to worry 'bout no job lack your husband. He's a God sent man and ain't nothin' none of y'all can do 'bout it.

I walked outer her yard den cause I wuz 'bout ready to beat her. You see, she took me fur a fool, she thought all dat stuff she told me I b'lieved. But she didn't know every time she told me her chillen loved me, I put a pin dere; when she sey dey like de way I iron, I put a pin dere; and when dey talked 'bout how good I cooked, I put a pin dere, and all twee dem pins I reads. And I know dey don't mean a thang they seys. So Irene don't pay 'em no mind.

And girl, dat same day I wuz fixin' to cross de street at a light where de bus stop, and a colored man stepped in the door of de bus and gave the driver a dime and told 'em he hoped dat would help out. I laughed 'til I cried.

The next time I worked fur dat ole 'omen, she said, "You know we could starve y'all maids for a month." I told 'er she wuz already starving [me] and I pity anybody who waits fur me to starve. Dey'll be waiting fur a long time. And you know outer all that talk she kept putting my fare (bus fare) wid my money so I could come to work, but I sided I better quit 'fore I have to beat her.

Now the other lady she wuz nice. She said dat she didn't blame me for sticking wid my people, and she told me dat if I owed dat 'omen next door any money to pay her and not go back over dere. And de way she told me, dat other 'omen musta planned to do somethin' to me, but she knowed not to do somethin' to me 'cause she heard me say heap o' time dat if you hit me, I hit back and I ain't big fur nothin' (weighs approx. 200 lbs.).

[Lee]: Do you see many colored folks riding the buses?

[Cook/Maid]: I see one or two sometimes.

[Lee]: What do you think of these people?

[Cook/Maid]: Girl, I do lack Rev. King seys. If dey wont to ride, let 'em ride. If they ain't got enough consciousness not to ride, I don't kere.

[Lee]: I see. Well, tell me this, what is it the people want before they'll ride the buses again?

[Cook/Maid]: All us wont is fur dem to stop makin' us stand and give white folks us seat and to git some colored drivers. And dat sho ain't askin' fur nothing.

[Lee]: Do you think you'll get what you asked for?

[*Cook/Maid*]: Dey folks ain't gona ride the buses if dey don't, and I ain't gona ride no more. I don't kere what dey do, dey ain't gittin no more of my dimes. Child, one day I wuz crossing de street by dis same light I wuz telling you 'bout and a white man got on the bus. He put a dime in, and de driver asked fur another nickel. Dat white man seyd, "Gimme back my dime. I'll walk wid de niggers fo I pay $.15." [. . .]

PV-ARC-LNT (February 2, 1956).

Spring . . . 9 . . .

Around the world, 1956 gave birth to new beginnings, fresh bursts of freedom sprouting from withering husks of the prewar order. The winning nonviolent movement in Ghana would render irreversible the overthrow of European colonialism in Africa, its last frontier. Poor nations of the South had banded together in Bandung, Indonesia, to create a "nonaligned" movement as an independent third force between the rival American and Soviet empires. In Moscow, the new Communist Party leader, Nikita Khrushchev, denounced Stalinist crimes at a party congress in February, sparking disaffection among communists worldwide and a democratic revolt in Hungary that Soviet tanks would crush in the fall.

In the United States the demise of Senator Joseph McCarthy diminished the anticommunist witchhunt that bore his name, opening up breathing space in the constricted vessels of American political culture for bold new ideas and initiatives. The South's doubly virulent mix of McCarthyism and white supremacy abated enough to allow a new generation of African American leadership to find footholds in the brittle wall of segregation. Young leaders like King, Ralph Abernathy, and Jo Ann Robinson in Montgomery, Fred Shuttlesworth in Birmingham, and Medgar Evers in Mississippi danced warily with pillars of the noncommunist American Left, white and black. They reached out for guidance from figures such as A. Philip Randolph, Ella Baker, A. J. Muste, and Norman Thomas, while holding them at arm's length. They energized and helped reconstruct a national black leadership network (ministers, educators, journalists, politicians) paralyzed by McCarthyism that would provide vital support in the southern crucible and, aided by white progressives, set the stage for the broadened civil rights movement of the 1960s.

Bayard Rustin, who exemplified both the strengths and weaknesses of the American Left as it self-consciously reconstituted itself, sought to draw King and the Montgomery movement into the orbit of a dynamic new politics that aspired to be an American moral equivalent of the Third World's nonaligned movement and of democratic dissent behind the Iron Curtain. This radical but pragmatic politics, which blended the Judaic and Christian prophetic traditions, the American egalitarian promise, libertarian socialism, and nonviolent activism, was anchored in an ambitious journal called *Liberation*, first published in March 1956. The editors included Rustin, Muste, Dave Dellinger, and Paul Goodman.

Writing to King in early March, Rustin enclosed the founding issue for him to read along with a draft of "Our Struggle," a feature article about Montgomery (written by Rustin) that would appear under King's name in the April issue. The March *Liberation* began with a manifesto entitled, "Tract for the Times," which set forth the political vision of the radical pacifist editors.

Rustin's presence in Montgomery had caused anxiety among MIA leaders and his New York colleagues partly because of an allegation that, soon after arriving, he had misrepresented himself as a correspondent for two major European newspapers, *Le Figaro* in Paris and the British *Manchester Guardian*.

Reverend Martin Luther King
309 Jackson
Montgomery, Alabama

Dear Reverend King:

I called your wife today and told her that I had gotten the matter cleared up with the *Manchester Guardian*. Actually, they had never offered any reward for my identification. In regard to *Le Figaro*, we are in process of getting that cleared up. For the record, at no time did I say that I was a correspondent for either of these papers. I did say that I was writing articles which were to be submitted to them and this is now in the process of being done.

Enclosed you will find an article which I should like you to revise and to give permission for being printed under your name in the April issue of *Liberation*. Also enclosed is a copy of *Liberation* so that you may know the nature of the magazine. This magazine is being widely distributed to the kind of moral leadership who are intensely interested in non-violence and many important leaders of the church. For this reason I emphasized the moral aspects of the problem. I hope you can see your way clear to give us permission to publish it, to revise it where you wish, and to get it back to me as soon as possible. I am working on a couple of other things for you for wider distribution.

Let me hear from you as soon as possible.

Sincerely yours,
Bayard Rustin

MLKP-MBU: Box 5 (March 8, 1956).

"Tract for the Times," by Editors of *Liberation*

The decline of independent radicalism and the gradual falling into silence of prophetic and rebellious voices is an ominous feature of the mid-twentieth century. Anxiety and apprehension have invaded the air we breathe. Advances in science and technology, which should have been our greatest triumphs, leave us stunned and uncertain as to whether human life and history have meaning.

Power is everywhere openly or secretly idolized. The threat of atomic or biological war, perhaps even the extinction of mankind, hangs over the earth. Hopes and ideals have become propaganda devices. But those who should furnish vision and direction are silent or echoing old ideas in which they scarcely believe themselves.

This failure of a new radicalism to emerge is an indication, it seems to us, that the stock of fundamental ideas on which the radical thinking of recent times has been predicated is badly in need of thorough reappraisal. Much of its inspiration appears to be used up. Old labels—principally in the Marxist and liberal traditions—simply do not apply any more, and the phrases which fifty years ago were guideposts to significant action have largely become empty patter and jargon.

The changes of recent years—represented by atomic power and by the beginnings of the Second Industrial Revolution and also by the rise of totali-tarianism—have filled many thoughtful persons with the strong suspicion that the problems of today must be attacked on a much deeper level than tradi-tional Marxists, Communists and various kinds of Socialists and Anarchists have realized. Proposals and calls to action couched in the old terms fail any longer to inspire much hope or genuine humane enthusiasm, because large numbers of people are aware, or dimly sense, that they do not touch the roots of the trouble.

There is no point, for example, in reshuffling power, because the same old abuses still persist under new masters. The vast energy devoted to reconstructing government is wasted if in a short time the new structure becomes as impervious to fundamental human decency and ethics as the old one. There is no doubt that there are forms of property relationships which are oppressive and destructive of true community, but if these are altered and the average individual finds his life as dull and empty as ever and the enslavement of his hours just as great, little or nothing has been achieved.

It is increasingly evident that nineteenth century modes of thought are largely incapable of dealing with such questions. The changes which are going on in the modern world—which call into doubt many assumptions which almost all nineteenth century revolutionists and reformers took for granted—require also changes in our deepest modes of thought. We require a post-Soviet, post-H-bomb expression of the needs of today and a fresh vision of the world of peace, freedom and brotherhood in which they can be met.

OUR ROOT TRADITIONS

In reexamining our thought—and especially the two great dominant traditions of liberalism and Marxism—we return in part again to root traditions from which we derive our values and standards. There are four of these:

1. There is an ancient Judeo-Christian prophetic tradition which gave men a vision of human dignity and a reign of righteousness, equality and brotherhood on earth. It taught them that building such an order of life was their task, and that a society of justice and fraternity could be built by justice and love and not by any other means.

2. There is an American tradition—far from having been realized, often distorted and all but lost—of a "nation conceived in liberty, and dedicated to the proposition that all men are created equal." It is a tradition which also emphasizes the dignity of man and asserts that government rests upon consent, and institutions are made for man, not man for institutions. Such names as Jefferson, Paine, Thoreau, Emerson, [Eugene] Debs, Randolph Bourne, the Quaker experiment in Pennsylvania, the Utopian community experiments, the Abolition movement, the Underground Railway, are associated with this tradition.

3. There is the heritage of the libertarian, democratic, anti-war, socialist, anarchist and labor movements in Europe and the United States in the latter half of the nineteenth century and the early years of the twentieth. Multitudes of common people, the impoverished and distressed, believed that through

these movements, with the help of modern science and technology, a "class-less and war-less world" had become possible and would in a comparatively short time be achieved.

4. There is a tradition of pacifism or nonviolence which has been exemplified throughout the centuries and in many parts of the world in great teachers and saints—or in such a figure as the Emperor Asoka—who have rejected war as accursed and unworthy of men and have insisted that injustice and violence cannot be overcome by injustice and violence but only by righteousness and peace. In particular, Gandhi stands in this tradition, not as an example to be slavishly imitated, but as a pioneer who in a series of great political and social experiments joined nonviolence and revolutionary collective action.

CRITIQUE OF LIBERALISM

In the light of these root traditions we can see that the greatness of liberalism has been its emphasis on humaneness and tolerance, its support of the liberties of the individual and its insistence on the free and inquiring mind and rejection of fanaticism and dogmatism. Its weakness has been its failure to come to grips with war, poverty, boredom, authoritarianism and other great evils of the modern world. These problems it has tended optimistically to leave to "education" and "good will," both of which have so far proved incapable of dealing with them successfully. Liberalism has tried to diagnose our troubles without going to fundamentals—the inequalities and injustices upon which our present social order is based and which no "good will" can wish away.

This failure to raise the embarrassing questions has made liberalism often shallow, hypocritical and dilettantish, all too often lacking in fundamental earnestness. Essentially the liberal accepts the existing order and wants to exploit it and share in it as much as the next man. At the same time he is troubled and wants the good conscience of repudiating its wrongs. Liberalism thus becomes a fashionable pose—for millionaires and generals as well as for intellectuals and editorial writers. It becomes a public ritual lacking roots in private life and behavior, and makes the liberal an easy prey of opportunism and expedience.

As against this liberal attitude a new quality of seriousness and personal honesty is necessary. In this respect what is wanted is not political liberalism but political fundamentalism. We are more interested in concrete situations than in rhetorical blueprints, in individual lives than in "global historical forces" which remain merely abstract. What matters to us is what happens to the individual human being—here and now. We will be just as flexible as the liberal, but we will strive to be more searching, and we will insist on spelling things out in terms of daily consequences, hour to hour, for everyone.

CRITIQUE OF MARXISM

Marxism, like liberalism, has much to teach both positively and negatively. Its fundamental demand for economic justice and its attack on the problem of poverty are permanently valuable. It touches the source of much that is wrong with the world in exposing the property nerve. But many of its attitudes are those of the outmoded bourgeois epoch which it tried to repudiate. Marx was to a greater degree than he himself realized a spokesman for nineteenth century thought patterns, now hopelessly out of date. His historical determinism, built up by analogy from now outmoded science, is an example. So also is the tendency to sacrifice the present for the future, so that human beings of today are regarded as pawns for bringing about something better in a tomorrow that never comes.

The most serious weaknesses of Marxism, however, are its omissions and its reactionary "realism" in respect to the instruments of revolution. Marx, for all his brilliant analysis of economic power, failed to analyze with equal profundity the questions of military and political power. Hence he underestimated the seriousness of the growth of the State and its emergence as an instrument of war and oppression. In trying to liberate mankind from economic slavery, he failed to see the looming horror of political slavery.

Closely related to this failure is Marx's inability to realize that social betterment cannot be brought about by the same old methods of force and chicanery characterizing the regimes which had to be overthrown precisely because they embodied such evils. It is an illuminating insight of pragmatism that means and ends condition each other reciprocally and that the ends must be built into the means. It is not sound, therefore, to expect to achieve peace through war, justice through violence, freedom through dictatorship, or civil liberties through slave labor camps. Such instruments create the social attitudes and habit patterns which they are ostensibly designed to remove. Dictatorship in any form, as well as spy systems, concentration camps, military conscription, restrictions on travel and censorship of books, papers and political parties must all be decisively rejected. What this means is that a truly radical movement today—if it does not want to fall into the trap which the Russian Communist movement has fallen into—must take these ethical problems much more seriously than many nineteenth century thinkers did, and must commit itself to an essentially democratic and nonviolent strategy.

One of the symptoms of our time is that many people are fed up with "politics" —by which they mean the whole machinery associated with political life. To become significant, politics must discover its ethical foundations and dynamic.

The politics of the future requires a creative synthesis of the individual ethical insights of the great religious leaders and the collective social concern of the great revolutionists.

It follows that we do not conceive the problem of revolution or the building of a better society as one of accumulating power, whether by legislative or other methods, to "capture the State," and then, presumably, to transform society and human beings as well. The national, sovereign, militarized and bureaucratic State and a bureaucratic collectivist economy are themselves evils to be avoided or abolished. Seizure of the war-making and repressive machinery of the State cannot be a step toward transforming society into a free and humanly satisfying pattern. It is the transformation of society by human decision and action that we seek. This is a more complex and human process in which power as ordinarily conceived plays a minor part. Political action in this context is, therefore, broadly conceived. It includes such developments as the Land Gift Movement in India and community and cooperative experiments in many lands. New political alignments in the narrower sense of the term may emerge from basic ethical and social changes, but preoccupation with or dependence upon the machinery of politics, or the violent seizure of power, are evils always to be avoided, and never more so than in the present crisis.

Similarly, we reject the faith in technology, industrialization and centralization *per se*, characteristic of both the contemporary capitalist and Communist regimes. Our emphasis is rather on possibilities for decentralization, on direct participation of all workers or citizens in determining the conditions of life and work, and on the use of technology for human ends, rather than the subjection of man to the demands of technology.

From the synthesis of the ethical and the political emerges a new attitude toward utopianism in social and cultural thinking. Under the impact of Marxism, utopianism became virtually a term of abuse. But this attitude itself was narrow and misjudged the scientific method, not seeing that the essence of science is its openness to new and creative insights and its willingness to test them experimentally. The utopian attitude is one that is permanently needed in human affairs. It represents the growing edge of society and the creative imagination of a culture.

As we recognize more and more the imaginative and speculative element in mathematics and science and as the mechanical determinism of the last century passes away, the outmoded "scientific" aspect of nineteenth century Marxism will begin to disappear, and Marx will then appear in his true light as one of the great visionaries and utopian thinkers of that century. With new conditions, modifications of his utopian thinking are necessary and new utopias will appear, to furnish direction and incentives for action.

The world *can* move toward the abolition of war and toward a society built on responsible freedom, mutuality and peace. Collective effort and struggle to achieve such a society should not be abandoned because the movements of an earlier day have been frustrated or wrecked.

The very presuppositions on which human relationships are based must be revolutionized. This makes it peculiarly difficult to live responsibly as individuals today and to carry on collective efforts for basic changes. In addition, the creation of a movement of dissent and social change in the United States is impeded by a sustained, war-based prosperity, with millions of unionists making a living at war jobs. This makes the task virtually as difficult in the United States as in Russia or other Communist-bloc countries.

The problem of war is one of special gravity for us, as for all our fellow men. It may be argued that for personal ethics there is no distinction between a war in which a few persons are killed at a time and one in which multitudes are wiped out. But from a sociological view, the H-bomb and what it symbolizes— possible extinction of the race itself—present mankind with a new situation. War is no longer an instrument of policy or a means to any rational end. For this reason, if for no other, a central part of any radical movement today is withdrawal of support from the military preparation and activities of *both* the dominant power blocs. Whatever differences may exist between Communist and "free world" regimes, in this decisive respect they are *equal* threats, two sides of the *same* threat to the survival of civilization. The H-bomb is not an instrument of peace in the hands of one and of war in the hands of the other. Nor is it a mere accidental excrescence in either of them but, rather, a logical outgrowth of their basic economic and social orders. [. . .]

Liberation will seek to inspire its readers not only to fresh thinking but to *action now*—refusal to run away or to conform, concrete resistance in the communities in which we live to all the ways in which human beings are regimented and corrupted, dehumanized and deprived of their freedom; experimentation in creative living by individuals, families, and groups; day to day support of movements to abolish colonialism and racism or for the freedom of all individuals from domination, whether military, economic, political, or cultural.

Liberation, March 1956.

King slightly revised Rustin's draft article on the bus boycott for publication in the second issue of *Liberation*. It was the first of numerous articles and chapter drafts that Rustin wrote for him.

"Our Struggle," by Martin Luther King Jr.

The segregation of Negroes, with its inevitable discrimination, has thrived on elements of inferiority present in the masses of both white and Negro people. Through forced separation from our African culture, through slavery, poverty, and deprivation, many black men lost self-respect.

In their relations with Negroes, white people discovered that they had rejected the very center of their own ethical professions. They could not face the triumph of their lesser instincts and simultaneously have peace within. And so, to gain it, they rationalized—insisting that the unfortunate Negro, being less than human, deserved and even enjoyed second class status.

They argued that his inferior social, economic and political position was good for him. He was incapable of advancing beyond a fixed position and would therefore be happier if encouraged not to attempt the impossible. He is subjugated by a superior people with an advanced way of life. The "master race" will be able to civilize him to a limited degree, if only he will be true to his inferior nature and stay in his place.

White men soon came to forget that the Southern social culture and all its institutions had been organized to perpetuate this rationalization. They observed a caste system and quickly were conditioned to believe that its social results, which they had created, actually reflected the Negro's innate and true nature.

In time many Negroes lost faith in themselves and came to believe that perhaps they really were what they had been told they were—something less than men. So long as they were prepared to accept this role, racial peace could be maintained. It was an uneasy peace in which the Negro was forced to accept patiently injustice, insult, injury and exploitation.

Gradually the Negro masses in the South began to re-evaluate themselves—a process that was to change the nature of the Negro community and doom the social patterns of the South. We discovered that we had never really smothered our self-respect and that we could not be at one with ourselves without asserting it. From this point on, the South's terrible peace was rapidly undermined by the Negro's new and courageous thinking and his ever-increasing readiness to organize and to act. Conflict and violence were coming to the surface as the white South desperately clung to its old patterns. The extreme tension in race relations in the South today is explained in part by the revolutionary change in the Negro's evaluation of himself and of his destiny and by his determination to struggle for justice. *We Negroes have replaced self-pity with self-respect and self-depreciation with dignity.*

When Mrs. Rosa Parks, the quiet seamstress whose arrest precipitated the non-violent protest in Montgomery, was asked why she had refused to move to the rear of a bus, she said: "It was a matter of dignity; I could not have faced myself and my people if I had moved."

THE NEW NEGRO

Many of the Negroes who joined the protest did not expect it to succeed. When asked why, they usually gave one of three answers: "I didn't expect Negroes to stick to it," or, "I never thought we Negroes had the nerve," or, "I thought the pressure from the white folks would kill it before it got started."

In other words, our non-violent protest in Montgomery is important because it is demonstrating to the Negro, North and South, that many of the stereotypes he has held about himself and other Negroes are not valid. Montgomery has broken the spell and is ushering in concrete manifestations of the thinking and action of the new Negro.

We now know that:

WE CAN STICK TOGETHER. In Montgomery, 42,000 of us have refused to ride the city's segregated busses since December 5. Some walk as many as fourteen miles a day.

OUR LEADERS DO NOT HAVE TO SELL OUT. Many of us have been indicted, arrested, and "mugged." Every Monday and Thursday night we stand before the Negro population at the prayer meetings and repeat: "It is an honor to face jail for a just cause."

THREATS AND VIOLENCE DO NOT NECESSARILY INTIMIDATE THOSE WHO ARE SUFFICIENTLY AROUSED AND NON-VIOLENT. The bombing of two of our homes has made us more resolute. When a handbill was circulated at a White Citizens Council meeting stating that Negroes should be "abolished" by "guns, bows and arrows, sling shots and knives," we responded with even greater determination.

OUR CHURCH IS BECOMING MILITANT. Twenty-four ministers were arrested in Montgomery. Each has said publicly that he stands prepared to be arrested again. Even upper-class Negroes who reject the "come to Jesus" gospel are now convinced that the church has no alternative but to provide the non-violent dynamics for social change in the midst of conflict. The $30,000 used for the car pool, which transports over 20,000 Negro workers, school children and housewives, has been raised in the churches. The churches have become the dispatch centers where the people gather to wait for rides.

WE BELIEVE IN OURSELVES. In Montgomery we walk in a new way. We hold our heads in a new way. Even the Negro reporters who converged on Montgomery have a new attitude. One tired reporter, asked at a luncheon in Birmingham to say a few words about Montgomery, stood up, thought for a moment, and uttered one sentence: "Montgomery has made me proud to be a Negro."

ECONOMICS IS PART OF OUR STRUGGLE. We are aware that Montgomery's white businessmen have tried to "talk sense" to the bus company and the city commissioners. We have observed that small Negro shops are thriving as Negroes find it inconvenient to walk downtown to the white stores. We have been getting more polite treatment in the white shops since the protest began. We have a new respect for the proper use of our dollar.

WE HAVE DISCOVERED A NEW AND POWERFUL WEAPON—NON-VIOLENT RESISTANCE. Although law is an important factor in bringing about social change, there are certain conditions in which the very effort to adhere to new legal decisions creates tension and provokes violence. We had hoped to see demonstrated a method that would enable us to continue our struggle while coping with the violence it aroused. Now we see the answer: face violence if necessary, but refuse to return violence. If we respect those who oppose us, they may achieve a new understanding of the human relations involved.

WE NOW KNOW THAT THE SOUTHERN NEGRO HAS COME OF AGE, POLITICALLY AND MORALLY. Montgomery has demonstrated that we will not run from the struggle, and will support the battle for equality. The attitude of many young Negroes a few years ago was reflected in the common expression, "I'd rather be a lamp post in Harlem than Governor of Alabama." Now the idea expressed in our churches, schools, pool rooms, restaurants and homes is: "Brother, stay here and fight non-violently. 'Cause if you don't let them make you mad, you can win." The official slogan of the Montgomery Improvement Association is "Justice without Violence."

THE ISSUES IN MONTGOMERY

The leaders of the old order in Montgomery are not prepared to negotiate a settlement. This is not because of the conditions we have set for returning to the busses. The basic question of segregation in intra-state travel is already before the courts. Meanwhile we ask only for what in Atlanta, Mobile, Charleston and most other cities of the South is considered the Southern pattern. We seek the right, under segregation, to seat ourselves from the rear forward on a first come, first served basis. In addition, we ask for courtesy and the hiring of some Negro bus drivers on predominantly Negro routes.

A prominent judge of Tuscaloosa was asked if he felt there was any connection between Autherine Lucy's effort to enter the University of Alabama and the Montgomery non-violent protest. He replied, "Autherine is just one unfortunate girl who doesn't know what she is doing, but in Montgomery it looks like all the niggers have gone crazy."

Later the judge is reported to have explained that "of course the good niggers had undoubtedly been riled up by outsiders, Communists and agitators." It is apparent that at this historic moment most of the elements of the white South are not prepared to believe that "our Negroes could of themselves act like this."

MISCALCULATION OF THE WHITE LEADERS

Because the Mayor and city authorities cannot admit to themselves that we have changed, every move they have made has inadvertently increased the protest and united the Negro community.

Dec. 1—They arrested Mrs. Parks, one of the most respected Negro women in Montgomery.

Dec. 3—They attempted to intimidate the Negro population by publishing a report in the daily paper that certain Negroes were calling for a boycott of the busses. They thereby informed the 30,000 Negro readers of the planned protest.

Dec. 5—They found Mrs. Parks guilty and fined her $14. This action increased the number of those who joined the boycott.

Dec. 5—They arrested a Negro college student for "intimidating passengers." Actually, he was helping an elderly woman cross the street. This mistake solidified the college students' support of the protest.

Two policemen on motorcycles followed each bus on its rounds through the Negro community. This attempt at psychological coercion further increased the number of Negroes who joined the protest.

In a news telecast at 6:00 P.M. a mass meeting planned for that evening was announced. Although we had expected only 500 people at the meeting, over 5,000 attended.

Dec. 6—They began to intimidate Negro taxi drivers. This led to the setting up of a car pool and a resolution to extend indefinitely our protest, which had originally been called for one day only.

Dec. 7—They began to harass Negro motorists. This encouraged the Negro middle class to join the struggle.

Dec. 8—The lawyer for the bus company said, "We have no intention of hiring Negro drivers now or in the foreseeable future." To us this meant never. The slogan then became, "Stay off the busses until we win."

Dec. 9—The Mayor invited Negro leaders to a conference, presumably for negotiation. When we arrived, we discovered that some of the men in the room were white supremacists and members of the White Citizens Council. The Mayor's attitude was made clear when he said, "Comes the first rainy day and the Negroes will be back in the busses." The next day it did rain, but the Negroes did not ride the busses.

At this point over 42,000 Montgomery Negroes had joined the protest. After a period of uneasy quiet, elements in the white community turned to further police intimidation and to violence.

Jan. 26—I was arrested for travelling 30 miles per hour in a 25 mile zone. This arrest occurred just 2 hours before a mass meeting. So, we had to hold seven mass meetings to accommodate the people.

Jan. 30—My home was bombed.

Feb. 1—The home of E. D. Nixon, one of the protest leaders and former State President of the NAACP, was bombed. This brought moral and financial support from all over the state.

Feb. 22—Eighty-nine persons, including the 24 ministers, were arrested for participating in the non-violent protest.

Every attempt to end the protest by intimidation, by encouraging Negroes to inform, by force and violence, further cemented the Negro community and brought sympathy for our cause from men of good will all over the world. The great appeal for the world appears to lie in the fact that we in Montgomery have adopted the method of non-violence. In a world in which most men attempt to defend their highest values by the accumulation of weapons of destruction, it is morally refreshing to hear 5,000 Negroes in Montgomery shout "Amen" and "Halleluh" when they are exhorted to "pray for those who oppose you," or pray "Oh Lord, give us strength of body to keep walking for freedom," and conclude each mass meeting with: "Let us pray that God shall give us strength to remain non-violent though we may face death."

THE LIBERAL DILEMMA

And death there may be. Many white men in the South see themselves as a fearful minority in an ocean of black men. They honestly believe with one side of their minds that Negroes are depraved and disease-ridden. They look upon any effort at equality as leading to "mongrelization." They are convinced that racial equality is a Communist idea and that those who ask for it are subversive. They believe that their caste system is the highest form of social organization.

The enlightened white Southerner, who for years has preached gradualism, now sees that even the slow approach finally has revolutionary implications. Placing straws on a camel's back, no matter how slowly, is dangerous. This realization has immobilized the liberals and most of the white church leaders. They have no answer for dealing with or absorbing violence. They end in begging for retreat, lest "things get out of hand and lead to violence."

Writing in *Life*, William Faulkner, Nobel prize–winning author from Mississippi, recently urged the NAACP to "stop now for a moment." That is to say, he encouraged Negroes to accept injustice, exploitation and indignity for a while longer. It is hardly a moral act to encourage others patiently to accept injustice which he himself does not endure.

In urging delay, which in this dynamic period is tantamount to retreat, Faulkner suggests that those of us who press for change now may not know that violence could break out. He says we are "dealing with a fact: the fact of emotional conditions of such fierce unanimity as to scorn the fact that it is a minority and which will go to any length and against any odds at this moment to justify and, if necessary, defend that condition and its right to it."

We Southern Negroes believe that it is essential to defend the right of equality now. From this position we will not and cannot retreat. Fortunately, we are increasingly aware that we must not try to defend our position by methods that contradict the aim of brotherhood. We in Montgomery believe that the only way to press on is by adopting the philosophy and practice of non-violent resistance.

This method permits a struggle to go on with dignity and without the need to retreat. It is a method that can absorb the violence that is inevitable in social change whenever deep-seated prejudices are challenged.

If, in pressing for justice and equality in Montgomery, we discover that those who reject equality are prepared to use violence, we must not despair, retreat, or fear. Before they make this crucial decision, they must remember: whatever they do, we will not use violence in return. We hope we can act in the struggle in such a way that they will see the error of their approach and will come to respect us. Then we can all live together in peace and equality.

The basic conflict is not really over the busses. Yet we believe that, if the method we use in dealing with equality in the busses can eliminate injustice within ourselves, we shall at the same time be attacking the basis of injustice— man's hostility to man. This can only be done when we challenge the white community to reexamine its assumptions as we are now prepared to reexamine ours.

We do not wish to triumph over the white community. That would only result in transferring those now on the bottom to the top. But, if we can live up to non-violence in thought and deed, there will emerge an interracial society based on freedom for all.

Liberation, April 1956.

April 3, 1956

Dear Dr. King:

[. . .] Several weeks ago, I wrote you. I have not received a reply but I know you are overwhelmed with work, and with many calls on you. I do not ask for a reply; I simply want you to know that I did write, for fear the letter went astray. I did not send it registered.

I am Lillian Smith, the writer, and am deeply with you in your fine non-violent efforts. As I said in my previous letter, this seems to me the right way. For the means you are using are in themselves so spiritually potent that they cannot fail to stir men's hearts and minds everywhere. Perhaps it will spread throughout the South. I hope so. You would be surprised, I believe, to know the strength of the admiration thousands of white southerners feel for what you are doing. I hear it everywhere I go.

Once, long ago, in 1940 I think it was, I heard an old Negro sharecropper pray. We were at a meeting in a small church in Arkansas; it was during the time when the sharecroppers had been evicted. There were many whites there from the unions trying to help; among them quite a few tough Communists whom I recognized. There were curious cross-currents in that meeting: snowing outside; people poor, hungry, cold; inside a fight going on between the Communist union organizers and the non-Communist ones. They had almost forgot the people; they had almost forgot the real cause: the human beings involved and their landlords. Then this old man got up to pray. He leaned on the chair in front of him—I can see his old knuckled hands even now—those hands pressed down hard on that chair as he stood there in silence. Even the Commies grew still as they watched him. Then he prayed about the landlords. And this is what he said: "Break their hearts, Oh God, give them tears. . . ." His hands beat silently on the chair. "Give them tears. . . . Make the tears flow, God, make them flow . . . until a flood comes, God. Wash away their pride, God, wash away their hate; wash away their stubborn ways. Flood our land with tears, God; it's been dry so long."

That is when I began to see plainly that the way of love is stronger than any other way. It can be resisted for a while; a time comes, when the human heart, even the hardest heart, will melt.

If I can be of help to you in any way, won't you call on me? I am telling people; I am urging the white southerners who believe in your way to let you know they do; that it is important for them to take a stand within their own hearts as well as for your group in Montgomery. But is there any other way I can help you? Would you want me to come down and speak to a few of your people? Would that help? or hurt? I want to help in any way I can.

My warmest greetings to you and to your congregation and to your people, who are my people, too; for we are all one big human family. I pray that we shall soon in the South begin to act like one.

Most sincerely yours,
Lillian Smith

[P.S.] My house up at Clayton was burned this winter by two young white boys; whether it was delinquency or racial feelings, I do not know—and I am not sure you can separate the two, wholly. They were very young. It is hard to believe they did it because of race. But this lawlessness of the young is a direct result of the lawlessness of their elders, many of whom do not hesitate to say they will not obey the highest law of our land when that law does not suit them. Such examples of disesteem for the law are bound to have a profound effect on the young. The burning of the house was quite a loss to me, as all my papers, 7000 letters on race relations, all my manuscripts, my work in progress—all clippings collected during these 20 years of work for racial integration—everything was burned. The boys were taken out of town and to another state by friends and family; there was not one word about the fire in the local paper. Fear. Fear eats up the goodness in us. That is why what you are doing, your emphasis on the power of love, on forgiveness, is so right, so true.

MLKP-MBU: Box 65.

Memo to [Fellowship of Reconciliation] Staff, April 7, 1956
From: Glenn Smiley, [Montgomery]

For some time I have been intending after discussions with John [Swomley] and Al Hassler, to write you regarding the program now underway in the South for the aid and guidance of nonviolence in this section. The program has been the outgrowth of four visits to the south and conferences with numerous people in New York, including A. Philip Randolph, Claude Nelson and others. It is significant to note that of the groups working in our field, it seems that the Fellowship of Reconciliation is the only one with a southern base of operation that could immediately enter the field with a positive program, and the value of Bob Cannon's office in Nashville cannot be overestimated at this point.

[*Generally speaking, the program has the following approaches:*]

1) An approach to the nonviolent movement under way in Montgomery and Orangeburg, S.C. This has included several visits to each place, contact with the leaders, distribution of literature, long conversations on nonviolence and pacifism as a whole, attendance at mass meetings, interviews, etc. In this fashion we have been able to have what may be considered a sizeable influence on the leaders of these movements, and a friendship that has been developed with Rev. King, Rev. Abernathy, Rev. McCollum, Dean Haines and others, has been most rewarding personally. In connection with this, and although it is still in the works, we are seeking to arrange next week a meeting of the various nonviolent leaders of the South within the Negro community, to consider problems of communication and overall strategy, as well as the ideological factors involved.

2) An approach to the white church, especially in the state of Alabama. This has included numerous conferences with individuals, pastors and laymen of churches, etc., and has resulted first, in the meeting of 10 ministers in Montgomery in March, for the planning of a larger meeting which was held Friday, April 6th at the YMCA camp, out 10 miles from Montgomery. At this meeting, 65 ministers from all over the state and northern Florida, gathered together to consider what might be done by the church under these circumstances. The meeting was a tremendous revival of faith and confidence on the part of the people present, and they in turn set up a further meeting which would be openly publicized and which would issue a public statement. We are continuing along this line with the help of both FOR and non-FOR ministers in the state of Alabama. In connection with this, there has been the encouragement of interracial ministerial associations' meetings, interracial meetings for prayer on the part of ministers, and an effort to re-establish the lines of communications which have been completely broken down in the four hard-core states of the South.

3) The holding of conferences, workshops, and seminars on nonviolence in colleges, universities and places. Bob Cannon has already held such workshops in Berea, Knoxville, Chattanooga, Nashville, etc. and Wilson Riles and I are now in the South holding such workshops at Morehouse, Paine College, Tuskegee, Claflin University. The effort here is to train as many student leaders as possible who might go back into communities this summer to help

relieve tensions and to insure a nonviolent approach to the problems that are to be faced. It is expected that the summer will be a crucial period in the South as far as this is concerned. In these workshops we are discussing the theory and practice of nonviolence, the experience that has been had abroad as well as in the U.S. in this field; the theology and philosophy of nonviolence, etc. We hope to use some socio-drama, literature.

4) Al Hassler is busy, along with professional help, on the preparation of a 15-minute documentary film prepared largely from news clips with a running commentary describing nonviolence, not only as it relates itself to Montgomery but to the race problem all over the world.

5) We are interested and are working on the preparation of literature to augment the supply already on hand and to provide more manageable pieces of literature dealing with nonviolence. In connection with a mailing just going out to the membership, Al Hassler has prepared a pamphlet and there is hope of reprinting the A. J. Muste pamphlet "What the Bible Teaches About Freedom" in the near future.

With regard to the support of such a program, the mailing has gone from New York and I am also writing some personal friends, non-FOR members on the west coast, giving them an indication of what we are doing and soliciting their help and prayers.

As an example, I have told them that if we had $250.00 we could distribute literature and books on nonviolence to scores of ministers and students throughout the South. If we had $800.00 it would enable me to stay close beside the men in Montgomery and Orangeburg who are desperately in need of guidance and help in this time of crisis. For $1000.00 we could hold 10 all-day workshops in 10 colleges and universities of the South and could distribute some literature. For $1000.00 we could prepare and present panels in scores of churches and ministerial associations in Alabama and South Carolina, raising the problem of race and the possibility of a Christian and not a Southern solution.

One of the things that is very important, it seems to me, is the fact that whereas before, we have had difficulty interesting Negroes in the South in nonviolence, at the present time, their interest is to the point of eagerness and they seem to welcome any help in this field. Our reception at the colleges has been uniformly enthusiastic.

In mentioning the above of course, I have not mentioned anything about what you are doing yourself in your own regions to help the nonviolent movement and I know of work that is significant in the Pacific-Southwest, the Middle Atlantic, the New England regions, and am assured that the other regions are not neglecting this important feature of our work.

[*I*] would appreciate help and suggestions regarding the above program as it is as always, an open-ended approach with eager acceptance of workable ideas for the South. It is my firm conviction that the FOR was created for such an hour, and I pray that we may be as adequate as possible.

FORP-PSC-P.

Smiley reported to King on his five-day visit to Montgomery in early April, accompanied by Wilson Riles, FOR's Southwest regional secretary.

April 13, 1956

Dr. Martin Luther King
309 S. Jackson
Montgomery, Ala.

Dear Martin:

We are sorry to have missed you while we were in Montgomery and I am especially sorry that our secretary from Los Angeles did not have the privilege of a conversation with you, as it would have enhanced his usefulness in securing support on the west coast. We did do a good deal of thinking on the problem and did hold the meeting of [*white*] ministers of which I spoke. Seventy ministers from all over the state and the northern tip of Florida attended the meeting at the YMCA camp near Montgomery, and discussed all day from 10:00 a.m. to 4:00 p.m. what could be done. Everyone was surprised at the turnout, as it was by invitation rather than by publicity, and strictly on the basis of a liberal approach to the problems in the state. I feel that this could very easily be the most significant thing I have done, in that it stands a good chance of being the beginning of a rebuilt "middle ground" in Alabama. The ministers agreed that although they had met with the promise of no publicity and no statements, that they would meet again sometime during the first two weeks of May in a *publicized* meeting and would make a statement then. This latter part should be held confidentially until they have had the opportunity to make the first move, but I believe that it will occur. There was a good deal of talk about reestablishing communications between the groups in the south, and a good deal of feeling of guilt and repentance that they had done so little and had allowed the church to be pushed about so much.

I also talked with [*Thomas*] Thrasher and some others about the possibility of establishing some prayer groups between a few of you in Montgomery and I hope that I was not too far wrong when I intimated to them that I felt you would be interested in getting together regularly with some members of the white ministerial group to pray for illumination and guidance in the problems that face the Christian church in the south. I mentioned this to Ralph and he thought it probably was a good idea.

I also mentioned to Ralph the fact that we are now preparing a 15-minute documentary film on nonviolence in the race question, about 7 minutes of it dealing with the Montgomery situation and the rest of it being devoted to experiences in South Africa and India, and the growing unrest of the world. If it turns out as good as we think it will—and it should be ready in about three weeks to a month from now—I was wondering if there is a possibility that we might show it first for one of the mass meetings in Montgomery. This is just a suggestion and would certainly appreciate your reaction to it. I suspect that we could arrange it from our end, although I have not talked with the man who is doing the picture. Also Wilson Riles and I were discussing the matter the other night, and wondered if there would not be some value in a boycott (if you would want to call it that, of the humiliating experience you suffer) in that the local *Advertiser* has a Negro sheet which is not sent to the white community and therefore it does nothing to forward the communication between the two groups, except to spread the poison of the racists among the Negro people. What a sentence! We were wondering if there is any value in casually suggesting that there is really no service to the Negro people, and further suggesting to some private capital that a sheet, or even a daily paper in Montgomery for Negro people might really serve the community more adequately than the *Advertiser* can do. Just to continue with our thinking, we thought that there might be a possibility that the *Atlanta Daily World* might issue a Montgomery daily edition, or that they would publish a daily sheet for you and airmail it to Montgomery for distribution. It does seem that Negro people are paying for being discriminated against in the *Advertiser* paper. I am not sure that this would serve as much pressure on the white community, although it would undoubtedly affect the advertising rates of the *Advertiser*, itself. Another possibility might be to have the paper printed at the Negro publishing house in Birmingham. Anyway, it is an idea presented for your consideration, and shall leave it with you.

Blessings upon you, and our prayers continue to be with you.

Sincerely,
[*signed*] Glenn
Glenn E. Smiley
National Field Sec.

cc to Ralph Abernathy

A. J. Muste (1885–1967), the veteran pacifist leader, invites Norman Thomas to join the Committee for Nonviolent Integration (CNI), an ad hoc organization formed to build national support for the Montgomery bus boycott and other desegregation efforts. It emerged from discussions among King, MIA leaders, Rustin, and other New York radical pacifists about how "outsiders" could assist the bus boycott. Muste served as CNI secretary; it was co-chaired by Rev. Donald Harrington of the New York City Community Church and Dean William Stuart Nelson of Howard University.

April 13, 1956

Mr. Norman M. Thomas
112 East 19th Street
New York, New York

Dear Norman:

A couple of days ago several members of the newly-formed Committee for Nonviolent Integration had a conference here in New York with the Reverend Martin Luther King Jr. of Montgomery, Alabama. He impressed upon us the need for our Committee and specifically approved of the initial list of projects, a copy of which is enclosed. From time to time he will propose additional projects related to the situation in Montgomery or to similar situations elsewhere in the South.

Also enclosed is a statement of the purpose and scope of CNI which has not only been passed upon by Mr. King but has also been discussed with Mr. E. D. Nixon, the local head of the Brotherhood of Pullman Porters in Montgomery who has also urged support of CNI, and with national officers of the Brotherhood.

Thirdly, I am enclosing a list of the persons who have agreed to serve on the Committee.

Our work would be greatly helped if a number of well-known persons, who may not feel able to give the time and assume the responsibility involved in joining the Committee, would agree to serve as Sponsors of our work. We earnestly hope you may be one of them.

A return card is enclosed for your convenience, but we should be pleased to receive any comments on, or suggestions about, our work which you may have.

Since we want to get printed material out promptly so that our work may get rolling throughout the country, as a number of groups are already waiting for such material, I hope we may hear from you at once, by telephone at our expense, if this letter is delayed in coming to your attention.

There are an awful lot of these things to belong to but if you can add one more, we certainly hope it will be this.

Sincerely yours, [*signed*] A. J.
A. J. Muste, Secretary pro tem.

NTP-NN.

Statement of Purpose of the Committee for Nonviolent Integration

April 13, 1956

The Protest of 40,000 Negroes in Montgomery, Alabama, (they prefer not to call it a boycott) against segregation and humiliating treatment on the city buses has attracted world-wide attention. This is as it should be.

The movement in Montgomery marks a decisive turning point in the life of Southern Negroes, and therefore in the whole life of the South and of the rest of the country.

It is a part of the revolt of the colored peoples of the world against old ideas and practices of white supremacy.

The Montgomery movement was not thought up or started, and it is not run, by Yankees, Communists, New Yorkers, or any "outsiders" whatsoever. It is a spontaneous revolt of the Negroes of Montgomery which raised up its own leadership in the Montgomery Improvement Association and in such men as the Reverend Martin Luther King Jr., and E. D. Nixon, local representative of the Brotherhood of Sleeping Car Porters.

The Montgomery movement and other struggles in the South mark the passage of Southern Negroes from an attitude of servility and passivity to a spirit of solidarity, fearlessness and hope and a demand for human dignity and first-class citizenship.

This is the most powerful dynamic at work in the South today for insuring a better life and a nobler culture for all its people.

The Montgomery movement is one of Nonviolent Resistance, deeply rooted in the religion of the Negro people of the South. The theme-song of the movement, sung to the tune of "Give Me That Old-Time Religion," contains the lines: "We know love is the pass-word to peace and liberty. Black and white all are brothers to live in harmony." Here is the pattern that may save this nation from the scourge of race war, while abolishing the curse of racial injustice and inequality.

The Committee for Nonviolent Integration and local committees associated with it are set up to assert publicly our appreciation of the struggle in Montgomery and similar efforts in other places and to gather all possible support for those who are carrying on these struggles now and in the future.

The CNI is an *ad hoc* arrangement to meet such needs as are revealed by the present emergency and to provide a channel into which those not already active in other groups may put their efforts. The main purposes of CNI are:

To provide such financial and other aid as may be needed and asked in Montgomery and other communities where non-violent efforts to abolish segregation are taking place.

To explain the spirit and method of nonviolent resistance and its meaning in a world fed up with violence.

To encourage workers, farmers, church people and other citizens inspired by the dynamic and nonviolent uprising in the South, to work on the problem of integration in education, employment, housing and other fields wherever they live, North, South, East or West. [. . .]

NTP-NN.

Support activities of the CNI included sending several hundred bicycles for a bicycle pool, which would also "provide a constructive outlet for the energies and skills of young Negroes in Montgomery"; sending new and used automobiles for the car pool; producing bus boycott pins and matchbooks to raise money; and helping to organize nonviolent workshops for southern black leaders.[1]

1. "Statement of Purpose of the Committee for Nonviolent Integration," April 13, 1956, NTP-NN.

Smiley wrote the following minutes for the May 12 Atlanta meeting of FOR activists and southern movement leaders. The Fellowship of Reconciliation organized the conference to foster communication, discuss strategy, and try to "consolidate the several movements." It drew eighteen participants, including King, his father, Abernathy, John M. Swomley Jr., and A. J. Muste. Muste praised the conference at Morehouse College as "the most significant I have attended in fifty years in the Christian ministry."[1]

The meeting began at 10:30 with a short devotional by Glenn Smiley and then the Chairmanship was turned over to Dr. Charles Lawrence, national chairman of the Fellowship of Reconciliation. An agenda was suggested which would include the following items: 1) The problem of communication; 2) The future of nonviolence in the South; 3) Recognition of the fact that a crisis period is upon us; 4) How can we achieve the unity of Montgomery; and 5) What has happened of late in the South.

Matthew D. McCollum reported on recent happenings in Orangeburg, S.C., laying particular stress upon the State College situation, where a strike has recently been conducted by students [*protesting white harassment, police surveillance, and WCC-led economic boycotts*]. Indications are that the college is fairly hard hit and that there may be some withdrawal of students and faculty members at the close of this year. Students have been dragging their feet on ordinary college functions, and are reported to have foregone most of the social events associated with the end of school. The annual Mother's Day event fizzled this year; usually 200 mothers are invited to the campus but this year only 8 letters were written and only three mothers answered.

A report was made about the farmers in Clarendon, Sumpter and Orangeburg counties and it was reported that the farmers refused crop loans are still in bad shape, although many farmers have already been helped by $40,000 loans run through the Victory Bank in Columbia, S.C. $11,800 has now come in for crop loans. [. . .]

The White Citizens Council vs. the NAACP trouble was discussed, and mention was made of how unfortunate it was that the oppressed had been equated with the oppressor in this fashion. Some liberal groups have contributed to this misunderstanding in the South.

The Montgomery situation was discussed by Martin Luther King and Ralph Abernathy. The May 11th case decision [Browder v. Gayle] will be rendered at an indefinite date and it was made clear that this was not the Rosa Parks case but the case of the four women who had sued the bus company [*and the city and state*]. The question was asked "Can this be duplicated elsewhere?," meaning the unity in Montgomery. [*South Carolina State College chaplain Henry*] Parker said that the Orangeburg situation is bad because there is no communication between ministers. King called attention to the fact that there is a personal and a collective passive resistance; personal resistance is a day-by-day affair and the collective resistance must be used with care in a controlled situation. McCollum called attention to the fact that it seemed to him that a collective passive resistance could only succeed if there is high moral goal, emotional content and a unifying theme. He felt that Orangeburg has not had the great central unifying theme at all. Smiley suggested state-wide meetings on nonviolence, and Parker called for the necessity of communication. James Thomas made mention of the fact that we must affect the power structure and wondered how we could get at this power structure in the various communities. Will Campbell from Mississippi called attention to the fact that the liberal forces in Mississippi are underground movements; there are 12 men who are doing a good job but they appear to be cowards, only because they live behind the "Magnolia Curtain." There was some discussion of the fact of whether it was right to lie in order to do good. Swomley stated that a South-wide strategy is the important factor and we should try to get onto a more healthy ground than an underground movement. [*Oscar*] Lee thought we needed people who would understand the nonviolent methods. There was considerable discussion on the part of many as to whether we can help start projects or whether we should wait until an incident occurred, and the general agreement seemed to be that incidents are occurring everywhere that resistance to the pattern of segregation appears. We need to train people so that when incidents occur, someone will be there to help. There is a need to call together men from each of the 11 states, allowing them to go back and teach others the methods of nonviolence. Another suggestion was two men from each major city for a meeting of several days to train in nonviolence, and it was finally decided that two conferences would be set up, one for Alabama, Georgia and Florida, meeting July 17–18, Tuesday and Wednesday, in Alabama; the second training conference would be for South Carolina, North Carolina and Virginia, and would be held probably in South Carolina. Two men from each major city up to the number of 40 were to be invited to the conference. A committee composed of B. R. Brazeal, M. L. King Sr., M. L. King Jr., R. D. Abernathy, and Glenn Smiley was appointed to work out the details of the two conferences. There was also considerable discussion of conferences for both white and colored ministers, to which would be invited people of varying points of view, and it was felt that for the most part this would be a job that might be done by the church in the various communities.

After expressions of appreciation for the hospitality of Morehouse College, the meeting adjourned at approximately 4:00 P.M. with prayer by Martin Luther King Jr.

While there may be varying opinions as to the accomplishments of the conference, one man's opinion, that of the writer of the minutes, was that it served two extremely worthwhile purposes: 1) It brought together leaders of widely separated constructive Protest Movements for purposes of getting acquainted and to learn and appreciate the problems of the others; 2) That we came to realize that this was a problem that was ours and not just "mine," and it seemed to me that we began to accept individual responsibility for collective action in this field. The Fellowship of Reconciliation feels grateful for the opportunity of having called it together and looks forward eagerly to participation in the workshops mentioned above.

Respectfully submitted,
Glenn E. Smiley

GESP.

1. Quoted in Glenn E. Smiley, "Report from the South, Number 2," August 15, 1956, GESP.

May 2, 1956

Dear Rev King

We are so proud of our people's and your pride. Please keep up the good work's. I am taking up a donation in my beauty shop for you all. We have taken up a donation in our church for you all. Now we are taken up one in my shop. You also have our prays. How can these devils keep us down, unless they stay with us? Please keep up the good work's. I am co-worker for the NAACP I am working just as hard as you are.

May God bless you and your menember's also your church and everything that you *undertake*

I am

Miss Sadie Bradford
Route 3, Gastonia, N.C.

MLKP-MBU: Box 16.

Juanita Moore to Martin Luther King Jr.

June 3, 1956

Dear Rv.

King offers of Member -S- also friend's it a pledgur to sit and read about the good work as well as fight you are have did which now do seam to lead to sucess altho i doe kno it comes only through God & good leadership an follars as well and as for me myself I am for ever grateful to God and you all for siting a exyempal for the deep S. as they call it. i my self is a widow with a 4 yeairs old Sun to suport is why i am writing this letter without a donation but please except my good wishes as well as prayer for i am ever praying to see the race get Jesurs which you all surtenly has peaid a grand part as well as sticking out your neck's Keep the good work up and ask God for what you wont for i no he is able he said he will fight your battle if you just keep still just trust him for his Word and dont get empatience i recieved your beautiful letter some time a go but not once had i forgotten it i still remain youse in Christ

Juanita Moore [*Baltimore, Md.*]

MLKP-MBU: Box 62.

Summer . . . 10 . . .

As spring turned to summer in Montgomery, the bus boycott's legal offensive heated up along with the air, pavement, and car pool radiators. The moral momentum of the *Browder* v. *Gayle* lawsuit was buttressed by a Supreme Court decision in late April in a bus segregation case from South Carolina.[1] In 1954 Sarah Mae Flemming had sued the South Carolina Electric and Gas Company, which operated city buses in Columbia, for violating her Fourteenth Amendment right to equal protection by forcing her to move to the black section of a bus. In February 1955 a federal district judge dismissed her lawsuit, but her appeal was upheld by the Fourth Circuit Court of Appeals in July 1955, which declared intrastate bus segregation unconstitutional. The Supreme Court's ruling on April 23, 1956, did not actually affirm the Fourth Circuit's decision but merely rejected the utility company's appeal as premature. Nonetheless, the narrow technical decision was widely perceived as striking down intrastate bus segregation—typified by the front-page *New York Times* headlines the next day: HIGH COURT VOIDS LAST COLOR LINES IN PUBLIC TRANSIT. EXTENDS BAN ON SEGREGATION TO INTRASTATE BUSES IN A SOUTH CAROLINA CASE. 13 STATES ARE AFFECTED. IMPACT OF RULING IS EXPECTED TO BE AS WIDE AS DECISION AGAINST SEPARATE SCHOOLS.

The hyperbole around the ambiguous decision spurred a number of southern bus lines to desegregate. Montgomery City Lines, reeling from the boycott, immediately ordered its drivers to end segregated seating. But Mayor Gayle and Police Commissioner Sellers resolved to continue enforcing the status quo. The split between the commissioners and the bus company widened on May 9, when the former obtained a court injunction from Montgomery Circuit Court judge Walter B. Jones compelling the bus company to cancel its desegregation order. Although he did not refer to the separate but equal doctrine of *Plessy* v. *Ferguson*, Jones quoted an 1899 Alabama Supreme Court finding that it "is not an unreasonable regulation to seat passengers so as to preserve order and decorum, and to prevent contacts and collisions arising from natural or well known customary repugnances which are likely to breed disturbances by a promiscuous sitting." He did not ignore the 1954 *Brown* decision, but he appealed to the moral and constitutional authority of the Tenth Amendment, according to which, he argued, "the power to regulate the intra-state carriage of passengers on buses in Alabama is a power reserved to the State of Alabama."[2] He thereby set the Tenth Amendment, which authorized "states' rights," on a collision course with the Fourteenth, which restricted them. Before year's end the latter would prevail over the former, but this constitutional conflict foreshadowed the social drama of the next decade.

Although the *Browder* lawsuit appeared to occupy the moral high ground, King's March conspiracy conviction followed by the city's injunction against the bus company, combined with the unpredictability of a three-judge federal panel of southern whites who ranged from segregationist to racial moderate, made a legal strikeout seem ominously possible. If they lost in this federal court, an appeal of *Browder* to the Supreme Court would take months, even a year or more.

Thus, much was at stake and tensions ran high when plaintiffs Aurelia Browder, Susie McDonald, Claudette Colvin, and Mary Louise Smith testified on behalf of themselves and the Montgomery black community in the old federal courthouse one block from the corner where Rosa Parks had been arrested. Browder was the first witness at the day-long hearing on May 11.

1. *South Carolina Electric and Gas Company* v. *Flemming*, 351 U.S. 901 (1956).
2. Quoted in Randall Kennedy, "Martin Luther King's Constitution: A Legal History of the Montgomery Bus Boycott," *Yale Law Journal* 98, no. 6 (April 1989): 1046.

IN THE DISTRICT COURT OF THE UNITED STATES
FOR THE MIDDLE DISTRICT OF ALABAMA
NORTHERN DIVISION

AURELIA S. BROWDER, and SUSIE MCDONALD, and CLAUDETTE COLVIN, by Q. Q. Colvin, next friend, and MARY LOUISE SMITH, by Frank Smith, next friend, and others similarly situated

Plaintiffs,

vs.

W. A. GAYLE, CLYDE SELLERS, and FRANK PARKS, individually and as members of the Board of Commissioners of the City of Montgomery, Alabama, and GOOD-WYN J. RUPPENTHAL, individually and as Chief of Police of the City of Montgomery, Alabama and THE MONTGOMERY CITY LINES, INC., a Corporation, and JAMES F. BLAKE and ROBERT CLEERE, and C. C. (Jack) OWEN. JIMMY HITCHCOCK, and SIBYL POOL, as members of the ALABAMA PUBLIC SERVICE COMMISSION.

Defendants,

Before Judge Rives, Judge Lynne, and Judge Johnson.

AURELIA BROWDER, Called as a witness first being duly sworn, testified as follows:

DIRECT EXAMINATION

MR. GRAY:

Q. State your name, Miss Browder?

A. Aurelia Browder.

Q. Where do you live?

A. 1012 Highland Avenue.

Q. Prior to December 5, 1955, did you live here in Montgomery?

A. Yes

Q. Prior to December 5, 1955, did you ride the City buses?

A. Yes. Two to four times a day.

Q. Have you been riding those buses since December 5, 1955?

A. No.

Q. Why did you stop riding them?

A. I had stopped riding because I wanted better treatment. I knew if I would cooperate with my color I would finally get it.

Q. Have you personally experienced any difficulty on the bus in connection with the seating arrangement?

A. Yes, several times.

Q. Will you please tell the Court what happened?

A. April 29 of last year I was on the Day Street Bus, I got a transfer from Oak Park Bus in front of Price Drug Store. After I rode up by the Alabama Gas Company bus driver had three of us to get up and stand to let a white man and a white lady to sit down.

Q. When you say three of you, do you mean yourself along with two other Negroes?

A. Myself and two other Negroes. I was sitting in a seat and another lady beside me. And the seat just across from me there was just one colored person in there. And he made all three of us get up because he said we was in the white section of the bus.

Q. If you were permitted to sit any place you wanted on the bus, would you be willing to ride again?

A. Yes, I would.

Q. That is all.

JUDGE RIVES: You may arrange to cross examine.

A. The Attorney for the Public Service Commission has no questions to ask this witness.

MR. KNABE: You say you stopped riding the buses about December 5, 1955, is that correct?

A. Yes, sir.

Q. And I believe you said you stopped riding at that time because you wanted better treatment, is that correct?

A. That is right.

Q. It is a fact, is it not, that at that time the Rev. King and several others, so called Improvement Association I believe, made such a demand, is that right?

A. No.

Q. They did make some requests, did they not?

A. I would not call it that.

Q. What would you call it then?

A. We, the Negroes, request the Rev. King, and not he over us.

Q. You didn't understand my question. Did Negro King ask three certain things at that time, did he not. One was, you said, for more courteous treatment on the part of the bus drivers, that is correct, isn't it?

A. The Reverend King did not ask that, the Negroes asked that.

Q. Very well, but he was the mouth piece for the Negroes, was he not?

A. We employed him to be our mouth piece.

Q. I see. And that is one of the things that you asked for, that is correct is it not?

A. That is correct.

Q. And then you asked for seating, first come, first served, didn't you?

A. Yes.

Q. And then you asked for the employment of Negro drivers, that is correct, isn't it?

A. Yes.

Q. And you said unless you were granted all three of them you would not return to riding on the bus, is that correct?

A. Yes.

Q. In other words, you did not stop on account of segregation but you stopped riding before segregation issue was ever raised, that is correct isn't it?

A. It is the segregation laws of Alabama that caused all of it.

Q. Just answer the question, isn't it a fact that your mouth piece took into . . .

A. No! He did not put it into us!

Q. Is it not true that he put into the newspaper a statement of his requests, and he specifically stated in that, that the segregation statutes were not involved? Do you know that, didn't you read what he put in the papers?

A. Yes, I did. [. . .]

SER-DNA.

"My Day," by Eleanor Roosevelt

NEW YORK, MAY 14—A few days ago I met Mrs. Rosa Parks, who started the nonviolent protest in Montgomery, Alabama, against segregation on buses. She is a very quiet, gentle person and it is difficult to imagine how she ever could take such a positive and independent stand.

I suppose we must realize that these things do not happen all of a sudden. They grow out of feelings that have been developing over many years. Human beings reach a point when they say: "This is as far as I can go," and from then on it may be passive resistance, but it will be resistance.

That is what seems to have happened in Montgomery, and perhaps it will happen all over our country wherever we have citizens who do not enjoy complete equality. It may be that this attitude will save us from war and bloodshed and teach those of us who have to learn that there is a point beyond which human beings will not continue to bear injustice.

Eleanor Roosevelt's My Day, vol. 3 (Mahwah, N.J.: Pharos Books, 1991), p. 99.

Recognizing that the bus boycott might continue indefinitely, on May 24 the MIA Executive Board decided on changes to "prepare ourselves for a long struggle."

Recommendations to MIA Executive Board, by Martin Luther King Jr.

1. In order to lessen the pressure that we have worked under for several months and prepare ourselves for a long struggle which might possibly last

several more months, our mass meetings will be reduced to once a week beginning the first week in June. This meeting will be held each Monday at 7:00 P.M., and the program committee shall be urged to limit the program to one hour and a half. If necessary situations arise special mass meetings will be called.

2. In order to valuably utilize the present relaxed phase of the bus situation and capitalize on the prevailing enthusiasm and amazing togetherness of the people, a strong emphasis shall be placed on increasing our political power through voting and increasing our economic power through the establishment of a bank. The committee on registration and voting shall seek to implement its program immediately. This committee shall meet weekly to discuss methods, findings and results. The Montgomery Improvement Association shall provide every avenue necessary to make the work of this committee successful. The Banking Committee shall meet immediately and make application for a charter through the Federal Home Loan Bank in Greensboro, North Carolina. If the charter is denied at this level a committee shall be immediately sent to Washington to appeal for a charter through the head office of all savings and loan banks. The program committee shall be requested to allot more time in the mass meetings to the voting and banking committees for purposes of getting the idea over to the people.

3. In order to give our numerous friends over the nation and the various newspapers an accurate account of developments in the bus situation, a bimonthly newsletter shall be released. The letter shall be edited by Mrs. Jo Ann Robinson, assisted by persons of her choice. Before the letter is released it shall be read and approved by the president, the vice-presidents, and the secretary of the Montgomery Improvement Association. Since the job of editor entails such a tremendous responsibility plus certain technical skills, a reasonable salary, recommended by the finance committee and approved by the executive board, shall be offered. It is hoped that this newsletter will very soon be expanded into a newspaper with an official staff, which will become the official organ of the Montgomery Improvement Association.

4. In order that there may be a reliable and orderly record of the bus protest plus an accurate record of the origin, growth and future development of the Montgomery Improvement Association, a History Committee shall be organized consisting of the following persons: Dr. L. D. Reddick, Chairman; Mr. N. W. Walton, Mr. J. E. Pierce, and Mrs. Jo Ann Robinson.

5. That an executive committee be established consisting of all officers of the association and all committee heads. The function of this committee shall be to make decisions on minor matters of policy when it is not possible to call

the whole executive board. Also this committee shall from time to time make recommendations to the executive board concerning vital matters of policy.

6. In order to maintain good public relations and keep the executive board well informed on the financial standing of the organization, a financial report of all receipts and disbursements shall be presented bi-monthly by the finance committee to the executive board.

HGP-GAMK.

The following undated minutes of the newly created executive committee, and the memorandum that follows, shed light on the MIA's inner workings. Rufus Lewis had just been replaced by Rev. Benjamin J. Simms as chairman of the Transportation Committee. The MIA paid full-time car pool drivers 4 dollars per day, plus fuel and maintenance, to drive automobiles made available by supporters. Those who drove their own cars were not paid but had expenses covered. The Transportation Committee contracted with several black-owned service stations for car pool drivers to charge gasoline at a discount to the MIA.

That chairman of transportation has authority to O. K. all bills pertaining to transportation with the approval of the transportation committee. This includes salaries of persons directly working with transportation, Carried—that chairman of Transportation committee has authority to make temporary replacements in emergencies with permanent replacements affirmed by the president—(carried).

FIRING

All firing of persons by this organization should be approved by the Executive Committee upon presentation by president only (carried). The chairman of transportation and Executive Assistant have temporary suspension power with suspension to be affirmed by the president. (carried)

REPAIRS

That Chairman of Transportation will be allocated 12 gallons of gasoline per week and the Association will pay forty per cent (40%) of the Chairman's repair bill. (carried)

HGP-GAMK.

Memorandum to All Day Drivers, June 30, 1956

SUBJECT: GENERAL INFORMATION

1. Report to Transportation Office if you desire to lay-off preferably a day ahead if possible.

2. Drivers are not authorized to place substitute drivers in their places without consulting the *Transportation Office*. The MIA assumes no responsibility in event of violation.

3. Permission for repairs and for adjustment on vehicles must be secured from the Transportation Office.

4. All drivers are expected to do the following:
(a) Make daily air pressure check of tires.
(b) See that vehicle is lubricated at proper time and battery checked.
(c) Oil change at proper mileage.
(d) Report at once to Transportation Office any repairs needed.
(e) Permission from office required on OIL CHANGE & LUBRICATION.

! ! DRIVE CAREFUL ! ! ! ! BE COURTEOUS ! ! ! ! KEEP GOOD BRAKES !

Rev. B. J. Simms, Director
Transportation Department

MLKP-MBU: Box 6.

Browder v. *Gayle* Decision

Aurelia S. BROWDER et al. v. W. A. GAYLE, etc., United States District Court, Middle District, Alabama, June 5, 1956, No. 1147

SUMMARY: Negro citizens in Montgomery, Alabama, brought a class action in federal district court against state and city officials, the company operating local buses in the city, and certain of its bus drivers, seeking a declaratory judgment and an injunction. The plaintiffs asked that the defendants' enforcement of state laws and city ordinances requiring racial segregation on the city bus lines be declared in violation of the United States Constitution and enjoined. Jurisdiction of the suit was assumed by the three-judge federal district court. The court, one judge dissenting, held that segregation violated the Equal Protection and Due Process clauses of the Fourteenth Amendment, the doctrine of separate-but-equal as applied to public transportation in *Plessy* v. *Ferguson* having been impliedly overruled. The court later issued a permanent injunction [*June 19*] but provided for its suspension.

Before [*Richard*] RIVES, Circuit Judge, and [*Seybourn*] LYNNE and [*Frank*] JOHNSON, District Judges.

RIVES, Circuit Judge.

[. . .] In the field of college education, beginning in 1938 and continuing to the present time, the [*Supreme*] Court has first weakened the vitality of, and has then destroyed, the separate but equal concept. [. . .]

The separate but equal concept had its birth prior to the adoption of the Fourteenth Amendment in the decision of a Massachusetts State court relating to public schools. Roberts v. City of Boston, 59 Mass. (5 Cush) 198 (1849). The doctrine of that case was followed in Plessy v. Ferguson, *supra*. In the School Segregation Cases, Brown v. Board of Education, 347 U.S. 483 (1954) and Bolling v. Sharpe, 347 U.S. 497 (1954) the separate but equal doctrine was repudiated in the area where it first developed, i.e., in the field of public education. On the same day the Supreme Court made clear that its ruling was not limited to that field when it remanded "for consideration in the light of the Segregation Cases and conditions that now prevail" a case involving the rights of Negroes to use the recreational facilities of city parks. Muir v. Louisville Park Theatrical Association, 347 U.S. 971 (1954).

Later the Fourth Circuit expressly repudiated the separate but equal doctrine as applied to recreational centers. Dawson v. Mayor and City of Baltimore, 4th Cir., 220 F.2d 386, 387. Its judgment was affirmed by the Supreme Court, 350 U.S. 877. The doctrine has further been repudiated in holdings that the cities of Atlanta and of Miami cannot meet the test by furnishing the facilities of their municipal golf courses to Negroes on a segregated basis. Rice v. Arnold, 340 U.S. 848; Holmes v. City of Atlanta, 350 U.S. 879.

Even a statute can be repealed by implication. A fortiori, a judicial decision, which is simply evidence of the law and not the law itself, may be so impaired by later decisions as no longer to furnish any reliable evidence.

We cannot in good conscience perform our duty as judges by blindly following the precedent of Plessy v. Ferguson, *supra*, when our study leaves us in complete agreement with the Fourth Circuit's opinion in Flemming v. South Carolina Electric and Gas Co., 224 F.2d 752, appeal dismissed April 23, 1956, 351 U.S. 901, that the separate but equal doctrine can no longer be safely followed as a correct statement of the law. In fact, we think that Plessy v. Ferguson has been impliedly, though not explicitly, overruled, and that, under the later decisions, there is now no rational basis upon which the separate but equal doctrine can be validly applied to public carrier transportation within the City of Montgomery and its police jurisdiction. The application of that doctrine cannot be justified as a proper execution of the state police power.

We hold that the statutes and ordinances requiring segregation of the white and colored races on the motor buses of a common carrier of passengers in the City of Montgomery and its police jurisdiction violate the due process and equal protection of the law clauses of the Fourteenth Amendment to the Constitution of the United States. [. . .]

LYNNE, District Judge, dissenting:

[. . .] My study of Brown has convinced me that it left unimpaired the "separate but equal" doctrine in a local transportation case and I perceive no pronounced new doctrinal trend therein.

Of course I appreciate the care with which the Supreme Court limits its pronouncements upon great constitutional questions to the narrow issues before it and the only issue in Brown involved a collision between the Fourteenth Amendment and state laws commanding segregation in the public schools. But in Brown the Court's opinion referred to Plessy v. Ferguson six times and to its "separate but equal" doctrine on four occasions. It epitomized its concept of that doctrine as follows: "Under that doctrine, equality of treatment is accorded when the races are provided substantially equal facilities, even though these facilities be separate." Its ultimate conclusion was, and this I conceive to be the rationale of its decision, "that in the field of public education the doctrine of 'separate but equal' has no place. Separate educational facilities are inherently unequal."

It seems to me that the Supreme Court therein recognized that there still remains an area within our constitutional scheme of state and federal governments wherein that doctrine may be applied even though its applications are always constitutionally suspect and for sixty years it may have been more honored in the breach than in the observance. Granted that the trend of its opinions is to the effect that segregation is not to be permitted in public facilities furnished by the state itself and the moneys of the state, as in the case of public schools, or public parks, [. . .] on the plain theory that if the state is going to provide such facilities at all, it must provide them equally to the citizens, it does not follow that it may not be permitted in public utilities holding nonexclusive franchises.

If that doctrine has any validity, this is such a case in which it has been applied fairly. According to its teaching not absolute, but substantial equality is required. Such equality is not a matter of dogma, but one of fact. Under the undisputed evidence adduced upon the hearing before us practices under the laws here attacked have resulted in providing the races not only substantially equal but in truth identical facilities.

In my opinion the holding of the Court in Morgan v. Virginia, 328 U.S. 373, that the attempt of a state to require the segregation of passengers on interstate buses results in the imposition of an undue burden on interstate commerce is wholly irrelevant to the issue before us. And equally inapposite is reference to Henderson v. United States, 339 U.S. 816, which held that rules and practices of interstate railroad carriers requiring the segregation of passengers in dining cars were offensive to Section 3(1) of the Interstate Commerce Act making it unlawful for a railroad in interstate commerce "to subject any particular person, . . . to any undue or unreasonable prejudice or disadvantage in any respect whatsoever. . . ."

The supremacy of the federal government in matters affecting interstate commerce is axiomatic. Cases involving the exercise of its power in that realm shed no light on Fourteenth Amendment problems. It does seem quite clear that by its terms the Congress is given the power and duty to enforce the Fourteenth Amendment by legislation. Thus the Congress would have the power, thus derived, to proscribe segregation in intrastate transportation. It is worthy of note that for sixty years it has not seen fit to do so.

While any student of history knows that under our system of government vindication of the constitutional rights of the individual is not, and ought not to be, entrusted to the Congress, its reticence to intrude upon the internal affairs of the several states should caution us against doing so where the path of duty is not plainly marked and when we must hold a clear precedent of the Supreme Court outmoded.

Because I would dismiss the action on the authority of Plessy v. Ferguson, I do not reach the procedural questions discussed in the majority opinion. I respectfully dissent.

Race Relations Law Reporter, August 1956, pp. 669–78.

The victory in *Browder* v. *Gayle* coincided with, and possibly helped precipitate, King's most severe test of leadership. It came not from without—from bombings, intimidation by White Citizens Councils, or intransigent city officials—but from within, from the threat to the MIA's carefully cultivated unity posed by Rev. Uriah J. Fields. He might have hesitated to challenge the leadership so brazenly before the June 5 *Browder* ruling, which seemed to make success unstoppable. Fields, twenty-five-year-old pastor of Bell Street Baptist Church, Korean War veteran, recent Alabama State student body president, and E. D. Nixon protégé, had been elected MIA recording secretary at its founding meeting. Six months later, at the end of May, the MIA was legally incorporated with a constitution and by-laws and its leadership structure reorganized. Rev. W. J. Powell replaced Fields as secretary—partly because the latter had not been attending meetings regularly, partly because King's inner circle did not fully trust him because of his tendency to act independently and impulsively. For instance, Fields had angered other leaders back in January when, identifying himself as MIA secretary, he published his *Montgomery Advertiser* letter asserting that "we have no intention of compromising" and prematurely floating a demand for the "annihilation" of bus segregation. Fields's letter, which may have strengthened white officials' resistance to serious negotiation, had spurred the MIA Executive Board to require its prior approval for all public statements except those made by King.[1]

Fields was absent from the board's May reorganization meeting. Discovering that he had been removed, he angrily denounced the leaders' decision at a mass meeting on June 11; but the large audience reaffirmed his ouster. After the meeting Fields announced to the press that he was resigning as MIA secretary because of "misappropriation of funds" by boycott leaders who were "misusing money sent from all over the nation." He said: "I can no longer identify myself with a movement in which the many are exploited by the few." The leaders had become "too egotistical and interested in perpetuating themselves." The MIA "no longer represents what I stand for."[2]

Although the young preacher acted out of resentment and his allegations were overblown, they were not entirely untrue. On some occasions, and possibly on a regular basis, King and a few other leaders who spoke and raised funds for the MIA around the country received honoraria above expenses. "We had a whole lot of money at that time and some of it we handled unwisely," MIA treasurer Nixon later stated. "There wasn't nobody stealing much of anything, but we just handled it unwisely." Not willing, in hindsight, to disagree with Fields's allegations, he said: "A lot of times a minister would go and make a speech and he'd think that he's entitled to some of it." Nixon admitted that he himself once accepted a $600 honorarium.[3] Not all speakers accepted personal fees, however; Rosa Parks and white Lutheran minister Robert Graetz were among those who did not.

Graetz later recalled that Fields's charges "reignited my own concerns about the way money was handled. I had raised several thousand dollars through speeches at fund-raisers, and each time, after paying for my travel expenses, I turned everything else over to the MIA. After one of those trips, however, when I brought the money in to be deposited, someone asked, 'Did you keep enough out for yourself?'

"I balked. 'I never keep any for personal use,' I replied. 'This money was raised for the movement.'

"'I know, but the other speakers normally keep an honorarium for themselves out of the money they raise.' I was shocked. I had no idea others were doing that. But I never changed my policy. I always turned in to the MIA everything above expenses."[4] Fields, however, had little opportunity to earn such fees, had he been inclined, since the Speakers Bureau rarely if ever asked him to represent the MIA. This might have contributed to his resentment and jealousy.

Moreover, funds were frequently expended on things unrelated to the car pool or administrative tasks, particularly as ad hoc relief to persons and families in need, a kind of improvised welfare program. Financial secretary Erna Dungee remembered: "We paid rent. We paid gas bills. We paid water bills. We bought food. We paid people's doctor bills. We even buried somebody. . . . Those were free rides as far as I was concerned. But they seemed to think this is what we had to do. We even bought washing machines. We did everything trying to get along with the people," to maintain morale and unity, at all cost. Dungee recalled that it was "usually the poorest ones" who came for help. King was "real sympathetic" to these people's needs. Though "he was against some of that," she stated, "he felt he had to go along with most of it."[5]

When Fields made his charges, King and Abernathy were in California, vacationing with their families and fulfilling speaking commitments. Realizing that Fields's allegations were a threat to the MIA's reputation, fund-raising, and internal cohesion, King immediately flew back to Montgomery and met with him. According to King's account, Fields recanted the allegations and admitted they had been motivated by his feeling of mistreatment by the executive board. At the next mass meeting, June 18, King declared that the MIA had not misappropriated any funds. With Fields beside him at the pulpit, he asked the audience to forgive the young pastor in a spirit of Christian love. "Let he who is without sin," King said, "cast the first stone."[6] Fields then read an ambiguous statement withdrawing his charges and apologizing, but claiming that he had been "misquoted, misinterpreted and misunderstood." His full statement was sent out later in June with the second issue of the MIA newsletter.

Reverend Fields's Retraction, June 18, 1956

These statements were issued by the Reverend U. J. Fields, who discontinued his connections with the Montgomery Improvement Association (MIA), for the purpose of correcting statements that he had been charged with making concerning certain leaders of the Montgomery Improvement Association.

These statements are being made voluntarily and without being pressured to do so by other persons.

It is with deep regret that the statements I made Monday night, June 11, 1956 about some leaders of the MIA and as to my reason for leaving the organization were misquoted, misinterpreted and misunderstood by people throughout the nation.

Therefore, this is an attempt to set the record straight by re-stating and using my personal signature to substantiate what I have to say about the MIA and its leaders.

First, allow me to state my reason for quitting the organization. I left the MIA because of "personality clashes" with several members of the Executive Board. (Reverend King was not involved personally). Our relations have always been cordial.

Secondly, I said what I did about the "few exploiting the many" and about money being misplaced (not misused) in anger and passion.

Certainly, there is no evidence available to me to indicate that money has been misplaced and there is no proof that money has been misused by the MIA. To my knowledge money sent to the organization has been used only for the purpose of transportation.

Surely, some leaders have enjoyed the privilege of visiting other cities and towns throughout the country, but I have no evidence at all that would allow me to truthfully say that money sent to the organization has not been brought back to the organization.

As for Reverend King, president of the MIA, I hold him in high esteem. In my association with him I have found him to be kind, understanding, honest and a dynamic leader. I feel that his integrity is beyond question, and it is to be regretted that the statements published involved him as has been observed.

I would like to take this opportunity to offer my apology to leaders of the MIA, Montgomerians, and our many friends and supporters throughout the nation for the statements that have been attributed to me as having said.

It is my desire that you will accept this apology in the spirit in which it has been made. My determination to work for equality, justice and first-class citizenship for all people has not changed in recent months. I shall continue in whatever way I can to do whatever is in my power to hasten the day when democracy will become a living reality for all Americans, irrespective of race, color or previous circumstance.

Signed:
Reverend U. J. Fields

HGP-GAMK.

King's deft handling of the Fields controversy buried it—and with it the prospect of an external investigation or audit of MIA finances that might have hurt its credibility. While the MIA was shaken by Fields's charges and the negative publicity, the unexpected opportunity for the leaders to win a well-publicized membership vote of confidence and for the MIA to project an image of unimpeachable unity, probably strengthened the organization, the movement, and King's leadership. King concluded that "nonviolence triumphed again, and a situation that many had predicted would be the end of the MIA left it more united than ever in the spirit of tolerance."[7] Yet Fields never unequivocally retracted his charges and returned to them in his 1959 bus boycott memoir.[8]

1. *Montgomery Advertiser*, January 5, 1956.

2. *Montgomery Advertiser*, June 12, 1956.

3. Nixon interview by Steven M. Millner, in David J. Garrow, ed., *The Walking City: The Montgomery Bus Boycott, 1955–1956* (Brooklyn: Carlson Publishing, 1989), pp. 550, 496.

4. Robert S. Graetz, *Montgomery: A White Preacher's Memoir* (Minneapolis: Fortress Press, 1991), p. 86.

5. Erna Dungee Allen interview by Steven M. Millner, in Garrow, ed., *The Walking City*, pp. 524–25.

6. Martin Luther King Jr., *Stride Toward Freedom: The Montgomery Story* (New York: Harper, 1958), pp. 154–55; *Montgomery Advertiser*, June 19, 1956.

7. King, *Stride Toward Freedom*, p. 157.

8. Uriah J. Fields, *The Montgomery Story* (New York: Exposition Press, 1959). Historian J. Mills Thornton III noted that Fields's strong reiteration of his allegations in this account "is particularly important because the book led to a grand jury investigation of the charges which, though it came to nothing in the immediate term, led in the longer term to the indictment of King for state income tax evasion." Thornton claimed that the Fields charges were "part of Nixon's discontent with King and his threats to resign as MIA treasurer," which he finally did a year after the bus boycott ended. (Personal correspondence from Thornton, September 8, 1994)

MIA Newsletter, June 23, 1956

Vol. 1, No. 2
530 South Union Street
Montgomery, Alabama
Telephone 5-3364
M. L. King Jr., President

RECENT HAPPENINGS

In the preceding issue of *MIA News Letter*, mention was made of the fact that a three-judge federal court had outlawed segregation of races on motor vehicles in Montgomery on the grounds that it violates the fourteenth amendment, and is, therefore, unconstitutional. The judges gave attorneys on both sides a period of two weeks to submit suggestions as to how the formal judgement given on the case could be carried out. That means briefly that: 1. The judges could call for an immediate end to segregation on busses. 2. The judges could grant an order restraining the immediate implementation of integration while the defendants—the City Commission, Public Service Commission and the Police Department—appeal the case to the Supreme Court and receive a verdict.

The two weeks period terminated on June 19. The formal judgement halted segregation on busses, but delayed the implementation of integration for an extended period of ten days to allow the defendants time for appeal. Negroes await the final judgement from the two possible decisions with great anticipation. No attempt has been made by Negroes to ride busses until segregation has been completely abolished. The car pool service is still in operation.

Between 30,000 and 40,000 Negroes are being transported daily by the car pool. There are very few complaints, if any, for service is wonderful. Hundreds of people are still driving their cars, wearing out tires and automobiles, relining brakes and mending automobile parts. They expend their own energy and devote long hours daily to the cause. They are tired, but they don't complain. They have been faithful for more than six months. They may have to serve many more. Nothing definite will be known for ten more days.

A REGRETTABLE INCIDENT

A month ago the MIA was incorporated into a permanent organization, with some new officers elected to serve the various posts. Prior to this time the MIA operated on a temporary, emergency basis to meet the unprecedented needs arising from the bus protest. Until the recent election, all officers were temporary.

The Reverend Uriah J. Fields, who had served as temporary recording secretary of the Executive Board of the MIA, was replaced by another minister, Reverend W. J. Powell of Old Ship A.M.E. Church. Reverend Fields, a student at Alabama State College, was busy with studies at the college, as well as with his regular pastoral duties at the Bell Street Baptist Church. He could not be present at all meetings and was, therefore, unable to render the type of service that the organization needed. He had not been present for several weeks before his replacement.

Reverend Fields resented the fact that he had been replaced, and in an emotional state, went to the press with false charges against the MIA.

Since its beginning the MIA has encountered much opposition from local authorities and a few disgruntled persons within its own rank. The charges made by Reverend Fields were so preposterous that the Association felt the accusations were unworthy of refutation.

Since that time Reverend Fields has been dismissed by his church, because of the false charges. But, in a spirit of Christ, he has regretted his retaliatory steps against the organization and has apologized to the Executive Board and to the MIA mass meeting public. He has also issued, of his own free will, a statement to the press retracting his accusations.

The Association regrets the unwarranted, false accusations made and also regrets the personal suffering encountered by the minister, who tried to retaliate against, what he later called, "personality clashes" with two men of the transportation committee. Reverend Fields admits with regret, the falsity of his accusations. He is a hard worker and is dedicated to the cause of civil rights. But in a moment of weakness, he lost self control. He was tired, for he has worked with 50,000 other Negroes for six months. He was angry and felt rejected. In a state of human passion and human frailty, he spoke falsely against an organization which he loves. The wrong has been righted, but the blur remains. The minister's mistake has been costly to himself and to the good name of the MIA, but 50,000 of his fellow comrades will neither desert nor forsake him. "To err is human," says Pope, "but to forgive is divine."

In the election of permanent officers, Reverend Ralph D. Abernathy was elected to the position of First Vice President, replacing Reverend Roy Bennett, who moved to California. Dr. Moses W. Jones, Second Vice President. Reverend A. W. Wilson, Parliamentarian and Mr. C. W. Lee, Assistant Treasurer. The other temporary officers were elected to regular [permanent] posts. [. . .]

VOTERS' CLINICS

A movement has gotten underway to encourage Negroes to register and to become qualified voters. Hundreds of volunteer workers are contacting non-registered, age-eligible people to exercise their constitutional right to qualify.

There are more than 50,000 Negroes in Montgomery, yet only 2,058 are registered voters. According to statistics, 34,000 Negroes are twenty-one years old and older. Of these, hundreds have tried, but failed to qualify as voters. They feel that voting is a privilege; that it is their constitutional right. Thus, they are going to try again in large numbers to secure their right of suffrage. [. . .]

HGP-GAMK.

On July 26 the MIA Executive Board approved King's recommendation to wait for the full Supreme Court to decide on the opposition's appeal of the Montgomery federal court's bus desegregation ruling, rather than seek an immediate decision from former Alabama senator Hugo L. Black (brother-in-law of Virginia Durr), the Supreme Court justice with Alabama jurisdiction.

[. . .] The President informed the body that the legal staff of the organization had decided that it would be wiser to wait until the Supreme Court reconvenes this fall and render a decision on our case than to appeal to one Supreme Court Justice for an immediate ruling on the same. The Executive Board accepted the thinking of its legal staff and agreed to continue as usual the promotion of the protest. [. . .]

MLKP-MBU: Box 30.

Fall . . . **11** . . .

For Montgomery's black community, buoyed by the *Browder* ruling, boycotting buses became a way of life. Late summer and autumn brought new legal and extralegal efforts by segregationists to shut down the prolonged mass protest. Insurance policies for car pool vehicles were mysteriously canceled. Rev. Robert Graetz's home was bombed; fortunately he, his wife, and children were away, visiting Highlander Folk School in Tennessee accompanied by Rosa Parks. Confidential information arrived (probably from Graetz's trusted local FBI contact) and rumors abounded that outside Citizens Council activists, provoked partly by emerging divisions in their own ranks, were conspiring to intervene, vigilante-style, to stop Montgomery's second civil war. There were reports too that a phalanx of white trade unionists would sweep into town and make citizen's arrests of car pool drivers.

Nevertheless, awaiting optimistically the Supreme Court's rendezvous with *Browder*, King and MIA leaders began to prepare people for riding desegregated buses and reconciling with the white community. This included planning a week-long commemoration of the bus boycott's first anniversary that would appraise the protest and provide more training in the powerful new tool of nonviolent direct action.

It was not only favorable legal developments that turned the tide toward the triumph of "justice over injustice." Overriding all odds, expectations, and stereotypes, the African American community had remained remarkably unified. In the early months it looked like the segregationists might succeed in solidifying the majority white community as well. But the fast-growing Citizens Council movement did not have comparable leadership at either the top or grass roots. King and his colleagues managed to keep their egos and ambitions under control and harnessed toward realizable common aims. The WCC, on the contrary, revealed itself as a muscular united front without a strong back to hold it up and keep it accountable to members. Petty jealousies, rivalries, and turf battles, and the lack of a positive unifying vision, tore holes in white supremacist armor and kept it from sustaining its community mobilization. Did the black movement's immersion in the black church culture have something to do with this contrast? Was white resistance too secular for its own good? But use of fundamentalist Christian symbols and commitments might have inhibited its means and undermined its ends. Defeat and desperation led to an escalation of white terror tactics in the aftermath of bus desegregation, which occurred four days before Christmas.

During the bus boycott both racial communities mobilized. Only the black community effectively *organized*. For this the women leaders and black churches were mainly responsible.

Montgomery Improvement Association leaders made repeated requests for the Justice Department to investigate violence and civil rights violations by white segregationists in Montgomery, to no avail.

September 4, 1956

Attorney General Herbert Brownell
Washington
District of Columbia

Dear Sir:

My name is Pastor Robert Graetz. I am a citizen of Montgomery, Alabama. At present I am serving as pastor of the predominantly-Negro Trinity Lutheran Church, in Montgomery, though I myself am white.

At about 3:00 A.M. on last August 25 a dynamite bomb was thrown into the front yard of my home. The blast damaged my home and several others in the neighborhood. It was apparently part of the reaction against us for working with the Negroes of Montgomery in their protest against inhuman treatment on the city's busses.

This, of course, was not the first time that dynamite has been used in an attempt to intimidate someone who was upholding an unpopular position. But there are other factors connected with the bombing and leading up to it which give many of us grave concern. These factors I shall attempt to describe below. Because of these things, we feel that the time has come when we must ask the Justice Department of the United States Government to make a thorough investigation of our local scene, particularly the notions of the members of our city commission.

On December 5, 1955, the Negroes of Montgomery began a boycott against the city buses which has continued nearly 100% effective until this day. A large percentage of the white population was so amazed that so many Negroes could be so dissatisfied about anything in the Southern way of life. They had to rationalize by saying that the Negroes were either intimidated or deceived by the NAACP or the Communists or by some other unknown outside agitator.

Our Police Commissioner is Clyde Sellers, who was elected by running on an anti-Negro platform. Sellers deliberately encouraged and distorted the above rationalization by accusing the Negroes publicly of using what he called "goon squads" to keep any other Negroes from riding the busses. He claimed that the majority of the Negroes really wanted to ride and were trying to do so. But that hundreds of them had been beaten up by the "goon squads." Yet only one case of intimidation by a Negro came to trial. And that was obviously a family quarrel. [. . .]

Not long after the big crack-down [*in January 1956*], bombs were thrown at the homes of two of the Negro leaders. Not much damage was done, fortunately, though there were people in both homes at the time of the bombings. I received reports that seemed to be fairly reliable, that some Negro men working in a tavern in Montgomery had heard Commissioner Sellers talking to some men about the bombings, presumably before the bombings took place. I was never able to check these reports out. At the same time, rumors began to circulate that the bombs had been thrown by a relative of Commissioner Sellers and that he had had an accident while preparing the next one to be thrown, and that he had blown his arm off. This latter rumor is not likely to be true, but it gives you an idea of the reputation that Sellers enjoys among the colored people.

This is not the full extent of Sellers' implication. On at least one occasion, and probably on many others as well, trusties from the prison have been sent to our meetings and services to spy. (They are colored, of course.) On the one occasion that I have direct knowledge of, the men were brought to the Dexter Avenue Baptist Church, where Dr. M. L. King is the pastor. The trusties were questioned by some of the church officers; and they explained that Sellers had brought them, and they were instructed to report to Sellers whatever they had heard.

A great many other things have happened, in which the personal rights of many of our citizens have been violated. Several white pastors attended one of the mass meetings of the Montgomery Improvement Association. After the meeting, Sellers and several policemen were waiting to get their auto license numbers. Later on some of them were threatened and intimidated. I am sure that there are more cases that I am not aware of than those that I know about. [. . .]

This brings us back to the episode of the bombing of my home. I do not believe that the bombing itself was as surprising or as dangerous as the reaction of the white officials. Mayor Gayle immediately branded the bombing as a publicity stunt on the part of the Negroes. And apparently the police have been ordered to find the colored people who did it, or at least someone that it can conveniently be blamed on. At least four colored men have been arrested in connection with the bombing. And the detectives who are working on the case, Detectives [Bard] and Anderson, are absolutely convinced that it was done by Negroes. As a matter of fact, due to the propagandizing of the mayor, many otherwise sensible white citizens are convinced that the mayor's theory is right. One further thing connected with the bombing. The small book in which I had my personal telephone numbers listed was missing when we returned after the bombing. The police deny that they had anything to do with it. But it is a rather strange coincidence, to say the least.

And what of the future outlook. Reports from my white friends indicate that tension is extremely high. Some white lawyers have commented on the drastic increase in police brutality where Negroes are concerned. (This is a recent report.) It should not be too long before we get a favorable ruling from the U.S. Supreme Court, outlawing segregation on our buses. And Sellers has promised publicly that our buses will never be integrated. The Central Alabama Citizens Council has stated in its official publication that they will use violence if necessary to maintain segregation. (I read this in the issue of about July 18.)

The Negroes know what Sellers is capable of. They know that all branches of the local government are stacked against them. So many of them, perhaps most of them are staying well-armed, ready to fight off the mob that could come any day. And as long as our local officials go on uncurbed, our local situation is potentially explosive.

On the basis of all those things, and others for the protection of our citizens and the preservation of law and order, we urge the Justice Department to make a thorough investigation of conditions in Montgomery, Alabama.

Yours sincerely,
(Rev.) Robert Graetz, Pastor
Trinity Lutheran Church

RGP.

Minutes of MIA Executive Board, September 13, 1956

The meeting was opened at 10:00 A.M. with the President, Rev. M. L. King Jr., in charge. [. . .]

After a brief opening, the President appointed a special committee with which he would work to see what could be done to change the bitterness or unfavorable attitude of some whites toward us. The committee appointed is as follows: Rev. W. J. Powell, R. D. Abernathy, S. S. Seay, B. J. Simms, H. H. Hubbard, J. W. Hayes, Mrs. Jo Ann Robinson.

The standing committee reports were then made in the following order:

TRANSPORTATION: The Transportation Committee's report was made by Rev. B. J. Simms, Chairman. He stated that Transportation is moving along satisfactorily on curtailed expense in spite of the fact that only seven station wagons are operating. People with private cars have responded wonderfully to the call for help when the majority of the station wagons could not be operated.

After some discussion of this report, it was moved and carried that the Board favored having a camera on every station wagon to make pictorial evidence of any and every accident. [. . .]

Rev. B. J. Simms appealed to the Executive Board from the ruling of the Executive Committee and Finance Committee which ruled that he was responsible for money turned in to him which was lost, and that he therefore replace the same. The Executive Board voted to sustain the Finance Committee and Executive Committee in their ruling.

Closing prayer was offered by Dr. H. H. Johnson.

Rev. W. J. Powell, Secretary
Rev. M. L. King Jr., President

MLKP-MBU: Box 30.

The likely source of Graetz's "information" was FBI agent Woodrow E. Draut, with whom he conferred regularly, informing him of bus boycott developments and getting useful intelligence back. Viewing the FBI as an ally, the Lutheran pastor considered this relationship beneficial to the movement.

Minutes of special meeting of the Executive Board of the Montgomery Improvement Association, Tuesday, September 18, 1956

The meeting was called to order by the President at 11:00 A.M. Opening prayer was offered by the Rev. S. Sanders. [. . .]

Rev. Robert Graetz was presented to give information which was responsible for the calling of this committee.

After Rev. Graetz had acquainted the body with confidential information which had come to him, the President stated that the course of action to be followed to meet the anticipated or possible danger was the question confronting the group.

After much discussion, it was moved and carried that this organization contact the U.S. Justice Department, the F.B.I., and influential local citizens in Washington, to acquaint them with the information which has come to us and seek their assistance and protection in this situation. It was further moved and carried that Governor James Folsom be contacted and informed of the situation before carrying out the decision of this body referred to immediately above.

The President appointed the following persons as members of the committee to contact the Governor: Rev. Robert Graetz, Mrs. Jo Ann Robinson, Attorney Charles Langford, Dr. M. L. King Jr.

It was agreed that if a personal contact could be had in Washington with the Justice Department or F.B.I., the Rev. Robert Graetz and Dr. M. L. King Jr. would constitute the committee.

Closing prayer was offered by Rev. G. Franklin Lewis.

W. J. Powell, Secretary
M. L. King Jr., President

MLKP-MBU: Box 30.

MIA Newsletter

Vol. 1, No. 4
530 South Union Street
Montgomery, Alabama
Telephone 5-3364
M. L. King Jr., President
September 21, 1956

RECENT HAPPENINGS

Since Negroes stopped riding busses in Montgomery ten months ago, every conceivable obstacle has been used to force them back to the public transportation lines.

The first attempt was at breaking the solidarity of the Negro resistance under the pretext that three Negro ministers had collaborated with officials to return to the bus under the same segregated policy. It was a miserable failure. The protesters stayed with the car pool.

The second attempt was the "get-tough policy" of officials which imposed hundreds of traffic tickets upon Negro drivers, both innocent and guilty, who were accused of violating traffic laws. Then, during a very short period of time at least sixty-four Negro drivers were arrested and jailed for minor traffic infractions. This policy hit heavily upon the purse strings of the Negro group, but it failed utterly, for Negroes paid their fines, paid for the alleged traffic violations, and stayed off the busses. The free car pool service continued to transport approximately 30,000 to 40,000 race members to and fro.

The third was an effort to disbar Attorney Fred D. Gray for an alleged "unauthorization" to represent a plaintiff in the federal suit which contested the Constitutionality of segregation laws on busses. That case was dismissed when proof was presented that the state and circuit officials had no jurisdiction in the matter. The federal suit was won, but integration was suspended because of an appeal to the U.S. Supreme Court, which is expected to act on the case when it reconvenes in October. Negroes continued to stay off the bus.

The fourth attack was through mass arrests wherein 100 Negroes, including twenty-four ministers, were arrested for "conspiracy against the bus company." Only one case was tried. The others were postponed depending upon the outcome of the first. That case involved the president of MIA, Dr. M. L. King Jr., who was found guilty. The case was appealed, and Negroes still stayed off the bus.

The fifth attack was brought against station wagon drivers, who were "trailed by officers," and arrested at various times for traffic infractions. Three station wagons have been involved in collisions with either city detectives, truck drivers or others where the situations were questionable. A suit by the same detectives in the collision has been brought against the church that owns the station wagon. This case comes up during the October term of the circuit court. Meanwhile the bus protest continued.

THE MOST RECENT

The newest and most recent of the attempts to end the protest has been effected through insurance companies, which for some strange reason have cancelled the insurance policies on all but seven of the twenty-four church station wagons. Whether pressure has been put upon the companies to force the cancellation, no one knows, but on Saturday September 8, the automobile insurance companies announced that they "could not take the risk" and cancelled the policies. Thus, seventeen station wagons have been out of operation since then. Efforts are being made to find "companies which *will* take the risk," so that these carriers can resume operation.

When the news was circulated, many of the private cars, which had been withdrawn from the car pool, were put back into service and no serious difficulty has been experienced. The protest continues and interest soars as the time nears for the re-convening of the Supreme Court.

A scant few of the city busses are still in operation with less than a third of the vehicles, according to the local press, in operation. Very few, if any, Negroes are passengers.

THE THIRD BOMBING OCCURS

The third home has been bombed in Montgomery in connection with the bus protest movement. This time it was the home of Reverend Robert Graetz, the white Lutheran pastor of a Negro church. Reverend Graetz is not only active in the bus protest, but the day before the bombing he extended an invitation to the white Ministerial Association to hear Reverend Doctor M. L. King Jr. speak at an inter-racial meeting (The Alabama Council on Human Relations). The invitation was publicized in the local press the day of the meeting and the press quoted a white minister saying that no "white ministers would attend." To make sure, two local press reporters, one with a camera, attended the meeting. As had been predicted, no white ministers appeared; however, many white laymen attended. That night Reverend Graetz' modern, ranch-style home was bombed. The injury was slight, and since they were out of town, the Graetz family was spared the frightening ordeal.

According to local newspapers of August 26, the mayor called the bombing a "publicity stunt." The local press quoted him as saying, ". . . It is a strange coincidence that when interest appears lagging in the bus boycott, something like this happens. . . . Perhaps this is just a publicity stunt to build up interest of the Negroes in their campaign. . . ." Then he reiterated a former statement that was made sometime before, that "white people did not care if the boycott lasts a 100 years."

Last January Reverend Graetz' car was damaged when someone put sugar into the gasoline tank and slashed two tires. His automobile insurance has been cancelled by two companies. He has had trouble getting more.

Immediately following the filing of the federal suit by Attorney Fred D. Gray to abolish segregation on public carriers, the local draft board changed his classification from 4-D (he is an ordained minister) to 1-A. The re-classification was appealed. Before the Appeal Board could study the case and give a decision, the lawyer was called in to take his physical for induction. The investigating committee upheld the re-classification decision and the local board gave the attorney a ten day notice to appear for induction. In the meantime Attorney Gray married. He became actively involved in the ministry of his church due to the six months extended leave of absence of his pastor.

The new evidence was submitted to the local board and to the Washington investigating committee. As a result of the new evidence General Lewis B. Hershey requested the local board to "re-open the case." The local board refused. The general then ordered a postponement of the lawyer's induction until further notice. The local board is, according to the local press of Monday, September 17, contemplating resigning if Attorney Gray is not inducted, or if General Hershey intervenes. [*Selective Service director Hershey overturned the induction order the next day, arguing that Gray had become a full-time pastor. In protest, fourteen southern draft board members resigned, six draft boards moved to halt inductions, and Alabama senator J. Lister Hill demanded a congressional investigation. Hershey's decision stood; Gray was not drafted.*]

THE NAACP STATUS

Any number of letters have come in from over the nation requesting information on the NAACP status in Alabama. Many expressed desire to know why the NAACP could be forced to cease operation, while the WCC (White Citizens Councils) continued to operate.

The following explanation was given by the legal minds of the MIA:

State Attorney General John Patterson, who brought the injunction against the organization, could bring suit against a foreign organization which has its charter in New York and which is, according to Attorney General Patterson, working against the laws of the state of Alabama. *He could* bring about the charge. A private citizen, or citizens *could not* bring such a charge.

Legal minds further explained that the WCC is not considered a foreign corporation, in spite of the fact that it had its origin in Mississippi. Each WCC is a local organization and has no connection with other similar organizations in other states. Thus, the WCC is allowed to continue its operation, while the NAACP has been banned, pending appeal.

NEW THREATS

According to press and T.V. reports, a leader of the North Alabama WCC, along with John Kasper, the recently sentenced segregation leader in the Clinton, Tennessee, racial uprising, was to come to Montgomery on Sunday, September 16, to divulge plans on how "they were going to break up the Negro bus boycott in Montgomery."

Accusing the Montgomery WCC of being too moderate in its fight against integration, the North Alabama leader and Kasper planned attempts to organize another WCC group, fashioned after the more radical group of the northerly section. Just how they had planned to force 50,000 Negroes back to the busses remains a mystery, for their engagement to speak in Montgomery was mysteriously cancelled. The method of approach may have been the contributing factor, for Mr. Kasper said in a T.V. broadcast that "anything goes" in his appeal to rabblerousing and mob violence "which should be used to prevent integration."

SPECULATION

It is expected that the Montgomery Federal Suit will be one of the first cases to be reviewed by the Supreme Court when it re-convenes in October, because of the injunctions against the suit. If the case is considered during the month of October, the Montgomery situation will, or should, be cleared up soon. If, on the other hand, the High Court does not get to this case before the first of the year, January, 1957, the bus protest will continue. The Montgomery people will be in for a long second winter if such is the case. The protest has already lasted ten months. There are no signs of weakening, even when the odds are against them, and things do not look so bright. They are determined to wait for justice.

Will it be in October? Or do Montgomery Negroes experience another, a second hard winter of protesting? It can be January, or March. It is anybody's guess.

PASSIVE RESISTANCE

It is necessary from time to time to reiterate the underlying philosophy of the Montgomery movement. It is a philosophy of passive resistance. This philosophy was ably expounded by Henry David Thoreau of this country and effectively practiced by Gandhi of India. Through this method Gandhi was able to free India from British domination. It has freed the hearts and minds of Negro Montgomerians, who are learning for the first time the real meaning of love.

Though Negroes refuse to cooperate with the evils of segregation on busses, they never resort to retaliatory violence against those who impose it. There is no bitterness, no hatred in their thoughts but there is a freedom that words cannot explain. The very souls of the masses are free. The people are happy as they walk or ride, whatever the case happens to be, and they go about their work as if nothing ever happened to create ill-will among the races.

Because of their cheerfulness, many white people respond with similar attitudes. A smile on the streets by one evokes a smile from the other. [. . .]

Edited by Jo Ann Robinson

HGP-GAMK.

Minutes of the meeting of MIA special committee to consider ways of creating the most wholesome attitude possible among the mass of whites of the city, Tuesday, September 25, 1956, 11:00 A.M.

Those present were: Rev. R. D. Abernathy, Dr. S. S. Seay, Dr. M. L. King Jr., Rev. W. J. Powell, Rev. B. J. Simms, and Mrs. Jo Ann Robinson.

The President made opening remarks in which he said that we must make friends with those who oppose us, we should make our motives clearly understood by the whites of our community, and that, in general, we must move from protest to reconciliation.

After much discussion of ways and means of accomplishing these objectives, the following recommendations were agreed upon to be presented to the Executive Board.

1. We recommend that the local newspapers be contacted in an effort to have them carry a series of articles on the spirit and motive of our movement without or with pay in order to clear up misunderstanding about the same, which articles will be written by persons associated with this organization and duly studied by authorized persons before publication.

2. We recommend also that this same basic information be mailed to influential and representative whites of this city, both those favorably disposed to our movement and those who oppose it. The mailing list for this group to be made up of all white ministers, the Men of Montgomery clubs, the business men of the city, the white women's organizations, civic and religious, and persons whose names might be submitted by members of the Executive Board.

3. Our third recommendation is that we authorize the President to work with local Radio and T.V. persons in an effort to get a local presentation of our side of this protest movement to the citizenry through these channels, and, if we fail here, to look forward to seeking to appear on "Meet the Press," a nationwide program.

Finally, it was suggested that an outline of the series of articles should be well planned in advance of any publication. Dr. Seay suggested the topic "I Believe in the Community" as the possible first article.

The meeting then adjourned.

W. J. Powell, Secretary
Dr. M. L. King Jr., President

MLKP-MBU: Box 30.

Robert Cannon, the Fellowship of Reconciliation mid-South field secretary, premiered the FOR's new film about Montgomery at an MIA mass meeting. In this meeting King directed the first nonviolent training exercise to prepare participants for desegregated buses. Smiley had taught him how to lead such nonviolent trainings.

October 3, 1956

Mssrs. Hassler and Smiley
21 Audubon Ave.
New York 32, N.Y.

Dear "Comrades":

Need I say it? The showing of our new movie to the mass meeting in Montgomery last Monday night was a howling success. I mean that literally as well as in its deeper sense. The meeting was, as usual, well-attended. The MIA leadership was in full force, including the new "hero" Pastor Graetz who came late and sat in the balcony. We were the only two white persons present.

A special significance was added to the premier showing. Either it was plain coincidence or something planned by King, but this meeting also marked the first in what is to be a series of mass training sessions in nonviolence. Now with the possibility looming that these people might wake up some morning to integrated busses, King and the MIA have decided to begin the process of training the people to [go] back to integrated busses with as much creative goodwill and quiet determination as they carried out with the boycott. The showing of our film tied in beautifully with this new emphasis in the mass meetings. King, displaying the marvelous gift of leadership he has with the people, pointed out that the end of the boycott may be quite near. Even though our hopes must not be raised too high, he said, it is nevertheless important to consider how we are to manage ourselves on integrated busses, because it is only to integrated busses that we plan to return (thundering applause here). Said King: "There will be some people who will not like this change and they will not hesitate to express themselves to you. There will possibly be some unpleasant experiences for us at the hands of people who will not immediately accept the idea of sitting with us on the bus. It is important that we begin to think seriously about how we are going to face up to these possibilities of abuse, slander, and embarrassment." Then the following took place:

King asked, "Now, I want just two persons to stand up and tell us how they plan to act on the busses. Suppose you sat down next to a white person on a bus. Suppose this person begin to make a fuss, calling you names, or even going so far as to shove you? What would you do?" The feelings over this were electric.

Two women stood up. King recognized one of them: "All right, Sister—" She began, "Well, if someone was to start calling me names, I guess I would be kinda upset, but mind you, I don't intend to move . . . I think I would just sit there and ignore her and let folks see how ignorant she was. But if she were to start pushin' me, maybe I would give her just a little shove."

At this point there were many murmurings of "No! No!" King then replied, "Thank you for your candid opinion. Now let me ask you this. If you were to shove this white person back, what would you achieve?" There were shouts of "Nothing!" in response to King, and the woman conceded the point. But King pursued it, addressing himself to the woman, "Now do you agree with the opinion expressed here that nothing would be achieved by treating the white person in question the same way you are treated?" She agreed. "Then why," King asked, "would you push that person back?" The woman replied, "Well, I guess I wouldn't."

The other woman was more forthright. She made this choice observation: "Now, I think most of us know the white folks pretty well. We have to remember that they are not used to us, but we're used to them. It isn't going to do us any good to get mad and strike back, 'cause that's just what some of them *want* us to do. (Cries of 'That's right!') Now we've got this freedom. It is something they can't take away from us. But we will *lose* it if we get mad and show them we are incapable of acting like good Christian ladies and gentlemen . . ." A wild applause followed this.

King then concluded, "This is good. Now you can see the seriousness of our task here. We are going to be doing some more of this in the meetings to come. Let's discuss and think this through together, for this is serious business. I want you to feel free to discuss and express your opinions about this, but I also want you to see what our Christian responsibility is to each other when we return to the busses of Montgomery."

The meeting was cut short in order to give more time to the film. King was most generous in his introduction. He pointed out how "the F.o.R. needs no introduction to us here. It is an organization of concerned Christians that has been with us from the very beginning." And so on. I was asked to say a few words of preface to the film. I pointed out how members and friends of the Fellowship have been thrilled and deeply moved by the courage and nonviolence of this movement for justice and human dignity. I mentioned how the F.o.R. for 40 years has sought to impress this same spirit upon the world. In commenting on the movie I tried to explain how because of its message—"your message," I said—the lives of people who have come into contact with its making have been visibly moved. (Toward the beginning of my remarks I tried to bring the courage of Negro students at Clinton and Sturgis [*public schools in Tennessee*] into the focus of the spirit of Montgomery.)

The thrill of seeing this movie with these history-making citizens of Montgomery will probably never be duplicated. I have often thought what it would be like to hear people cheer and applaud the virtues of nonviolence and Christian love the same way people go nuts over seeing "our boys" march to war or the impressive fluttering of Old Glory in the winds. That night my wondering was answered. The appearance of Rosa Parks on the screen brought the house down. King's remarks in his church with the white reporter were followed by an ovation-like applause. For me any shadow of a doubt that "Walking to Freedom" had "made its point" was quickly eliminated by King's whole-hearted reaction to the showing. He was obviously deeply moved and followed the showing with a brilliant, short summary of the power of nonviolence.

I got a thrilling indication of the priceless leadership this movement has when Ralph Abernathy got up and made this unforgettable remark:

> "Children, I know how much this film has meant to you. But it is not something to be laughed at. When you see the feet of our people walking the streets with worn-out, scuffed, and turned in shoes you should feel *glad* inside and proud of those feet! You should have joy in your hearts for this movement and be able to say, 'Thank you, Jesus!'"

So went the premier showing of "Walking for Freedom." King is quite certain the MIA will buy a copy. I suggest you send down a copy immediately, because in any event they are willing to use the film under the second condition mentioned in Al's recent letter on the use of the film. Besides, Bob Graetz is eager to get his hands on it. We discussed this, and he plans to have it shown before white groups in Montgomery, Mobile, and Birmingham. And when Graetz says he will do it, it is as good as done. King agrees with my contention that there is ample need to show this film among the Negroes of Montgomery itself, because now a small percentage of the 46,000 or more Negroes attends the mass meetings. He has asked me to send him a note this week as a reminder to him to bring the matter of purchase before the MIA.

I felt lonely without you guys there, and I mean this. I was holding out a last-minute hope that at least one of you could make it. Anyway, I hope I have been able to convey to you a meaningful sense of the impact the film made on the mass meeting.

My thanks to you both for allowing me to represent you at such an event.

in fellowship,
[*signed*] Bob
Robert L. Cannon

FORP-PSC-P.

Minutes of MIA Executive Board, October 10, 1956

[. . .]
4. Objectives of the [*first anniversary*] celebration
    1. Take notice of the year of protesting
    2. Stress non-violence and non-cooperation
    3. Evaluation of the movement
    Recommendations
    1. Pamphlet to announce the activities
    2. Invite reps from all types of [*organizations*]
    3. Get Mr. Lewis Lautier (Negro press men)
    4. Get professional man to take over public relations campaign
5. Set up local publicity committee with paid secretary
b. National campaign plans re-committed
Committee ordered to bring further report on local campaign
a. Accepted. Committee ordered to continue

President empowered to look for public relations man, promoter and secretary to work on celebration.

MLKP-MBU: Box 30.

Executive Board of MIA—10:30 A.M. [*October 24, 1956*]

Meeting called to order by Pres. M. L. King Jr.
Opening prayer by Rev. A. W. Murphy.
[. . .]
    4. Statement concerning Savings & Loan association:
    In order to start association must have several persons who are willing to leave about 35,000 in Escrow for three years. $400,000 necessary to obtain Charter—In so many instances applications are turned down—have to apply to higher authority. In meantime we should be doing something—probably a Credit Union in name of MIA and would serve purpose of helping our people from the "Loan Sharks" downtown—take about 30 ds to organize—*Committee to look into this possibility*—all angles ie, name, requirements, etc. A safe venture though not as large as a Savings & Loan Association.
    Committee: R. B. Binion, A. W. Murphy, Co-Chairman, Thos. Gray, P. E. Conely, Mrs. Irene West, Mrs. Jimmie Lowe, Rev. H. J. Palmer. Committee to meet immediately and have report by next Board meeting.
    5. Discussion of First Anniversary Observance:
    The other side of picture presented (Pessimistic 2 hours long). Suggestion (Lowe): Delineate the word anniversary and supply another word—in order not to suggest a victory. A week of rededication to the principles of non violence and passive resistance. A rededication of our lives to struggle for Freedom and justice.
    (a) Program Committee—Rev. R. D. Abernathy
    Place: Still unable to get a place for our mammoth celebration (Sunday). Ala State Arena unobtainable. We might contact Dr. Foster of Tuskegee for use of facilities but committee was not too optimistic as Tuskegee also receive funds from the state. Next—A Mammoth tent. Still not certain as to place.
    The committee has made progress as to program and contacting persons who were named as program participants. Everyone except Mr. Grover Hall has accepted for the first day. Has not to date heard from [*Ralph*] McGill, nor Roy Wilkins. Had not heard directly from Mahalia Jackson, but she has accepted [*along with*] Mrs. King. A. Philip Randolph will not be able to come due to ill health. All program participants have accepted excepting three.

Alternates are being contacted. Report from committee accepted and authorized to continue its work [. . .]

(c) Publicity Committee—Mrs. Rosa Parks

Publicity report stands from previous report. Publicity to begin immediately.
Miscellaneous:

Rev. Palmer reported neglect on organization's part of the general Negro
public. Mistreatment of Negroes on a general scale throughout the city. Reprisals are more severe than any of us realize. Dr. Jones: We are deeply
concerned—Look into job losing and do something about it. Several suggestions were discussed—super market, etc. Insurance reports are better than in
ten years. Organized [*white*] groups to make them worse.

MLKP-MBU: Box 6.

To the President and Members of the Executive Committee of the Montgomery Improvement Association, Inc.

Dear Brethren:

For nearly seven months I have labored and given my all to the association
and the people of Montgomery for the cause of freedom. I have done my best
in spite of many hindrances and obstacles placed in my path. In spite of the
above road blocks and difficulties in my path, I have labored without stint and
given my all to the movement. I have now, after careful consideration, decided that I cannot, under the present condition, continue in the position as
Director of Transportation. I am therefore submitting my resignation to be
effective at once or no later than Wednesday, October 31, 1956. In submitting
my resignation I wish it known that I am not severing my association with
the organization and that I will therefore continue to cooperate with all my
heart towards the successful attainment of our goal of dignity and freedom for
all.

In closing, I wish to thank all who supported me in my efforts to effect a
workable transportation system for our people, for without support and encouragement I could not have gone on under the existing conditions of which
I have had to work.

Respectfully submitted
(Rev.) B. J. Simms, Director
Transportation

MLKP-MBU: Box 30 (October 26, 1956).

Virginia Foster Durr to Myles Horton

November 5, 1956

Dear Myles:

Aubrey [*Williams*] told me that you had written to him about Rosa Parks. I think you are among many who want to help her and I have collected $600 or so for her over the past year but even with what she had gotten from Highlander that is hardly enough to live on and she has had a hard time. As you know she has a terrible problem with her husband [*alcohol abuse*] and her Mother is sick a lot and she has real troubles and cannot leave them. If she could she would be at Highlander like a shot as she adores it and thinks it is the most wonderful place in the world. [. . .]

Now this is what I have been working on. She is the Secretary for this District of the Co-ordinating Committee to Register and Vote. This is a group that grew out of but is not affiliated with the NAACP (of course now in Alabama it could not be) and it is headed by a Mr. [*W. C.*] Patton of Birmingham who has been the head of the NAACP. I don't know anything about him but I do know Rosa and Mr. Nixon and our idea is and has been to set up a Voters Service Bureau here with Rosa in charge at $35.00 a week and it could be in Fred Gray's office which would be $25.00 a month rent and the telephone and mailing etc. could be as little or as much as was necessary. She would not only encourage people to register and vote but keep up with them afterward and keep them informed as to the issues etc. The whole operation even with the telephone and mailing would only come to about $3000 per yr. and another two or three thousand voters here would make all the difference. I cannot help but think that money for this could be raised somewhere. I have written to Jim [*Dombrowski*] about it and to Clark [*Foreman*] and Corliss [*Lamont*] and Palmer [*Webber*] and so on and so forth but so far no money except a few hundred that Rosa has had to use to live has been forthcoming. Is this anything that Highlander could help with under its charter? I think money could be raised for this and offices set up several places in the South and Highlander could be the co-ordinating force, (that is if the NAACP would be friendly) but I think whatever the official attitude we have right here a person and an opportunity. Let me know what you think of this and any ideas you might have. It looks to me as though the ECLC [*Emergency Civil Liberties Committee*], the SCEF [*Southern Conference Educational Fund*] and Highlander and the NAACP (this is always the stumbling block) could co-operate on something like this and it could be a pilot project. If you are interested I know you could put it over. Think about it hard and let me know what you think. Why don't you and the children come down here for Thanksgiving and stay with us. We have plenty of room with the girls gone and would love to have you.

Lots of love, Va.

November 15, 1956

Dear Myles:

Thanks for your letter. I simply don't believe I can write plainly enough to make myself understood! I write of course in great haste usually and that may be the trouble. Of course I did not intend or think that Highlander could finance the whole $3500. I have written to Jim, Clark, Palmer, Corliss etc. etc. all over the country to try and get this pilot project going. It has been [*ripe*] in other places and I think Montgomery is ripe for it as the Negroes have just gone through such a stern course of discipline and see the vital necessity of getting the vote if they are to survive assaults on them. I wish that Mrs. R. [*Roosevelt*] and Senator [*Herbert*] Lehman and so on could see how much good it would do the Democratic Party if they would take an interest in this kind of thing. I see in the NYT that Tenn. was lost due to the Negro vote in Shelby Co. going Republican. I know if I enlist your support and enthusiasm with this that you can help in it a great deal and it could be a part of the Highlander program even if not done in the Highlander.

Rosa has already left on her tour for the NAACP and will end it up in Brooklyn on the 20th. [. . .] I am convinced that the Negro vote, North and South is the only thing that will prevent widespread violence and riot. I wish you could be in New York when she gets there as she needs direction, she is timid and shy and yet she has the courage of a lion. [. . .]

I am still riding the same old horse or so it looks. I am convinced as I have been for LO these many years that the South will not be safe until at least the elementary rights of free citizens are enjoyed here. After that there will be other battles but now it seems to me this is the most important one. Don't you agree with me?

Lots of love, VA

HRECR-WHi: Box 11.

On November 13, the same day that Montgomery Circuit Court judge Eugene Carter granted the city's request for an injunction to shut down the MIA's car pool system, the Supreme Court, in a summary disposition without dissent, upheld the Montgomery federal court's June 5 ruling for the plaintiffs in

Browder v. *Gayle*. The eleven words overturned the 1896 *Plessy* v. *Ferguson* ruling that had given constitutional sanction to segregated public transportation for sixty years. *Brown* v. *Board of Education* had implicitly nullified *Plessy*; this decision did so explicitly. The bus boycott continued, however, until Montgomery's black citizenry implemented the high court's ruling five weeks later by desegregating the buses.

The motion to affirm is granted and the judgment is affirmed.

U.S. Reports, 352 U.S. 903 (1956).

The MIA Executive Board met the next day, November 14; excerpts from an audiotape recording of the meeting appear below. Two mass meetings that evening affirmed the executive board's recommendation, proposed by King, to end the bus boycott when the Supreme Court decision was enforced, expected within days. Because of final appeals, however, the desegregation order was not put into effect until December 21. During the interim, as another winter set in, protesters walked the last leg of their crusade along Montgomery's cold, slick streets.

[*King*:] All of us have a basic responsibility to seek to implement this noble decision. Let all of us be calm and reasonable. With understanding, good will and Christian love, we can integrate the buses of Montgomery with no difficulties. [*Applause*] Executive Board of the Montgomery Improvement Association, what is your pleasure?
[*Rev. Solomon S. Seay Sr.*:] Mr. Chairman.
[*King*:] Brother Seay?
[*Seay*:] We wish to make the motion that we accept the recommendations from our president and go along with the entire idea.
[*New speaker*:] I second the motion.
[*King*:]: It has been moved and properly seconded that this recommendation from the president and Executive Board of the Montgomery Improvement Association will be accepted. It is carried unanimously. I should first make you intelligent of what is happening legally. You, I am sure, might be a little confused because we are in so many court cases. [*Laughter*] And the kind of difficulty following this injunction, this means that the transportation system as we have had it set up is no longer in operation. I'm sure you understand why the station wagons were not operating this morning, why the automobiles were not operating, why the various dispatchers were not at their stations. It was because this injunction was issued and if we disobeyed the injunction all

of us could be cited for contempt of court and be heavily fined and arrested, so that is why the car pool is broken up.

You might also know that today we were in court. We were in the Federal court today before Judge [*Frank*] Johnson, requesting a restraining order, that is an order that the city could not file any court proceedings to halt the car pool. I don't believe that we are ever going back to any segregated buses. [*Cheering, applause*] Now there is a possibility that we could go back to the buses tomorrow morning on a segregated basis and have no trouble. Wouldn't have a bit of trouble; everything would be all right. [*Laughter*] But there is a danger that if we will go back on a *non*-segregated basis some trouble will be developed. Not that we are afraid of trouble. We don't mind getting arrested, that isn't the point. But we feel that this mandate is so close there's no point in getting a lot of folk arrested and we have to spend out a lot of money for meaningless litigation. (*Yes, That's right*) Once that mandate is here, we are clear, we have the authority to move and we will not put the bus company on the spot. [. . .] If there is anything about this Christian faith that means anything to us, it says to us that lives can be changed! (*Yes*) There is a Nicodemus standing before Jesus asking about it. (*Yeah*) Jesus cries out "You must be born again," but he implies that you *can* be born again. [*John* 3:2–7] We must live by that and we must believe it.

SBC.

Attorney Clifford Durr recounted the legal history of the bus boycott to his friend Carey McWilliams, editor of *The Nation* magazine. Durr played a major advisory role in the legal efforts but stayed in the background, partly for fear of white persecution and damage to his law practice, partly because Virginia Durr's brother-in-law was Supreme Court Justice Hugo Black. The Durrs did not want any perception of bias to prevent Black from ruling in favor of the bus boycott's constitutional challenge.

November 16, 1956

Dear Carey:

Confirming our telephone conversation, here is a brief summary of the situation:

Shortly after the Negroes filed their suit in the three Judge Federal Court and while that suit was pending, the Bus Company came out with a statement that, on advice of Counsel and in reliance on the Supreme Court's Actions in the South Carolina Bus case it was instructing its drivers to let all passengers sit where they pleased.

The City promptly filed a bill in the Circuit Court of Montgomery County asking for a writ of mandamus against the Bus Company requiring it to enforce the segregation laws. This was promptly granted by Judge Walter B. Jones, notwithstanding the pending suit in the Federal Court.

A Week or so [*four weeks*] later the three Judge Court entered its opinion and order declaring the State and City segregation statutes and ordinances unconstitutional and enjoining their enforcement. However, in its order the Court stayed the injunction pending an appeal to the Supreme Court. The Negroes did not oppose the stay, apparently feeling that the enforcement problem would not be so great once it was backed up by the Supreme Court.

During this time, the Negroes were getting along quite well with their car pool operation which was working quite efficiently and notwithstanding the constant harassment of arrests for the most minor traffic violations.

During the latter part of October, following the injunction issued against the car pool in Tallahassee, Florida, the White Citizens Councils began shouting that the City Commission of Montgomery should follow the same course. The City Commission thereupon adopted a resolution directing the City Attorneys to file appropriate proceedings.

The Negroes thereupon sought to beat the City to the punch by filing a bill in the Federal District Court seeking to enjoin the City from interfering with the car pools. This was set by Federal Judge Johnson for hearing on November 14th. A couple of days later the City filed its bill in the Montgomery County Circuit Court and Judge Eugene Carter set it down for hearing on the 13th.

Following the hearing and on the same day, Carter issued the injunction sought by the City and the Negroes promptly announced that they would comply. So the car pool, as such, is no longer operating.

In the course of the hearing in the Federal Court the next day [*actually on November 13*] news came of the Supreme Court's action. The Negroes proceeded with their case but stated to Federal Judge Johnson that once the Supreme Court opinion was effective, they would return to the busses and would not any longer need the car pool. The Supreme Court rule allowing twenty-five days for filing a motion for rehearing was not called to Judge Johnson's attention and, being a new Judge, I doubt that he was aware of it. Anyway, before the day was over he issued his opinion and order saying that while he thought the Federal Court had jurisdiction, the facts presented did not make out such a case of irreparable injury as to justify the granting of the injunction. Whether the result would have been different if the 25 day rule had been called to his attention I do not know. In view of the excitement over the news of the Supreme Court decision, the oversight on the part of the Negro attorneys is certainly understandable.

The situation now is about as follows:

1. The Supreme Court has declared the segregation laws unconstitutional but the local Federal Courts are not in a position to enforce the opinion.

2. Judge Walter B. Jones' Order says in effect that if any Negro tries to exercise the rights which the Supreme Court says he has, then he gets arrested by the City Police.

3. Carter's Order that if a Negro doesn't have a car to ride in he must walk or ride the busses still stands.

You can see the explosive potentialities of the conflicting opinions of the State and Federal Courts. The Negroes are still off the busses, but the weather is getting bad and a lot of them have a long way to go to their jobs. King has done a remarkable job of selling his people on the idea of non-violence but there are 50,000 Negroes in Montgomery and he cannot control them all. The WCCs are shouting defiance of the Supreme Court and the Kluxers are too. The Prophecies of violence in the local press sound mighty like threats of violence. What if a few Negroes fresh from their term of military service say "To Hell with this business of walking in the rain. We are going to ride the busses and we are going to sit where the Supreme Court of the United States says we can sit."

On the white side, the voices of reason have been pretty well silenced. There are a few bold spirits like Tom Thrasher of the Church of the Ascension who are still doing what they can but their voices are drowned out.

I hope I am unduly disturbed. It seems to me that if Law isn't observed it has got to be enforced or we go back to the jungle and I hear no quiet but firm voices from the direction of Washington.

This is just for you personally. I am not one of the bold spirits who dare to speak out—at least not yet.

We will let you know of developments. Suppose you have seen about the Symposium on Non-Violent Resistance which the Montgomery Improvement Association is sponsoring from December 3–6.

Sincerely,
Clifford J. Durr

Dear Carey:

[...] I wish to correct one of the remarks you made on the Southern election picture which I thought was fine and agreed with entirely. Lister Hill, John Sparkman and Folsom did campaign very hard for the Democratic ticket But not in Alabama. Neither did Kefauver campaign hard in Tennessee and he lost that. I hope you all will begin to draw a better line between such men as Hill, Sparkman, Folsom even, Kefauver, Gore, Fulbright etc. and such as Eastland, Stennis, Talmadge. The thing to do is to Split the South, not weld it together.

Va. Durr

CJDP-A-Ar.

The MIA created a public relations committee to coordinate plans for the Institute on Nonviolence and Social Change the first week of December.

Responsibilities of the MIA Public Relations Committee

1. Complete arrangement for Program
   a. Finish contacting speakers.
   b. Follow up letter of thanks and request for Biographical material.
   c. Proceed in getting official program printed.
   d. Have letterheads printed (35,000).
2. Press, Radio and TV Releases
   a. Release total program to Montgomery Advertiser by Tuesday, Nov. 13.
   b. Release statement to Mass meeting Monday night, Nov. 12.
   c. Release total program to all Negro News Papers and request that a representative be sent to Montgomery to cover the workshop. Wednesday, Nov. 14.
   d. Seek time on Radio and TV to announce the Workshop. Week after the third Sunday.
   e. Have placard and hand bills printed announcing workshop.
   f. Release weekly article to newspapers featuring individual speakers.
3. Issue Letters to All Churches and major organizations of the nation for financial contributions.
   a. Draw up mailing list of pastors of all denominations across the nation.
   b. Draw up mailing list of funeral directors, physicians, beauticians, nurses, and teachers across the nation.

MLKP-MBU: Box 30 (November 1956).

Job Description for Promotional Director

I. Promote attendance and general interest for workshop on state level.
   a. Contact all major ministerial alliances across the state.
   b. Contact all major civic groups across the state.

    c. Distribute placards and hand bills over the state.

    d. Make contact with school principals across the state.

    e. Make contact with choirs across the state for state mass meeting.

    f. Explain the practical use of badges and a special dedication day.

II.   Promote financial effort on state and local level

    a. Draw up mailing list of pastors of all denominations across the state.

    b. Draw up mailing list of funeral directors, physicians, farm agents, home demonstration agents, teachers, beauticians.

    c. Distribute 30,000 envelopes among churches of Montgomery and vicinity for anniversary contributions. Have each church to submit two solicitors for this purpose.

MLKP-MBU: Box 30 (November 1956).

Ralph Abernathy and Martin Luther King Jr. to Alabama Clergy

November 30, 1956

Dear Reverend,

The U.S. Supreme Court has ruled that we have the right to sit with dignity in the Montgomery City Buses. Yet, it appears we may have to continue our struggle just as we all have to work hard to get school integration following the Court's decision of 1954.

To continue our effort in the Spirit of Jesus, we are calling upon our people in Montgomery to rededicate themselves to non-violence and the love of God in our continuing struggle for freedom and dignity.

From December 3–9, one full year since the beginning of the bus protest, we are holding an *Institute on Non-Violence and Social Change*. Many important Negro and White Leaders from all over America are coming to Montgomery. But, Rev. King, Rev. S. S. Seay and I know that our Institute cannot be a success without you "who labor in the vineyard of the Lord." For you are the shepherd of His flock.

We would like you to be with us for the whole time and certainly hope you will, but we especially want and need you for two major events during the Institute:

1. On Dec. 7, we are urging Pastors from all over the State to attend an all day Ministers Seminar. Dr. Harry V. Richardson, President of Gammon Theological Seminary and Rev. James H. Robinson, of Harlem's famous Church of the Master have been invited to lead the discussion. Another

feature of the Seminar will be a sermon by the Rev. Gardner Taylor, Pastor of the new million dollar Concord Baptist Church in New York.

2. On Sunday afternoon, Dec. 9, we plan a mammoth State-Wide Religious Service. At that Service Dr. J. H. Jackson, President of the National Baptist Convention, will speak. We are depending on you to make these great meetings a success. We also want to give you the opportunity to share in raising much needed funds to help us carry on the struggle here in Montgomery.

Since the Supreme Court Decision on transportation on Nov. 13, many people all over the South are watching to see how we behave here. If we do well, if we protect our people who face hardship, if we can press our struggle into new areas—then people in other cities and states will be inspired to greater action. We believe that you, your Church, and your community will definitely feel the results of the Movement in Montgomery. We urgently need funds for the following purposes:

(a) To give aid to the 200 men and women who sacrificed to drive in our car pool. Many of them are "marked men" who will not be able to get work for some time.

(b) To issue literature and to hire a secretary to *build a credit union* to help people stand on their own feet in time of economic boycott or crisis.

(c) To help us continue our effort to establish the first Negro bank in the state of Alabama.

(d) To help us continue the *voting Clinics*, where we help people to register and teach them voting procedures.

(e) To keep our office open to insure that our people are trained to meet the new situations with dignity and a Christian spirit.

We are sending you some special envelopes for your congregation and hope you will raise as much as you can. We want you to make your Church's report at the State-Wide Mammoth Service following Dr. Jackson's sermon.

We trust you will do all you can to attend the Institute and raise funds to help us continue the struggle for justice in Montgomery.

We remain,

Yours for His Cause,
Rev. Ralph D. Abernathy, Institute Chairman
Dr. Martin Luther King Jr., Pres.

BRP-DLC.

Winter: Return of the Light ... 12 ...

On December 3 King opened the Institute on Nonviolence and Social Change, which commemorated the movement's first anniversary, with an address before several thousand townspeople and visitors at Holt Street Baptist Church. "God decided to use Montgomery as the proving ground for the struggle and triumph of freedom and justice in America," he declared to the assembly. "It is one of the ironies of our day that Montgomery, the Cradle of the Confederacy, is being transformed into Montgomery, the cradle of freedom and justice. . . .

"All of the loud noises that you hear today from the legislative halls of the South in terms of 'interposition' and 'nullification,' and of outlawing the NAACP, are merely the death groans from a dying system. The old order is passing away, and the new order is coming into being. We are witnessing in our day the birth of a new age, with a new structure of freedom and justice." He called for reconciliation, redemption, creation of the beloved community. "It is this type of understanding goodwill that will transform the deep gloom of the old age into the exuberant gladness of the new age."[1]

The seven-day educational marathon featured workshops and mass meetings led by distinguished guests on the dynamics of the "new and powerful weapon" of nonviolent direct action, culminating in a huge Sunday service with Rev. J. H. Jackson, president of the National Baptist Convention. On the second night Smiley moderated a forum on nonviolent social change at Bethel Baptist Church, which included ministers T. J. Jemison, architect of the 1953 Baton Rouge bus boycott; C. K. Steele, leader of the ongoing bus boycott in Tallahassee; and Fred Shuttlesworth, organizer of Birmingham bus protests.

The next evening, December 5, Baptist educator Nannie Burroughs enthralled her listeners by likening the bus boycott to the American Revolution. "Work as if all depended upon you," she concluded, "and pray as if all depended upon God." Georgia novelist Lillian Smith sent regret that she was not able to come because of a recurrence of cancer. A friend, Dr. Walter Alford of New York, delivered her address. The attentive audience "sensed the sadness of the occasion" due to her illness, wrote reporter Inez Baskin. "A feeling of sympathy permeated the atmosphere."[2]

"The Right Way is Not a Moderate Way," by Lillian Smith

I want to take my stand by your side because I respect the creative means you have chosen to use to secure your legal rights as American citizens.

These means are nonviolent. This way is the way of good will and intelligence and truth, and love. You have refused to use the crude and dangerous weapon of hate. You have refused to lie. You have not succumbed to retaliation or to resentment. You have used no harshness of word or of act.

You have behaved under stress like mature men and women—not like a mob.

But you have not been "moderates" nor have you kept in the middle of the road. No. You have shown the world that there are two extremes and they cannot be put in the same moral category. There is the extreme of hate, yes; but there is also the extreme of love. There is the extreme of the lie, yes; but there is also the extreme we call the "search for truth." There is the habitual thief who is certainly an extremist; there is the habitually honest man who is an extremist, also. But would you put the thief and the honest man in the same moral category? Would you put the person whose life radiates love in the same moral category with the men whose life radiates hate? Are they equally harmful? Or equally good? Those who think so have abandoned the concept of morality and the concept of *quality*, and sanity in human affairs.

So: You have been extremists: good, creative, loving extremists and I want to tell you I admire and respect you for it.

Moderation is the slogan of our times. But moderation never made a man or a nation great. Moderation never discovered anything, never invented anything, never built a skyscraper, never invented an airplane, never wrote a poem, never painted a great picture, never wrote a great play, never discovered a country, never explored a new frontier, never built a civilization and never dreamed a great religion. These great thrusts of the human imagination and spirit came out of daring to meet ordeal in a new way. It would be difficult to imagine Jesus as a "moderate." Imagine Leonardo da Vinci being a moderate. Imagine Gandhi as a moderate. Imagine Shakespeare or Einstein as a moderate. Imagine Lindbergh being a moderate. He may be one now but he was not one when he flew the Atlantic. It was the act of a daring extremist if there ever was such; but it was a creative act; it was not the act of a destroyer, nor the act of a hating man, nor the act of a violent man.

You have done many good things, down here in Montgomery. But one of the best, one of the most valuable, has been the fact that you have dramatized for all America to see that *in times* of ordeal, in *times of crisis*, only the extremist can meet the challenge. The question in crisis or ordeal is not: Are you going to be an extremist? The question is: *What kind of extremist* are you going to be?

Here, in Montgomery, you have decided what kind of extremist you are. You have chosen the way of love and truth, the way of nonviolence and understanding, the way of patience with firmness, the way of dignity and calm persistence.

You have done this as others keep talking about moderation.

What do people mean when they use that fuzzy word, moderation? Why do the mass magazines keep talking about it? What is the meaning of this hypnotic word?

Let's take it step by step: Let's be as fair as we can. Many mean simply this: "We want to freeze things as they are. We want to be neutral. We don't want to move a step either way. Things suit us as they are: Why should we change them? Change is painful so let's don't change." There are others, a few men of good will but with only a moderate amount of brains who intend no harm at all when they lean back on this slogan. They mean in a vague way: "Let's be tactful; let's talk in a quiet voice; let's don't stir things up; let's do a little bit but let's sleep through it and then maybe some day we'll wake up and find that everything has settled itself without our having to do anything about it." And there are the few sincere, even intelligent people who want moderation simply because to them it is a synonym for *doing nothing*. They are too frightened to move, to think, to find a new way to meet the challenge. It is known by all of us that our minds don't work well if we become too frightened, although they work best of all when we are a little frightened.

People behave this way in other crises too; not simply this one of race relations. There are people who react in a similar way when they are told they have cancer. They decide to be moderate and do nothing. Why? Because they are scared. And because they are very frightened they convince themselves that if they do nothing, the cancer will go away.

The tragic fact is, neither cancer nor segregation will go away while you close your eyes. Both are dangerous diseases because they spread, they metastasize throughout our country—and indeed, throughout the whole earth. Because this is so: because you cannot wall these problems in, you don't have time to lose with cancer nor today, do we have time to lose since the Supreme Court has spoken on segregation. The critical moment is on us. Now is the time to deal with it.

Why is there a crisis now when for 50 years we have not felt segregation had reached a critical peak? Why has the Supreme Court's decision precipitated this crisis?

As I see it, this is why:

The Supreme Court is the highest legal voice in our land. It interprets the U.S. Constitution for us. We are not free, in this country ruled by law, to interpret the law for ourselves as [*Georgia senator-elect*] Herman Talmadge says he does and that "everybody can do." The Supreme Court has spoken: It has said, segregation in the public schools must go because it is unconstitutional. The Supreme Court has, therefore, said in effect that all legal segregation must go. Once saying this, the crisis was upon us.

Why? Because now, if we do not take segregation out of our schools, we are defying the Supreme Court, we are subverting the Constitution. If we do not get rid of segregation in buses and trains and planes, we are defying the highest law-interpreting body of our land. If we do not now get rid of all forms of public segregation, we are subverting our form of government.

But to say the Supreme Court's decision precipitated the crisis is only half a truth. It spoke its decision. The actual crisis came because we did not listen. The ordeal began when the governmental leaders of our southern states spoke out and said they would not obey the Supreme Court's decision. It takes two to make a crisis. And these political leaders, these governors, these attorneys-general, these U.S. Senators who defy the Supreme Court and force us to defy the Supreme Court have, in effect, started a revolution against the legal structure on which our free and democratic government is based.

This is how the ordeal started; this is the situation we are now faced with: a different situation from that of three years ago.

Three years ago we had segregation. And it was the same old unchristian, undemocratic way of life we have had for fifty years and have now; and people, colored and white, were harmed by it. But the situation is different. Different because segregation is now against the law of our nation. Different because to maintain it we have to defy our own government.

How we deal with this critical situation will determine our moral health as individuals, our cultural health, our health as a nation, and as a leader of democracy throughout the world.

You know how the destructive extremists are dealing with it in the South. But how are the rest of the white southerners dealing with it? May I trouble the waters, a little, by telling you?

A few—perhaps far more than you know—are dealing with it creatively and honestly and with courage. There are many white southerners opposed to segregation; there are many more who are not opposed to segregation but who believe it is more important to obey the law of the land than it is to have segregation. Some of these are speaking out: some in their pulpits and some in their editorial chair. Some are meeting in small groups and probing deeply into this trouble in order to try to understand it. Others are taking, here and there, a bold stand. Some are losing their jobs, of course. They are the creative, nonviolent "extremists" who are quietly, with wisdom and tact and goodwill trying to bring change about as quickly as possible. How about the rest of the white southerners? the moderates? those who are neither good extremists nor bad extremists? How about them?

Most are doing nothing. That does not mean they are not worried. It means they are suffering from temporary moral and psychic paralysis. They are working harder to be moderates and neutrals than they are working to meet the crisis. They are driving straight down the middle of the road with their eyes shut and you know what happens in traffic when you do that. But they are trying to believe there is no traffic. They are telling themselves nobody is on the road but themselves. They are, you see, trying very hard not to be extremists, they are trying to be neither good nor evil.

And all the time these moderates are doing nothing or almost nothing, men like Herman Talmadge, men like Senator Eastland are shouting at the tops of their voice; certain newspaper editors are writing violently against the good extremists and begging everybody to please freeze and do nothing. And the mobs gather; and the crosses are burned; and the houses are dynamited; and the brave ones who speak out lose their jobs and so it goes, on and on. The White Citizens Councils mushroom, the Klan wakes up and wraps itself in its pillow case and sheet; and Negroes and whites working for integration are boycotted and penalized and cheated.

But the big middle group turn away and try not to see, whispering, "I must be moderate; I must not get worried; I must not mind when innocent people are hurt and brave people lose their jobs and lives."

And how are the moderates getting along? How are they faring? What kind of price are they paying for their moderation, for this desire of theirs to prolong segregation?

May I suggest how high this price is?

In order to maintain the status quo, to maintain segregation as long as possible even though the Supreme Court has spoken, to drive in the middle of the road, the white people are having to give up their freedoms. What freedoms?

Let me name a few:

a. *The freedom to do right.* There are white Christians in the South who know segregation is wrong. They want to do right. But they are not free to do right. Every day they do what they know in their hearts is contrary to their Christian beliefs.

b. *The freedom to obey the law.* The Supreme Court has spoken. But we in the South are not free to obey the law. We obey our dictators instead; these are sometimes our governors; other times these dictators are our business employers, our school superintendents, or our Boards of Trustees of the church.

c. The freedom to speak out, or to write, or teach what one believes is true. We have almost lost this basic freedom now in the South. The penalties are heavy for those who dare speak out anyway. Loss of jobs; boycott; ostracism; violence, sometimes.

d. And of course, having lost those three big freedoms, we have also lost our freedom from fear. In old Reconstruction days, white people were afraid of freed Negroes. Or so they said. Today, they are afraid of each other and themselves. They fear. And that is the saddest loss of all, in this great, free country of ours.

The risk is too big, people say. Young brave men say "the risk is too great. I'd like to do something but the risk is too big."

I say, "The time has now come when it is dangerous not to risk. We must take risks in order to save our integrity, our moral nature, our lives and our country. We must do what we do with love and dignity, with nonviolence and wisdom, but we must do something big and keep doing it."

I was talking to a group of white students in one of our southern universities. They had sort of sneaked me in. Yes, really. They were afraid for people to know Lillian Smith was on the campus. So everything was hush-hush. I teased them a little. And they laughed. But they felt ashamed, too. Some of these young men had come home from Korea a few years ago. They knew what danger is; and had gladly run risks. Now, they were not running any more risks.

Not only the loss of our freedoms but the loss of our old gallant courage, is part of the high price we are paying today for our do-nothing attitude toward segregation. And worst of all, is the loss of belief. One young man said, "I'd risk anything for something I believed. I just don't think I believe in anything much, anymore."

Then I told them about your creative project in Montgomery. They had heard a little, of course. But they listened, these young white men and girls. And they grew excited and interested, and thrilled.

Do you realize that in helping yourselves to secure your freedom you are helping young white southerners secure theirs, too? This is a big thing. This is how the creative act works: it always helps somebody else besides you. In dramatizing that the extreme way can be the good way, the creative way, and that in times of ordeal it is the only way, you are helping the white South find its way, too. You are giving young white southerners hope. You are persuading some of them that there is something worth believing in and risking for. You are stirring their imaginations and their hearts, not simply because you are brave and are running risks but because you know that the means we use are the important thing: that the means must be right; the means must be full of truth and dignity and love and wisdom.

Because you are doing this, I want to close my greeting to you by saying thank you. Thank you for what you are doing for yourselves and what you are doing also for the entire South. Thank you for dramatizing before the eyes of America that the question is not, "Are you an extremist?," but "What kind of extremist are you?" Thank you for showing us all that there is always a creative, good, nonviolent way to meet ordeal.

MLKP-MBU: Box 6.

1. King, "Facing the Challenge of a New Age," December 3, 1956, MLKP-MBU: Box 10.
2. Inez J. Baskin, "New Plan of Non-Violence Rises from 'Cradle of the Confederacy,'" *Norfolk* (Va.) *Journal and Guide*, December 15, 1956.

December 7, 1956

Mr. A. J. Muste
LIBERATION
110 Christopher Street
New York 14, N.Y.

Dear Mr. Muste:

I too am very sorry that it will not be possible for me to come to the meeting but I cannot and doubt if I will get to New York for another year. I go up to see my daughter once a year and have a day or so in New York and that is the extent of my travelling.

But this is, in my opinion, no great loss as I think that a Negro should speak of what is happening in the South today. I am suggesting that Dr. Lawrence Reddick of the Alabama State Teachers College be asked in my place and I think you will find him a great addition and a man who has the knowledge and historical background of the whole southern liberal movement.

I went to hear Mr. Smiley on yesterday at the Institute on Non-Violence and thought he spoke very well. It is certainly appreciated by the Negro Community that your group has come to their help and aid so generously. I am not quite clear about the extent of the non-violence theory but in answer to a question on yesterday, Mr. Smiley said he did approve of the legal application of force as demonstrated in Clinton, Tennessee, to back up the edict of the Supreme Court, which relieved my mind a lot, as I think it is a great mistake to say that no "force" of any kind should be used even to back up the Supreme Court Decision.

In my opinion, I think the struggle that is going on in the South today is historically the most important struggle in the country and no progress can be hoped for unless and until this sore spot in the South, this cancer, is cut out and cured. It seems to me that the function of the liberal groups in the country is to act in this crisis and not talk about how to get together. People are welded together by struggle and by doing something—not by discussion and by argument alone. The struggle here in the South is far from being won and there is a long hard road ahead and no better way can be found, in my opinion, for the liberal forces to get together and accomplish something than by helping to bring this struggle to a successful conclusion.

Sincerely,
Virginia Durr

FORP-PSC-P.

Liberation magazine editors devoted the December 1956 issue to the bus boycott.

Liberation's Salute to Montgomery

ELEANOR ROOSEVELT

I think December 5th is an important date for all of us in the U.S. to remember. The bus protest carried on by the colored people of Montgomery, Alabama, without violence, has been one of the most remarkable achievements of people fighting for their own rights but doing so without bloodshed and with the most remarkable restraint and discipline, that we have ever witnessed in this country. It is something all of us should be extremely proud of for it is an achievement by Americans which has rarely before been seen.

RALPH J. BUNCHE

For the past year Martin Luther King and his fellow Negro citizens of Montgomery have been doing heroic work in the vineyards of democracy. Their patient determination, their wisdom and quiet courage are constituting an inspiring chapter in the history of human dignity. They have steadfastly refused to barter away their dignity and may God bless them for that.

ROY WILKINS

Long known as the first capital of the late Confederacy, the City of Montgomery, Alabama, now has a new and more righteous claim to fame. Once the war capital of an alliance dedicated to human slavery, it is now the peace capital of a new liberation movement. Formerly a more or less complacent Southern town, it has become a center of activity providing a demonstration of the effectiveness of non-violent resistance to racial tyranny.

The rebirth of Montgomery came with the spontaneous protest of the city's Negro population against the humiliation of Jim Crow. This upsurge of protest was channeled into constructive action by the Montgomery Improvement Association under the inspired and dedicated leadership of Martin Luther King Jr., Ralph Abernathy, and E. D. Nixon.

The Montgomery protest is an historic development. It demonstrates before all the world that Negroes have the capacity for sustained collective action. It refutes the white supremacist's false charge that Negroes are content with discrimination and segregation. It validates the role of local leadership in social action programs. It reveals the economic strength of the Negro. It affirms the value of a calm approach to potentially explosive issues. And finally, it demonstrates that 50,000 persons can work together as a unit without military discipline and without degenerating into a mob.

HARRY EMERSON FOSDICK

Montgomery, Alabama, has become one of the most significant places in the world. The idea of non-violent resistance is not traditionally at home in the United States. Many of us who regard it as basically Christian have wondered how it ever could be made at home here. Now, in Montgomery, it is actually at work on an impressive scale.

Racial prejudice and discrimination are a fundamental denial of the Christian gospel. Atheism itself is no more complete a rejection of everything the church stands for, from monotheism to the teachings of Jesus. Yet many churchmen today are supporting in America a system of racial inequality and injustice which denies the faith, disgraces us among free peoples and furnishes a major weapon of propaganda to the Communists. The dignified, resolute and peaceable protest of the Montgomery Negroes against such inequality and injustice is a godsend, to our country, and a lesson that, North as well as South, we need to learn.

In the North the tensions caused by racial prejudice are less acute than in the South, but let no Northerner pride himself that we are free from the curse, or from the Christian responsibility it involves. Violence will never solve the problem: only the persuasive influence of patient, resolute, sometimes heroic good will, will help: and the Negroes of Montgomery, Alabama, are pioneering a method which all Christian churchmen should welcome, and be prepared, when it is necessary, to practise.

JOHN HAYNES HOLMES

Montgomery is destined to hold the same place in the heroic history of the Negro in America as Lexington and Concord in the history of this country. In both instances the people of a whole region rose up against those among them who would deny liberty and justice. Montgomery set the noble example of putting aside the weapons of force and violence and turning to non-violence for their weapons. Men showed their willingness, the eagerness, to suffer and even to die for their rights; and when that moment comes in the life of a people, the victory is already sure.

In the present struggle there can be no doubt as to its outcome. The forces of righteousness are on our side. God is with us—which means that every force for good in this vast universe is lined up in support of the deliverance of humankind from tyranny. The victory may seem slow in coming. The waiting for it may seem interminable. We perhaps may not live to see the hour of triumph. But the great Theodore Parker, abolitionist preacher in the days before the Civil War, answered this doubt and fear when he challenged an impatient world. "The arc of the moral universe is long, but it bends toward justice."

A. PHILIP RANDOLPH

In this moment of history when dynamic, centrifugal, social impulses for human dignity, equality, justice and freedom have been unloosed, especially, within the area of the South that will never be contained until Negroes are fully free, it is important to note that the protest of jim crow buses in Montgomery, Alabama, by fifty thousand Negroes in that city, marks the most dramatic expression of the civil rights revolution which is now under way.

This Montgomery movement for human rights has introduced in the complex of social change in human relationships in the South, a new quality of action; namely, non-violent, good-will, direct action. It is love instead of hate; good-will instead of ill-will; peace instead of war.

This philosophy of non-violent, good-will, direct action, which stems from Judeo-Christian ethic, was implemented by the life and work of the noble saint of India, Mahatma Gandhi. Its great social significance and value in the field of social action for the achievement of human brotherhood consists in the fact that it rejects the old doctrine of an eye for an eye and a tooth for a tooth and shocks and frustrates the enemy by enduring and absorbing violence without offering violent resistance but, on the contrary, peaceful non-resistance or spiritual and moral resistance. [. . .]

Z. K. MATTHEWS

I am sure that all the world over lovers of freedom have been thrilled by the magnificent way in which the people of Montgomery and other places in the States have stood up and fought for the elementary rights which some of their fellow countrymen seek to deny them. Their example has been an inspiration to others faced with similar problems in other parts of the world.

In our own country [South Africa] Africans in one of our main African townships—Evaton in the Transvaal—have for months carried on a bus boycott against burdensome fares bearing hard upon people of the lower income group. Although the people concerned suffered much hardship, including violence at the hands of those anxious to break the boycott, the people stood their ground and won the battle in the end, proving once more the power of non-violent resistance to oppression in various forms.

At the present time African women in different parts of the country have embarked on non-violent protests against the Government's plans to extend the hated "pass system" to African women in the same way as it has applied to African men in the past. The biggest demonstration, involving 10,000 women, took place in August at the Union Buildings in Pretoria, the administrative capital of the Union. Others have taken place in other centers.

At a time like this when the world seems to stand on the brink of another futile resort to arms to settle disputes, it is good to know that the banner of non-violent resistance as a method of settling differences, whether at the local, state or national level, is being kept high in some places.

"We Are Still Walking," by Martin Luther King Jr.

When the Supreme Court ruled on November 13th that segregated buses are illegal, it must have appeared to many people that our struggle in Montgomery was over. Actually, the most difficult stage of crisis had just begun.

For one thing the immediate response of some influential white people was to scoff at the court decision and to announce that it would never be put into effect. One pro-segregationist said: "We are prepared for a century of litigation." The leader of the Montgomery Citizens Council stated: "Any attempt to enforce this decision will inevitably lead to riot and bloodshed." It is clear that all our tact and all our love are called for in order to meet the situation creatively.

Even more important, our own experience and growth during these eleven and a half months of united nonviolent protest has been such that we cannot be satisfied with a court "victory" over our white brothers. We must respond to the decision with an understanding of those who have opposed us and with an appreciation of the difficult adjustments that the court order poses for them. We must be able to face up honestly to our own shortcomings. We must act in such a way as to make possible a coming together of white people and colored people on the basis of a real harmony of interests and understanding. We seek an integration based on mutual respect. We have worked and suffered for non-segregated buses, but we want this to be a step towards equality, not a step away from it.

Perhaps if I tell you of our first mass meeting the night after the Supreme Court's decision, it will indicate what was going on in our minds.

After our opening hymn, the Scripture was read by Rev. Robert Graetz, a young Lutheran minister who has been a constant reminder to us in these trying months that white people as well as colored people are trying to expand their horizons and work for the day-to-day applications of Christianity. He read from Paul's famous letter to the Corinthians: "Though I have all faith, so that I could move mountains, and have not love, I am nothing. . . . Love suffereth long and is kind."

When he got to the words: "When I was a child, I spoke as a child, I understood as a child, I thought as a child, but when I became a man I put away childish things" [1 Corinthians 13], the congregation burst into applause. Soon there was shouting, cheering, and waving of handkerchiefs. To me this was an exciting, spontaneous expression by the Negro congregation of what had happened to it these months. The people knew that they had come of age, that they had won new dignity. They would never again be the old, subservient, fearful appeasers. But neither would they be resentful fighters for justice who could overlook the rights and feelings of their opponents. When Mr. Graetz concluded the reading with the words: "And now abideth faith, hope and love, but the greatest of these is love," there was another spontaneous outburst. Only a people who had struggled with all the problems involved in trying to be loving in the midst of bitter conflict could have reacted in this way. I knew then that nonviolence, for all its difficulties, had won its way into our hearts.

PECULIAR PEOPLE

Later, when Rev. Abernathy spoke, he told how a white newspaper man had reproached him for this outburst on the part of the congregation. "Isn't it a little peculiar," he said, "for people to interrupt the Scripture that way?" "Yes it is," said Abernathy, "just as it is peculiar for people to walk in the snow and rain when there are empty buses available; just as it is peculiar for people to pray for those who persecute them; just as it is peculiar for the Southern Negro to stand up and look a white man in the face as an equal." Pandemonium broke loose.

In my talk, I tried to discuss the basic philosophy of our movement. It is summed up in the idea that we must go back on the buses not as a right but as a duty. If we go back as a right, there is a danger that we will be blind to the rights of others. We Negroes have been in a humiliating position because others have been chiefly concerned with insisting on their own rights. This is too narrow a basis for human brotherhood, and certainly will not overcome existing tensions and misunderstandings.

Secondly, if we insist on our "rights," we will return to the buses with the psychology of victors. We will think and say—by our manner if not our words—that we are the victors. This would be unworthy of us and a barrier to the growth we hope for in others.

In the past, we have sat in the back of the buses, and this has indicated a basic lack of self-respect. It shows that we thought of ourselves as less than men. On the other hand, the white people have sat in the front and have thought of themselves as superior. They have tried to play God. Both approaches are wrong. Our *duty* in going back on the buses is to destroy this superior-inferior relationship, from whichever side it is felt. Instead of accepting the division of mankind, it is our duty to act in the manner best designed to establish man's oneness. If we go back in this spirit, our mental attitude will be one that must in the long run bring about reconciliation.

There is a victory in this situation. But it is a victory for truth and justice, a victory for the unity of mankind.

These eleven months have not been at all easy. Our feet have often been tired. We have struggled against tremendous odds to maintain alternative transportation, but we have kept going with the faith that in our struggle we had cosmic companionship, and that, at bottom, the universe is on the side of justice. We must keep that perspective in the days that are immediately ahead.

KLAN STAGES PARADE

The night the Supreme Court decision was handed down, the Ku Klux Klan tried to intimidate us. The radio announced that the Klan would demonstrate throughout the Negro community. There were threats of bombing and other violence. We decided that we would not react as we had done too often in the past. We would not go into our houses, close the doors, pull the shades, or turn off the lights. Instead we would greet them as any other parade.

When the Klan arrived—according to the newspapers "about forty carloads of robed and hooded members"—porch lights were on and doors open. The Negro people had gathered courage. As the Klan drove by, people behaved much as if they were watching the advance contingent for the Ringling Brothers Circus or a Philadelphia Mummers Parade. Many walked about as usual; some simply watched; others relaxed on their stoops; a few waved as the cars passed by. This required a tremendous effort, but the Klan was so nonplussed that after a few short blocks it turned off into a side-street and disappeared into the night. [. . .]

GROWTH ON BOTH SIDES

[. . .] We have all inherited a situation that is extremely difficult. We are therefore gratified when we find members of the white population making a serious effort to change. There are many evidences of growth on the part of both white and Negro people in Montgomery.

A year ago the intolerable behavior of a prominent member of the white group was largely responsible for prolonging the protest. In fact, considerable tension arose from his initial intransigence. At the beginning we felt that this gentleman treated us rather rudely. But now he talks with us in a dignified and courteous manner and says that he understands us better. He told me that he respects persons who have deep convictions and are willing to stand up for them at the cost of personal suffering.

There are encouraging indications that hundreds of other white persons have come to feel similarly. They are under tremendous pressure to conform to the views of the more reactionary elements, or at least to remain discreetly aloof. But we are trying to encourage them to act firmly in line with their deeper convictions. That is why we are publicly asking all persons of good will to comply with the Supreme Court order.

One anonymous phone caller, whose voice I have come to recognize, has been calling me for months to insult and threaten me and then slam down the receiver. Recently he stayed on the phone for half an hour, giving me the opportunity to discuss the whole underlying problem with him. At the end of the call he said: "Reverend King, I have enjoyed talking with you, and I am beginning to think that you may be right." This willingness to change deeply ingrained attitudes buoys us up and challenges us to be open to growth, also.

APPEAL TO THE CHURCHES

We are appealing especially to church people to examine their lives in the light of the life and teachings of the great religious leaders. They teach that all men, whatever their race or color, are children of one Father and therefore brothers, one of another. He that loveth not his brother whom he hath seen can not love God whom he hath not seen.

Churches, by disseminating these teachings, have had much to do with the increasing sensitiveness on the issue of race relations and the undoubted advances which have been made in recent years. However, the churches have fallen woefully short of practicing what they preach. They have contributed to the confusion, the hesitation, the bitterness and violence.

We are convinced that great gains can be made if religious men will seek to practice true love toward their brothers and sisters. This conviction underlies our own attempts to be fearlessly non-violent in the present situation. It is the basis on which we are appealing to our white brothers to see beyond the narrow concepts of the past.

CAN NOT BE SOLVED BY POLITICS

Discussion has tended to concentrate on such aspects as Supreme Court decisions and the maintenance of law and order against mob rule. We do not wish to minimize these issues. They have an important bearing on the peace of our land. But the racial problem, North and South, cannot be solved on a purely political level. It must be approached morally and spiritually. We must ask ourselves as individuals: What is the right thing to do, regardless of the personal sacrifices involved?

Within the Negro churches, one of the lessons we have learned is that the church is not living up to its full responsibilities if it merely preaches an other-worldly gospel devoid of practical social connotations. It must concern itself, as Jesus did, with the economic and social problems of this world, as well as with its other-worldly gospel. As our church has played a leading role in the present social struggle, it has won new respect within the Negro population.

LONG RANGE PROGRAM

From this perspective, it is obvious that our interest in brotherhood extends far beyond the desegregation of the buses. We are striving for the removal of all barriers that divide and alienate mankind, whether racial, economic or psychological. Though we are deeply involved in the bus protest, we have also worked out a long-range constructive program. Recently we agreed on six continuing goals:

1. To establish the first bank in Montgomery to be owned and operated by Negroes. We have found that in the present situation many Negroes who are active in the protest have been unable to secure loans from the existing banks.

2. To organize a credit union. As a result of the protest, there is a strong desire among the Negroes to pool their money for great cooperative economic programs. We are anxious to demonstrate that cooperation rather than competition is the way to meet problems.

3. To expand the voting clinics, with which we have been trying not only to teach Negroes the techniques of registration and voting but also to provide impartial discussion of the underlying issues.

4. The establishment of training institutes in the methods and discipline of non-violent action. We have begun to see the tremendous possibilities of this method of tackling human problems.

5. Until the NAACP, which has been outlawed in Alabama, is able to function again in the State, we hope to be able to take on some aspects of the excellent work it has carried on.

6. To give aid to those who have sacrificed in our cause. Many of them are marked men and women who will be unable to work in Montgomery for a long time. We cannot build a movement if we do not stand by those who are victims in the struggle. Spiritual solidarity is meaningless if it does not extend into economic brotherhood.

UNANTICIPATED RESULTS OF NON-VIOLENCE

Everyone must realize that in the early days of the protest there were many who questioned the effectiveness, and even the manliness, of non-violence. But as the protest has continued there has been a growing commitment on the part of the entire Negro population. Those who were willing to get their guns in the beginning are coming to see the futility of such an approach.

The struggle has produced a definite character development among Negroes. The Negro is more willing now to tell the truth about his attitude to segregation. In the past, he often used deception as a technique for appeasing and soothing the white man. Now he is willing to stand up and speak more honestly.

Crime has noticeably diminished. One nurse, who owns a Negro hospital in Montgomery, said to me recently that since the protest started she has been able to go to church Sunday mornings, something she had not been able to do for years. This means that Saturday nights are not so vicious as they used to be.

There is an amazing lack of bitterness, a contagious spirit of warmth and friendliness. The children seem to display a new sense of belonging. The older children are aware of the conflict and the resulting tension, but they act as if they expect the future to include a better world to live in.

We did not anticipate these developments. But they have strengthened our faith in non-violence. Believing that a movement is finally judged by its effect on the human beings associated with it, we are not discouraged by the problems that lie ahead.

Liberation, December 1956.

Montgomery Board of Commissioners Statement on Supreme Court Decision, December 17, 1956

We have been advised that our petition for rehearing has been denied in connection with the case involving the segregation of the races on buses operating exclusively on the streets of Montgomery.

This decision sweeps away the wise and long-standing ordinance of the City of Montgomery, which experience over the years has shown, has contributed to the peace and social order of our City. An ordinance of the City admitted as valid by the United States Supreme Court for over half a century is nullified by a Court which could find no reason for ruling as it did, and hence could write no opinion to tell the people of Montgomery why their ordinance was unconstitutional.

The Supreme Court of the United States, repudiating all former decisions rendered years ago, by a court composed of the wisest jurists of the nation, has now set itself up as a fourth department of government. In addition to the judicial power given it by the Constitution, it has gone out of its orbit as a judicial body, and has now arrogated to itself the right to be and to act as super-lawmaking body, over the Congress, the State Legislatures, and to assume powers which are denied to it by the Federal Constitution.

For a layman it comes as a shock to learn that the fundamental law of this country, that is, the Constitution, can mean one thing today and something entirely different tomorrow. If the separation of the races was legal in 1896, and during the years thereafter, it is hard for the average citizen to understand how the meaning given to it at that time can be changed 60 years later by nine men sitting on the United States Supreme Court to mean something directly opposite.

This decision in the bus case has had a tremendous impact on the customs of our people here in Montgomery. It is not an easy thing to live under a law recognized as constitutional for these many years and then have it suddenly overturned on the basis of psychology and not by amending the Constitution.

The City of Montgomery, having at heart the welfare of both the white and black races and carrying out the wishes of 90 percent of our people, has done all in its power to uphold the City Ordinance providing for the separation of races on the buses. It has faithfully fought the effort to nullify this ordinance through all the courts of the land, and with every legal weapon available. The people of Montgomery realize that the good order and peace of our city imperatively requires the separation of the races on the buses, each race being given equal and identical accommodation.

Now that our wise, time-tested, and proper ordinance for the separation of the races on buses has been declared void, we have neither State nor City law providing that the races be given separate but equal seats on the buses. Although we consider the Supreme Court's decision to be the usurpation of the power to amend the Constitution, which belongs to the people and not the Court, we have no alternative but to recognize it. That is not to say, however, that we will not continue, through every legal means at our disposal, to see that the separation of the races is continued on the public transportation system here in Montgomery.

The City Commission will not let up in its efforts to convince the Supreme Court at Washington, that the City authorities have under their general police power, a power until recently never questioned by any court in the land, the undoubted right to regulate bus service on the streets of Montgomery.

The negro race, whose National Association for the Advancement of colored people has secured this decision, should not be led into conduct which will embarrass the race and lead to blood-shed, engender conflict and disorder on the buses and bring the curse of tragedy to our City. It is hoped that those recent comers to Montgomery, who claim to be the leaders of the boycott-crusaders here, and who have day in and day out, in nearly every state in the Union for over a year, denounced the white race, will cease their hypocritical and unjustifiable attacks upon the people of Montgomery and their Board of Commissioners and will counsel the members of their race not to act unwisely.

The City Commission, and we know our people are with us in this determination, will not yield one inch, but will do all in its power to oppose the integration of the negro race with the white race in Montgomery, and will forever stand like a rock against social equality, intermarriage, and mixing of the races in the schools. In these matters, for the common good of all the people of Montgomery, and for the public peace and quiet of this City, there must continue the separation of the races under God's creation and plan. In so doing, we know that the best interest of both races will be served.

SBC.

"Negroes Get Bus Classes: Montgomery Ministers and Others Give Instructions Regarding Integration"

Montgomery, Ala., Dec. 14 (AP)—Negroes awaiting the end of bus segregation in Montgomery are being schooled by their leaders to remain peaceful "even if others strike first." And to guide them, the Rev. Ralph D. Abernathy disclosed in an interview today that an effort will be made to have a Negro clergyman or civic leader aboard "every bus day and night" during the early stages of integration.

The U.S. Supreme Court has ruled city and state bus segregation laws unconstitutional but the formal order has not been issued pending action on a request for city and state authorities for a rehearing. If the court acts on the rehearing petition Monday, the integration notice may reach Montgomery later next week.

Meanwhile, Abernathy said as many as 1,000 Negroes are attending weekly classes designed to "prepare our people for the return to the buses and for integration in general." He did not elaborate on the latter. The weekly instruction periods, held in Negro churches, are conducted by the Montgomery Improvement Assn., the organization which has directed the long mass Negro boycott against segregated city buses. Abernathy is vice president of the MIA. Ministers and other MIA leaders along with officers of civic clubs and volunteers in each neighborhood are acting as instructors, the Baptist minister said. Besides the weekly classes, Negro civic clubs also are urged to spread the doctrine of nonviolence at their meetings.

"We are trying to get over the idea of courtesy," Abernathy explained. Abernathy said his people are being told, in substance:

1. "If anyone argues with you, at least we feel the channel of communication has been opened. If we can discuss it, that's good. But we must remain calm, talk in the spirit of love, and maybe we can win them."

2. "If they strike or push us, the strong thing to do is to refrain from striking or pushing back. We must be calm and reason with them. We must say to them, 'If you want to hit me again, do it, because I'm not going to hit you back. If you want to fight me, you will say to everyone on this bus that you are weak.'"

3. "If they threaten us with arrest, for disorderly conduct, we must go to jail peacefully because if they arrest one of us for violating no law, there are 50,000 other Negroes they'll have to arrest, too."

Abernathy said the presence of Negro ministers and lay leaders on the buses "will give our people strength and let them know someone is with them. And it will help show them how to act."

In other fields of integration—the Negro minister did not disclose any plans for specific action—Abernathy said his people at the weekly meetings are told to "encourage cleanliness and politeness" and to take part in "campaigns to beautify their homes and their lawns." [. . .]

Chattanooga Times, December 15, 1956.

In addition to the series of mass nonviolent training sessions being conducted, Glenn Smiley drafted a code of nonviolent conduct for desegregating buses that the MIA distributed at mass meetings just before the boycott ended on December 21.

Integrated Bus Suggestions

This is a historic week because segregation on buses has now been declared unconstitutional. Within a few days the Supreme Court Mandate will reach Montgomery and you will be re-boarding *integrated* buses. This places upon us all a tremendous responsibility of maintaining, in face of what could be some unpleasantness, a calm and loving dignity befitting good citizens and members of our Race. If there is violence in word or deed it must not be our people who commit it.

For your help and convenience the following suggestions are made. Will you read, study and memorize them so that our non-violent determination may not be endangered. First, some general suggestions:

1. Not all white people are opposed to integrated buses. Accept goodwill on the part of many.

2. The *whole* bus is now for the use of *all* people. Take a vacant seat.

3. Pray for guidance and commit yourself to *complete* non-violence in word and action as you enter the bus.

4. Demonstrate the calm dignity of our Montgomery people in your actions.

5. In all things observe ordinary rules of courtesy and good behavior.

6. Remember that this is not a victory for Negroes alone, but for all Montgomery and the South. Do not boast! Do not brag!

7. Be quiet but friendly; proud, but not arrogant; joyous, but not boisterous.

8. Be loving enough to absorb evil and understanding enough to turn an enemy into a friend.

NOW FOR SOME SPECIFIC SUGGESTIONS:

1. The bus driver is in charge of the bus and has been instructed to obey the law. Assume that he will cooperate in helping you occupy any vacant seat.

2. Do not deliberately sit by a white person, unless there is no other seat.

3. In sitting down by a person, white or colored, say "May I" or "Pardon me" as you sit. This is a common courtesy.

4. If cursed, do not curse back. If pushed, do not push back. If struck, do not strike back, but evidence love and goodwill at all times.

5. In case of an incident, talk as little as possible, and always in a quiet tone. Do not get up from your seat! Report all serious incidents to the bus driver.

6. For the first few days try to get on the bus with a friend in whose non-violence you have confidence. You can uphold one another by a glance or a prayer.

7. If another person is being molested, do not arise to go to his defense, but pray for the oppressor and use moral and spiritual force to carry on the struggle for justice.

8. According to your own ability and personality, do not be afraid to experiment with new and creative techniques for achieving reconciliation and social change.

9. If you feel you cannot take it, walk for another week or two. We have confidence in our people. GOD BLESS YOU ALL.

THE MONTGOMERY IMPROVEMENT ASSOCIATION
THE REV. M. L. KING JR., PRESIDENT
THE REV. W. J. POWELL, SECRETARY

MLKP-MBU: Box 3.

December 19, 1956

Mr. Carey McWilliams
Editor, THE NATION
333 Sixth Avenue
New York 14, New York

Dear Carey:

[. . .] You have doubtless seen the papers and know of the Supreme Court's action on Monday overruling the motion for a rehearing. The Mandate of the Court is on the way and something should be happening in the next few days as the local District Judge has said his injunction will issue automatically as soon as the mandate of the Court gets here.

I am feeling a little better and more optimistic than at the time of my last letter. While the City officials continue to breathe defiance publicly, off the record they are saying that the Supreme Court has spoken and there is nothing else they can do but comply. The white business leaders definitely do not want any incidents and they likewise are quietly bringing pressure on the City officials in the right direction. The non-violent line of the Negro leaders seems to have gotten across to the Negroes and I think all of these factors working together including the good will of the Christmas season (to say nothing of the concern of the merchants over the Christmas trade) make things look pretty hopeful. There may be, of course, a few violent incidents but I really don't believe we will have any serious trouble in this way.

There is still talk of shutting down the busses entirely but the bus line has too much at stake to permit this without a real court fight. I understand that the operations here were fairly profitable before the boycott and there is a three-quarter million dollar deficit to make up.

Virginia joins me in best wishes for a Merry Christmas.

Sincerely yours,
Clifford J. Durr

CJDP-A-Ar.

"My Day," by Eleanor Roosevelt

HYDE PARK, DECEMBER 24—Throughout the country our eyes are turned on Montgomery, Alabama, as the Supreme Court's order ending segregation on buses goes into effect. The Negroes celebrated this order at mass meetings on Thursday night and they have already gone back to using the buses on a nonsegregated basis. Their spiritual leader, Rev. Martin Luther King Jr., cautioned them not to allow any violence. "This is a time when we must observe calm dignity and wise restraint," he said. "Emotions must not run wild."

Only one or two minor incidents occurred the first day of nonsegregation on buses. The Negroes in Montgomery had been given careful schooling in a nonviolent approach to any difficulties that might arise. Special emphasis had been laid on "remaining peaceful even if others strike first." It is to be hoped that everything will continue to move quietly, for this experiment of nonsegregation is already in force in the airlines in the South, and in the North there is no place where one may not sit next to an individual of any nationality or color in public conveyances. Once it is accepted, I am sure it will seem as natural for the people of the South as it does for the people of the North.

Eleanor Roosevelt's My Day, vol. 3 (Mahwah, N.J.: Pharos Books, 1991), p. 112.

Rustin to King: Memo on the Montgomery Bus Boycott, December 23, 1956

Montgomery possessed three features which are not found in other movements or efforts:

1. It was organized; used existing institutions as foundations so that all social strata of the community were involved. It thus had the strength of unity which the school integration efforts have lacked, thereby leaving the fight to heroic but isolated individuals. Montgomery could plan tactics, seek advice and support, develop financial resources and encompass a whole community in a crusade dominating all other issues. The reason there were those who did not want to give up the boycott is due in part to the consciousness that this welding of a comprehensive, unified group had a quality not to be lost. The fellowship, the ideals, the joy of sacrifice for others and other varied features of the movement have given people something to belong to which had the inspiring power of the Minute Men, the Sons of Liberty, and other organized forms which were products of an earlier American era of fundamental change.

2. The actions of the people won the respect of their enemy. The achievement of unity, the intelligence in planning, the creation of a competent, complex system of transportation, the high level of moral and ethical motivation, all combined to give the closed mind of the white southerner an airing it has never before had. It is not only the Negroes' self-respect which was won—but the respect of white people, who though they retain basic prejudice, have lost something in the course of this year that begins

their long struggle to genuine understanding. In short, Montgomery has contributed to the mental health and growth of the white man's mind, and thus to the entire nation.

3. Montgomery was unique in that it relied upon the active participation of people who had a *daily* task of action and dedication. The movement did not rely exclusively on a handful of leaders to carry through such fundamental change.

B. The more advanced white people must be encouraged to develop more open relations through various agencies so that a beginning toward Negro-White relationships can be organized. Special recognition, in the form of honoring speeches, or if possible, formal events, must be accorded such figures as Rev. Turner of Clinton, Attorney Lee Grant, the superintendent of schools in Louisville. It must be pointed out that their devotion to the principles of morality, respect for law, the decent human response to their fellow men, express the truest and [*finest*] traditions of our nation.

C. Similarly, the new southern Negro leaders must recognize that they built upon the work of those men who for decades fought a more lonely fight . . . The Randolphs, Wilkins, Bunches.

D. The movement must now widen to political areas. Representation in all levels of political life from the exercise of the ballot to the holding of office and participation in administrative agencies, is a next most vital step. (Here consultation with men who led great national movements, such as [*Walter*] Reuther, Randolph, [*Jacob*] Potofsky, [*Michael*] Quill, should be set up. Note that all have a special social outlook and all except Reuther represented minorities in trade union and social life).

E. Regional groups of leaders should be brought together and encouraged to develop forms of local organization leading to an alliance of groups capable of creating a Congress of organizations. Such a Congress would create both the alert leadership capable of reacting promptly and effectively to situations and possessing ties to masses of people so that their action projects are backed by broad participation of people who gain experience and knowledge in the course of the struggles. We will be sending a prospectus on this later. The final stage may be the conference of leaders on transportation but its broader perspectives must be implicit in the deliberations.

F. The next stage must see the development of a strategy group of national leaders who will be able to guide spontaneous manifestations into organized channels. They will be able to analyze where concentration of effort will be fruitful and while not discouraging any effort, be mobile enough to throw reserves and support to areas where a breakthrough is achievable. The assessment of urban centers as areas of concentration should be studied against rural centers to determine possibilities of setting up practical goals so that the whole movement can balance successes with setbacks.

G.   The fight of the Negro for integration and equality is a vital component in the fight of the common man, Negro and white, to realize higher living standards, higher education, and culture, and a deeper commitment to moral and ethical principles. It is contributing to the movement of America to achieve a nation [*capable*] of utilizing its vastly impressive industrial might for the benefit to all.

BRP-DLC.

On Sunday, December 29, King spoke to a convention banquet of the black Omega Psi Phi fraternity in Baltimore. After his address he and his wife were driven to Washington by Harris and Clare Wofford, authors of a book on the Indian independence struggle, *India Afire*. The two couples were joined in the crowded car by Rustin and New York attorney and civil rights fund-raiser Stanley Levison, who met King for the first time. Along the Maryland highway— where the racially mixed group would likely have been barred from sitting together in a roadside restaurant—the six discussed Rustin's and Levison's ideas for a new civil rights organization. Rustin later recalled the conversation:

"I believe that you have got to have a South-wide organization," he suggested to King, "which I think you must now head up, and that that South-wide organization should be made up of key boycott leaders across the South, not involving Urban League or NAACP, because if you bring all those organizations together, you will have to compromise to their needs. But you're in a very strong position now, to set up an organization, but to set it up so that you are the key, and to set it up in a way where your board is only advisory.

"He said: You can't set up an organization like that!

"I said: I can show you how to do it.

"So he said: Okay, draw up the plans. And I drew up the plans for the SCLC, which then became the organization Dr. King worked with after the conclusion of the boycott."[1]

As they were riding, Levison, who soon became one of King's closest friends and advisers, was struck by his frank openness about his leadership role. "There was a certain tension in the air," Levison recalled. "Dr. King broke it by starting to talk. He said, if anybody had asked me a year ago to head this movement, I tell you very honestly, that I would have run a mile to get away from it. I had no intention of being involved in this way. He said that as I became involved, and as people began to derive inspiration from their involvement, I realized that the choice leaves your own hands. The people expect you to give them leadership. You see them growing as they move into action, and then you know you no longer have a choice, you can't decide whether to stay in it or get out of it, you must stay in it."

Another impression hit Levison: "He didn't seem to be the type to be a mass leader. There was nothing flamboyant, nothing even charismatic about him as he sat in an ordinary discussion. He looked like a typical scholarly kind of person—very thoughtful, quiet, and shy—very shy. The shyness was accented, I felt, with white people. . . . There was a certain politeness, a certain arm's length approach, and you could feel the absence of relaxation. As the years went on this vanished. But it was as if Dr. King's Southern background, largely with the black community, had its effect on him as far as thinking comfortably and easily in the company of white people."[2]

1. Bayard Rustin, "The Reminiscences of Bayard Rustin" (New York: Oral History Research Office, Columbia University, 1988), p. 151.
2. Stanley Levison interview, Moorland-Spingarn Research Center, Howard University, pp. 9–10.

As the new year arrived Glenn Smiley organized an Atlanta conference, sponsored by Fellowship of Reconciliation, to train southern activists in nonviolent methods and discuss next steps after the Montgomery victory.

Dear Friend:

We, the undersigned, call you to join with us in a three-day conference on NONVIOLENCE AND THE SOUTH, to be held on *January 8, 9, &10, 1957 at Atlanta University in Atlanta, Georgia.*

Coming as it does, in the midst of the titanic nonviolent struggle to desegregate the buses in Montgomery, Tallahassee and Birmingham, following a month after the week-long Institute on Nonviolence (Montgomery, Dec. 1956) and preceding by four months another large Institute on the same subject, to be held in Tallahassee in May, the January conference in Atlanta is perhaps of crucial importance in preparing leadership for the nonviolent movement in the South.

Leadership: The Rev. Dr. Martin Luther King Jr.; the Rev. Ralph D. Abernathy; Mme. Magda Troome (a leader in the nonviolent resistance to the Nazis in France during World War II); the Rev. John M. Swomley, Jr. (National Secretary, Fellowship of Reconciliation); the Rev. C. K. Steele (Talla-hassee); the Rev. Matthew McCollum (Orangeburg); the Rev. Glenn E. Smiley (Field Secretary, Fellowship of Reconciliation).

Dates: First session begins 4 P.M. Tuesday, Jan 8. Concluding 1:30 PM Thursday, Jan. 10. Please come for the entire three days, so as to benefit from the whole program as it builds to climax.

Program: 1) Get-acquainted warm-up session, framing the problem, and tracing the spread of nonviolence as its solution. 2) Addresses by Mme. Troome, Dr. King, and Mr. Swomley. 3) Socio-drama; the acting-out of antici-pated crisis situations. 4) Singing and prayer sessions. 5) Discussion meeting; Theory and Practice of Nonviolence.

Costs: Room and board at Atlanta University; $5 a day, or $10 for the entire conference. Some accommodations in private homes if requests are received in time.

Fill out enclosed card and mail at once, telling us you are coming.

Sincerely yours,
Glenn E. Smiley (For the Committee) [. . .]

FORP-PSC-P (January 1957).

Before it adjourned on January 10 the FOR conference issued a press release, signed by twenty-six participants, aimed at white Christian ministers espe-cially in the South.

Fellowship of Reconciliation Press Release

For immediate release

A group of Southern White and Negro Christians have met in Atlanta to consider the increasing acts of violence in the South all over against the significant nonviolent movement for justice and brotherhood. We are in-spired by the courage of White and Negro citizens—clergy and lay—who are daily exposed to the violence and terror of our time, but who in love them-selves refrain from the use of violence.

The increasing violence in such cities as Birmingham, Tallahassee, Mont-gomery and at Koinonia Farms in Americus, Georgia, has led us to believe that a deep spiritual vacuum exists in the white community of the South today. In this hour of great spiritual travail we appeal to the white ministers of the South to utilize all their spiritual resources to the end that the spirit of our Lord might be brought to the solution of these acute problems.

We applaud the valiant efforts of white clergymen, exemplified by the minister in Clinton, Tenn., to express a moral authority to counter violence and lawlessness. We appeal to the white clergy to initiate such acts of reconciliation in these troubled areas as will mend the deep cleavages between the people. We are deeply concerned about the moral responsibility of Christian leaders and officials in the face of the wanton destruction of Churches, homes, and the assaults on persons. We appeal to the ministers of other communities to assert their leadership now to the end that the conditions of justice and a climate of love will be so present that it will preclude that violence in their communities.

We unite in prayer and penitence with people of goodwill everywhere that God may heal our broken communities.

FORP-PSC-P.

MIA Press Release Announcing Southern Negro Leaders Conference

For immediate release

Bus Protesters call *Southern Negro Leaders Conference on transportation* and *non-violent integration.*

KING, STEELE AND SHUTTLESWORTH ISSUE URGENT PLEA.

In an effort to coordinate and spur the campaign for integrated transportation in the South, a conference has been called for January 10th and 11th in Atlanta, Georgia.

The emergency conference call was issued by Rev. M. King Jr. of Montgomery, Rev. C. K. Steele of Tallahassee and Rev. F. L. Shuttlesworth of Birmingham. Negro leaders from troubled areas all over the South are expected to attend to share thinking, to discuss common problems, to devise a unified strategy and to plan mutual economic assistance.

A. Philip Randolph, a vice-president of the A.F.L.-C.I.O. and International President of The Brotherhood of Sleeping Car Porters, will deliver one of the opening addresses. Mr. Randolph of New York, Dean of Negro leaders, will attend the conference as a fraternal representative from the North.

Rev. King will open the conference by presenting eight working papers. These will include such subjects as:

(1) Dealing with violence directed toward the Negro communities.

(2) The role of law in the struggle.

(3) A unified strategy in the campaign for integrated buses.

(4) Economic sharing.

(5) Dedication to non-violence.

(6) The relation of registration and voting to all efforts for justice.

In their call, the Negro leaders said:

"We are convinced that most white southerners are prepared to accept integration as the law of the land. On the other hand, a small but willful minority, dedicated to violence is resorting to threats, shootings, cross burning and bombings.

"In this manner, they seek to intimidate Negroes and to frustrate our highest laws. They believe we will retreat from the realization of democracy for all.

"This conference is called because we have no moral choice, before God, but to delve deeper into the struggle—and to do so with greater reliance on non-violence and with greater unity, coordination, sharing and Christian understanding."

The leaders announced that the conference will convene at 2 P.M. at The Ebenezer Baptist Church, 407 Auburn Avenue, Atlanta, Georgia. The two-day working session will be closed to the public. However, following the consultations, a public *statement to the nation* will be issued. A press conference will be held at the end of the last session, Friday evening, January 11th.

BRP-DLC (January 7, 1957).

The Southern Negro Leaders Conference in Atlanta, convening January 10, overshadowed the FOR gathering that immediately preceded it. At the second, larger meeting the leaders spent the first day discussing several "working papers" that Rustin had drafted to guide their thinking about strategy, tactics, and the shape of a new civil rights organization.

"Working Paper #1: The Meaning of the Bus Protest in the Southern Struggle For Total Integration"

In analyzing the Bus Protest certain factors emerge:

1. These protests are directly related to economic survival, since the masses of people use busses to reach their work. The people are therefore interested in what happens in busses.

2. The people know that in bus segregation they have a just grievance. No one had to arouse their social anger.

3. In refusing to ride the busses the people pledge a daily rededication. This daily act becomes a matter of group pride.

4. Unlike many problems, such as integrated education, there is no administrative machinery and legal maneuvering that stand between the people and

the act of staying off the busses, or sitting in the front seats. The situation permits direct action.

5. The campaign is based on the most stable social institution in Negro culture—the church.

6. The protest requires community sharing through mass meetings, contributions, economic assistance, hitchhiking etc.

7. The situation permits and requires a unified leadership.

8. The method of non-violence—Christian love, makes humble folk noble and turns fear into courage.

9. The exigencies of the struggle create a community spirit through community sacrifice.

NOTE:

The underlined words are 9 qualities required for any mass movement. When a group of people have developed them in one area, these qualities can be transferred to any other constructive one through education by action, the final quality.

It is important that Bus Protest action arise in other areas of the South for the following reasons:

1. There is a real question as to whether any of the present can succeed if Montgomery, which has become a symbol, is defeated. But there is a question as to whether Montgomery or any other campaign can succeed unless many more areas of protest spring up.

2. Those who use violence believe that their tactics will cause us to retreat. When we, in the face of violence, delve deeper into the struggle, and when other areas of protest emerge, then, and perhaps only then, will reactionary forces see the futility of their violence.

3. The masses of white people are perhaps prepared to accept integration in transportation. The Supreme Court decision enabled them to move farther in the direction of acceptance. If additional communities join the struggle, they will no doubt move closer to acceptance. If the present protests fail, it is likely they will move towards reaction.

4. More bus protests will encourage the Negro people who are on the move to become more self-respecting, more determined to act in areas other than the buses.

5. Additional protests involving direct action will frustrate both "the century of litigation" tactic and the kind of legal subterfuge now being experienced in Atlanta and Tallahassee.

6. They will also create the kind of situation in the eyes of the world that may cause a more responsible attitude in the executive branch of the government.

THIS PAPER IS DESIGNED TO RAISE TWO QUESTIONS. In a sense, the most important part of our entire discussion. These questions are:

I. Do we need a coordinating group for advice and council among the present protest groups?

II. Should such a council try to stimulate bus protests in other areas of the South?

BRP-DLC.

"Working Paper #2: The Next Step for Mass Action in the Struggle for Equality"

If one examines carefully the three branches of our government, legislative, judicial and executive, one sees the following: The legislative branch for 80 years has been impotent: Congress has not passed any civil rights legislation since Reconstruction days. With the exception of such Executive Orders as the wartime measure on FEPC [*Fair Employment Practices Committee*], we have not been able to look to the executive branch, and today, that branch is confused and woefully inactive. Progress in the past thirty years has sprung mainly from judicial decision.

The industrialization of the South now emerges as a new factor, affecting the political structure of the South. The one party system is breaking up. Republicanism is coming south with new industrialization. This before long may lead to a two party South competing for Negro votes. Negro voting in such a situation can also hasten the decline of the one party system which has been able to exist primarily because of the Negro's enforced economic and social position.

In any event, the time has come to broaden the struggle for Negroes to register and to vote, for the simple reason that until this happens, we cannot really influence the legislative branch of the government. In addition, until the Negro votes on a large scale, we shall have to rely more and more on mass direct action as the one realistic political weapon.

This raises some interesting problems:

1. How can we utilize the bus protest to stimulate interest in voting?

2. Should voting clinics become a major part of the constructive program of the bus campaign?

3. If so, how do the voting clinics operate? Are they to discuss merely the technique for registering and voting, or should political issues also be discussed?

4. How are test cases on voting to be carried in the courts in those areas where the NAACP has been outlawed? Should bus protest groups back such cases until the NAACP is free again?

5. What broad campaign in the South should be carried on to stimulate interest in and educate Negroes to see the basic significance of voting?

6. Should all churches, able to do so, become centers of voting education?

BRP-DLC.

"Working Paper #3: Unified Planning for Bus Integration"

The first mass assault on the busses occurred in Baton Rouge, La. Montgomery followed and because of its long and sustained nature, its world wide publicity and the mass arrests of its leaders, it has become the symbol of the struggle. For Negroes, it must succeed. For defenders of segregation it must fail.

However, there is a question as to whether bus integration can succeed in the South, unless it succeeds in Montgomery. On the other hand, can it really succeed in Montgomery unless and until there are protests in many states and cities of the South?

It is therefore imperative that we examine the following problems:

1. Broadening and strengthening specific bus protests throughout the South.
2. Mutually supporting one another in the protest movement.
3. Creating the machinery for stimulating new protests and coordinating the bus protests into a single movement.

To help us examine these problems, the following questions are submitted:

1. Where and how new areas of protest can grow?
2. How can financial burdens be shared?
3. How can white persons of goodwill be drawn into the protest?
4. What is the best way to encourage and support victims of reprisals?
5. How can mass morale be maintained in periods of set-back?
6. How can the unavoidable suffering be made a badge of honor?
7. How can leaders identify with the people at every stage of the struggle?
8. What constructive program is essential for daily commitment, and eventual success?

BRP-DLC.

"Working Paper #4: The Relationship of Community Economic Power Groups to the Struggle"

In the past we have given all too little attention to the economic power groups in the struggle for equality. However, the bus protests have clearly revealed certain economic facts.

1. The Negro's dollar is a factor in the economic organization of the community.

2. His refusal to ride had a catastrophic effect on the economics of the bus companies.

3. The unintended but nonetheless direct effect of the protest on down town merchants is real, indeed.

These very real economic facts have at certain stages caused bus companies, formerly unsympathetic to our cause, to see that they need the revenue of Negro riders. Add to this the legal "subterfuge" and the "century of litigation" tactics and it is clear to see that the bus companies are not prepared to lose money to save segregation. At this point two things occur:

1. The political leadership and the bus officials part company. The opposition is divided.

2. The bus companies may be prepared to make common cause with protest leaders.

If this analysis is correct, the following questions are worthy of discussion.

1. When can protest leaders approach bus officials to devise common strategy?

2. How can we foster that period in the struggle?

3. Should Southern Negro leaders arrange conferences with the home offices of the companies working in more than one city of the South?

4. Can some approach be made to local businessmen in terms of the economic consequences in the present transportation confusion?

BRP-DLC.

"Working Paper #7: The Role of Law in Our Struggle: Its Advantages and Limitations"

Historically, the major emphasis in our struggle to obtain civil rights has been legal and legislative. For forty-six years the National Association for the Advancement of Colored People has brilliantly and successfully represented Negro Americans before the courts of the land. From time to time, widespread campaigns to enact favorable legislation have been waged. However, since the Supreme Court decision of May 17, 1954, a new stage has been set.

While there is still much legal work to be done, there is ample and convincing evidence that *the center of gravity has shifted from the courts to community action*. It is on the community level that court decisions must be implemented. The job before us now is to demonstrate that our cause is basic to the welfare of the community; and we must challenge our white fellow citizens: to win them to believe in and to practice democracy. Law will be very important in this process, *but something new must be added*.

In other words, we must determine when pursuing a legal course is helpful and when it will merely strengthen the tactics of the White Citizens Councils, such as the "century of litigation" threat. An example of this is seen in Birmingham where the bus protestors were first arrested and charged with *disorderly conduct rather than violation of jim crow bus laws*. Another example is the new seating arrangement proposed for the busses in Tallahassee.

We must recognize in this new period that *direct action is our most potent political weapon*. We must understand that our refusal to accept jim crow in specific areas challenges the entire social, political and economic order that has kept us second class citizens since 1876. Those who oppose us, understand this, and that is why they resist our every effort with every instrument at their command, including violence.

Should we refuse at any point to reject the legal interpretations of the South, or should we challenge custom, we will not be engaged in *civil disobedience*, but we will be exercising *civil obedience* to the highest law of the land. Our job is to reinforce the process of persuasion [*as*] the basis for law and order. We must not be afraid to explore new ways. We must not be timid, and must be prepared to pay the price involved in making this new approach to the solution of our problems.

This thinking leads to certain questions:

1. What new problems are posed by the "century of litigation" tactic? To what extent does this tactic require extra-legal mass action?

2. Under what circumstances are mass arrests strategically desirable or necessary? For example, could the people [*in*] Tallahassee adopt this tactic now?

3. Can we develop in our communities a core of people who are disciplined to face and accept going to jail? What steps have been taken in this direction?

4. Are we prepared to fully support such people wherever arrests occur?

5. When "states of emergency" are proclaimed by state and local officials, for the purpose of frustrating our struggle, what can we do to hold the initiative?

6. How do we educate the Negro masses and the leaders on the significance of such tactics?

7. What is behind the current attack on the NAACP?

(a) What is its significance to our struggle?

(b) How do we meet the challenge?

BRP-DLC.

The churches and parsonages of Ralph Abernathy and Robert Graetz were among four churches and two homes bombed on the night of January 10. King and Abernathy immediately drove back to Montgomery, leaving Coretta Scott King, Fred Shuttlesworth, and C. K. Steele to chair the conference in their absence. King returned to Atlanta the next afternoon.

Call for Action on Bombing of Churches

Today sixty Negro leaders from twenty-nine communities in ten Southern States gathered here in Atlanta to discuss among other things, the violence directed toward Negro People, who struggle for freedom in the South.

As our conference opened, we were shocked to learn that early this morning four Negro churches and the homes of two ministers in the service of Christ were bombed by dynamite and T.N.T.

To destroy the homes of a man is a deplorable and a lamentable act. But the willful destruction of the house of God is beyond description.

(1) This conference calls upon every American Christian to protest that this grievous act could occur in our nation. In the name of God.

(2) We call upon every Christian church in the nation to set aside the Sunday of Brotherhood week in February, as a day of repentance and prayer that such an atrocity could occur in a nation dedicated to our Saviour, Jesus Christ. Each church should beseech Almighty God to restore law and order to our land.

(3) We forward these suggestions to Dr. J. H. Jackson and to Bishop D. Ward Nichols requesting that they, through their denominations, ask the National Council of Churches to forward these ideas to every church in the nation.

MLKJrP-GAMK (January 10, 1957).

THE PRESIDENT
THE WHITE HOUSE

DEAR MR. PRESIDENT:

EXTREME VIOLENCE CONTINUES TO BE DIRECTED TOWARD NEGRO PEOPLE IN THE SOUTH WHO MERELY SEEK RIGHTS GUARANTEED EVERY AMERICAN CITIZEN

BY THE UNITED STATES CONSTITUTION. NEGROES, WHO SEEK TO VOTE, ARE DRIVEN FROM THEIR LAND IN MISSISSIPPI ON THREAT OF DEATH. IN TENNESSEE, NEGRO CHILDREN HAVE BEEN ATTACKED. IN FLORIDA, STONING AND CROSS BURNING ARE USED TO OBSTRUCT JUSTICE. NEGRO LEADERS ARE THREATENED. IN ALABAMA, CHRISTIAN CHURCHES LITERALLY HAVE BEEN DESTROYED BY DYNAMITE AND T.N.T. NUMEROUS INDIVIDUALS, INCLUDING WOMEN, HAVE BEEN BEATEN ON THE STREETS. THE HOMES OF NEGRO AND WHITE LEADERS HAVE BEEN BOMBED. MEN AND WOMEN, BLACK AND WHITE, SITTING PEACEFULLY IN BUSES HAVE BEEN ATTACKED BY SNIPERS. A FORT-NIGHT AGO, A 15 YEAR OLD NEGRO GIRL WAS BRUTALLY BEATEN. A FEW DAYS AGO THE LEGS OF A WOMAN EIGHT MONTHS PREGNANT WERE SHATTERED BY A GUN FIRED INTO A PUBLIC CONVEYANCE. A STATE OF TERROR PREVAILS.

AS WE HAVE DEMONSTRATED, THE QUESTION BEFORE THE NATION IS NO LONGER WHETHER THERE SHALL BE SEGREGATION OR INTEGRATION, BUT RATHER, WHETHER THERE SHALL BE ANARCHY OR LAW. THE MAINTENANCE OF LAW AND ORDER IN THE NATION FINALLY RESTS SQUARELY ON THE EXECUTIVE BRANCH OF GOVERNMENT—DIRECTLY UPON THE PRESIDENT. BUT BEYOND YOUR CONSTITUTIONAL POWER, AS PRESIDENT, YOU POSSESS AND CAN WIELD AN IMMENSE MORAL POWER. WE, THEREFORE, URGE YOU TO USE THE WEIGHT OF YOUR GREAT OFFICE TO POINT OUT TO THE PEOPLE OF THE SOUTH THE MORAL NATURE OF THE PROBLEM FACED AT HOME AND ABROAD BY THE UNSOLVED CIVIL RIGHTS ISSUES AND THE VIOLENT RACIAL DISORDER THAT WILL ARISE AGAIN AND AGAIN UNTIL THESE ISSUES ARE SOLVED.

WE ASK YOU TO COME SOUTH IMMEDIATELY TO MAKE A MAJOR SPEECH IN A MAJOR SOUTHERN CITY URGING ALL SOUTHERNERS TO ABIDE BY THE SUPREME COURT'S DECISIONS AS THE LAW OF THE LAND. AS THE LEADER OF A GREAT NATION WHICH PROCLAIMS ITS DEFENSE OF FREEDOM ABROAD, YOU WILL UNDERSTAND OUR URGENT PLEA THAT YOU MAKE THIS TRIP TO DEFEND, BY WORDS OF WISE COUNSEL, AMERICAN CITIZENS UNJUSTLY AND BRUTALLY ATTACKED AT HOME. RESPECTFULLY,

THE REV. M L KING JR MONTGOMERY, ALABAMA
THE REV C K STEELE, TALLAHASSEE FLORIDA
THE REV F L SHUTTLESWORTH, BIRMINGHAM ALABAMA
THE REV T J JEMISON BATON ROUGE LOUISIANA.
FOR SOUTHERN NEGRO LEADERS CONFERENCE ON TRANSPORTATION AND NONVIOLENT INTEGRATION MEETING IN ATLANTA, GEORGIA, JANUARY 10–11 1957, APPRECIATE REPLY BY WIRE TO
REV M L KING JR 530 S. UNION STREET MONTGOMERY ALA.

DDEP-KAbE (January 11, 1957).

A STATEMENT TO THE SOUTH AND NATION
issued by the
SOUTHERN LEADERS CONFERENCE ON TRANSPORTATION
AND NON-VIOLENT INTEGRATION

attended by
60 NEGRO LEADERS FROM 29 COMMUNITIES
of ten Southern States

called by Rev. M. L. King Jr., Rev. F. L. Shuttlesworth, Rev. C. K. Steele

at Ebenezer Baptist Church
407 Auburn Ave., Atlanta, Ga.
(Rev. M. L. King Sr., Pastor)
Thursday–Friday—January 10–11, 1957

All over the world men are in revolt against social and political domination. The age old cry for freedom and human dignity takes on a significance never experienced before. For in a very real and impelling sense no man, no nation and no part of the universe is an island unto itself.

Asia's successive revolts against European imperialism, Africa's present ferment for independence, Hungary's death struggle against communism, and the determined drive of Negro Americans to become first class citizens are inextricably bound together. They are all vital factors in determining whether Twentieth Century mankind will crown its vast material gains with the achievement of liberty and justice for all, or whether it will commit suicide through lack of moral fibre.

Because America is one of the two most powerful nations on earth and, even more, because our power and our prestige are pledged to freedom and civil liberties for the individual and constitutional government for the nation, the unresolved problem of Civil Rights becomes the most crucial issue of our culture. This is so because the nation, in proclaiming freedom, shines as a beacon of hope for the oppressed of the world and yet denies even elementary democratic rights to its Negro minority. But beyond this moral embarrassment, all of the nation's institutions remain stunted and frustrated by the contradiction between what America practices and what America proclaims.

The church has the high task to provide the American people with moral leadership. And while the major denominations have spoken out clearly for brotherhood, the task of many local churches is made more difficult by the moral compromise in part imposed upon them by the Civil Rights conflict.

Even the Congress of our land is shackled. It is unable to enact urgently needed social legislation. Federal aid to education and increased social security bills for the benefit of white and Negro people die in congressional committees because the division over Civil Rights permits a small political minority to capture and control the legislative branch of our national government.

Thus the entire nation suffers because our democratic vitality is sapped by the civil rights issue. This is even more true of the South. In her unwillingness to accept the Negro as a human being, the South has chosen to remain undeveloped, poorly educated and emotionally warped.

Through recent Supreme Court decisions, declaring that discrimination based on race violates the Constitution, the issue has been joined. There is no turning back. The nation must now face the reality that America can never realize its vast economic, social and political potential until the struggle for Civil Rights has been decisively won.

We are convinced that the great majority of white Southerners are prepared to accept and abide by the Supreme Law of the Land. They, like us, want to be law-abiding citizens. Yet a small but determined minority resorts to threats, bodily assaults, cross-burnings, bombing, shooting and open defiance of the law in an attempt to force us to retreat. But we cannot in clear conscience turn back. We have no moral choice but to continue the struggle, not for ourselves alone but for all America. We have the God given duty to help save ourselves and our white brothers from tragic self-destruction in the quagmire of racial hate. We must continue to stand firm for our right to be first class citizens. Even in the face of death, we have no other choice. For if in carrying out this obligation we are killed, other, more resolute even than we, will rise to continue the drive to free the United States of the scourge of racial conflict.

In dedication to this task, we call upon all Negroes in the South and in the nation *to assert their human dignity.* We ask them *to seek justice and reject all injustice,* especially that in themselves. We pray that they will *refuse further cooperation with the evil element which invites them to collude against themselves in return for bits of patronage.* We know that such an assertion may cause them persecution; yet *no matter how great the obstacles and suffering, we urge all Negroes to reject segregation.*

But far beyond this, *we call upon them to accept Christian Love in full knowledge of its power to defy evil.* We call upon them to understand that *non-violence is not a symbol of weakness or cowardice,* but as Jesus demonstrated, *non-violent resistance transforms weakness into strength and breeds courage in face of danger.* We urge them, no matter how great the provocation, to dedicate themselves to this motto:

"Not one hair of one head of one white person shall be harmed."

We advocate non-violence in words, thought and deed, we believe this spirit and this spirit alone can overcome the decades of mutual fear and suspicion that have infested and poisoned our Southern culture.

In this same spirit, we place the following concerns before white southerners of goodwill:

1. We call upon white Southern Christians to realize that the treatment of Negroes is a basic spiritual problem. We believe that no legal approach can fully redeem or reconcile man. We urge them in Christ's name to join the struggle for justice. They, as individuals, can begin now:

(a) By working to see that all persons, regardless of color or creed, who seek the saving grace of Christ are accepted as equals in their churches.

(b) By encouraging schools and colleges controlled by the church to set an example of brotherhood.

(c) By speaking out in moral terms and by acting on the basis of their inner convictions, and accepting as Negro Christians must, the consequences of the Christian imperative. In this way they may well reduce the violence directed toward the Negro community; restore order and hasten reconciliation.

2. We call upon every white Southerner to realize that the major choice may no longer be segregation or integration, but anarchy or law. We remind them that communities control their destinies only when order prevails. Disorder places all major decisions in the hands of state or federal police. We do not prefer this, for our ultimate aim is to win understanding with our neighbors. In a profound sense, the lawlessness and violence our people face is blood upon the hands of Southern Christians. Far too many have silently stood by as a violent minority stalks over the southland. We implore men of goodwill to speak out for law and order.

As citizens and as representatives of equal rights movements all over the South, we cannot ignore the vital role that government could play in easing tensions and in helping Negroes secure their constitutional rights.

In recent years the Judicial Branch of government has behaved in a responsible manner. But not since Reconstruction days has the Congress passed any civil rights legislation. Since 1952, the Executive Branch has not clearly given direction to millions of confused citizens on questions relating to civil rights.

We therefore have called upon the Executive Branch of our government in the following manner:

1. Today this conference wired Dwight D. Eisenhower, President of the United States, asking him to come south immediately, to make a major speech

in a major southern city urging all southerners to accept and to abide by the Supreme Court's decisions as the law of the Land. We further urged him to use the weight of his great office to point out to the South the moral nature of the problems posed at home and abroad by the unsolved civil rights issue.

2. We also wired Vice President Nixon urging him to make a tour of the South similar to the one he made on behalf of Hungarian refugees. We told him that through such a trip he could report to the President and the American people the economic boycotts, and reprisals, and bombing and violence directed against the persons and homes of Negroes who assert their rights under the Constitution. We further indicated that thousands of Negroes had fled Mississippi within the last year with no moral or financial help from their government.

3. In light of the Supreme Court decision in transportation and the Attorney General's December meeting with federal district attorneys from the South, we today requested that Mr. Brownell grant an interview with representatives of this conference to discuss the responsibility of the Department of Justice in maintaining order in several areas where Negroes, and whites who stand up for justice, fear for their lives.

We have made this statement, believing that the trials of the present are not in vain. For we are convinced that if Negroes of the South steadfastly held to justice and non-violence in their struggle for freedom, a miracle will be wrought from this period of intense social conflict and that a society based on justice and equality for all, will gradually emerge in the South. Then we shall all be emotionally relieved and freed to turn our energies to making America truly "The land of the free and the home of the brave."

MLKP-MBU: Box 2.

President Eisenhower did not respond directly to the movement leaders' telegram but perfunctorily through an aide.

Among many African American activists who reached out to King during the bus boycott was Malcolm X, who was then little known. Although King personally responded to most letter writers, he did not reply directly to letters from the young Nation of Islam leader; he would meet Malcolm only once, seven years later, in March 1964. King's secretary responded for him, starting a personal correspondence with "Mr. X," whom she came to admire, that continued for several years.

February 1, 1957

Mr. Malcolm X
25-46 99th Street
E. Elmhurst 69, New York

Dear Mr. X:

This is to acknowledge receipt of your letters to Rev. M. L. King Jr.

Rev. King has read your letters and articles with great interest. He wants to thank you for your kindness in sending them.

Yours very truly,
(Mrs.) Maude L. Ballou
Secretary to Rev. King

MLKP-MBU: Box 67.

Selected Bibliography . . .

Books

Branch, Taylor. *Parting the Waters: America in the King Years, 1954– 63.* New York: Simon and Schuster, 1988.

Carson, Clayborne, Stewart Burns, and Susan Carson, eds. *Birth of a New Age, 1955–1956: Papers of Martin Luther King Jr.* Vol. 3. Berkeley: University of California Press, 1997.

Garrow, David J. *Bearing the Cross: Martin Luther King Jr. and the Southern Christian Leadership Conference.* New York: William Morrow, 1986.

——, ed. *The Walking City: The Montgomery Bus Boycott, 1955–1956.* Brooklyn: Carlson Publishing, 1989.

Reddick, L. D. *Crusader Without Violence: A Biography of Martin Luther King Jr.* New York: Harper, 1959.

Wright, Roberta Hughes. *The Birth of the Montgomery Bus Boycott.* Southfield, Mich.: Charro Press, 1991.

Memoirs

Abernathy, Ralph D. *And the Walls Came Tumbling Down: An Autobiography.* New York: Harper and Row, 1989.

Fields, Uriah J. *The Montgomery Story: The Unhappy Effects of the Montgomery Bus Boycott.* New York: Exposition Press, 1959.

Graetz, Robert S. *Montgomery: A White Preacher's Memoir.* Minneapolis: Fortress Press, 1991.

Gray, Fred D. *Bus Ride to Justice.* Montgomery, Ala.: Black Belt Press, 1994.

King, Coretta Scott. *My Life with Martin Luther King, Jr.* New York: Holt, Rinehart and Winston, 1969.

King, Martin Luther, Jr. *Stride Toward Freedom.* New York: Harper, 1958.

Parks, Rosa. *Quiet Strength.* Grand Rapids, Mich.: Zondervan Publishing House, 1994.

——. *Rosa Parks: My Story.* New York: Dial Books, 1992.

Robinson, Jo Ann Gibson. *The Montgomery Bus Boycott and the Women Who Started It: The Memoir of Jo Ann Gibson Robinson.* Edited by David J. Garrow. Knoxville: University of Tennessee Press, 1987.

Articles

Gardner, Tom, and Cynthia Stokes Brown. "The Montgomery Bus Boycott: Interviews with Rosa Parks, E. D. Nixon, Johnnie Carr and Virginia Durr." *Southern Exposure* 9, no. 1 (1981): 12–21.

Garrow, David J. "The Origins of the Montgomery Bus Boycott." *Southern Changes* 7 (October 1985): 21–27.

Kennedy, Randall. "Martin Luther King's Constitution: A Legal History of the Montgomery Bus Boycott." *Yale Law Journal* 98 (April 1989): 999–1067.

Thornton, J. Mills, III. "Challenge and Response in the Montgomery Bus Boycott of 1955–1956." *Alabama Review* 33 (July 1980): 163–235.

Valien, Preston. "The Montgomery Bus Protest as a Social Movement." In *Race Relations*, edited by Jitsuichi Masuoka and Preston Valien. Chapel Hill: University of North Carolina Press, 1961.

Theses and Dissertations

Abernathy, Ralph D. "The Natural History of a Social Protest Movement: The Montgomery Bus Boycott." M.A. thesis, Atlanta University, 1958.

Gilliam, Thomas J. "The Montgomery Bus Boycott of 1955–1956." M.A. thesis, Auburn University, 1968.

Millner, Steven M. "The Montgomery Bus Boycott: Case Study in the Emergence and Career of a Social Movement." Ph.D. dissertation, University of California, Berkeley, 1981.

Yeakey, Lamont H. "The Montgomery, Alabama Bus Boycott, 1955–56." Ph.D. dissertation, Columbia University, 1979.

Dramatization

Burns, Stewart. *Jim Crow on Trial: Voices from Montgomery*. Stanford University, 1996.

Film and Video

Eyes on the Prize: Awakenings (1954–1956). Boston: Blackside, 1987.

Jim Crow on Trial: Voices from Montgomery. Stanford University Center for Professional Development, 1996.

Martin Luther King Jr.: From Montgomery to Memphis. Chicago: Phoenix/BFA Films and Video, 1969.

Index . . .

Men of Montgomery, 44, 155, 157, 182, 183,
291
MIA. *See* Montgomery Improvement
Association
Mississippi, 32, 120, 259, 342
Montgomery: history, 1–2; demographics, 2
Montgomery Advertiser, 19, 87, 94, 95, 99,
101, 103, 115, 122, 254, 304
Montgomery bus boycott. *See* Bus boycott—Montgomery
Montgomery city commissioners, 28, 40,
42, 46, 50, 58, 60, 61, 97–99, 107–8, 112,
157, 265, 278, 302, 324, 325; "get tough"
policy, 19, 42, 43, 47, 125, 130, 132, 152,
180, 283, 287; false settlement, 120–22;
reject MIA jitney service, 140, 147, 264;
statement on bus desegregation, 323–25
Montgomery City Lines, 41, 42, 61, 66, 67,
68, 92–93, 97–101, 106, 107, 157, 181, 263,
264, 265, 301–2
Montgomery County Circuit Court, 19,
45, 59, 77, 87, 162, 211–12, 299, 302
Montgomery Improvement Association
(MIA), 1, 4, 13, 14; founding, 10, 41, 87,
88–89; transportation committee, 13,
89, 103, 123, 137, 174, 197–98, 269, 270,
279, 285, 297; finance committee, 13,
89, 123, 285; executive board, 19, 28, 43,
46, 47, 88, 120–24, 128–30, 148–50, 205,
267–69, 274, 276, 279, 280, 285–86,
295–97, 300–301; strategy committee,
123, 205–6; newsletter, 268, 277–79,
286–91; executive committee, 268–69,
285, 297; postboycott goals, 322
Montgomery Voters League, 7–8
Moore, Amzie, 119
Moore, Gladys, 70–73
Moore, Juanita, 260–61
Moral witness, 24
Morehouse College, 27, 28, 161, 257, 259
Morgan, Juliette, 33 (n. 5), 101
Mount Zion AME Zion Church, 10, 88
Murray, Pauli, 200
Muste, A. J., 20, 21, 26, 46, 199, 200, 235,
236, 252, 255–56, 257, 313

Nation of Islam, 346
Nation, The, 301
National Association for the Advancement
of Colored People (NAACP): Montgomery branch, 8, 9, 26, 96, 110, 149,
150, 151; Montgomery Youth Council,
8, 96; Alabama state conference, 8, 298;
lawyers, 19, 57, 110, 129, 130, 149, 196,
339; Atlanta branch, 26; national, 26,
31, 32, 37 (nn. 59, 61), 110, 116, 119, 150,
151, 170, 186, 188, 199, 248, 260, 283,
324, 331; banning in Alabama, 28, 29,
46, 289–90, 307, 322, 338; attack on,
341
National Baptist Convention, USA, 5, 27,
171, 306, 307
National City Lines (Chicago), 19, 42, 99
National Council of Churches, 21, 171,
172, 341
National Deliverance Day of Prayer, 45
National Urban League, 331
Nelson, Richard, 57
"New Negro," 12, 208, 244–45
New Testament, 23, 195, 301
New York Times, 161, 263
Nichols, Bishop D. Ward, 341
Nicodemus, 301
Niebuhr, Reinhold, 23, 195
Nixon, E. D., 5, 6, 7–8, 9, 10, 11, 13, 32, 34
(n. 17), 39, 40, 43, 46, 77, 78, 86, 87, 88,
128, 130, 152, 160–61, 164, 165, 200, 201,
219, 247, 255, 315; and U. J. Fields con-
troversy, 274, 277 (n. 8)
Nixon, Richard M., 30, 39, 51, 346
Nkrumah, Kwame, 47, 51
Nonviolence: nonviolent philosophy, 17,
18–19, 24–25, 167, 168, 169, 195, 290–91,
314, 317, 318, 319, 321, 325, 345; Christian, 17, 23–25, 30, 195–96, 207; Gandhian, 18, 20–24, 167, 195, 204, 205, 207;
FOR vs. Randolph traditions, 20–23, 31;
nonviolent resistance, 21, 30, 33, 109,
174, 200, 202, 209, 210, 214, 239, 248, 256,
257, 258, 281, 315, 317, 326–27, 336, 344,
346; as MIA policy, 130, 164, 175, 247,
328; education and training in, 200–201,

252, 259, 292–94, 322, 325, 326–27, 329, 332–33; results of, 322–23

Old Testament. *See* Hebrew Scriptures
Omega Psi Phi, 331
Orangeburg, S.C.: protests, 28, 45, 160, 251, 252, 258

Pacifists. *See* Radical pacifists
Palmer, Rev. H. J., 148, 149, 150, 151, 174, 296, 297
Parker, Henry, 186
Parker, Rev. Henry, 258
Parker, Theodore, 316
Parks, Commissioner Frank, 40, 42, 78, 97, 99, 140, 148, 153, 265
Parks, Raymond L., 35 (n. 20), 86
Parks, Rosa L., 6, 35 (n. 33), 36 (n. 42), 46, 89, 90, 95, 150, 188, 267, 274, 294; bus arrest, 8–9, 41, 72–73, 83–84, 95–96, 99, 106, 108, 126, 156, 181, 209, 221, 222, 229, 246; trial, 10, 84, 87; and Highlander, 81, 82, 124, 155, 156–57; radio interview, 82–86; legal appeal, 150, 258; post-arrest consequences, 227; post-arrest activities, 274, 281, 297, 298, 299
Patterson, Carrie, 29
Patterson, Ala. Attorney General John, 46, 289
Patton, W. C., 109–10, 148, 150, 151, 298
Paul, Saint, 318
Personalism, 14
Pierce, James E., 268
Plato, 215
Plessy v. Ferguson, 27, 28, 34 (n. 15), 264, 270, 271, 272, 273, 300
Pollard, Mother, 10
Poll tax, 9, 59, 95
Populists, 3
Powell, Rev. Adam Clayton, Jr., 116, 171–72, 204
Powell, Rev. W. J., 14, 137, 274, 278, 285, 286, 291, 292, 327
Prague, xii
Pratt, Ann Smith, 10, 14
Prayer Pilgrimage, 32, 51

Presley, Elvis, 48
Progressive Democratic Association, 9, 34 (n. 17), 40, 61, 77, 152

Radical pacifists, 20–23, 195, 237–42, 255
Randolph, A. Philip, 7, 20, 21, 22, 26, 32, 46, 119, 159, 160–61, 171, 199, 204, 235, 250, 296, 330, 334; article by, 316–17
Rape, 7, 8
Rauschenbusch, Walter, 23
Reconstruction, 2, 337, 345
Reddick, Lawrence D., 268, 313–14
Reese, Jeanetta, 44, 128, 129, 149, 166, 175
Reuther, Walter, 330
Richardson, Harry V., 305
Ricks, Inez, 16
Riles, Wilson, 159, 251, 253, 254
Rives, Judge Richard T., 27, 46, 265, 271–72
Robinson, Rev. James H., 200, 305
Robinson, Jo Ann, 6, 10, 11, 12, 15, 16, 30, 32, 35 (n. 33), 40, 57, 58, 77, 97, 139, 235, 285, 286, 291; starts bus boycott, 9, 41, 86–87; edits MIA newsletter, 268
Rogers, Sidney, 82–86
Roosevelt, Eleanor, 46, 203–4, 267, 299, 314, 328–29
Roosevelt, Franklin D., 20, 160
Rowan, Carl T., 120, 121
Ruppenthal, Police Chief Goodwin J., 99, 148, 265
Rustin, Bayard, 20–23, 26, 27, 28–30, 36 (n. 52), 37 (n. 61), 44, 195, 199–201, 203, 236–37, 255; arrival in Montgomery, 159–60, 164–70, 171–72, 204, 205; writings, 208–11, 243–49, 329- 31, 335–41

St. John AME Church, 157, 216
Salinger, Neil, 163
Satyagraha, 20. *See also* Nonviolence: Gandhian
School desegregation, 8, 46, 57, 271, 329
Scott, C. A., 161
Scott, Judge John B., 10
Scottsboro Boys, 3, 35 (n. 20)
Seay, Rev. Solomon S., 8, 14, 123, 129, 130,

Voting rights, 8, 32, 57, 227, 279, 298, 306, 322, 335, 337–38, 342

Walker, Martha K., 64–66
Walton, Norman W., 268
War Resisters League (WRL), 21, 22, 26, 159, 207
Washington, Booker T., 3
West, Irene, 296
White, Walter, 109
White Citizens Council (WCC), 40, 42, 43, 81, 91, 103, 112, 117, 118, 139, 140, 142, 149, 152, 153, 168–69, 182, 184, 185, 189–91, 206, 208, 224, 247, 273, 281–82, 284, 290, 302, 303, 311, 318, 340; vs. NAACP, 258, 289–90

Wilkins, Roy, 26, 46, 109–10, 119, 148, 296, 315, 330
Williams, A. D., 26
Williams, Aubrey, 96, 125, 139, 298
Williams, Samuel, 37 (n. 59)
Wilson, Rev. A. W., 163, 196, 279
Wofford, Clare, 29, 331
Wofford, Harris, 29, 195, 331
Women's Political Council (WPC), 6, 7, 11, 39, 40, 57, 58, 59–61; starts bus boycott, 9, 41, 86–87
Women's rights, xi
Worthy, William, 169, 199
WPC. See Women's Political Council

Young Communist League, 21